Diplomacy's Value

A volume in the series

CORNELL STUDIES IN SECURITY AFFAIRS

edited by Robert J. Art, Robert Jervis, and Stephen M. Walt

A list of titles in this series is available at www.cornellpress.cornell.edu.

Diplomacy's Value

CREATING SECURITY IN 1920s EUROPE AND THE CONTEMPORARY MIDDLE EAST

BRIAN C. RATHBUN

Cornell University Press

ITHACA AND LONDON

First published 2014 by Cornell University Press

First printing, Cornell Paperbacks, 2014

Printed in the United States of America

Library of Congress Cataloging-in-Publication Data

Rathbun, Brian C., 1973– author.
  Diplomacy's value : creating security in 1920s Europe and the contemporary Middle East / Brian C. Rathbun.
     pages cm — (Cornell studies in security affairs)
  Includes bibliographical references.
  ISBN 978-0-8014-5318-2 (cloth : alk. paper)
  ISBN 978-0-8014-7990-8 (pbk. : alk. paper)
  1. Diplomacy. 2. Europe—History—1918–1945. 3. Arab-Israeli conflict—1993—
Peace. I. Title. II. Series: Cornell studies in security affairs.
  JZ1405.R37   2014
  327.4009'042—dc23   2014013178

Cornell University Press strives to use environmentally responsible suppliers and materials to the fullest extent possible in the publishing of its books. Such materials include vegetable-based, low-VOC inks and acid-free papers that are recycled, totally chlorine-free, or partly composed of nonwood fibers. For further information, visit our website at www.cornellpress.cornell.edu.

Cloth printing   10 9 8 7 6 5 4 3 2 1
Paperback printing   10 9 8 7 6 5 4 3 2 1

*To Beth, Rose, and Charli for being so kind
to me when I was less than diplomatic.*

Contents

Preface and Acknowledgments

This book has a very personal beginning. After my wife and I finished graduate school, she was hired to work as a diplomat for the U.S. State Department. After the initial excitement that accompanies one's first grown-up job (better said, vicarious excitement, because I was unemployed, having been beat out for that very same job by this wonderful woman I had married), I realized that I had absolutely no earthly idea what Nina would be doing. She was similarly clueless, having received the same apparently inadequate Ph.D. education I had. How could it be that after six years of graduate school at Berkeley we had no real understanding of what comprises most of interstate relations—communicating via diplomacy? I noted this as a future research topic. Ten years later, this is the result.

When I finally started looking into diplomacy as a concept and a phenomenon, I felt better. No one else seemed to have any idea either. I found a half-dozen reviews of the literature on diplomacy, all complaining that no one had studied it and no one knew how it worked. They provided a few requisite quotes from diplomats who claimed that their brilliant skill was simply intuitive and inexplicable and then went onto a list of the various functions of the diplomat—smiling at cocktail parties, acting pretentious, and so on. Yet, frustratingly, none of these works really did anything about this enormous gap in our scholarly knowledge.

To make progress, I first had to understand that diplomacy was, at least conceptually, very different from foreign policy. Diplomacy is not the formulation of foreign policy interests; it is the pursuit of them without recourse to force. This can be done in different ways. State leaders can engage in coercive bargaining, pragmatic statecraft, or reasoned dialogue. There are different diplomatic styles used to pursue the same goals.

[ix]

I had the perfect laboratory to test these arguments—1920s Europe. I had been interested since graduate school in this somewhat neglected period in great power politics. After I published my first book, I turned back to it, hoping to make the case again that parties defined the national interest differently. In hindsight, this would have been a mistake, a mere retread of my first book. And it would not have worked in any case. The definition of the national interest was not in dispute in the domestic politics of France, Britain, and Germany between the wars. This had frustrated me when I first took up the topic, but when I reopened it, I saw that this fact served my new theoretical purposes. Foreign policy goals were not contested, but diplomatic style was.

It indicated, yet again, that important elements of state behavior are not structurally determined. Diplomacy is the exercise of agency. Those with different diplomatic styles take the same interests and go about achieving them in very different ways. Indeed, it is hard to think about diplomacy in any meaningful way if it is simply endogenous to attributes of the environment such as the position of a state in the distribution of power. If the powerful always get what they want, then the neglect of diplomacy in the international relations literature is forgivable. Yet they don't, and it isn't.

It is not enough, however, simply to show that diplomacy matters. I wanted to say something about what diplomatic styles we could expect states to pursue. Here I drew again on psychological attributes of decision makers, in particular social and epistemic motivations. These two factors combine to produce a number of diplomatic styles that we find implied in different schools of international relations theory. In other words, not only do we have realist and liberal scholars, we also have realist and liberal practitioners, and we can predict who they are likely to be. Scholarly debates are replicated in the real world with real consequences.

I envision this book as the last in a triptych of books that one might think of as neo-idealist in character. They are idealist in that a major takeaway from all of them is that we are not destined to a competitive world of power politics; leaders exercise considerable agency in their foreign policy choices. In *Partisan Interventions*, I contend that states often intervene with military force for humanitarian purposes. In *Trust in International Cooperation*, I show they are capable of trusting other states to effectively create multilateral security institutions. And in this book, *Diplomacy's Value*, I demonstrate that liberal and realist diplomacy enables states to reach win-win outcomes that they would otherwise not have achieved through coercive bargaining. The books are neo, however, in the sense that they are neither naïve nor normative. All three are based on rigorous objective analysis with a careful research design. The last two make the case that decision makers can reach cooperative outcomes even when motivated primarily by egoistic ends. But also, always, there are opponents of humanitarian intervention, multilateralism, and reasoned diplomacy. These outcomes are by no means predetermined. Particular political parties favor them, while others do not. I do not think that we are on a long march to a liberal paradise.

I was fortunate enough to be put through the fire by Iain Johnston, Todd Sechser, Wayne Sandholtz, Jacques Hymans, Mark Haas, Jon Mercer, David Welch, Vincent Pouliot, Robert Trager, Paul Sharp, Jennifer Mitzen, Marcus Holmes, Mark Trachtenberg, Jordan Branch, Arthur Stein, Andrew Moravcsik, Burcu Bayram, Aaron Rapport, Mai'a Davis Cross, and audiences at Princeton University, the University of Texas–Austin, UCLA, and McGill University. Any remaining mistakes I blame on them for not catching.

Heather McKibben helped me immensely in situating my argument against the alternatives and showing how they are often more complementary than competitive. Dustin Tingley greatly influenced my thinking about case selection. Ron Krebs was instrumental in helping me distinguish foreign policy from diplomacy. Andrew Moravcsik made me deal with the role of interests and beliefs in isolating the causal importance of diplomatic style. Nina brought me down to size repeatedly by saying, "Yes, of course," to every insight I thought I had generated about the diplomatic process, as diplomats will do. Robert Jervis was one of the reviewers for Cornell University Press. His endorsement was one of the highest points of my professional career. Another anonymous reviewer was also superb. Anyone who has worked with Roger Haydon at the press knows how he combines humor with professionalism to make publishing a book painless. It was great fun to do this again with him. I thank my graduate student Mark Paradis for research assistance. The Center for International Studies at the University of Southern California and the Social Sciences and Humanities Research Council of Canada were generous in providing me with research support.

A theme in this book is that by combining efforts one can create value. This is also true in my life. Nina and I have done this with our two sons—Max and Luc. These precious little boys make me want to be a better person, father, and scholar, although with various degrees of success. If you two ever read this, know that your dad loves you.

[1]

The Value and Values of Diplomacy

What is the value of diplomacy? How does it affect the course of foreign affairs independent of the distribution of power and foreign policy interests? Despite the centrality of diplomacy to international affairs, little is known about how it works. The notion that diplomacy matters probably strikes most as intuitively obvious, yet most accounts of diplomacy are personalistic accounts of the triumphs of particular state representatives, with little effort made to disentangle the effects of their actions from the broader environment or to offer a general theory about the origins of their choices (Sharp 2009: 1–2; Sartori 2005).

Diplomacy is given little attention in international relations scholarship because of the structural bias of the discipline. Diplomacy is a process that individuals engage in. A theory of diplomacy must be a theory of agency (Cross 2007). If its successes or failures are merely a function of the larger geopolitical environment, then diplomacy per se is essentially unworthy of study. If power is the only currency in international politics, a focus on diplomacy adds little value to our understanding of international affairs.

International relations theorists are not good at theorizing about agency. Books and articles on international relations tell us more about what states cannot do or must do than what they can do or choose to do. By reducing important outcomes to structural features beyond agents' control, such as the ability to send costly signals, prominent traditions in international relations theory have long treated diplomacy implicitly or explicitly as automatic, unproblematic, and ultimately unimportant (Fearon 1994, 1995; Gartzke 1999; Schultz 2001). This raises an obvious question: If diplomacy lacks value, why do states spend so much time engaging in it?

[1]

A theory of diplomacy would offer a set of propositions about how states go about communicating and pursuing their interests, which in turn affects their ability to successfully negotiate agreements. Demonstrating that diplomacy matters in international relations requires showing two things. First, diplomats must have a choice about what to do. If those in a position of leverage always adopt coercive bargaining, then diplomacy matters little. Second, decision makers' actions must have an effect on outcomes independent of other factors. If the strong always get their way, diplomacy is not important. If states find agreement merely because their interests are closely aligned, then diplomacy does not deserve the credit for pushing on an open door.

Decision makers choose from a variety of *diplomatic styles*—coercive bargaining, pragmatic statecraft, and reasoned dialogue—in predictable ways. These different conceptions of diplomacy are found, generally implicitly, in the international relations literature, but we need to identify those who are predisposed to using them. I argue that they are the product of different psychological motivations revealed in decision makers' ideological predispositions.

The particular combination of diplomatic styles used by state leaders gives way to interactions of a certain character, what I will call the prevailing *spirit* of negotiations. Parties might engage in *value claiming* negotiation behavior, using leverage to extract the greatest benefits possible. Alternatively, they might engage in *value creating* behavior, an exchange of concessions and honest information in the pursuit of mutual benefits. Value creating is most likely when all parties embrace reasoned dialogue. A dialogue is not a monologue. Coercive bargaining not only makes value creating more difficult but also induces coercive bargaining on the part of those otherwise inclined toward integrative negotiation. Whereas value creating takes two, value claiming can be brought on by only one.

Most important, the spirit of negotiations has an effect on international outcomes independently of the distribution of power and interests. Behavioral research on negotiation in economics and psychology shows that, by holding their cards close to their vest, those engaged in value claiming are harder pressed to reach mutually beneficial outcomes, even in situations of potential integration, in which each side can obtain what it values most provided it concedes on items of less importance. Value creating helps avoid this dynamic by revealing the existence of joint gains in the first place. And individuals vary in their preference for different negotiating strategies, even given the same set of incentives. Negotiating behavior is not endogenous; negotiating outcomes are not epiphenomenal.

I find the same applies to international relations. Diplomacy cannot bring about agreements where there is no outcome that both sides prefer to the status quo. It can, however, frustrate or facilitate agreement where there is the potential for success based on the underlying distribution of preferences. Diplomacy allows states to reach outcomes that might have been unexpected but also to miss out on opportunities that are within their grasp. This is the added value of diplomacy in explaining international events. And, as is the case in psychological experiments, individuals in the same strategic setting approach diplomacy differently. Their behavior is not reducible to their environment.

In this book, I demonstrate the role played by diplomacy using a hard case—relations among France, Germany, and Britain in the 1920s, in the aftermath of World War I. As is well known, the Germans deeply resented the punitive peace that, in addition to requiring reparations, dismembered their territory, permanently demilitarized the Rhineland, saw the country occupied in the west by tens of thousands of foreign troops, and disarmed the vanquished state to the point that it could have been easily overrun by Poland, not to mention France. Despite the condition of Germany, France was terrified of an eventual *revanche* by its more economically and demographically powerful neighbor and sought in the immediate postwar years to hold Germany down through every legal means possible in the Versailles Treaty. French fear was a "seemingly insuperable obstacle" to reconciliation in the 1920s (Stambrook 1968: 234). The French military even marched into the Ruhr area of Germany in 1923, seizing its industrial assets to force Germany to pay its reparations.

Yet it was in this environment, when the European powers were, in Lord Curzon's words, "relapsing . . . into the deepest slime of prewar treachery and intrigue," that Germany made a remarkably successful bid for reconciliation with its wartime adversaries (in Jacobson 2004: 17). The German foreign minister, Gustav Stresemann, announced what he called a "peace offensive on a grand scale," proposing a treaty of mutual guarantee in which France and Germany would each renounce the use of force to change their mutual border. Britain would come to the aid of either country should it fall victim to aggression by the other. Stresemann's proposal reflected his pragmatic statecraft. He believed that Germany in its weakened state had to seek mutually beneficial accommodations with its former adversaries.

His proposal found a favorable reception in Britain, whose foreign secretary was similarly pragmatically inclined, and in France, led by a liberal government that favored reasoned dialogue. The value creating negotiation that ensued yielded success in the Treaty of Locarno, signed and ratified in October 1925. The three protagonists identified an outcome that left them all better off. Despite its total lack of military power or any other type of bargaining leverage, Germany was able to achieve all its aims. The agreement was followed by a significant alleviation in the occupation conditions of the Rhineland. To account for this unlikely success, a theory of diplomacy is necessary; this forms the bulk of the empirical focus of the book.

This case is not only theoretically hard for diplomacy; it is empirically important. An analysis of the 1920s corrects the often-mistaken impression that the period was simply a prelude to a second world war that was inevitable given the distribution of power and the outstanding grievances between France and Germany. In fact, the diplomacy of the 1920s offered the possibility of a lasting peace among the European powers. Only the twin tidal waves of the Great Depression and the rise of Nazi Germany overturned this new state of affairs. As Arthur Balfour, the elder statesman who had served as both prime minister and foreign minister of Britain, states, "the Great War ended in November 1918. The Great Peace did not begin until October 1925" (quoted in Grayson 1997: 35).

I also apply the argument to Israeli-Palestinian negotiations from the late 1980s to the early 2000s, focusing on the rise and fall of the peace process that began in Oslo, with a particular focus on the Israeli side. The ability of my psychological theory of diplomacy to explain the initiation, consolidation, and subsequent decline of talks between the two sides demonstrates its relevance for a contemporary and still ongoing conflict.

THE ARGUMENT

Although the existing international relations scholarship does not offer anything close to a theory of diplomacy as agency, we do find different conceptions of diplomacy, alternative styles that policymakers might use to realize their interests. Rationalists highlight *coercive bargaining*, in which states use threats and exploit their leverage to pressure other states to concede. They make high demands, refuse to budge to demonstrate their credibility, and hold issues dear to the other states hostage. Diplomacy is a game of high-stakes poker in which states have no incentive to show their cards or believe the cheap talk of others. Realists, in contrast, emphasize *pragmatic statecraft*. Here the far-sighted diplomat focuses on securing the most vital of interests, conceding on issues of less importance to avoid creating unnecessary conflict with others. Good diplomacy is chess rather than poker. Finally, liberals highlight the possibility of *reasoned dialogue*, in which diplomacy is a process of argumentation in which state representatives aim to persuade others of their point of view while listening closely to their claims as well. Reason implies

[4]

moderating demands to arrive at an outcome of mutual benefit but also indicates the primary instrument that states use—the giving of reasons. This is enlightened, civilized diplomacy of a liberal variety. It is marked by good faith and goodwill.

The first step in building a theory about diplomacy is to recognize that these different styles of diplomacy are a menu from which decision makers choose and that they very well might choose differently even in the same structural circumstances. This choice, of course, implies agency. From there, we proceed to link the adoption of these alternative styles to particular attributes of decision makers that lead them to prefer one style of diplomacy over another. To do so, I draw on the psychological literature on negotiation. Experiments show that, even in the same structural setting, individuals negotiate in different ways.

Psychologists point to the role played by two motivational goals: social motivation and epistemic motivation. These are attributes of individuals. Negotiators intrinsically have different preferences as to what they regard as the ideal distribution of benefits. Some are *prosocial*, valuing gains for others as well as for themselves. They are value creators who seek joint value for the pair. Others are *proself*, simply egoistic value claimers who think only of themselves. Proselfs make lower offers, reveal less information, and hold out longer than prosocials in negotiations. In terms of foreign affairs, proselfs think only of their own states, whereas prosocials think also of others. Those with a proself motivation are inclined toward coercive bargaining; prosocials are inclined toward reasoned dialogue.

Some proselfs, however, are more adaptable. Social motivations are based on heuristics, cognitive shortcuts with which individuals develop expectations about what interactions with others will generally be like. Heuristics impede the objective evaluation of one's situation at any particular time. Those with greater epistemic motivation demonstrate a greater willingness to transcend these cognitive obstacles and develop an accurate understanding of their environment—I call them pragmatists. This is the diplomatic style highlighted by realists. It is separated from coercive bargaining by a greater level of epistemic motivation. Pragmatists use both distributive and integrative tactics, adapting to the particular strategic circumstances in which they find themselves.

My argument therefore amounts to a behavioralization of existing international relations traditions. The question is not, What is *the* nature of diplomacy? Instead, it is, *Who* acts like a coercive bargainer, a pragmatic statesman (or stateswoman), or a reasoned interlocutor? We should think of realism, rationalism, and liberalism not as theories that capture the singular essence of diplomacy but, rather, as sets of prescriptions that guide the behavior of some (but not all) decision makers. Psychology provides a microfoundation for more macro-oriented international relations theories.

One negotiating style alone, however, does not determine the character of the interaction among states. Diplomatic styles interact to create a certain spirit of negotiation. Prosocials' preference for value creating is driven by an expectation of reciprocal concessions and open exchange. It will prevail when both sides have the prosocial motivations that drive liberal diplomacy—it takes two. In the absence of this reciprocity, prosocials punish proselfs by adopting the latter's negotiating style. Coercive bargaining by any one side prohibits negotiating pairs from reaching win-win outcomes that benefit both by inducing value claiming negotiation among all parties. Pragmatists adapt to their environment. They are likely to create value with prosocials but to claim value against those proselfs with lower epistemic motivation who prefer coercive bargaining.

This spirit of negotiation, whether value creating or value claiming, in turn affects the outcome. Psychologists and behavioral economists studying negotiation have long found arguments relying on structural features incomplete. Outcomes in experiments do not vary simply as a function of the structural setting, such as the distribution of power and interests. Even in games of integrative potential, in which players value various items differently, only pairs of negotiators who both practice value creating are consistently able to maximize joint value.

I hypothesize that those whose diplomatic interactions are marked by value claiming are less likely to find a mutually beneficial agreement. This is true even in situations of potential integration, in which each side can obtain what it values most provided it concedes on items of less importance. The agreements reached in climates of value claiming will reflect the distribution of power and leverage in the situation.

I find that this combination of diplomatic styles affects outcomes independently of the distribution of power and interests by comparing the expectations of my argument against a structural baseline. Crude bargaining theories argue that diplomatic style should reflect the bargaining leverage of a state, with the stronger state engaging in coercive bargaining. The outcome of negotiations will reflect the interests of the more powerful parties, defined in terms of either material influence or satisfaction with the status quo. Value creating is more likely when parties' interests are asymmetrical, that is when they value different issues on the negotiating agenda differently and can engage in trade-offs and logrolls in which each side gains what it values most.

I find, instead, that states exercise agency, often *not* adopting the diplomatic style that reflects their structural position. Diplomatic style might enable states to punch above (or below) their weight. Structure is

[6]

important but not determinate. Depending on the combination of diplomatic styles, easily obtainable outcomes might go unattained while more unlikely successes are achieved. Even where the potential for joint gains is present, integrative deals are hardly guaranteed. Value creating negotiation is still necessary to reveal the very possibility of such agreements. And even when outcomes reflect the crude distribution of bargaining leverage, diplomacy is still a crucial part of the story. It is only when both sides embrace a coercive bargaining style that such outcomes emerge.

This still leaves an unanswered question: Where do the social and epistemic motivations underlying diplomatic style come from? And how can we generate expectations about who is likely to engage in which type of diplomacy, independent of their negotiating behavior? The difference between prosocials and proselfs is based on values. Those engaged in diplomacy can decide to reach their interests with or without regard for the interests of others. How states pursue value is a function of their values. Edward H. Carr (1964) famously claimed that politics are not a function of ethics, but ethics of politics. He was wrong. A theory of the value of diplomacy requires a theory of the values in diplomacy.

A prosocial motivation in international affairs reflects a particular set of "moral foundations" (Graham et al. 2011). Prosocials care for others, and they value fairness and equality in outcomes. They have a greater commitment to self-transcendence values than proselfs do (Schwartz 1992). This is liberal morality, based on Enlightenment thinking, which judges ethical behavior on how one treats other individuals regardless of what group they are in. A proself motivation in foreign affairs reflects a different set of moral foundations, those of respect for authority and loyalty to the in-group. Proselfs are convinced that in-groups must demonstrate solidarity and preserve order to protect the group from dangers both within and without. Conservation values of conformity and tradition help maintain cohesion and stability within the group. We must be careful to avoid a false dichotomy between ethical prosocials and Machiavellian proselfs. The behavior of the latter is also morally driven, just by different sets of considerations.

Social motivations and moral foundations are revealed in political ideology. The policy positions of the left and right emerge naturally from the particular set of values they embody and represent in politics. The left typically emphasizes self-transcendence values based on the moral foundations of providing and caring for others. Leftists believe in the equal worth of all individuals. The right, in contrast, values the community more highly and sees the need for strong authority structures, whether law and order at the state level or traditional values at home, to control bad behavior and protect the group from instability, diversity, and change. Armed with these insights, political ideology presents a way of

[7]

measuring social motivation independent of diplomatic behavior. We expect that those on the left will generally prefer reasoned dialogue, whereas those on the far right will use coercive bargaining.

Individuals also vary systematically in their degree of epistemic motivation, a cognitive rather than an ethical difference. Those without epistemic motivation exhibit a need for closure. They are less open to new information and more disinclined to question their beliefs. Although those who are ideologically extreme have a propensity toward closed-mindedness, studies consistently show that the right demonstrates a lower degree of epistemic motivation than the left. For this reason, variation in epistemic motivation is a particularly strong cleavage among conservatives. Pragmatic statecraft should find its support primarily in the center right, where the proself motivation is present but where epistemic motivation is somewhat higher, thereby facilitating pragmatic adaptation to different circumstances based on a more objective perception of the environment.

The Cases

I present two cases. First, I show how my argument explains the pattern of diplomatic relations in 1920s Europe. Bilateral efforts to provide France the security it so desperately desired failed twice. In 1922, although there was a deal that both Britain and France preferred to no agreement, under which Britain would have issued a security guarantee to defend France against German aggression, it fell through due to distributive bargaining and coercive diplomacy on both sides. This value claiming was not a function of the structural circumstances but, rather, the product of choices about how to negotiate that were consistent with the conservative ideological predispositions of both governments. Britain, although it valued a security guarantee in its own right, decided to try to use its bargaining leverage to extract greater gains on other issues from France as a condition for negotiating. And even the much weaker France made high demands, refused concessions, played hard to get, and denigrated the British offer. This diplomatic style was unsuited to the circumstances, given France's lack of bargaining leverage.

Then, after both conservative governments were replaced by those with leftist ideological orientations, the liberal diplomatic style of both produced value creating negotiation and a tentative agreement on a win-win outcome called the Geneva Protocol, even though the foreign policy goals of the two countries were now actually further apart. Open, informative, and honest negotiations between two prosocial governments yielded a win-win outcome in the form of the Geneva Protocol, in which

[8]

the Labour government of Britain acquiesced to an extension of the sanctions of the League of Nations that the French government desired in exchange for the convocation of a disarmament conference and the institution of compulsory universal arbitration for all disputes among parties to the protocol. The agreement, however, was killed off by the British Tories when they returned to power because they had a different set of foreign policy goals.

It was Germany, despite a complete lack of bargaining leverage, that transformed the security situation in Europe. Under the center-right foreign minister, Gustav Stresemann, the Germans proposed a treaty of mutual guarantee in which both France and German would renounce the use of force along their mutual border, with Britain brought in to guarantee the security of either state in case it became the victim of aggression by the other. This was a realist strategy resting on the instrumental consideration of French interests and the pragmatic use of short-term concessions to secure vital interests in the longer term. Stresemann sought to gain the trust of France to facilitate an early evacuation of the Rhineland and, eventually, border revisions in the east. This effort at conciliation, however, cannot be reduced simply to the German structural position of weakness. Stresemann's proposals were opposed by his coalition partners on the far right. These conservatives shared the foreign minister's goals but not his diplomatic style.

Whereas the French right denigrated the value of the offer, the leftist coalition government in France was willing to engage in an open exchange of ideas, given its diplomatic style of reasoned dialogue. Although the left shared the foreign policy goals of the right and still feared and distrusted Germany, it nevertheless pursued liberal diplomacy. The center-right British foreign secretary, Austen Chamberlain, fit Stresemann's program into his own realist strategy of drawing a rehabilitated Germany into a new concert of Europe, returning the country to great power status safely. He took the far-sighted view that reconciling France and Germany was in British interests because Britain would inevitably be drawn into any renewed conflict between the historical adversaries. Consequently, he was prepared to pay the short-term price of guaranteeing the security pact. Chamberlain prevailed over more conservative critics in his cabinet, who, although sharing the goal of dampening tensions between France and Germany, favored a different diplomatic style. They again wanted to extract a greater price from France for the British offer of security. Under the foreign secretary's leadership, Britain set out to broker a deal between the two sides by convincing them to practice pragmatic statecraft vis-à-vis one another rather than the coercive bargaining that had marked their bilateral relations in recent years.

[9]

Stresemann's unlikely gambit paid dividends. The Treaty of Locarno was drafted at a conference marked by a spirit of value creating negotiation between realists and liberals in which good faith and goodwill prevailed. The security treaty was quickly followed by a package of alleviations to the Rhineland occupation that created the impression of a simple quid pro quo integrative deal of the kind that rationalists might expect based simply on the structure of interests. But Britain and France were prepared to offer such concessions only as a reward for the new pragmatic diplomacy of Germany. Indeed, had Germany proposed such an exchange at the beginning of its peace offensive, as Stresemann's far-right colleagues had wanted, it would have undermined the foreign minister's reassurance strategy by confirming French and British biases about the bottomless German appetite. Only careful pragmatic statecraft by Germany had made success possible.

The French leftist coalition tried to consolidate this new "spirit of Locarno," but the value creating that had prevailed previously among the three countries was undermined when the conservatives under Raymond Poincaré returned to power in France. Although the occupation was of declining importance to the French and there was a win-win outcome available in which France would offer early evacuation in exchange for a renegotiated reparations settlement, the conservatives used the occupation coercively to extract greater concessions from Germany. The coercive French diplomatic style induced value claiming by others. Stresemann, the pragmatist, adapted to the new situation and took a similarly confrontational line, demanding an immediate and unilateral end to the Rhineland occupation. When the parties convened at a conference on reparations and the occupation at The Hague, only the British threat to unilaterally withdraw their forces from the Rhineland induced the French to seriously negotiate an early end to the occupation. After an extended period of brinksmanship during which a breakdown of negotiations was a strong possibility, the two sides finally settled on an outcome weighted toward the more powerful French. The last chance of the European powers to consolidate the peace before the onslaught of the Great Depression and the rise of fascism in Germany was over.

In chapters 8 and 9, I extend my analysis to the peace process between Palestinians and Israelis, which demonstrates remarkable parallels to 1920s Europe. Pragmatists on the weaker side, in this case, the Palestinians, made efforts at rapprochement toward the stronger side, the Israelis, by renouncing claims to territory in the hopes of ending a military occupation. Pragmatic leaders in an interested third party, the George H. W. Bush administration in the United States, tried to play the role of honest broker, despite their greater historical ties with the stronger party. Nevertheless, true progress was made only when the pragmatic

Palestinians teamed up with the prosocial Israeli Labor government. The combination of diplomatic styles generated a value creating dynamic that fostered the two Oslo accords. Much as the return of coercive bargaining on the stronger French side contributed to undermining the spirit of Locarno, the return of the Likud Party to power in Israel changed the character of negotiating to value claiming. Benjamin Netanyahu's successor on the left, however, Ehud Barak, also failed to commit fully to a liberal diplomacy of dialogue, creating suspicions on the Palestinian side that impeded, alongside Yasser Arafat's intransigence and Palestinian mismanagement, a peace deal at Camp David.

Overall, the two cases show that diplomacy adds value to accounts of international relations. Diplomacy can both make agreements that should be easier to reach more difficult and make agreements that should be hard to achieve more attainable. The Locarno period is particularly well suited for analyzing the effects of diplomacy because it presents a hard case for value creating, given the distrust and discord that had characterized prior relations among France, Britain, and Germany. The same is true of the Palestinian-Israeli case (chapter 8). I address the difficult methodological problems faced by those who study diplomacy in the next chapter.

Defining Diplomacy

In the remainder of this chapter, I review the academic literature on diplomacy. First, however, we need a working definition of *diplomacy*. This is a different question from how diplomacy works. All definitions of *diplomacy* use some combination of two primary components: (1) that diplomacy involves communication between states through the collection, interpretation, and dissemination of information about the interests of a state and of others (Bull 1977: 158; Watson 1981: 20) and (2) that diplomacy involves peaceful conflict resolution through negotiation when interests diverge or do not wholly overlap (Watson 1981: 33; Sharp 2009: 1).

Even though diplomacy involves the peaceful resolution of conflicts, this does not require the absence of the implicit or explicit threat of coercion or even force. Hedley Bull writes that the goal of diplomacy is to "secure [other states'] cooperation or neutralize their opposition in carrying it out—by reason and persuasion if possible, but sometimes by threats of force or other kinds of coercion" (1977: 158). Nor need the exchange of information be completely genuine and based on good faith. Yet this does not obviate the need for communication in diplomacy. In describing Niccolò Machiavelli's views on diplomacy, Geoffrey Berridge writes of the diplomat: "Much of the information that he obtains will be false and misleading, but he owes his own prince his judgment. As a result, he must compare information from different sources, weigh it, and finally declare what he himself believes to be the truth" (2001: 89).

Going forward it is important to distinguish foreign policy from diplomacy. Diplomacy is a part of foreign policy but not identical to it (Nicolson 1980: chap. 1). It is important to distinguish foreign policy *interests*, the specific ends that states pursue, from the way they peacefully pursue them through communication and negotiation, which is diplomacy. Style is not substance, and we want to distinguish the independent effect of the former, looking for variation in diplomatic style among those who share the same conception of the national interest. Diplomatic style is also motivated by something more than hawkish or dovish *beliefs*, which reflect different attitudes about the nature of the adversary and the utility of military force (Jervis 1976; Tetlock 1983b). While doves might prefer a diplomatic style of reasoned dialogue, if diplomacy simply reduces opposition to the use of organized violence or a benign depiction of one's interlocutors, it does not add much to our understanding of international politics.

It seems uncontroversial, therefore, to adopt a definition of *diplomacy* as the nonviolent and negotiated pursuit of state interests through the communication and exchange of information, even if the threat of coercion, either economic or military, might be present or part of the process and if the dialogue might be less than genuine (Steiner 2004: 3; de Callières 2000: 6–7). Nevertheless, within this broad notion of diplomacy, there is still room for several different types of diplomacy. In a review of the limited international relations literature on diplomacy, we find three: coercive bargaining, pragmatic statecraft, and reasoned dialogue.

Three Diplomatic Styles

Those who have engaged the subject of diplomacy have attributed our ignorance to the role played by power in international relations theory. In this vein, James Der Derian writes, "It could well be that diplomacy has suffered from theoretical neglect to the extent that power politics has profited in theory and practice. When diplomacy is construed as a continuation of war by other means, as is often the realpolitik case, then little intellectual energy needs to be wasted on the illumination of power's shadow" (1987: 92).

If power is the only currency in international politics, diplomacy per se does not matter. The successes and failures of diplomats are reducible to the distribution of material capabilities. Long before the advent of structural realism, François de Callières, in one of the classic works on diplomatic practice, explained this conception: "When a prince or a state is powerful enough to dictate to his neighbours the art of negotiation loses its value, for then there is need for nothing but a mere statement of the prince's will" (2000: 83). Diplomacy is epiphenomenal to power and serves as a post hoc window dressing, the "silken glove over the iron fist" (Sharp 2009: 58). Adam Watson describes this logic as the "cynical claim that the capacity and the will to use force is what 'really' influences the relations of states, while diplomacy serves as its instrument registering and clothing its verdicts" (1981: 55). Diplomats are substitutable and mere "transmission belts" for forces larger than themselves (Cross 2007: 2).

Recent international relations scholarship takes up diplomacy only to dismiss it implicitly or even explicitly. Rationalist bargaining theory argues that diplomatic communication is often uninformative and cheap since states have incentives to misrepresent their preferences. James Fearon writes that because of incentives to dissemble, "diplomacy may not allow rational states to clarify disagreements about relative power or to avoid the miscalculation of resolve" necessary to maintain peace (1995: 391). Signals must be costly to be believed, but this is something out of the control of diplomats or any decision makers. If, as some rationalists argue, effective diplomacy is equivalent to credible signaling and if, for instance, democratic states have an advantage in doing so given their transparent political institutions, those who are engaging in diplomacy are just as unimportant to the outcome as in neorealism. Anyone who can operate a telegraph could send a costly signal in a democracy, yet the most skilled diplomat would still be a useless bloviator in an autocracy. If domestic institutions do the work, then agency is unimportant. They are simply another type of structure.

I would also not consider recent rationalist work on "cheap talk" diplomacy to capture diplomacy as agency. The attempts by Sartori (2005) and Trager (2010) to demonstrate the effect of costless signals also implicitly rely on costs. Communication not accompanied by a direct and immediate cost might have an effect on outcomes, but only if it carries with it the possibility of a future cost for the sender, such as the interruption of other aspects of a mutually beneficial relationship or the undermining of a state's reputation for honesty. Sartori writes: "A cheap talk signal may have eventual negative consequences, but the message itself is costless to send" (2005: 10). As Trager points out, Sartori's model is only based on cheap talk in a semantic sense. The game theory literature counts as cheap talk any signal that does not incur costs directly and immediately upon its transmission. Sartori can claim cheap talk status only through a

[13]

technicality (Trager 2010: 349). Yet the same could be said of Trager's model, in which threats become credible only because they put at risk existing mutually beneficial relationships.

Paul Sharp captures the essence of a crude neorealist position, but it could apply just as easily to rationalism, which is also a structural approach.

> Someone has to gather and disseminate information. Someone has to communicate threats, promises and bargaining positions. And, less certainly, someone has to perform the tasks associated with the more concrete aspects of representation such as negotiation. These functions occur automatically, however, and we lump them together as "diplomacy" for convenience. That term does not convey any sense that these functions, taken together, make an independent contribution to what happens, or explaining what happens, in international relations at the system level. . . . If diplomacy matters in systemic theories, therefore, it does so only occasionally as one of those contingent factors *about which it is neither possible nor necessary to theorize.* (2009: 54–55; emphasis added)

I argue instead that it is both possible and necessary to theorize about diplomacy. This is not easy. Diplomacy is shrouded in mystery (Sharp 2009: 2). It is frequently referred to as an "art," even a "black art" because it can be used for both good and evil purposes (Neumann 2003: 353; Morgenthau 1948: 15; Cross 2007: 1). Drawing on Pierre Bourdieu, Vincent Pouliot (2008; 2010) conceives of diplomacy as the most important "practice" of international relations. In his view, however, practices are intuitive feels for the situation that cannot be explained by those engaged in them, a common sense that cannot be articulated. He writes that "seasoned diplomats are at pains to explain their craft in abstract, social scientific terms" (Pouliot 2008: 258).

Diplomacy is undoubtedly an art in the sense that it a creative process of agency in which its practitioners make something new that did not previously exist. Even so, we might still say something systematic about it. Even as we struggle to explain how particular artists arrive at their specific results, we can at the very least identify certain common schools of painting and music. Next, I explore three such styles.

Diplomacy as Coercive Bargaining

Even though most contemporary rationalist literature on coercive bargaining minimizes the role of agency, insights of great use can be recovered from the first generation of thinking in this vein. Thomas Schelling offers a particular conception of diplomacy, one marked by exploiting

[14]

leverage. "The power to hurt is bargaining power. To exploit it is diplomacy—vicious diplomacy, but diplomacy," writes Schelling (1966: 2). This might include holding issues hostage that are of importance to others as bargaining chips so as to obtain benefits for oneself, even if conceding those issues would be of little cost. Harold Nicolson describes coercive bargaining thus: "Fundamental to such a conception of diplomacy is the belief that the purpose of negotiation is victory, and that the denial of complete victory means defeat. . . . The strategy of negotiation thus becomes an endeavor to outflank your opponents, to occupy strategical positions which are at once consolidated before any further advance is made" (1980: 53).

The coercive bargaining approach is premised on a particular framing of the international environment, that of the deterrence model. As Robert Jervis (1976) and Philip Tetlock (1983b) have long pointed out, in this particular characterization of state interaction, the adversary is seen as implacably hostile. The environment is zero-sum and fixed-pie in nature. Therefore, any efforts to reassure or cooperate will be taken as a sign of weakness and exploited. This differs from the spiral model, in which conflict is seen as a product of the strategic situation rather than the inherent disposition of the other side. In the former, international relations is a game of chicken; in the latter, it is a prisoner's dilemma. Coercive bargaining theorists are not concerned about spirals of hostility as unintended consequences of state behavior because the malign intentions of the other are taken for granted (Jervis 1989: 192).

This framing leads to a particular set of prescriptions. States should start from the premise that others are misrepresenting their preferences and not reveal their own. A state should understate how interested it is in an agreement, inflate its reservation price, and engage in brinksmanship to obtain the best possible outcome. Refusing concessions and holding out demonstrate resolve. It is best if others make concessions first to avoid commitment problems with later compliance and to be able to pocket concessions made by others and to ask for more without spending any capital.

The challenge posed by diplomacy in coercive bargaining is making the other believe in one's resolve: "The hardest part is communicating our own intentions. . . . Nations have been known to bluff; they have also been known to make threats sincerely and change their minds when the chips were down. . . . A persuasive threat of war may deter an aggressor; the problem is to make it persuasive, to keep it from sounding like a bluff" (Schelling 1966: 35). Schelling's early hypothesis was that, by escalating crises and risking or even fighting wars over issues of little importance, states would indicate that they were highly resolute in future conflicts of more significance.

[15]

Coercive bargaining is not as simple as a crude neorealist argument in which the powerful state generally wins. In terms of card games, diplomacy is poker, not war. Schelling stresses the "difference between the unilateral, 'undiplomatic' recourse to strength" that we could say characterizes neorealism and "coercive diplomacy based on the power to hurt." "International relations often have the character of a competition in risk taking, characterized not so much by tests of force as by tests of nerve," he writes. "Particularly in the relations between major adversaries . . . issues are decided not by who can bring the most force to bear in a locality, or on a particular issue, but by who is eventually willing to bring more force to bear or able to make it appear that more is forthcoming" (Schelling 1966: 94).

Any observer of international relations is familiar with the types of behaviors that Schelling describes—saber-rattling and threatening messages—and the use of leverage to achieve more favorable outcomes. But I argue that coercive bargaining is just this—one style that does not describe all diplomacy or even the behavior of all diplomats in the position of being able to exploit their leverage. In other words, I seek to behavioralize Schelling's insights, specifying more precisely who will engage in this type of behavior. As Erik Gartzke notes, "Winning at poker has as much to do with judging human personalities as it does with weighing the cards" (1999: 570). Schelling's intention, after all, was not to describe how diplomacy actually worked but to admonish state representatives to practice better diplomacy (Jervis 1989: 188).

Diplomacy as Pragmatic Statecraft

As previously noted, numerous students of diplomacy have attributed the dearth of knowledge about diplomacy to the dominance of realist thinking in the discipline (de Callières 2000: 83; Sharp 2009: 58; Watson 1981: 55). Classical realists, however, place significant importance on diplomacy, even as they articulate a particular notion of what good diplomacy entails (Berridge 2001). Hans Morgenthau offers the most compelling realist conception of good diplomacy as prudent statecraft, going so far as to offer several "rules of diplomacy" (1948: esp. chap. 31).[1] Above all, realist diplomacy is pragmatic in nature, which has a number of elements.

First, the practitioner of pragmatic statecraft focuses on securing vital interests while conceding others. Having identified the truly important state goals, Morgenthau cautions states to "promote the national interest

---

1. This is the same conception of diplomacy reviewed in Craig and George (1983: 11–16).

[16]

with moderation and leave the door open for compromise in the form of a negotiated settlement" (1948: 534). The distinctiveness of the pragmatic approach to diplomacy is most evident when it is compared with Schelling's coercive style. In pronounced contrast to Morgenthau, Schelling stresses the "interdependence of commitments" (1966) and advises states to take a hard and uncompromising line on matters of less importance so as to gain a reputation for resolve in matters of greater significance down the line. Being pragmatic, in contrast, involves setting priorities. Good statecraft is good chess-playing; one sometimes sacrifices pawns to protect the king.

Second, pragmatic statecraft is oriented toward the long term. The skilled chess player is able to see several moves ahead. Morgenthau describes "the mind of the diplomat" as "complicated and subtle. It sees the issue in hand as a moment in history, and beyond the victory of tomorrow it anticipates the incalculable possibilities of the future" (1948: 547). The realist should keep his or her eye on the prize, pragmatically making short-term sacrifices for long-term gains.

Third, pragmatic statecraft emphasizes the importance of cold and objective decision making. Diplomacy is "sang-froid," sober and emotional detachment that facilitates long-term thinking and the careful ranking of priorities (de Callières 2000: 12). The primary impediment to good diplomacy is what Morgenthau calls the "crusading spirit"—missionary zeal that distracts from the real national interest and needlessly inflates fear of the adversary (1948: 544). Moralizing distracts from the national interest. Morgenthau asks those engaged in diplomacy to "give up the shadow of worthless rights for the substance of real advantage" (1948: 545; see also de Callières 2000: 25, 94). The realist is not afraid to admit hard truths, even if they are emotionally costly.

Objectivity is also paramount in evaluating the intentions and power of others, a primary function of diplomacy. States want to avoid both understating and overstating the actual dangers in the international environment. Objectively evaluating the interests of other states requires seeing the world through their eyes. One of Morgenthau's rules is that "diplomacy must look at the political scene from the point of view of other nations" (1948: 553). Classical realist statecraft involves instrumental empathy. Truly understanding where others are coming from allows for more prudent decision making. This includes understanding that others might regard oneself as threatening. Ken Booth and Nicolas Wheeler (2008) call this "security dilemma sensibility." Without it, one risks unnecessary provocation not in the interests of the state (Jervis 1989: 193).

Fourth, pragmatic statecraft is situational, adapting to the particular environment and using the appropriate tools for the time. Morgenthau describes diplomacy as "quick adaptation to new situations, clever use of a psychological opening, retreat and advance as the situation may require, persuasion, the quid pro quo of bargaining and the like" (1948: 530). Coercion and force are not necessarily the most cost-effective way of reaching one's goals. Morgenthau recommends "not to advance by destroying the obstacles in one's way, but to retreat before them, to circumvent them, to maneuver around them, to soften and dissolve them slowly by means of persuasion, negotiation and pressure" (1948: 546; see also de Callières 2000: 12). There is certainly a place for force and coercive bargaining, but there is no one-size-fit-all strategy.

As is clear by the prescriptive nature of so many of the passages quoted here, classical realists understand diplomacy as an agent-driven process in a way that rationalists often do not. For Morgenthau, good diplomacy is not something that occurs automatically or unproblematically. Statecraft is a craft (de Callières 2000: 69; Morgenthau 1948: 549; Sharp 2009: 55). Applied appropriately, diplomacy serves as a source of additional power for the state to reach its goals, independent of the threat of force. If used correctly, diplomacy is a "multiplier" that helps states punch above their weight (Morgenthau 1948: 591; de Callières 2000: 11; Sharp 2009: 64). On the other hand, when wielded ineffectively, states might squander their power by overstating national goals or creating encircling alliances (Jönnson and Hall 2005: 15). Power does not speak for itself. But classical realism, although it takes diplomacy seriously, does not yet offer anything like a theory of diplomacy that identifies who is likely to behave in this pragmatic fashion. It has not been behavioralized.

Diplomacy as Reasoned Dialogue

Both coercive bargaining and pragmatic statecraft stand in contrast to what I call *liberal diplomacy*, by which I mean a conception of diplomacy that one can tease out of a diverse set of literatures, including the Grotian tradition of the English School and certain recent strands of constructivism. Liberal diplomacy is the pursuit of joint gains through the exchange of information and arguments. It is reasoned dialogue. Liberalism as a system of thought is predicated on the noncoercive pursuit of one's interests that respects the other's autonomy and interests. Individuals are regarded as fundamentally equal, with none superior to the other (Dworkin 1977). Reasoned dialogue is not like a card game but rather like solving a puzzle, trying to find an outcome that leaves both sides as satisfied as possible.

Liberal diplomacy proceeds in good faith and with goodwill. In terms of the former, those in the Grotian tradition prefer the term *dialogue* rather than *bargaining* (Watson 1981). The latter term implies, of course, a more coercive process than do other terms, such as *negotiation*. As opposed to the Middle Eastern bazaar with buyer and seller far apart, shouting and disinclined to budge, the English School sees diplomacy as a "civilized" process of patient discussion. In diplomacy, states "transform crude bargaining about objects of interest and desire into discussions about the moral and rational bases for particular claims and policies" and "make those whose claims and policies are said to be inconsistent with any notion of restraint into shared problems" (Sharp 2009: 42).

Liberal diplomacy overlaps considerably with Jürgen Habermas's conception of communicative action, which has been used by some constructivist international relations scholars to capture how the process of argumentation might lead to a reasoned consensus (Müller 2004; Lynch 2002; Risse 2000; Mitzen 2005). Diplomacy in this conception is a process of talk and persuasion rather than threats. Reason entails remaining open to and objectively evaluating new arguments, as well as offering one's own in an effort to persuade the other side. It means giving reasons for one's positions. If reason is to be relevant to international relations, diplomats, like any other actors, must be prepared to change their views in the face of a good argument. Habermas conceives of communicative action as an ideal type rather than an actual description of politics, much less international politics. Nevertheless, we can easily conceive of empirical instances in which this type of diplomacy is more prevalent than others.

Liberal diplomacy also rests on goodwill. It is motivated by the desire to find value for both sides. In the liberal mindset, one does not regard the other purely instrumentally, as a means to an end (Doyle 1997: 217). Hedley Bull writes, "The extent to which diplomacy can play any role or serve any function in the international system is therefore bound up with the extent to which states visualize foreign policy as the rational pursuit of interests of the state which at least in principle at some points overlap with the interests of other states. Diplomacy can play no role where foreign policy is conceived as . . . the pursuit of self-regarding interests that take no account of the interests of others" (1977: 164). Diplomacy is more than "simply the determined assertion of the national will" (Neumann 2003: 353).

Liberal diplomacy is based on a sense of both equality and empathy. One must recognize that others have interests as well. The essence of being reasonable is to take the interests of others into consideration. Alan Gewirth writes, "A reasonable person is one who takes due account of the interests of other persons, respecting their rights as well as one's own and maintaining a certain equitableness or mutuality of consideration between oneself and others" (1983: 225). Similarly, communicative action requires the ability to see things through the eyes of others (Risse 2001).

[19]

Marc Lynch writes, "strategic action is defined by the orientation to-wards achieving predefined egoistic ends, treating the other as an object to be manipulated, while communicative action is characterized by the orientation towards achieving understanding, treating the other as an equal participant" (2002: 192). In this ideal speech situation, in which reasoned dialogue can prevail, Nicole Dietelhoff and Harald Müller explain, "Discourses need to guarantee that asymmetric power resources of participants do not influence the discursive interplay: only converging perceptions and viewpoints of the participants lead to a rational consensus. Everyone affected must be able to take part and should have an equal opportunity to speak and to listen to others. These criteria underline the necessity that actors empathise with each other; they are required to . . . emancipate themselves from the egocentricity of their preferences so they are able to reflect about them as one among alternative sets of preferences" (2005: 169).

This is not, however, pure altruism or the suppression of one's own interests. Liberal diplomacy involves the pursuit of fair compromises and win-win outcomes through creative problem solving. John Owen writes, "Liberals have transformed, rather than transcended, selfishness" (1997: 35). Francis Watson writes, "It is a function of the diplomatic dialogue to mitigate and civilize the differences between states and if possible to reconcile them, without suppressing or ignoring them" (1981: 20). Sharp writes of "dampening passions and moderating egos by reducing ignorance and elevating reason" and "the resolution of conflicts by procedures that encourage fair compromise" (2009: 39). Liberals are not teleological utopians who believe in the natural harmony of interests (Doyle 1997: 211; Zacher and Matthew 1995: 110; Keohane 1989: 11); however, unlike in realism, others are not regarded as pure means to egoistic ends. Nicolson writes of this style, "There is probably some middle point between the two negotiators which, if discovered, should reconcile their conflict interests. And to find this middle point all that is required is a frank discussion, the placing of cards upon the table, and the usual processes of human reason, confidence and fair-dealing" (1980: 54).

Coercive bargaining stands in clear contrast to liberal dialogue in that the former is a process of information gathering rather than information sharing through argumentation or deliberation. There is neither good faith nor goodwill. Indeed, the foundation of the rationalist bargaining approach is that information cannot be shared credibly unless it is backed by a costly signal. In coercive bargaining, actors start from the assumption that others are not negotiating in good faith. "Actors know each other as *strategists*, and they must thus fear that apparently innocent and useful information is untrue" (Müller 2004: 398). And the goal is to seize as much of the pie as possible by inflating one's demands and using pressure to secure an individually beneficial outcome.

Liberal diplomacy potentially allows state representatives to reach mutually beneficial outcomes through communication. "Relative power may play a role in determining whether or not state leaders decide to try to cooperate, but persuasion is, to a significant extent, out of the grasp of power. The ability to persuade is in the hands of the diplomats," writes Mai'a Cross (2007: 4). Yet liberal scholars have not articulated a theory of diplomacy. Grotians are more taken with broader historical trends in the practice of diplomacy. For their part, Habermasian constructivists have been content so far simply to conceptualize a kind of diplomacy distinctive from coercive bargaining without specifying when and by whom it is likely to be adopted (Reus-Smit 1999: 28). Again, the solution offered in this book is to behavioralize the insights of liberal international relations scholars, identifying those diplomats who are more inclined to engage in the kind of reasoned dialogue they highlight. Liberal diplomacy should be facilitated by egalitarian-mindedness and genuine empathy, a prosocial stance toward international relations. In the next chapter, I begin this task of converting the insights of international relations theory into a theory of diplomacy.

[2]

Creating Value

A Psychological Theory of Diplomacy

Although diplomacy is arguably the most prevalent activity in inter-state relations, rigorous theoretical and careful empirical work on diplomacy in international relations is extremely sparse (Der Derian 1987: 91; Sharp 2009: 1–2). Those few scholars who have explicitly engaged the subject complain that "IR [international relations] theory . . . has yet to give a theoretical account of what diplomacy is" (Jönnson and Hall 2005: 24). James Der Derian notes that "diplomacy has been particularly resistant to theory"; he cannot find "a substantial theoretical work on the subject in the contemporary literature of international relations" (1987: 91).[1] There is considerable research in recent years on diplomacy as a practice (Adler-Nissen 2014; Pouliot 2010; Neumann 2012; Sending 2011; Reus-Smit 1999). Yet the aim of this work is not to specify a theory of when diplomacy matters independently of other factors and how to establish that empirically.[2]

In this chapter, I build a theory of diplomacy, looking for guidance in three psychological literatures—on negotiation, political ideology, and moral values. The sections in this chapter link together disparate findings in these fields to develop a theory of diplomacy as agency. Like

---

1. Perhaps the most prolific student of the process, Paul Sharp admits that "what diplomacy is remains a mystery. . . . What we know about diplomacy has typically come from former diplomats themselves or from historians who document but do not explain its precise mechanisms" (2009: 1–2).

2. Those working in this vein generally understand diplomacy as a macro-level institution of international society, rather than a micro-level process in which individuals seek interests for their state. The two are not incompatible but operate at different levels of analysis with a different degree of historical sweep.

diplomats themselves sometimes do, I hope to create value through the combination of these different strands of research.

I first review the literature on negotiation, laying out the difference between value claiming and value creating. Formal rationalist work attributes negotiation behavior and outcomes to features of the structural situation, such as the distribution of power and interests. This vein of research, however, has difficult explaining how negotiators resolve the dilemma when they have incentives to engage in both value claiming and value creating, and it problematically assumes that all negotiators interpret the same environment identically. Studies inspired by social and cognitive psychology show that attributes of the negotiators matter in addition to structure. Particular combinations of epistemic motivation and social motivation lead to different negotiating styles that demonstrate a remarkable parallel to the conceptions of diplomacy uncovered in chapter 1. These affect how political actors interpret their task and predispose negotiators toward value claiming or value creating independent of their situation.

I then develop a series of hypotheses about which kind of negotiating will prevail when different diplomatic styles interact. Because international relations theory does not yet offer a theory of diplomacy, the primary rival to a psychologically driven account is a purely structural account derived from microeconomic bargaining theory in which diplomacy is endogenous and epiphenomenal to situational factors. Structural theories provide a baseline from which to judge the effect of agency. Nevertheless, as we will see, rationalism and psychology are not mutually exclusive. Structure matters, but it is hardly the whole story.

Establishing the effect of diplomacy poses some thorny methodological issues of measurement and causal inference. Diplomatic outcomes might be epiphenomenal to the distribution of power and interests. Diplomatic style might be endogenous to those same factors. And the selection of cases might be biased in favor of finding an effect for diplomacy. In the last section, on research design, I explain how I chose the appropriate cases to solve these problems as well as how I rigorously measure psychological motivations and diplomatic styles in a nontautological way. In short, social and epistemic motivations are embedded in the political ideology of actors, allowing us to measure them independently of behavior. We then look for variations in diplomatic style among political parties in the same country that share the same foreign policy interests and beliefs, thereby showing that diplomatic style is not endogenous. Particular combinations of diplomatic styles are capable of yielding successful outcomes when others are not, even though the distribution of power interests is more or less constant; this shows that diplomacy is not epiphenomenal. And the core of the book revolves around a case in which

[23]

the preconditions for diplomatic success and value creating were completely absent at the beginning, mitigating the danger of selection bias.

NEGOTIATING STYLES: CREATING OR CLAIMING VALUE

Both the formal and the psychological literatures generally distinguish between types of negotiation. *Value claiming*, sometimes called distributive or contending negotiation, is marked by noncooperative behavior—one side making significant demands of the other side and refusing to make or only grudgingly making concessions. Value claiming is marked by the heavy use of "positional commitments," in which parties insist on specific settlements tilted highly in their favor and threaten to walk away unless their demands are met. The aim is to pressure the other side into making concessions, coercing others into deals closer to one's ideal point. Concessions from others are derided as inadequate yet quickly pocketed without reciprocation. Holdouts and delays can be used to extract as much as possible from the other side. One never reveals private information about his or her "reservation point," the lowest possible outcome he or she would be ready to accept. Indeed, value claiming revolves around trying to make the other side believe that point is as high as possible. All sources of leverage are used. One might hold an issue of value to the other (but not necessarily to oneself) hostage, refusing to concede on it so as to extract concessions on more important issues (Odell 2000; De Dreu and Boles 1998; Beersma and De Dreu 1999; Olekalns, Smith, and Kibby 1996; Pruitt and Lewis 1975; De Dreu and Carnevale 2003; McKibben 2014; Weingart et al. 2007).

Value creating, on the other hand, aims at a win-win outcome in which both sides secure their most important goals. Also called cooperative, integrative, or problem-solving negotiation, value creating proceeds through reciprocity rather than coercion. In contrast to withholding information, value creating is possible only if states honestly and openly reveal their preference structure. Information exchange is crucial because only then is the potential for a win-win deal revealed. If states do not have asymmetrical preferences, those engaged in value creating will act creatively, trying to draw in other issues through side payments that make a mutually beneficial package deal. One concedes on issues of lesser importance, rather than holding them hostage, in exchange for concessions by the other side on those issues that one values more. Integrative negotiation avoids the use of threats and the brinksmanship of value claiming negotiation.

Note that the integrative style does *not* imply that one is "failing to work diligently to gain value for one's own side" (Odell 2000: 32). Value

[24]

creating is no less self-interested than is value claiming (Odell 2000; De Dreu and Boles 1998; Beersma and De Dreu 1999; Olekalns, Smith, and Kibby 1996; Pruitt and Lewis 1975; De Dreu and Carnevale 2003; McKibben 2014; Weingart et al. 2007). Indeed value claiming negotiating, if it fails, can often result in a lower individual outcome than integrative negotiating, leaving potential gains on the table. Value creating is designed to "expand rather than split the pie" (Odell 2000: 21). It rests on reciprocity, in which concessions and information are exchanged so that both sides might benefit.

Perhaps the most common experimental scenario used in negotiation research involves two negotiators trying to reach a solution on three or more interconnected issues on which the pair has contrasting but also asymmetrical interests. In other words, each side would prefer to prevail on all the questions at hand, but the matter of most importance to each is different. For instance, participants in an experiment try to strike a deal on the sale of an appliance. They must agree on the price but also on the financing and the speed of delivery. The buyer would prefer the cheapest price, the least interest on financing, and the fastest delivery. The seller has the opposite preferences. There might nevertheless be potential outcomes that benefit both of them more than others; the key is to find them. For instance, the seller might care much more about price and the buyer about financing. In this way, integrative negotiation does not so much create value as it discovers it (Odell 2000; De Dreu and Boles 1998; Beersma and De Dreu 1999; Olekalns, Smith, and Kibby 1996; Pruitt and Lewis 1975; De Dreu and Carnevale 2003; McKibben 2014; Weingart et al. 2007).

Whereas the central problem in value claiming is demonstrating resolve, the main challenge in value creating is conveying cooperative intentions. Particularly in interactions among parties whose previous relations are marked by prior antipathy and conflict, value creating is likely to involve a process of reassurance (Glaser 2010; Kydd 2005; Ramsay 2011). One's interlocutors must be convinced that one is negotiating in good faith.

Value claiming negotiation should be familiar to students of international relations because it is the basis for the models of coercive bargaining discussed in chapter 1, which were pioneered by Thomas Schelling and have been elaborated more recently in bargaining theories of war (Schelling 1966; see also Fearon 1994, 1995; Schultz 2001). Value creating, with its emphasis on good faith and goodwill, parallels the liberal conception of diplomacy as reasoned dialogue. While reasoned dialogue also offers the potential for a fundamental reappraisal of one's interests arising from participation in the diplomatic process over the long term, I focus on the more simple process of discovering the potential for joint gains while holding interests constant.

[25]

The Structural Baseline: Microeconomic Bargaining Theory

Microeconomic bargaining theory, generally rationalist and formal in character, makes two primary claims regarding negotiation. First, the choice of negotiating strategy should be a function of one's bargaining leverage. This source of influence might be defined in various ways, such as satisfaction with the status quo, a restricted win set due to domestic political opposition, or material power. Those in a position of leverage should adopt a coercive bargaining strategy, something first observed by John Nash (1953) and subsequently applied to international relations (Moravcsik 1998; Morrow 1999; Muthoo 1999; Voeten 2001). Those lacking such leverage should pursue a conciliatory strategy of concessions or side payments, known as "obliging." Applied to diplomacy, a crude structural model would predict that diplomacy is endogenous to structure.

Second, rationalists expect that outcomes will reflect the distribution of bargaining leverage (Krasner 1991; Fearon 1998; Moravcsik 1998). In other words, the strong do as they will and the weak as they must. Applied to diplomacy, a crude structural model would expect diplomacy to be epiphenomenal. Outcomes are weighted toward status quo states or those with the power to coerce.

A more sophisticated set of structural arguments maintains that the underlying preference structure affects negotiating strategies as well as the outcome. Value creating strategies are more likely to be used when parties value different issues on the negotiating agenda differently, facilitating a package deal. When parties have symmetrical preferences—that is, the same preference function—negotiation takes on a zero-sum character and value claiming prevails (Axelrod and Keohane 1985; McGinnis 1986; Martin 1992, 1994; Lohmann 1997; Tollison and Willett 1979; Sebenius 1983; Martin 1994; Davis 2004; Morgan 1990). In such fixed-pie situations, states will resort to distributive bargaining. Where the pie can be expanded, they are able to create value. In any case, diplomatic style is still endogenous to the structure of interests, and the effect of diplomacy continues to be epiphenomenal.

Microeconomic bargaining theory has much to tell us about how states negotiate and forms the foundation of the argument that I advance. It reminds us that for successful diplomacy to take place there must be an overlap in the bargaining space between states and that states engage in a communicative process of conveying their interests to each other. If there is no outcome that both parties do not prefer to the status quo, no amount of diplomacy can overcome this short of a truly transformative process of persuasion. Nevertheless, bargaining theory is incomplete in a number of ways.

[26]

Given uncertainty, negotiators always face an incentive to engage in value claiming, even in situations with integrative potential. The very existence of joint gains is not revealed unless states engage in value creating negotiation (Pruitt and Lewis 1975; De Dreu, Koole, and Steinel 2000; Olekalns and Smith 2009: 347–48). The distribution of interests is not something that states necessarily know as they consider negotiating with one another. Finding an outcome that creates value requires players to reveal private information about which issues are most important to them and how far they can actually compromise without crossing their red lines. As Mara Olekalns and Philip Smith explain, "The decision to offer accurate information to the other party is a critical one. Without information about underlying interests, negotiators are unable to identify mutually beneficial outcomes" (2009: 347–48; see also Tomlinson, Dineen, and Lewick 2009; Pruitt and Lewis 1975). Experimental research shows that value creating is necessary to facilitate the striking of integrative deals in which both sides obtain what they value most (Schei and Rognes 2003; Weingart et al. 2007; De Dreu, Giebels, and Van de Vliert 1998; Beersma and De Dreu 1999; Pruitt and Lewis 1975; Schultz and Pruitt 1978; De Dreu, Koole, and Steinel 2000). A favorable distribution of interests is not sufficient for generating a win-win outcome.

Yet parties to a negotiation, even in the presence of potential joint gains, still have an incentive to maintain a value claiming negotiating strategy and conceal their underlying preferences (De Dreu, Koole, and Steinel 2000; O'Connor and Carnevale 1997). They can inflate the value of low-priority issues for use as bargaining chips (Olekalns and Smith 2009: 347–48; Risse 2000: 21). Even if they decide against this course, they will nevertheless fear that others will exploit their forthrightness (Jervis 1970; Fearon 1995; Schultz 2001; Glaser 2010). Or, just as problematically, they might not be believed when attempting such honest communication. At the heart of the rationalist approach to strategic interaction is an assumption of distrust among political actors (Kydd 2005; Rathbun 2012). States cannot believe others' representations of their interests.

In other words, value creating negotiation can be impeded by a kind of prisoner's dilemma logic. Olekalns and Smith write, "Despite these benefits, there is a strong temptation to withhold or misrepresent information as a way of increasing bargaining power and individual outcomes. Moreover, the decision to offer accurate information is high risk because it makes negotiators vulnerable to exploitation by the other party" (2009: 347–48). This dynamic might impede states from recognizing the existence of an underlying distribution of preferences that allows for value creating in the first place. This is the same conundrum highlighted by rationalists in distributive zero-sum games. By withholding

[27]

private information, even in fixed-pie situations, both parties risk not reaching an agreement that might have left both better off (Fearon 1995). Thomas Risse summarizes, "The successful joint search for better overall solutions requires creativity, effective communication, and mutual trust, whereas success in the distributive battle depends on strategic, and even opportunistic, communication and withholding of available information—and a good deal of distrust against potential misinformation" (2000: 21).

This lack of trust can make even coming to the table difficult (Ramsay 2011). If decision makers believe that others have malign intentions, they will refuse even to negotiate because any private information shared might be used against them in the event that talks break down (Schultz 2005; Larson 1997). Decision makers are also more likely to believe that there is no outcome that will leave both sides satisfied; that the greedy other will make unacceptable demands that can never be conceded; that the offer to negotiate reflects an ulterior motive; or that any agreement will be violated in the future, what rationalists call a commitment problem (Fearon 1995).

Value creating therefore requires both the structural fact of a potential package deal and also the agency that uncovers it. Rationalists argue that states might engage in a costly signaling process to reassure others about their cooperative intentions, which might *create* the trust necessary to facilitate value creating negotiation (Kydd 2005; Glaser 2010). Because the recipients of signals of assurance are uncertain of others' intentions and fear exploitation (most classically to be the "sucker" of a prisoner's dilemma), states seeking better relations must make unilateral and costly gestures of conciliation that leave themselves vulnerable so that their peaceful and cooperative intentions will be believed (Glaser 1994; 2010; Kupchan 2010; Jervis 1976). Implicitly in this vein, Kristopher Ramsay (2011) argues that states might honestly indicate their willingness to compromise, thereby revealing private information that demonstrates a serious intent to negotiate. Ramsay calls this cheap talk, but in revealing something about their reservation price, this is surely a costly action. Nonrationalists make similar arguments, stressing that these signals should not be made contingent on immediate reciprocal concessions (Larson 1997; Etzioni 1962; Osgood 1962; Nincic 2011).

These are important insights, and signals of this sort are undoubtedly crucial for generating value creating negotiation. Nevertheless, rationalist theories are incomplete in a number of ways. First, taking such steps toward reassurance presumes what Ken Booth and Nicolas Wheeler (2008) call "security dilemma sensibility," the understanding that the other side is wary of one's actions, something that should not be taken for granted. In fact, in the cases that are difficult for diplomacy, those examined in this book, such a sensibility is distinctly lacking. Security dilemma sensibility requires states to objectively view the situation both from their own standpoint and from that of others.

Second, even when such costly signals are made, there is no guarantee they will be perceived as reassuring. Rationalists generally assume that all individuals will have the same prior beliefs and information and will interpret their environment similarly (Rathbun 2007; Yarhi-Milo 2014; Schultz 2005; Fearon 1995: 392). Clearly, such an assumption is not likely to hold up to empirical scrutiny. It is well known in the psychological literature on international relations that decision makers often operate on the basis of assumptions and heuristics that lead them to pay more attention to some pieces of information than others (Tetlock 1998). They often engage in belief assimilation and belief perseverance, drawing inferences from information that allows them to maintain a certain image of the other (Jervis 1976; Tetlock 1998; Yarhi-Milo 2014; Mercer 1996). This creates the possibility that seemingly objective costly signals will be judged by some as cheap talk whereas objective cheap talk will be regarded as credible signals. This subjectivity "opens the door for negotiators' attributions and perceptions to shape how negotiations unfold" (Neale and Fragale 2006: 27). Who will read the signals in which way is an open question.

BEHAVIORAL NEGOTIATION THEORY: AGENCY AND INDIVIDUAL ATTRIBUTES

The poor record of microeconomic bargaining theory in explaining negotiation behavior has spawned an interest in social cognition approaches to negotiation built on previous work in behavioral economics. As Margaret Neale and Alison Fragale write, "Traditional economic theories, as well as conventional wisdom, suggest that negotiations should be rational transactions guided by the principle of utility maximization. . . . Unfortunately, in reality, negotiations are rarely this straightforward, and negotiations often fail to play out according to the predictions of rational choice models" (2006: 27). This psychological-inspired literature on negotiation provides solutions to the problems we have identified. It explains how individuals' characteristics lead them to engage in very different negotiating behaviors in the same strategic situation based on how they interpret the environment. When this literature is applied to international relations, it indicates how diplomacy might be neither endogenous nor epiphenomenal to structure. I begin with the literature explaining individual behavior and then proceed to how different individual behaviors combine to produce different outcomes.

[29]

The literature to date highlights two individual motivations: social and epistemic. The former is the "desire to attain certain distributions of outcomes between oneself and the other party"; the latter is "the need to develop a rich and accurate understanding of the world" (De Dreu and Carnevale 2003). These directly parallel the two main themes of the behavioral economics literature: that individuals are not exclusively egoistic and that they are often less than rational (Kahneman 2003). As Neale and Fragale explain, "Unlike traditional economic models of negotiator behavior, the social cognition approach to negotiation recognizes that two negotiators, facing the same objective circumstances, may have different goals, express different behaviors, and obtain different benefits, simply because these two negotiators perceive their circumstances differently" (2006: 27). There is a very large psychological literature on the importance of individual-level differences in negotiation that has not yet been tapped by international relations scholars.

The Value Difference: Social Motivation

Social motivation is the most powerful predictor of individual-level differences in negotiation analysis to date (Deutsch 1960; McClintock 1972; Messick and McClintock 1968). Prosocial motivation is marked by a concern for not only one's own outcome but that of others as well. Prosocials want to maximize joint benefits. They are also concerned with guaranteeing an equal distribution of gains (De Cremer and Van Lange 2001). In contrast, proselfs have only egoistic interests. Social motivation is either primed in experiments through a treatment, so as to reduce omitted-variable bias, or captured as an intrinsic quality through measures of social value orientation. It has consistently been found that individuals have dispositional tendencies to prefer different distributions of benefits for themselves and others that substantially influence behavior in experimental settings. Research has indicated that priming social motivation and capturing intrinsic individual differences through prenegotiation surveys yield the same pattern of results in experimental behavior (De Dreu and Carnevale 2003).

These motivations help decision makers resolve the dilemma they face between value creating and value claiming behaviors. Prosocials generally prefer value creating negotiation; proselfs prefer value claiming negotiation (Olekalns, Smith, and Kibby 1996; Pruitt and Lewis 1975; Fry 1985; Beersma and De Dreu 1999). Proselfs offer less and demand more. In experiments, proselfs make less conciliatory first offers and lower overall concessions than prosocials (De Dreu and Boles 1998; De Dreu and Van Lange 1995; Carnevale and Lawler 1986; Van Lange 1999; Van Lange and Kuhlman 1994; De Cremer and Van Lange 2001; Liebrand et al.

1986) and make higher demands of others (De Dreu and van Lange 1995; Olekalns, Smith, and Kibby 1996; De Dreu and Van Kleef 2004). Proselfs engage in more positional commitments, in which they draw a line they claim they will not cross (Carnevale and Lawler 1986). Proselfs also make more threats and give more warnings (De Dreu, Giebels, and Van de Vliert 1998; see also Beersma and De Dreu 1999; Tomlinson, Dineen, and Lewicki 2009; Weingart et al. 2007; Sorenson, Morse, and Savage 1999).

Committed to equal outcomes, prosocials often forgo gains so that others might also share in the spoils (Kuhlman and Wimberley 1976; Kuhlman and Marshello 1975; McClintock and Liebrand 1988). In "take-some and give-some" games, in which experimental participants move after an initial offer has been made, there is a dominant egoistic strategy of retaining all chips for oneself. Nevertheless, prosocials give significantly more than proselfs (Van Lange 1999; De Cremer and Van Lange 2001). In situations in which the decision about allocation must be made simultaneously, before knowing what the other does, prosocials give as much as they expect others to give, whereas proselfs donate less. Because the experiment is a one-shot game, there is no strategic reason to be generous (Van Lange 1999). Prosocials express a greater interest in the welfare of others in post-experiment surveys and less interest in maximizing their own utility (De Cremer and Van Lange 2001; De Dreu and Van Lange 1995). Concern for one's own outcomes and lack of concern for the other's outcomes are both associated statistically with lower levels of concessions and higher level of demands in negotiation settings (De Dreu and Van Lange 1995; Sorenson, Morse, and Savage 1999).

Rationalist bargaining theories expect those with the bargaining leverage that comes with an exit option, such as being more satisfied with the status quo, to exploit it. But experimental research indicates that prosocials do not take generally take advantage of such opportunities; only proselfs do. In a game with integrative potential, having a one-sided exit option in the form of a payoff leads proselfs to engage in more coercive bargaining with more threats, leading to higher individual outcomes. Giving prosocials such power does not lead to a change in behavior (Giebels, De Dreu, and Van de Vliert 2000). Proselfs are more opportunistic and exploitative negotiators (Van Lange 1999). They meet weakness with higher demands (De Dreu and Van Kleef 2004). And they have been found to exploit asymmetric information about other's type, whereas prosocials have not (Schei and Rognes 2003).

Proselfs and prosocials differ in terms of their values. That the term *value* indicates both the price that individuals place on something and the moral principles that guide individuals in life is an indication that we cannot separate negotiation from ethical considerations. Even selfish behavior can have a moral motivation or justification. Individuals have a general tendency to regard themselves as fairer, more moral, and more honest than the average other and consequently believe that they deserve more in negotiations (Kramer, Pommerenke, and Newton 1993; Messick et al. 1985; Rothbart and Hallmark 1988; Thompson and Loewenstein 1992; Paese and Yonker 2001). Individuals often exhibit ego defensiveness, seeing themselves as more entitled than others. They also might engage in reactive devaluation, in which others' offers are seen as insufficient and insulting (De Dreu and Carnevale 2003). Both behaviors are particularly common among proselfs. Self-righteousness is still a kind of righteousness.

The Cognitive Difference: Epistemic Motivation

Those with different social motivations adopt different negotiating styles because they have unique framings of the same situation. Negotiating strategies are accompanied by particular mindsets that operate as simplifying heuristics (Carnevale and Pruitt 1992; De Dreu and Boles 1998). Proselfs are more likely than prosocials to adopt a fixed-pie framing, viewing negotiations in distributive and zero-sum terms even when there is the potential for outcomes of mutual benefit (De Dreu and Boles 1998; De Dreu, Weingart, and Kwon 2000; De Dreu, Koole, and Steinel 2000). They are guided by notions such as "winner take all" and "your loss is my gain" (De Dreu and Boles 1998). Prosocials, in contrast, see more possibility for joint gains because they are more likely to frame negotiations in mixed-motive terms, in which interests are only partially incompatible (Olekalns, Smith, and Kibby 1996; Golec and Federico 2004). They view negotiations more as a problem to be solved than as a game to be won.

Heuristics provide cognitive shortcuts that tell individuals how the world generally works and what their interactions with others will generally be like. Individuals generally expect others to share their social motivation, which is known in the literature as the egocentric bias (Iedema and Poppe 1994; Kuhlman and Wimberley 1976). Not surprisingly, given their different framings of the same situation, prosocials expect negotiations to be more friendly than do proselfs (De Dreu and Boles 1998).

Nevertheless, as shortcuts, heuristics can distort reality and interfere with the accurate interpretation of information. Behavioral economists and psychologists use heuristics to explain how individuals are less than rational (Kahneman 2003). These simplifying devices lead individuals to engage in confirmatory information searches, searching out and interpreting incoming stimuli to be in line with preexisting beliefs (De Dreu and Van Kleef 2004). For instance, prosocials are more open to signals of cooperative intent than proselfs because these signals confirm their pre-existing beliefs in the joint benefits of cooperation. In contrast, proselfs demonstrate considerable reactive devaluation, denigrating even the generous offers of others (De Dreu and Carnevale 2003: 248).

In addition, psychological researchers point to the important role played by epistemic motivation, "the need to develop a rich and accurate understanding of the world" (De Dreu and Carnevale 2003: 235), in moderating the use of heuristics during negotiation (De Dreu et al. 2006; De Dreu, Koole, and Oldermsa 1999). Epistemic motivation encourages openness to, and the complex processing of, new information. Those who are lower in epistemic motivation demonstrate more of a need for closure. Their information processing is marked by "seizing" and "freezing." They feel an urgency to make a decision quickly and are disinclined to revisit it because they are uncomfortable with uncertainty and ambiguity (Kruglanski and Webster 1996; Webster and Kruglanski 1994). Those who lack epistemic motivation are less committed to developing a completely objective view of the situation they are in. De Dreu and Peter Carnevale summarize: "Individuals at the high need for closure end of the continuum are characterized by considerable cognitive impatience, leaping to judgment on the basis of inconclusive evidence and rigidity of thought. At the other end of the continuum, individuals with low need for closure may prefer to suspend judgment, engaging in extensive information search and generating multiple interpretations for known facts" (2003: 262).

Those with epistemic motivation are more likely to revisit and revise their beliefs in light of disconfirming evidence than are those with the same prior beliefs and social motivation because they are more open to information (Tetlock 2005; Baron 1994; Mitzen and Schweller 2011; Stanovich and West 1998, 2000). In the case of negotiations with those viewed from past experience as hostile, uncooperative, and intransigent, they will be more receptive to signals of reassurance to the contrary than will proselfs who have a higher level of cognitive closure. The latter are more likely to engage in belief perseverance and belief assimilation. Those with epistemic motivation are also more able and more motivated to look at a situation from the point of view of others. When they interact with those with whom they have had past conflicts, this allows for the security dilemma sensibility often necessary to initiate negotiations. Finally, those with greater epistemic motivation are better able to admit the hard truth of their relative weakness when they are in unfavorable bargaining positions, a weakness that can make coercive bargaining fruitless. All these behaviors require cognitive effort, the hallmark of those with epistemic motivation.

[33]

THEORETICAL EXPECTATIONS

We now have the tools to behavioralize the diplomatic styles we uncovered in chapter 1. The combination of epistemic and social motivation produces the four different diplomatic styles seen in figure 1, three of which we have already explored. Prosocials with high epistemic motivation are liberals who prefer reasoned dialogue. As reviewed in chapter 1, reason involves both a commitment to finding the truth through an exchange of information and arguments and a desire to find value for the other side as well as oneself. The former tendency is indicative of epistemic motivation, the latter of prosocial motivation.

Proselfs with low epistemic motivation are inclined to be coercive bargainers. Proselfs with high epistemic motivation are predisposed toward being realist advocates of pragmatic statecraft. Whereas the former are prisoners of their heuristics, the latter should be better able to adjust to their situation. They will be highly attuned to structure and adopt behaviors typically associated with both coercive bargaining and reasoned dialogue styles. I refer to integrative and distributive tactics used by pragmatists. *Tactics* are different from styles in that they are temporary. The term captures how pragmatists move back and forth between distributive and integrative negotiation, neither of which captures their general style. The pragmatist style is to have no fixed tactics. The realist uses all the tools in his or her toolkit.

Epistemic motivation

		Low	High
Proself		Coercive bargaining	Pragmatic statecraft (realist)
Social motivation **Prosocial**		Obliging	Reasoned dialogue (liberal)

FIGURE 1 Diplomatic styles.

The common thread of the pragmatist style is a global understanding of the situation, which requires more cognitive effort. More than others, pragmatists should (1) stress the priority of vital interests over peripheral considerations and the need to make painful tradeoffs; (2) self-consciously adopt an objective and unemotional appraisal of the environment, including the interests of other states; and (3) emphasize the necessity of thinking in steps toward a long-term goal.[3] Pragmatists evaluate not just the present but also the future, not just one of their interests but all of their interests, and not just their own interests but those of others. These are all driven by an explicitly egoistic instrumentalism. Pragmatists should find themselves better able to overcome the fixed-pie bias in situations in which there is integrative potential. Less committed to their heuristics, pragmatists will be open to signals of both cooperativeness and hostility. Epistemic motivation should encourage perspective taking, in which one puts oneself in another's position, the instrumental empathy that realist theorists prescribe.[4] To the extent that pragmatists pursue more integrative, conciliatory, and cooperative policies, they are nevertheless driven by instrumental proself motivations rather than by any normative commitment to reciprocity and joint gain, as prosocials are.

Prosocials with low epistemic motivation are the rosy-eyed idealistic utopians who Edward H. Carr (1964) warns about, those who are naively oblivious to wolves in sheep's clothing. They engage in "obliging." For reasons that I explain later, however, prosocials with a low epistemic motivation are likely to be relatively rare in politics, particularly international politics, and therefore we can focus primarily on the other three styles of diplomacy. Therefore, when I refer to prosocials in the empirical cases I present, I mean prosocials with high epistemic motivation.

Whether value creating or value claiming comes to prevail among negotiators is a function of the combination and interaction of diplomatic styles. The choice made by one country of how to negotiate is not always monadic in nature but often depends on the choices made by other states. This combination is what affects the character of the interaction among

---

3. This is not the same as having a longer time horizon, a greater discounting of present benefits, or a higher evaluation of future benefits. It is not that pragmatists are better able to deny themselves the immediate gratification of smaller gains and wait for larger gains down the line. They are more likely to point to the value of short-term benefits and even costs as steps in a gradual process rather than to denigrate them as insufficient and reject them. On the difference, see Rapport (2012).

4. This is different from genuine empathy in that it is instrumental in character.

the parties. Although value claiming and value creating are terms that also might be used to capture the negotiating styles of particular units, I reserve the use of these expressions to capture the spirit of negotiations. When referring to the individual use of value claiming, I refer to coercive bargaining, coercive diplomacy, or distributive negotiating. When referring to the individual use of value creating, I refer to reasoned dialogue, integrative negotiating, or liberal diplomacy.

In what particular combination of diplomatic styles is value claiming or value creating more likely to prevail? The most consistent finding in the social motivation literature on negotiation is that prosocial dyads are better able than proselfs to reach joint outcomes that benefit both partners (Schei and Rognes 2003; Weingart et al. 2007; De Dreu, Giebels, and Van de Vliert 1998; Beersma and De Dreu 1999; Pruitt and Lewis 1975; Schulz and Pruitt 1978; De Dreu, Koole, and Steinel 2000; De Dreu et al. 2006; De Dreu and Boles 1998; De Dreu, Weingart, and Kwon 2000; Olekalns, Smith, and Kibby 1996; Carnevale and Lawler 1986). Considering the literature review above, this is not particularly surprising since each party has a preference for the same style of negotiation.

Research shows that proself dyads consistently leave gains on the table compared to prosocials because they do not share information or reciprocate concessions. These dyads are less able to reach integrative outcomes in which both sides obtain what they value most, even when such a possibility exists given preference structures (Schei and Rognes 2003; Weingart et al. 2007; De Dreu, Giebels, and Van de Vliert 1998; Beersma and De Dreu 1999; Pruitt and Lewis 1975; Schulz and Pruitt 1978; De Dreu, Koole, and Steinel 2000). This leads to my first two hypotheses.

- *Hypothesis 1:* Value creating negotiation will prevail among prosocials practicing liberal diplomacy, making mutually beneficial agreements easier to reach.
- *Hypothesis 2:* Value claiming negotiation will prevail among proselfs practicing coercive bargaining, making mutually beneficial agreements more difficult to reach.

In the former case, negotiations will proceed more quickly and outcomes are less likely to simply reflect the distribution of bargaining power. In the latter case, successful agreements are harder to reach and stalemates are more likely. Negotiations will be slower and more arduous, with both parties engaging in brinksmanship bargaining. Agreements that are reached will probably reflect the crude distribution of bargaining power if the weaker side finally capitulates. This does not indicate that diplomacy is epiphenomenal. Such outcomes emerge when a particular type of negotiation prevails. Diplomacy is still necessary to explain when pure structure prevails.

Pragmatists, given their higher epistemic motivation, should find it easier to recognize when it makes more sense to engage in value creating than in value claiming. Pragmatists are particularly likely to shift to integrative negotiating when they face prosocials and when they have less power (or expect to have less power in the future), that is, when coercive diplomacy is inefficient and inappropriate for the particular situational circumstances. Research shows that prosocials do not behave differently toward prosocials and proselfs pursuing a tit-for-tat strategy (McClintock and Liebrand 1988). These findings open up the possibility of collaboration between pragmatists and prosocials in a Baptist-bootlegger coalition to reach the joint gains of an integrative deal, particularly if the pragmatist is not in a position to exploit the other side's weakness in a proself manner (Schei and Rognes 2003).

- *Hypothesis 3:* Proselfs higher in epistemic motivation (pragmatists) will adapt their diplomatic style to the structure of the situation more easily than proselfs lower in epistemic motivation (coercive bargainers) when there is the possibility of joint gains, thereby making value creating with a pragmatic or prosocial partner easier.

Value claiming negotiation, however, is likely to prevail in any dyad that contains a coercive bargainer. Distributive negotiation induces a lowest-common-denominator effect on interactions with those with other diplomatic styles. Research shows that prosocials' commitment to value creating negotiation is contingent on reciprocity. Prosocials' commitment to equality and fairness places limits on their other-regarding behavior (De Cremer and Van Lange 2001). Reaching equal outcomes requires that others contribute to the group as well. In mixed-motive cooperation games, prosocials do not consistently choose the outcome that maximizes joint gains if the other is not cooperating (Kuhlman and Marshello 1975; Kuhlman and Wimberley 1976). Consistent with their emphasis on joint gains, prosocials demonstrate a greater degree of "compensatory" trust, being willing to put up with a few defections to elicit cooperation (Kramer et al. 2004). Nevertheless, in a phenomenon known as *behavioral assimilation*, they defect against defection, indicating again that their interest in joint gains hinges on a commitment to reciprocity and equality (Stouten, De Cremer, and van Dijk 2006; Kanagaretnam et al. 2009; Kelley and Stahelski 1970; Kuhlman and Marshello 1975; Kuhlman and Wimberley 1976; McClintock and Liebrand 1988; Rotter

[37]

1980). Prosocials begin with a *general* preference for value creating, but this might change their behavior vis-à-vis *specific* partners. Dialogue takes two; it is not a monologue.

This alerts us again to the important point that concern for other's outcomes does not imply a lack of consideration for one's own gains. It is the combination of a concern for one's own outcome *and* the outcome of others that tends to drive instances of win-win value creating (De Dreu, Weingart, and Kwon 2000; Kimmel et al. 1980; Pruitt and Lewis 1975; Sorenson, Morse, and Savage 1999; De Dreu et al. 2006). Prosocials want to expand the pie, not simply let others eat all of it.

Prosocials have been found to shift from an integrative to a distributive negotiating style when the number of proselfs in a group increases (Weingart et al. 2007; Beersma and De Dreu 1999). Indeed, research shows that the joint outcomes of prosocials and proselfs in experiments tend to be as low as those between proselfs (Fry 1985; Beersma and De Dreu 1999). Prosocials significantly award generosity and punish stinginess (De Cremer and Van Lange 2001; Van Lange 1999; see also Liebrand et al. 1986; Kanagaretnam et al. 2009; Van Lange and Kuhlman 1994). They are less honest with proselfs than with other prosocials (Steinel and De Dreu 2004).

Reciprocity is a morally laden principle of behavior for prosocials, not an instrumental one of the kind generally seen in the international relations literature, which is based on long-term egoistic considerations (Keohane 1984). Prosocials attribute behavior by others to moral characteristics, holding prosocials to be more moral than defectors. Prosocials believe that honesty will have a greater effect on the level of cooperation of others than proselfs do (Kanagaretnam et al. 2009; Liebrand et al. 1986; Van Lange and Kuhlman 1994). Similar findings are found in negotiation studies. Prosocials believe distributive strategies to be morally inappropriate (De Dreu and Boles 1998).

Pragmatists, too, are unlikely to engage in value creating vis-à-vis a coercive bargainer because it leaves them vulnerable to exploitation. There is no instrumental gain from cooperative negotiation. Therefore,

- *Hypothesis 4:* Coercive bargaining by proselfs with low epistemic motivation will induce value claiming on the part of others, leading to negotiations with a value claiming character.

By crossing the three types of negotiators, we generate different types of potential dyads and expectations for the spirit of diplomatic interactions (see figure 2). Because obligers are relatively rare empirically, I do not include them in the figure 2.

[38]

	Coercive bargaining	Pragmatic statecraft	Reasoned dialogue
Coercive bargaining	Value claiming likely		
Pragmatic statecraft	Value claiming likely	Value creating possible	
Reasoned dialogue	Value claiming likely	Value creating possible	Value creating likely

FIGURE 2 Interaction of diplomatic styles.

METHODOLOGY: DEMONSTRATING THE ADDED VALUE OF DIPLOMACY

My hypotheses do not give us a firm and specific prediction about the success of diplomacy in any particular case. The nature of any agreement, that is the ultimate outcome, depends on other factors that must be treated exogenously on a case-by-case basis, the most important of which is the structural environment. We must know the distribution of interests and whether it creates the possibility for a mutually beneficial outcome. We must know the distribution of power and which side is favored. Only then can we know whether diplomacy has added value. Evaluating the influence of the character of diplomatic interaction, the added value of diplomacy, therefore requires careful reconstruction of the diplomatic environment to generate the structural baseline. This forms the null hypothesis that might emerge from a simple rationalist bargaining model in which the powerful or satisfied prevail.

The study of diplomacy poses particularly difficult methodological problems, particularly regarding causal inference, case selection, and measurement. First, it might be the case that the effect of the character of the interactions, value creating or value claiming, is epiphenomenal. For

[39]

instance, parties whose reservation points are close together might find agreement easy to reach, but this has little do with diplomacy. This problem is exacerbated by the danger of selection effects. States have a number of reasons not to begin negotiations unless they believe somewhat strongly that they are likely to bear fruit (Ramsay 2011). Therefore, the set of cases marked by the convocation of formal negotiations is likely to be unrepresentative and biased in favor of successful agreement. This has nothing to do with diplomacy per se but, rather, reflects a large zone of possible agreement.

I use a number of strategies to overcome these obstacles. The solution to the epiphenomenality problem lies in rigorous research design. We are looking for cases in which diplomatic style varies but other structural factors, such as the distribution of power and interests, do not. A longitudinal research design in which some combination of states with the same attributes is negotiating the same issues over some restricted period of time is appropriate to this task. This is akin to a fixed-effect model in statistics. The 1920s are well suited for this task in that the same three countries negotiated over the same issues over the course of a decade with little or no change in underlying preferences. Yet the governments of these countries frequently changed hands, altering the diplomatic style and therefore the character of the interactions. There are instances of all the types of combinations specified in figure 2.

Second, to cope with the problem of selection bias, the important case is one in which the likelihood of success was low but in which the parties nevertheless pursued diplomacy and found success. This describes the Locarno process of 1925, the core of the book, in which relations among the parties were initially marked by profound mistrust. Because value creating depends on the open and honest sharing of information, relations among former adversaries are particularly disadvantageous to successful diplomacy. The hostility of Germany to the Versailles regime is well known. The peace settlement left it bitter but also diplomatically weak, a tough nut for diplomacy to crack. French politicians of all political stripes were terrified of a German *revanche*. Franco-German relations deteriorated further when France under Raymond Poincaré invaded the Ruhr in 1923 to force Germany to pay reparations. And the geopolitical environment was made all the more difficult by the tremendous domestic instability in France and Germany, each of which saw constant collapses in governing coalitions. Politicians faced powerful incentives to exacerbate tensions to prove their patriotic credentials. My second case, the Israeli-Palestinian conflict, is also marked by suspicion and hostility.

These cases also allow us to observe the behavior of actors with different diplomatic styles from the same starting point in regards to their beliefs about their interlocutors. For instance, it might be that prosocials

[40]

find value creating easier because they have more trust in the other side than do proselfs, which in other work I have found generally to be the case (Rathbun 2012). This would be a simple case of prosocial "doves" versus proself "hawks" (Schultz 2005). In these cases, however, distrust of the other is pronounced and invariant among all political actors in the same country. In the terms of Rathbun (2012), whereas prosocials have more "generalized trust," this does not apply to their historical adversaries; they do not have "particularized trust." Although trust might certainly facilitate value creating (Wheeler 2013), in these cases the parties began the process in its absence. As we will see, this makes epistemic motivation particularly important because it allows cognitively open individuals to revisit and revise their beliefs (Larson 1997).

Overall, the cases demonstrate instances in which agreement was extremely likely, given overlapping win sets or the potential for integrative negotiation, but nevertheless failed as well as cases in which diplomatic style overcame a structural environment rocky for diplomatic success, making us more confident in asserting that diplomacy added value to the outcome. So as not to be accused of cherry picking particular successes and failures, however, I engage all the efforts by Britain, France, and Germany to resolve issues of security during the 1920s.

But even if we demonstrate an independent effect of diplomatic style, we must be careful to consider the possibility that diplomatic style was induced by structure at some point earlier in the causal chain. Microeconomic bargaining theory expects that diplomatic style is strongly influenced by one's interests and power. This is the endogeneity problem. My solution to this issue is discussed more extensively in the next section. I establish that there was significant variation *within* a country in the preference for diplomatic style on the part of those with the same interests and information. If so, diplomatic style was not endogenous. This variation was evident both cross-sectionally at any point in time and longitudinally as one government took over from another.

Measurement

An argument relying on psychological motivations raises some difficult measurement issues. When the subject is the decision making of political elites, particularly when the cases are historical, these two motivations are difficult, if not impossible, to measure directly through the traditional psychological survey instruments. Indeed, those measures might not even be applicable. A prosocial in his personal life may not necessarily be a prosocial in diplomacy, and vice versa. We are looking for some way of predicting either prosocial or proself behavior on behalf of one's group in the arena of international politics as diplomats

[41]

take on the function of representing their nation-state in interactions with others. The psychological research on negotiation centers on how individuals interact with other individuals. These might very well be related, but we should not assume so.

The most direct way of measuring social motivation is to seek out evidence of how decision makers think about joint gains. It is not the case, as reviewed above, that prosocials are self-abnegating. The difference between proselfs and prosocials is in their degree of concern for the outcome of others. In the context of international relations, a proself position is an exclusively nationally oriented one. A prosocial position is a more internationalist, egalitarian, and universalist one. Social motivation is also evident in the heuristics that individuals exhibit, proselfs being marked by their fixed-pie and prosocials being marked by their expanding-pie characterizations of the situation. The most direct way of measuring epistemic motivation is looking for evidence about how decision-makers describe their thinking process. Reference to costs and benefits, feasibility, and anticipation of the reactions of others are all markers of a more epistemically motivated political actor.

These direct measures of our psychological attributes, however, are not easy to obtain and come with particular pitfalls. For social motivation, the danger is tautology. We risk measuring social motivation by reference to the negotiating and bargaining behavior of our actors such as their bargaining offers. For epistemic motivation, the danger is a lack of data. It is likely that those who lack epistemic motivation will be less inclined to describe their decision making since it will be less salient in their minds. Deliberate and effortful thought is a valence issue; no one wants to admit that they do not do it. Most of our data about key decision makers comprise what they do, and they generally act without explicit reference to their psychological motivations.

These issues lead me to supplement my direct measure with an indirect measure of these motivations. Making use of the latest advances in political psychology, I propose the innovation of capturing these constructs through political ideology. John Jost and colleagues make the case for political ideology as a motivated social cognition (2003). They argue that political ideology is driven by a number of underlying psychological motivations, which include those that other researchers have identified as crucial for understanding the psychology of negotiation.

As I have previously argued, the motivational difference between prosocials and proselfs is based on values, and value differences are at the heart of the distinction between left and right (Schwartz, Caprara, and Vecchione 2010; Barnea and Schwartz 1998; Piuko, Schwartz, and Davidov 2011; Caprara et al. 2006; Duriez and Van Hiel 2002; Cohrs et al. 2005). Values are "trans-situational goals that vary in importance and

[42]

serve as guiding principles in the life of a person or a group" (Schwartz 2007: 712). In Shalom Schwartz's scheme of universal values, those who identify with the left score more highly on "self-transcendence" values, marked by "benevolence," that is concern for the welfare of close others in everyday interaction, but more importantly "universalism," "understanding, appreciation, tolerance, and protection of *all* people and nature" (Schwartz 1992: 12, emphasis added). Schwartz himself refers to these as "prosocial" attitudes.

Left and right are distinguished in large part by their commitment to equality and the welfare of others, both of which Paul Van Lange has found to predict social motivation in interpersonal settings (Van Lange 1999; Jost et al. 2003). A preference for social hierarchy is one of the defining principles of conservatism, whereas a preference for egalitarianism is an attribute of the left. The left has an "approach" orientation. It wants to provide for others, which explains its support for state programs to help the most disadvantaged (Janoff-Bulman, Sheikh, and Baldacci 2007).[5] Helping those in the most need, of course, also serves to make society more equal, which is historically at the heart of distinguishing left from the right, even as the particular disadvantaged groups the left has sought to empower have evolved over time. More than fifty years ago, Seymour Martin Lipset wrote, "By 'left' we shall mean advocating social change in the direction of greater equality—political, economic, or social. By 'right,' we shall mean supporting a traditional, more or less hierarchical social order, and opposing change towards greater equality" (1954: 1135). This definition has maintained a broad consensus over time (Gerring 1998; Putnam 1973).

The left also identifies more strongly with the moral foundations of protecting others from harm and caring for their well-being as well as ensuring fairness and equality (Graham, Haidt, and Nosek 2009). Although there is great cultural and individual variation in moral values, social scientists have isolated a finite number of distinct moral systems, that is, discrete sets of different ethical values (Graham, Haidt, and Nosek 2009; Haidt, Graham, and Joseph 2009; Haidt and Joseph 2004). Fairness/reciprocity and harm/care are grouped by Haidt and his colleagues under a broader rubric of the "ethics of autonomy" (Schweder et al. 1997). These "individualizing foundations" form the backbone of liberal

---

5. Although some might object that the left is less libertarian than conservatives, liberal and conservative support for state action has a different basis. Whereas conservative enthusiasm for government is almost exclusively premised on preventing negative outcomes through institutional restraints, liberal support for government action aims at positively providing for society, harnessing the power of the state to redistribute wealth or reach collectively more optimal resource allocation (Dworkin 1985; Janoff-Bulman, Sheikh, and Baldacci 2007).

philosophical thinking, dating to the Enlightenment, in which morality is about how well or poorly individuals treated other individuals (Turiel 1983). David De Cremer and Paul Van Lange (2001), seeking a better understanding of what drives prosocial behavior, evoke the twin morally defined motives of social responsibility and justice, which parallel the constituent elements of the ethics of autonomy.

Whereas the left demonstrates a more universal prosocial motivation, the right is marked by its concern for the security, safety, and stability of the in-group, which Jost et al. (2007) calls the "existential motive." Hierarchy serves this motivation because it preserves social stability (Jost et al. 2003). The right sees adherence to traditional moral values and deference to authorities that coerce and punish violators of social norms as necessary checks on individual freedoms to protect society from those who would do others harm (Altemeyer 1998). Right-wing authoritarians resolve the trade-off between personal autonomy and social order in favor of the latter (Feldman 2003). They place a great stress on conformity and tradition because diversity and change are seen as threats to social cohesion and stability (Feldman and Stenner 1997). The left, in contrast, comes down in favor of greater political liberty, both in the United States and in other advanced democracies (Inglehart 1977; Inglehart and Flanagan 1987; Kitschelt 1988a, 1988b, 1994; Kitschelt and McGann 1995). The left see less threat to society from free expression. It is more comfortable and supportive of diversity (Duckitt 2001; Duckitt and Fisher 2003; Feldman and Stenner 1997; Janoff-Bulman 2009b; Jugert and Duckitt 2009; Stenner 2009; Van Leeuwen and Park 2009). The right also makes more intense distinctions between in-groups and out-groups and emphasizes loyalty to the former (Duckitt 2006; Duckitt et al. 2001; Jugert and Duckitt 2009; Van Leeuwen and Park 2009).

The right embraces the moral foundations of in-group/loyalty and authority/respect and Schwartz's conservation values. Authority/respect concerns the maintenance of social hierarchies to maintain social order. This moral foundation highlights the values of obedience, respect, and role fulfillment. In-group/loyalty stresses individuals' obligations to their group to preserve its cohesion, particularly against out-groups (Graham, Haidt, and Nosek 2009; Haidt, Graham, and Joseph 2009; Haidt and Joseph 2004). These moral systems serve the same function as others—constraining self-interested action to benefit society as a whole. They simply do so by subordinating individual needs to the needs of the larger community. They are "binding foundations" based on the "ethics of community" (Graham, Haidt, and Nosek 2009; Haidt, Graham, and Joseph 2009; Haidt and Joseph 2004).

The right identifies more strongly with conservation values, a set of principles that closely match the ethics of community, including

[44]

conformity, tradition, and security (Schwartz, Caprara, and Vecchione 2010; Barnea and Schwartz 1998; Piuko, Schwartz, and Davidov 2011; Caprara et al. 2006; Duriez and Van Hiel 2002; Cohrs et al. 2005). Conformity restrains the individual expression that would violate social expectations and norms. Tradition involves respect for the customs of one's society. Security indicates a high valuation of the safety of one's society. All these values promote social order, stability, and predictability by suppressing the individual, binding him or her to the in-group. They inhibit individualism by restricting change across time and variety across space (Stenner 2009). Jesse Graham and colleagues (2011) report a strong association between this cluster of values and the binding moral foundations of in-group/loyalty, authority/respect, and purity/sanctity.

Left and right also differ in terms of epistemic motivation. Those who are more ideologically extreme are less likely to be epistemically motivated because it is more painful for them to change their beliefs or depart from their core values. There is evidence for this in the literature on political psychology (Rathbun 2004; McClosky and Chong 1985; Tetlock 1988). Extremists have what psychologists call a directional motivation or motivated bias, a desire to reach a specific conclusion (Jost et al. 2003). Their beliefs determine their level of epistemic motivation. Therefore, we expect the relationship between political ideology and the political spectrum to be curvilinear.

In addition, there is reason to think that the right will demonstrate something more of a need for closure than the left (Tetlock 1983a, 1984; Van Hiel and Mervielde 2003). Individuals also have nondirectional motives, those that reflect the desire to arrive at a belief independent of its content (Jost et al. 2003). Those who demonstrate a need for closure are uncomfortable with ambiguity and uncertainty and therefore have been found to gravitate toward particular beliefs that provide predictability. The right might therefore be expected to exhibit lower levels of epistemic motivation because conservative values promise more stability. Their lower level of epistemic motivation contributes to the adoption of their specific beliefs. Consistent with this theory, the need for closure is associated with support for a socially conservative program of traditional morality, social conformity, and strong law-and-order policies (Altemeyer 1998; Duckitt 2001; Duckitt and Sibley 2009; Kossowska and Van Hiel 2003).

Jost et al. argue that people on the right also have an "epistemic motive," a motivation to avoid uncertainty because they find it threatening (2007: 990). As a consequence, even though epistemic motivation is curvilinear in relation to the political spectrum, we can expect it to decline somewhat more precipitously on the right than on the left. Therefore variation in epistemic motivation will induce a particularly salient cleavage within the right, which is otherwise unified in terms of social motivation, in terms of diplomatic style.

On the basis of this review, we can use political ideology as another measure of social and epistemic motivations (see figure 3). Placement on the center left captures prosocial and high epistemic motivation, which should lead to a preference for liberal diplomacy and reasoned dialogue. Center-right placement indicates a combination of proself and high epistemic motivation that should induce pragmatic statecraft. Far-right placement serves as a proxy for the combination of proself and low epistemic motivation, which should lead to coercive bargaining. The far left, prosocial combined with low epistemic motivation, will be idealists who engage in obliging diplomacy. Recall, however, that because of the weaker relationship between leftist ideology and epistemic motivation described before, this group should be relatively rare; this was confirmed in the case studies that follow. In addition, the competitive pressures of international politics select out the pursuit of purely idealistic policies, and the far left of the spectrum during this period is occupied by communist parties with Marxist ideologies that fit uncomfortably within the framework offered here, something I take up in the appendix to this chapter.

Of course, political ideology alone is not sufficient to measure social and epistemic motivations because ideology might also be capturing other factors that also affect foreign policy behavior, such as different

Epistemic motivation

		Low	High
Proself		Right	Center-right
Social motivation			
Prosocial		Far left	Left

FIGURE 3 Political ideology and psychological motivations.

[46]

conceptions of the national interest and different beliefs about other states, like how threatening they are. In the case studies that follow, I take these into account.

Rather than relying solely on the ideological placement of individual decision makers, I devote much attention to the political orientation of their domestic political support base, particularly the positions of their political parties. Political parties are aggregations of like-minded individuals. In past work (Rathbun 2004, 2012), I have shown that we can think of them as vehicles for bringing ideology into the foreign policy process. The behavior of foreign policy elites such as the prime ministers and foreign ministers must be our main focus of analysis given the centralized, high-stakes, and often secretive nature of diplomacy. But the social and epistemic motivations of leaders should be consistent with the diplomatic style preferred by their party or coalition base. Where it is not, we should expect (and indeed find) cabinet and parliamentary dissension that constrains and alters behavior. Although individuals are undoubtedly important in the cases that follow, it is possible to exaggerate their influence. Devoting attention to broader party orientations also leads to a more generalizable theory and more methodologically sound empirical conclusions because it enables us to more easily measure motivations independently of behavior.

A focus on parties also helps solve the endogeneity issue. If we see predictable variation in diplomatic style across the political system within the same country, whether judged through cross-sectional variation at time between the government and opposition or longitudinally as governments turn over from one side to the other, we can be more confident that diplomacy is not endogenous to structure and also that style has its origins in social and epistemic motivations. Thinking of parties as carriers of psychological motivations allows us to hold structure and the issues under negotiation constant with variation only in diplomatic style. We must, however, also be cognizant of the need to control for shifts in foreign policy goals that also accompany a change in a government party coalition. In each country under study, there is an easily identifiable left-right spectrum, described in the appendix to this chapter.

Nevertheless, the personal ideological position of those key decision makers is likely to be particularly causally important when parties are larger and encompass greater ideological variation or in coalition governments in which parties distribute key ministries. I expect that larger catch-all parties will demonstrate more ideological variation than smaller, more ideologically coherent parties. For instance, the British Tories were (still are) the main party of the British right, whereas the German People's Party (DVP) and German National People's Party

(DNVP) competed with each other on the conservative side of the political spectrum. In the former case, we expect internal divisions that correspond roughly to the ideological extremity of party members. When there is predictable variation within a government, the inclinations of the foreign minister and the head of government, who are responsible for diplomacy, will be particularly important.

Political actors other than politicians certainly matter as well. In the cases that follow, elected decision makers were often constrained by their militaries. I treat the latter's preference as largely exogenous and incorporate them into the story on an as-needed basis. The cases also generally neglect the positions and actions of professional diplomats. This is made possible by the high profile of the issues under discussion, which meant that decisions were made at the highest levels of government by political leaders rather than by bureaucrats. By virtue of their importance, security discussions were highly political and required a strong domestic basis of support from the parliament of each state. Nevertheless, a study of the issues of more day-to-day diplomatic interaction would probably need to explore the diplomatic style of regular diplomats, as others have done (Neumann 2012).

Political parties also have other, more self-serving interests. They seek reelection and need to deliver material benefits to their members, something that might be affected by foreign affairs (Downs 1957; Fordham 1988a, 1998b; Narizny 2007; Gaubatz 1991). It could be that the different diplomatic styles adopted by political parties are a consequence of these other functions of political parties. I consider this possibility on a case-by-case basis in the empirical chapters that follow. Security issues might have distributional implications for domestic political groups that could also explain party cleavages over diplomacy; however, there is more unity on national security goals because of their life-and-death nature, particularly in the aftermath of a major war, lessening this concern. National security issues also provide instances in which parties are more united on foreign policy goals, thereby allowing us to more easily distinguish between differences over substance and over diplomatic style. Nevertheless, I do not just assume, but empirically establish, this unity.

To measure diplomatic style (coercive bargaining, pragmatic statecraft, and reasoned dialogue) and the spirit of negotiations (value claiming vs. value creating), I draw from the inventory of behaviors identified in psychological work associated with different types of negotiation. We are judging style, which is monadic, and the spirit of negotiations, which is dyadic, simultaneously by the same actions. Where necessary, I distinguish the preferred diplomatic style of a state from the type of negotiating it engages in light of others' behavior. This is tricky but unavoidable.

Coercive bargaining by any particular party (or value claiming by multiple parties) has the following elements:

- *Lack of information exchange*: Negotiators will not reveal their own private evaluation of different offers or their reservation point. Nor will they believe the representations of others who are also presumed to be engaged in coercive bargaining.
- *Pessimism*: Practitioners of coercive diplomacy can convey aloofness by expressing their skepticism that a deal can be reached. Optimism suggests weakness and a lack of resolve. The more this is feigned, the more this is coercive bargaining. Distributive negotiators will overstate, rather than understate, the differences between the sides to drive a harder bargain.
- *Ego defensiveness and reactive devaluation*: Value claimers will denigrate the sufficiency and generosity of others' offers. Instrumentally, this puts pressure on others to concede more. More genuinely, it reflects the feeling that their side deserves more than the other side. Ego defensiveness will inhibit empathetic understanding of the needs and constraints faced by the other side.
- *Offer inflation*: Negotiators open with high demands, which conveys the impression that they will settle only for a deal with major concessions, anchors the negotiation at points favorable to their reservation price, and allows some room for concessions while still commanding a larger share of the pie. The further opening bids are from their reservation price, the more coercive the bargaining.
- *Coercive linkage:* Value claiming parties will attempt to hold issues dear to the other side hostage to force the others to offer better terms on issues they care about. If an issue is of some worth to others, but not to them, they still have an incentive to hold onto it as a bargaining chip and demand compensation.
- *Staging*: Value claimers will insist that others make concessions before they do. This prevents commitment problems in which they have to trust that others will come through on their promises. It also allows them to pocket others' concessions and to ask for more without having spent any of their negotiating capital. This might include demanding prior concessions as a condition of even coming to the table.
- *Indifference and brinksmanship*: Negotiators should not be quick to concede but, rather, should hold out for eventual concessions. By not appearing eager, they convey resolve. In the event that a deadline is set, value claiming parties will play a game of brinksmanship.

- *Positional commitments*: Negotiators will use as a favorite technique staking out absolute take-home points and pledging not to agree on anything short of their obtainment. If done publicly, this creates a costly signal of resolve by making it harder to back down.
- *Cheap talk*: Negotiators will regard efforts by other side to persuade as cheap talk in value claiming, not as efforts to explain the others' position or arrive at an accommodation.

Liberal diplomacy by any one party (or value creating by multiple parties) has the following elements:

- *Honest information exchange*: Value creating parties will share accurate private information about their true preferences, feeling less concerned about exploitation, and be more inclined to believe the representations of others.
- *Optimism and earnestness*: Value creating parties will indicate their optimism that a deal can be reached to encourage the other side to negotiate in good faith. They will understate their differences with the other side rather than overstate them.
- *Recognition of generosity*: Value creating parties, in an indication of empathy, will recognize when others have made significant concessions and attempt to place themselves in others' shoes. They will not denigrate others' offers. When done publicly, this sends a signal of conciliation.
- *Fairer offers*: Value creating parties will present offers that more closely shadow their reservation point, if they have one, and include value for the other side as well as an indication of a commitment to equality and mutual benefit.
- *Integrative linkage*: Parties use integrative negotiation, which involves connecting issues, not to coerce a better deal but, rather, to find outcomes in which each side gains what it values most. Side payments can be used as positive concessions.
- *Staging*: Parties negotiate issues simultaneously, rather than holding them up to force concessions on other issues, even if an eventual integrative deal requires progress on both. Decision makers might consider unilateral concessions without immediate compensation to demonstrate cooperative intentions.
- *Argumentation*: Parties attempt to persuade others to concede to their point of view rather than to coerce them. The use of argumentation will be seen as an indication that the other side is open to dialogue.
- *Retaining flexibility*: Negotiators rarely draw lines because they impede the flexibility necessary to make trade-offs across issues.

[50]

Sources

Methodologically, I chose to engage in careful qualitative analysis, relying predominantly on primary documents. This kind of work is well suited for establishing the causal impact of diplomacy by establishing the structural baseline that also contributes to the outcome, which must be treated as an exogenous factor on a case-by-case basis. Because the distribution of interests, in particular, is private information, it cannot be measured through behavioral observation, making it difficult to put together a large data set. Historical case work is also necessary for establishing diplomatic style because observing behavior is not enough. For instance, if a state leader draws a red line that he or she promises not to cross, this might appear to be a coercive bluff aimed at extorting a better deal. On the other hand, it might also be a genuine representation of the reservation price of his or her country and therefore honest, integrative negotiating behavior. The action does not speak for itself; only by knowing the private information held by the leader can we judge.

The primary sources of the period are quite comprehensive in most cases. Both Germany and Britain have assembled enormous bound collections containing almost all the documents relevant to the cases examined in this book in their original languages. There is also a complete collection of cabinet minutes for both the British and German governments in their original languages. Where these collections proved to be insufficient, I conducted my own archival research. The documentation of French diplomacy is by far the worst.[6] My findings on France must therefore be treated more tentatively. Still, I have attempted to triangulate using German and British sources as much as possible. Indeed, most students of French foreign affairs rely as heavily on these sources as they do on the French archives.

THE HISTORICAL CONTEXT AND THE PLAN OF THE BOOK

A bit of background is necessary to set the scene. Under the terms of the Versailles peace treaty, Germany was permanently forbidden to construct fortifications or maintain troops on the left bank of the Rhine and

6. For instance, Keeton complains that Briand, by far the most important French politician for the purposes of this book, "read little and wrote less" (1987: 107). He "never answered letters and never gave written promises" (29). This, he contends, was true of the French as a whole. They "committed little to paper, and often discarded what they did" (208).

50 kilometers to the east of the river. The left bank was divided into three zones, occupied and administered by French, Belgium, and British troops and to be evacuated in 1935 provided that Germany met its treaty obligations. The Cologne zone was set to be freed in 1925, the Koblenz area in 1930, and Mainz in 1935. The German army was reduced to 100,000, its navy was reduced to a token number of ships, and its air force was abolished, all monitored by an Inter-Allied Commission of Control of foreign officials whose expenses were paid by Germany. The Alsace-Lorraine was returned to France, Eupen-Malmedy was given to Belgium, colonies were turned over to the allies, upper Silesia was given to Czechoslovakia, and unification with Austria was forbidden. West Prussia became part of Poland, creating the Polish corridor to the sea and dividing Germany into two noncontiguous parts. Germany lost 10 percent of its population and land. The League of Nations took over the Saar for fifteen years, with control of its valuable coalmines given to the French. Yet the French were still obsessed with security and sought a bilateral guarantee of its borders from Britain.

Figure 4 presents an overview of expectations about the particular types of interactions, based on the ideological orientations of the governments in the three countries. In chapter 3, I compare a coercive bargaining dyad with a liberal dyad (the upper left and lower right boxes in figure 4) as France and Britain twice engaged between 1922 and 1924 in an effort to negotiate an increase in French security, first under rightist governments in both countries and then under leftist governments. Unable to come to an agreement, they tabled the issue. In chapter 4, I pick up the story in 1925 as Germany entered the mix, creating a pragmatic-integrative Franco-German dyad, a pragmatic-pragmatic Anglo-German dyad, and a pragmatic-integrative Anglo-Franco dyad that made value creating possible. Here I set the table, making the case that the particular combination of diplomatic styles in the three countries laid a fertile foundation for Germany to propose a multilateral security arrangement among the three countries, and I consider what might have been had other political forces been in power. In chapter 5, the most diplomatic of the chapters, I delve deeply into the minutiae of exchanging notes and formulating responses that allowed the three countries to get to the table, convening formal negotiations. When all sides laid their cards on the table, it resulted in the Treaty of Locarno and a dramatic improvement in relations that raised the prospect of a complete settlement of remaining issues between France and Germany; this is detailed in chapter 6. In chapter 7, I show the deterioration of relations following the 1926 shift in the French government to the right that turned the tables. As the Franco-German and the Anglo-Franco dyad shifted to value claiming, the three powers found it difficult to capitalize on the momentum of Locarno. In

[52]

	Coercive bargaining	Pragmatic statecraft	Reasoned dialogue
Coercive bargaining	1. Franco-Anglo relations, 1922–1923		
Pragmatic statecraft	2. Franco-German relations, 1926–1929 Franco-Anglo relations, 1926–1928	4. Anglo-German relations, 1925–1928	
Reasoned dialogue	3. Franco-Anglo relations, 1928–1929	5. Franco-German relations, 1925–1926 Franco-Anglo relations, 1925–1926 Anglo-German relations, 1928–1929	Franco-Anglo relations, 1924

Value creating likely
Value creating possible
Value claiming likely

FIGURE 4 Expectations and case studies.

chapter 8, I supplement the European cases with one from the Middle East. I note how many of the processes discussed in the earlier chapters repeat themselves in negotiations between Palestinians and Israelis, indicating the added value of the argument. In the final chapter, I draw lessons from the 1920s experience for the Middle East.

APPENDIX: THE POLITICAL PARTY SPECTRUM IN INTERWAR FRANCE, GERMANY, AND BRITAIN

Party positions in interwar France, Germany, and Britain are understandable through the political psychological concepts explored in this chapter, allowing us partly to infer psychological motivations from ideological placement, providing this is supplemented with other measures

[53]

In Britain, the parties were, from left to right, Labour, Liberal, and Conservative. Labour had supplanted the Liberals as the main alternative to the Conservatives (Tories) by the 1920s. The Liberals had split during World War I and played only the most marginal of roles in interwar politics.

Even the Conservatives in this oldest and most established of democracies represented the ethics of community rather than the ethics of autonomy. The Tories believed that there was a natural and beneficial hierarchy of classes in English society that preserved stability and allowed the community to function effectively as a whole. The interests of the nation were more important than that of any individual. Whereas radical liberals (and, later, Labour) spoke of rights, conservatives emphasized duties and loyalty to the church, king, country and the empire. Tories embraced only gradual change because anything else was disruptive to societal stability. They revered the British past and traditions, which held society together. Strong authority and law of order were necessary. The Tories were also the strongest advocates of adherence to traditional moral values (Baker 1993: xiv, 15, 127, 141, 198, 247; Smith 1997: 79; Hearnshaw 1967: 22–38; Barnes 1994: 315–22). The moral foundations and values of the Conservatives, in particular their lack of universalism and their intense loyalty to the nation-state, made them the natural party of empire (Barnes 1994: 336–38; Smith 1997: 79).

Labour represented universalist, self-transcendence values, which Jonathan Haidt and collaborators call the ethics of autonomy (Graham, Haidt, and Nosek 2009; Haidt, Graham, and Joseph 2009; Haidt and Joseph 2004). The aim of the nationalization of industry, for instance, was the creation of a new utopian society marked by solidarity. The Labour election manifesto, *Labour and the Nation*, identified the egalitarian foundations of its domestic policies: "The Labour Party . . . is a Socialist party. Its aim is the organization of industry and the administration of the wealth which industry produces in the interest, not of the small minority (less than 10 percent of the population) who own the greater part of the land, the plant and the equipment without access to which their fellow-countrymen can neither work nor live, but of all who bring their contribution of useful service to the common stock. . . . It is the practical recognition of the familiar commonplace that 'morality is in the nature of things' and that men are all, in very truth, members one of another" (Labour Party 1928).

In Germany, the main parties were, from left to right, the Social Democratic Party (SPD), German Democratic Party (DDP), Center Party, German People's Party (DVP), and German National People's Party (DNVP). There were also some minor regional parties. The Nazis (National Socialist German Workers' Party) also had a small representation in parliament, although not of any discernible influence during the period under study.

The left-right divisions in Germany during the interwar years were the starkest of the three countries under study. The core issues were social reform, with the looming possibility of a communist revolution, and the stability of the recent transition to democracy, with the recurring prospect of a reactionary return to an aristocratic and autocratic government. The SPD, DDP, Center Party, and DVP were all committed to the preservation of a liberal form of government, that is, to the ethics of autonomy. They often came together in great coalitions. The DNVP, on the other hand, was largely hostile to the Weimar regime, and this intensified greatly in 1929 (Wright 2002; Mommsen 1996; Hiden 1996; Craig 1978).

However, the DVP, Center Party, and DDP frequently aligned with the DNVP on social issues, generally opposing any steps in the direction of social democracy, in what were known as bourgeois coalitions. Although the SPD was formally a Marxist party, it was not a truly revolutionary party, preferring to work within the confines of the political system to bring about gradual social change while maintaining democracy in a way not true of the communists (Eley 2002; Berman 2006; Berger 1994). The SPD was the strongest supporter of the Weimar Republic (Berger 1994: 177). Suzanne Miller identifies its core principles as the rights of democratic freedom, the demands for social justice, and the idea of solidarity. In other words, the SPD believed in self-transcendence values (Miller 1976: 16–31). It was the most prosocial of the parties.

In France, party labels were far more unstable. The French Third Republic was highly factionalized. Parties constantly dissolved and reformed. Politicians frequently quit their parties to remain in positions of power when their colleagues left the government. Fourteen of nineteen new interwar parties were formed as breakaways from existing parties; the other five were formed from scratch. Names meant little (Kreuzer 2001: 6). The Left Radicals, for instance, were a conservative and center-right party. The Radical Socialists were more centrist than the Socialists. The term *radical* indicates a link with the liberal values of the French Revolution.

We can, nevertheless, generally distinguish between a left and right bloc. The former was composed primarily of the Socialist Party, the primary vehicle of the French left, and the Radical (sometimes called the Radical Socialist) Party, the primary vehicle of the French center-left, or liberals. The latter was the equivalent of the British Liberal Party, the defenders of the democratic gains of the French Revolution against its conservative and authoritarian opponents. The Radicals shared values with the Socialists, although the latter were more extreme (Keiger 1997: 63, 65).

They were all in favor of "solidarism," social reform and welfare to help those in need. Their program was "universal suffrage, freedom of the press, . . . the separation of Church and State, secular free and compulsory schools, income tax, a state-controlled economy, social insurance, and far-reaching social reforms" (Kayser 1960: 325). This dual commitment to individual liberty and providing for the less well-off in society is an indication of a belief in the prosocial ethics of autonomy.

The French right unified under what was called the Bloc National, later renamed the Union Nationale. Its constituent parties frequently changed their names and used different monikers in and outside of the parliament. It represented conservation values, seeking to prevent any radical overhaul of French society, particularly in regards to the Church, and generally opposing social reform that redistributed wealth and power to the masses. Class politics was thought to undermine the solidarity of the French people (Keiger 1997: 39, 40, 64). As a consequence of its values, the right was more nationalistic and proself in social motivation. The large number of former military members who served in the early postwar right-wing coalitions gave the Bloc National the nickname of the "Blue Horizon," after the color of their uniforms (Keiger 1997 267).

For a number of reasons, I have excluded formally communist parties from the analysis. First, in no country did the communist parties have any effect on outcomes. Second, communists in the three countries were universally opposed to any effort at western reconciliation among Britain, France, and Germany. Such a reconciliation was seen as a precursor to a capitalist alliance against the Soviet Union; their position was driven not by diplomatic style but by revolutionary foreign policy goals. Third, communists fit uneasily on the left-right spectrum that forms the basis of how I capture social and epistemic motivations. It is not the case, for instance, that Marxists are simply more extreme than Social Democrats on issues of social welfare—Marxists and Social Democrats are qualitatively different (Eley 2002; Berman 2006). The ideology of the former is not based on the fundamental value of all human beings. Marxists do not have the individualizing moral foundations that are the basis of prosocial motivation. They would not score high on self-transcendence. As Howard and Donnelly (1986) argue, communist ideology is not based on a notion of rights. This is evident in the communist preference for authoritarian government, which would make Marxists more favorable to coercive bargaining than liberal diplomacy. Unlike social democracy, communist ideology is fundamentally divisive, drawing a strict division between the classes. It is not universalist in content, only in application (Berman 2006).

I stress that I am describing relative differences across the political spectrum. It is certainly the case that the ideological fulcrum of left-right

[56]

varied systematically across countries. The German far right, for instance, was significantly more conservative than the British far right during this period. Nevertheless, in all three countries, the points of ideological contestation between left and right were very similar, even in Britain—social reform and the extent of democratic participation and individual freedom (McCrillis 1998). Social and political egalitarianism went hand in hand. "In the Left's tradition," writes Geoff Eley, "some notion of social justice was practically inseparable from the pursuit of democracy" (2002: 18). Even the differences in leftist ideology between, for instance, the more radical German SPD and the more evolutionary and gradualist British Labour Party are often overstated and belie a set of core fundamental values (Berger 1994: chap. 5).

Readers might object to the application of the political psychological studies on which I rely to a very different period. Studies have consistently shown, however, that, although the issues of political contestation have changed over time as democracies have matured and changed, the new elements of conflict are simply grafted onto old political cleavages (Kitschelt and Hellemans 1989; Inglehart and Flanagan 1987). For instance, it is not surprising that the left, which historically backed democratic inclusion and political equality against the right, is now the primary advocate for the rights of women, gays and lesbians, and racial minorities.

[3]

Tabling the Issue

Two Franco-British Negotiations

European foreign relations in the wake of World War I were preoccupied with the question of French security. This was to great degree the product of structural circumstances. Germany was France's immediate neighbor, and France could not take the same wait-and-see approach as Britain. In addition, France had suffered losses in the Great War that were disproportionately larger than those of Germany or Britain. Demographically it was estimated that the German population would in a few decades outnumber that of France by 20–30 million, giving Germany a decisive advantage, particularly in the number of men of fighting age. Nevertheless, French insecurity was also undoubtedly psychological, a consequence of their wartime experience. Arnold Wolfers, whose *Britain and France between Two Wars* is still, more than seventy years later, the most trenchant analysis of the foreign policy of the two countries, writes, "France was obsessed by the fear of a new war with Germany," even though it was "not normal for the policy of a great power, especially a victorious power, to be based so openly on the fear of future attack by its vanquished opponent" (1940: 11). The French saw the Germans as naturally aggressive and bent on revenge.

This fear was invariant across the political spectrum. Although politicians were deeply divided on matters of domestic politics during the 1920s, there was great unity as regards the threat posed by Germany (Wolfers 1940: 29). The French left and right had identical foreign policy goals and beliefs.

France wanted most a firm commitment by Britain to protect it in case of renewed conflict with Germany (Wolfers 1940: 76).[1] France simply

1. Wolfers writes, "If there was one conviction which all Frenchmen shared, it was the belief that outside of their own military preparedness an *entente* with Britain must become the

could not do it alone. It had made significant concessions on security to the allies in the postwar settlement, forgoing the annexation of the Rhineland to gain a formal security guarantee from the United States and Britain. When the Versailles Treaty was not ratified by the United States in 1919, however, this guarantee fell by the wayside.

Members of the British government, composed of a conservative coalition under David Lloyd George, privately expressed a willingness to provide a security guarantee even without the Americans. The British felt a commitment to the sanctity of the French western borders to be in their interest given the changing nature of military technology that made the Rhine, rather than the Channel, the new strategic border of Britain. In December 1921, they agreed to negotiations with the French, putting the issue formally on the table. This should have been an easy case for diplomacy given the overlap in interests.

Yet a deal was never consummated. How can we explain this unlikely failure? The inability to conclude an agreement had major consequences. It left Britain without a potential means of restraining France in the latter's coercion of Germany to make good on its reparations payments. In 1923, against British wishes and without British participation, the French military invaded and occupied the German Ruhr, seizing industrial assets as compensation for the failure of Germany to pay.

In 1924, the issue was put on the table again under much less favorable conditions. Anglo-Franco relations were still tense given French behavior vis-à-vis Germany, and the new left-wing Labour government in Britain had very different foreign policy goals than its predecessor. The Labour government under Ramsay MacDonald was generally opposed to exclusive alliances, favoring instead more universalist efforts at disarmament and arbitration through the League of Nations. The new government of France, a coalition of the left, still badly wanted an alliance, but Britain refused to renew negotiations along the lines considered a few years earlier because of the change in British interests.

Nevertheless, the two sides negotiated a new protocol to the League of Nations that was mutually beneficial to both sides. By making peaceful conflict resolution through means of third-party mediation a requirement, the Geneva Protocol institutionalized the peaceful conflict resolution that the British left so desired. By providing for League sanctions in the case of noncompliance, it met to some degree the French need for security. The French also committed to the convocation of a general

cornerstone of France's system of security. . . . Her entire post-war foreign policy might therefore be characterized not only as an effort to keep Germany in her place but also as a continuous struggle to get Britain to pledge her support against Germany" (1940: 76).

disarmament conference that the British valued so highly, the successful conclusion of which was a condition for the protocol to come into force.

The Geneva Protocol episode ultimately ended in failure due to domestic differences over foreign policy. The British Conservatives, who returned to power in December 1924, had little interest in a universalist scheme that increased British obligations under the League of Nations. The security issue was tabled for the time being. But diplomacy had brought the two countries to the precipice of agreement before the change in government. How was it that the two countries had been better able to negotiate a deal when their interests were further apart than when they were more closely aligned?

Both the successes and failures of bilateral negotiation between the two powers can be explained through a focus on diplomatic style. In 1922, both governments pursued coercive bargaining that we expect from conservative parties lower in social and epistemic motivation. Although a simple guarantee was in Britain's interest, Lord Curzon, the very conservative foreign minister, sought to exploit the greater French interest in a pact. He insisted that France make concessions on a host of outstanding bilateral issues between the two countries before Britain would even begin negotiations on the content of a security pact. By rationalist logic, the behavior of Britain might not be surprising given its greater leverage. But France, even in its much weaker bargaining position, embraced a similar style of diplomacy when rationalists would, instead, expect significant concessions. Governed by a conservative coalition, the French also bid high, asking the British for a full-scale alliance in which they would coordinate their positions on all major issues and make commitments of specific forces to be placed at the service of the French in case of aggression. Diplomatic style was not endogenous to structure. The conservative premier, Raymond Poincaré, denigrated the British offer of a mere security guarantee and pretended not to be interested in the conclusion of the pact. The combination led to value claiming negotiation, which left a potentially more beneficial outcome for both sides on the table.

When in 1924 the French government again reached out to its wartime ally, both France and Britain were governed by parties with a prosocial motivation. Just as in psychological experiments in which prosocial dyads are better able than proself pairs to reach joint gains through value creating negotiation, the French and British left did what their rightist counterparts could not do. French and British representatives both made significant concessions, indicated their interests honestly and without overstatement, and commented on the atmosphere of goodwill and good faith. Diplomacy was not epiphenomenal. Despite the now greater disparity in foreign policy preferences, the prosocial character of both governments and their liberal diplomacy facilitated integrative negotiation. Diplomatic style prevailed over foreign policy substance.

THE FAILURE: CONSERVATIVE GOVERNMENTS AND
THE BILATERAL TREATY NEGOTIATIONS OF 1922

Negotiating with a Big Club: The *Coup de Cannes*

Given the different structural circumstances of France and Britain, it is not surprising from the point of view of formal and rationalist bargaining theory that France first placed the idea of a security treaty on the table. The French alternative to no agreement was the exposed position France currently occupied vis-à-vis Germany. Even if France overstated the threat posed by Germany, Britain was more isolated and therefore less concerned about a German *revanche*. Premier Aristide Briand, who was also serving as foreign minister, explained the French position. France had "suffered so much from the proximity of Germany." It "cannot contemplate without horror the possibility that such havoc may be experienced again. France cannot forget that the German population exceeds her own by 20 millions; that democracy is still for the great majority of Germans no more than an empty phrase, and this people, highly disciplined, industrious, gifted with a fertile genius for organization, but dominated by an active political and intellectual propaganda . . . which encourages a spirit of aggression and inflates the desire for revenge, may someday render vain the disarmament provisions of the Treaty of Versailles." For this reason, "the best guarantee against any such eventuality would be the certainty on the part of Germany that France would not be found isolated in the face of a German attack" (Cmd. 2169, No. 35). Briand instructed his ambassador to Britain in early December 1921 to bring up the topic of a bilateral alliance informally with the British foreign secretary, Lord Curzon, in a "purely private, unofficial and confidential capacity" (Cmd. 2169, No. 23). The foreign secretary consented to an exchange of views that quickly led to formal negotiations in Cannes in January 1922.

France's greater need for security should have made it adopt a conciliatory and concessionary diplomacy. Yet, even though France was in the role of *demandeur*, its initial offer was almost outrageously high. Rather than the simple guarantee that had fallen through in 1919, in which Britain unilaterally pledged to guarantee France against unprovoked aggression, the ambassador proposed at Briand's instruction "something much more definite and precise, nothing less than a defensive alliance" (Cmd. 2169, No. 23). In a private meeting, Briand suggested a "very broad alliance in which the Two Powers would guarantee each other's interests in

[61]

all parts of the world, act closely together in all things and go to each other's assistance whenever these things were threatened" (Cmd. 2169, No. 33). And Britain was asked to do this without U.S. help.

The French government was pursuing a coercive bargaining style. Briand was historically a center-left politician, a former socialist who had left the party when he accepted a ministerial post before the war, something that was anathema to the socialists at the time (Unger 2005: 78, 98; 101–2, 181–84; Oudin 2004: 98–99, 120–26, 144–46). After departing from his political base he was beholden to a coalition of rightist parties called the Bloc National. The moderating force of the French center-left Radicals had left the cabinet in November 1919, leaving Briand as the only non-conservative politician in the cabinet. He established an "uneasy alliance with a coterie of conservative ministers" (Hall 1978: 1126).

The somewhat audacious nature of the French demands became more evident in a draft treaty presented in Cannes. France asked Britain to intervene with all its military forces not only in the case of a direct invasion of French soil but also in the event of any German violation of its treaty obligations to remain disarmed and to keep the Rhineland demilitarized. Great Britain and France were also to collectively agree on the strength of their respective military, naval, and air forces. France wanted a military convention, a specific commitment of particular British assets to its defense in advance. France also called for a constant collaboration between the general staffs of the two countries. Even the language betrayed the bold opening offer of the French. Briand wrote that there was "no more effective guarantee of a durable peace than a *vast* international arrangement of this nature based on the close union of France and Great Britain" (Cmd. 2169, No. 35, emphasis added). France was particularly interested in a British guarantee of the security of French allies in Eastern Europe. Its proposals made allusions to an agreement of "two stages," one for direct attack on France and the other for indirect attack on French allies. The French mentioned Poland specifically (Cmd. 2169, No. 23).

Briand did moderate his coercive diplomacy with aspects of liberal diplomacy. He tried to persuade the British of the advantages of a global alliance for Britain. It would allow for France to reduce its land armaments, which was a major British goal (Cmd. 2169, No. 33). It would deter the Germans, which was in the interests of Britain as well as France (Cmd. 2169, Nos. 23, 33). Briand expressed a willingness to consider side payments to the British, calling them an "indispensable part" of an agreement. Briand understood there was "no passion in the hearts of the British" for an alliance, an expression of empathy that took the edge off France's coercive diplomacy (Cmd. 2169, No. 23).

For their part, the British were genuinely desirous of a security pact of the kind they had been prepared to make in 1919, a unilateral guarantee of French security. It "did not throw heavy obligations upon us" but "would be of great value to France," the cabinet concluded privately (CC 1 (22)). It would also be in the interests of Britain, as Lloyd George recognized. This kind of guarantee would serve to deter Germany in a way that it had not been when Britain had remained noncommittal in the run up to the Great War (Cmd. 2169, No. 34). The British cabinet even concluded that it had a "moral obligation" to defend French soil because the 1919 guarantee had fallen through (CC 1 (22)). The pact was more attractive if Germany were to subsequently be brought into the arrangement through a nonaggression pact with the other Western European powers, as Briand thought possible (Cmd. 2169, No. 33). The cabinet believed this "would make for a general easement in Europe" (CC 1 (22)).

Lord Curzon told Briand that there was "general concurrence" in the cabinet that Britain might give France a "complete guarantee against invasion" on its western frontier (Cmd. 2169, No. 33). Nevertheless, as Curzon stated, "opinion in Great Britain was hardly prepared for so broad an understanding as that" envisioned by France. The British cabinet rejected any kind of close military cooperation such as institutionalized staff talks or a military convention. It concluded in January that an "Anglo-French alliance of a bi-lateral character was open to serious objections as it would leave us no longer free. France would endeavor to induce us to increase our Army so that we should be able to send large military forces to the Continent or wherever they were required by France" (CC 1 (22)). The British also refused any type of indirect guarantee through a commitment to use force in the event of German violations of its Versailles Treaty obligations. The British draft treaty simply stated, "In the event of a direct and unprovoked aggression against the soil of France by Germany, Great Britain will immediately place herself at the side of France with her naval, military and air forces." Otherwise, it offered only to "concert together" if any treaty provisions were breached or consult if there was confusion as to its interpretation (Cmd. 2169, No. 38). The cabinet also limited the geographic scope of the treaty, concluding it was "beyond our resources to deal with certain military problems such as the defence of Poland" (CC 1 (22)). Curzon stated that Britain was "not very much interested in what happened on the eastern frontier" and even less interested in being drawn into military operations "in any eventuality" in other parts of the world (Cmd. 2169, No. 33; see also No. 34). He spoke of "enormous undefined responsibilities" in the French scheme (Cmd. 2169, No. 23).

Yet, indicative of a coercive bargaining style, the British also decided to use the pact to extract other benefits. Even though they valued a bilateral (or trilateral if, which was possible, Belgium was to be associated) security guarantee in its own right, they held it hostage. From the beginning, they linked the successful conclusion of a security agreement with France to the resolution of a number of outstanding issues between the two countries in the favor of Britain, such as differences over the nationalist uprising in Turkey (Hall 1978). At the exploratory meeting with the French ambassador, Curzon made this linkage diplomatically but unmistakably:

> I said in conclusion, there was one further question upon which he had not touched. Did he contemplate, in his outlook, that the consideration of a treaty of alliance between France and ourselves should or should not be accompanied by a general clearing up of all the questions upon which we disagreed, and which were a source of a good deal of unpleasant bickering and quarrel in so many parts of the world? What was the good of an alliance—and indeed, could an alliance be entered into which allowed such questions as Morocco and Egypt, to mention two subjects only where the French view appeared to be sharply opposed to our own, to remain unsettled? If the French Government therefore wished us to examine the question of an alliance, they ought to tell us very plainly whether the discussion ancillary thereto should not embrace the whole field of agreement or disagreement between the two Powers. (Cmd. 2169, No. 23)

In his formal memorandum to Briand outlining the position to be taken by his government at Cannes, the Prime Minister Lloyd George stated that the British opposed "any piecemeal treatment of the questions by which the conference is faced. On the contrary, they consider it absolutely necessary that the problem should be treated as a whole." Lloyd George stressed the necessity for Britain, given its heavy reliance on trade, of global economic recovery following the destruction of the war. He made a security pact contingent on the convocation of a conference to deal with this question. "Great Britain fully recognizes France's ground for anxiety, and desires to do all in her power to allay it, but she cannot agree to postponing the question of the reconstruction of Europe, while meeting France's desires in regard to her reparations and her security." But this was not all. The prime minister called for a "complete entente" that also included a French limitation on submarine construction and concessions in the direction of Britain on the Near East problem of Turkey (Cmd. 2169, No. 34).

As Sally Marks writes, "Clearly, Britain intended to extract a stiff price for the limited guarantee of French soil she offered" (1982: 538). Britain was governed by Conservatives and a rump Liberal Party that had been devastated by splits over policy toward the war. It was effectively a conservative coalition, with the Tories supplying the vast majority of the ministers. The few Liberals in cabinet came from the right wing of their party that had not decamped to the opposition. Still, given the strength of the British bargaining position, the British adoption of a coercive diplomatic style is less surprising than similar behavior by the French.

Coercive Bargaining before the Ruhr Crisis: Poincaré's Diplomacy

Briand was punished by the French right for his diplomatic style at Cannes. When aspects of the British proposals became public, showing that the British were driving a hard bargain, pressure on Briand not to concede grew rather than softened. He narrowly escaped a parliamentary recall, but the right-wing French cabinet summoned the premier back to Paris. In what was known as the "coup de Cannes," Briand was sacked and replaced by the much more conservative Raymond Poincaré, who cabinet members thought would more stubbornly defend French interests through coercive bargaining. The phrase played on the triple meaning of *Cannes*—as a place but also as the French word for a "caning" and a "golf club." Briand had been photographed receiving a golf lesson from Lloyd George, which was taken as a metaphor for French subservience and weakness, drawing nationalist ire. His punishment by the conservative cabinet was likened to his being beaten by a wooden stick (Hall 1978: 4; Keiger 1997: 276). The rightist French government, despite its lack of negotiating strength, was not going to simply concede. Because no pact had been concluded, Briand was fired for his diplomatic style rather than his foreign policy substance.

Poincaré expected a value claiming process in which both sides held firm, conceding only gradually and out of necessity. He predicted that it would not be easy to find common ground (DD, No. 32). He would wait for a formal response from Britain "so that we can ourselves measure the limit of our concessions" (DD, No. 32). John Keiger writes that Poincaré exhibited a "lack of ability to concede points in a spirit of negotiation [that] was worsened by a complete lack of tact in expressing his own point of view" (1997: 287). He demonstrated a "withering stubbornness" (Keiger 1997: 294). The British had anticipated such a shift in diplomacy, earlier recognizing that they had an interest in maintaining Briand in power. According to Jules Laroche, French bureaucrat, at the now infamous golf outing Briand had gotten in the way of a drive by a member of the British delegation. Lloyd George had pulled him quickly back and gesticulated at his forehead, saying in broken French: "Watch out, if the ball hits here, Briand zap! And then . . . Poincaré!" (in Keiger 1997: 276).

The conservative premier had a thoroughly proself motivation in diplomacy, writing, "The best way to love mankind is first of all to love that portion of humanity which is near to us, which surrounds us and which we know best. Instead of scattering our affections and wasting our energies let us concentrate and use them productively in that corner of soil where nature rooted us." This was a moral commitment based on the foundation of loyalty. *"La patrie* is therefore the material heritage which our ancestors have bequeathed to us and which we must, in turn, pass on to our descendants. It is not simply our land, it is also our national soul . . . evoked in us by the name of France" (in Keiger 1997: 70).

Although it is tempting to reduce his negotiating behavior simply to his personality, the new premier's diplomatic style went part and parcel with the psychological motivations embedded in conservative ideology, common to the French right. "Poincaré's *not very original* bargaining technique was to begin by asking for more on the basis of carefully prepared evidence in the expectation of settling for less," writes Keiger (1997: 257, emphasis added). This was what his colleagues were expecting from his appointment.

With Briand gone, there was no longer any check on the conservatives' instincts to engage in coercive bargaining. Poincaré met with Lloyd George as the British delegation passed through Paris on its way back to London following the aborted Cannes conference. Still a few days away from formally taking office, he denigrated the British offer of a guarantee, saying it had "very little effective value in France without a military convention," according to the British minutes of the meeting. "He said that he would rather have a military convention without a treaty than a treaty without a military convention." Poincaré described a treaty without a convention as "useless" because the guarantee was "illusory." Rather than a simple promise to come to the aid of France, he wanted specific commitments from the British as to the military forces they would devote to French defense (CP 3612 (22)).

When Poincaré officially became premier, his government submitted to the British another draft treaty that differed little from its first (Cmd. 2169, No. 39). Britain would still be obliged to intervene militarily in cases of violations of the Versailles Treaty. Anything else was "altogether insufficient security" (Cmd. 2169, No. 40); it "would restrict to a dangerous extent . . . the circumstances in which the assistance of Great Britain is contemplated," requiring Germany to actually breach French borders (CP 3961 (22); see also Cmd. 2169, No. 41). The French even objected to the use of the word *soil* by Britain because an attack could come by air or sea as well (CP 3961 (22); see also Cmd. 2169, No. 41).

The French backed away from a demand for a full military convention but called for a formal "entente" between the general staffs in the treaty itself, in which the two countries would constantly coordinate military plans (Cmd. 2169, Nos. 39–41). The French also spoke of a "general entente," a pledge to confer together and find a common policy on every issue that might endanger the peace (CP 3961 (22); see also Cmd. 2169,

Nos. 40–41). This was an effort to extract more British help in the event of a German attack to its east (Cmd. 2169, No. 40). Poincaré's only concession was to express a willingness to remove the general entente and the staff talks from the treaty. They would still, however, be formalized through an exchange of letters accompanying the treaty, to be signed and published by the two governments (DD, No. 25).

Poincaré took all these actions in a security environment that should have made him more conciliatory rather than less. This indicates that diplomatic style was not endogenous to structure. As discussions with the British were taking place, Germany signed the Treaty of Rapallo with the Soviet Union, raising the specter of Russian-German cooperation against the West. This convinced the French premier that Germany was "destined" to disrupt the peace. Yet he believed that it reinforced his argument about the necessity of a stronger guarantee from Britain in Eastern Europe and in the Rhineland. He dug in his heels further (DD, No. 32). Poincaré even referred in private correspondence to the "price" that Britain would have to pay for consolidating and tightening the relationship between the countries (DD, No. 37).

We might conclude that Poincaré did not in fact, despite the obvious French security interest, value a guarantee from Britain or that he radically misconstrued the bargaining environment. Yet privately the leader said that "he would make any sacrifice" to gain a pact with Britain (Marks 1982: 541). He also understood the weakness of the French bargaining position. Marks writes that the conservative leader "wanted the treaty badly but was determined not to appear eager" (1982: 540–41).

The lack of fit between the conservative French government's style of diplomacy and the French structural position is exposed further by the efforts made by Charles de Saint-Aulaire, the French ambassador to Britain, to soften Poincaré's position. He cautioned the premier about how difficult it would be to pass an agreement of the type that he envisioned in the British Parliament. He advised that the French should conclude a pact as soon as possible, lest the political winds shift unfavorably. Shifting away from coercive diplomacy, St. Aulaire noted to Lord Curzon the "high moral value" of a treaty along the lines that Britain envisioned, "even if it does not have the precision we would like" (DD, No. 31). He tried to reassure the British that Poincaré was in fact eager to conclude a treaty and that it was only a matter of extending it for longer than the British envisioned (DD, No. 49) He objected to the accusation that the French scheme was a "refusal disguised as an offer" (DD, No. 36). Saint-Aulaire expressed to the British his confidence that the two sides could find a formula that both agreed on (Cmd. 2169, No. 42). His efforts, indicating a more pragmatic and realist style of diplomacy perhaps more typical of professional diplomat, were for naught. Poincaré resented the ambassador's efforts to "make me a part of a conversation that you had on the pact" (DD, No. 32).

Value Claiming Subtracts Value: The Collapse of Negotiations

In the face of French intransigence, the British elected to stall so as to coerce the French to make concessions. After he returned home, Lloyd George told his cabinet that, given the latter's weaker bargaining position, the British would wait for the French to come to them: "In their present hostile attitude towards me it did not seem to be desirable that we should take the initiative. After some weeks have elapsed and the French began to feel themselves isolated in Europe and began to realize that we did not regard the pact as of supreme importance to ourselves, it was likely that they would approach us in a more reasonable frame of mind" (CC 2 (22)). Lord Curzon reported of the "extreme importance which the French Government attach to the conclusion of the Pact, upon which the existence of Monsieur Poincaré's Ministry may be said in fact to depend, and left me with the impression that while we hold it in suspense . . . we may find in it a powerful level for securing a favourable settlement of the other issues" (CP 3664 (22)). He concluded, "It would be unwise on our part to abandon the very powerful form of pressure which its non-conclusion enables us to exercise" (CP 3760 (22)). This was a "policy of aloofness" typical of coercive bargaining (Cohrs 2004: 39).

In another act of coercive diplomacy, the British exploited the parallel but separate negotiations with the Belgians to coerce the French in their direction. They reasoned that if they could induce the Belgians to accept a treaty without a military convention, it would confer "certain tactical advantages" in negotiations with the French (CC 2 (22)). And although initially the British were inclined to sign a separate guarantee pact with the Belgians, who proved more docile in negotiations, they rethought their position to put further pressure on the French. British ministers realized that securing the Belgian frontier went a long way toward providing French security and would therefore undermine the value of a guarantee by Britain of France. A senior civil servant wrote to Curzon that "it might be wise to delay the signature of the Anglo-Belgian pact until agreement on the Anglo-French pact was further advanced, as otherwise we might find Poincaré more difficult to deal with in view of the fact that, as regards her Belgian frontier, France would be automatically secure. It seems to me that there is some force in this point." Curzon replied, "Your point about the Anglo-Belgian treaty is a new one and worth considering." Subsequently they put the Belgians on ice (in Marks 1982: 542).

Curzon also tightened the linkage (CP 3760 (22); Cmd. 2169, No. 44). He continued to make any deal with the French hinge on the resolution of other outstanding issues between the countries. Curzon, however, did not imagine a package deal in which the British gained what they valued most while simultaneously conceding what the French most valued. Rather, he took an even more coercive line, demanding that France make concessions on those items even before renewed discussions of a security treaty. Curzon instructed the ambassador: "His Excellency, I said, would remember that when the subject was first discussed with M. Briand at Cannes the British Prime Minister had clearly laid down that the ground must be cleared of certain matters still in dispute between the two Governments before the Pact could be concluded. . . . When the whole of these matters had been concluded then would be the time to resume the discussion . . . of the Pact" (Cmd. 2169, No. 45).

Here Lord Curzon seems to have been acting on his own authority and in line with his own more conservative ideology. His biographer, Harold Nicolson, who also worked with him in the Foreign Office, observes that Curzon embraced the moral foundations of loyalty, authority, and the ethics of community that drive a proself motivation in diplomacy (Nicolson 1937: 13). Curzon believed that "God had personally selected the British upper classes as an instrument of the Divine Will. It was interpreted in terms of unsparing self-sacrifice, of a religious ideal of duty" (1937: 16). He was a "nationalist and an imperialist to the depths of his soul" with little sympathy for prosocial sentiments that took others' interests into account (1937: 42–44). The foreign secretary was not pragmatic, Nicolson claims: "Curzon . . . was not by nature and adaptable man. . . . He never learnt the . . . lesson of contemporary politics, namely that elasticity is the supreme advantage" (1937: 13, 32). He once said, "There are two constituents of successful diplomacy. . . . One is knowing one's own mind, the other is letting other people know it" (in Nicolson 1937: 43).

Yet, even though British behavior was consistent with rationalist bargaining theory, it was ineffective against the French conservatives, given their simultaneous adoption of coercive diplomatic style. Even though he lacked the bargaining strength, Poincaré acted as indifferently as the British. So as not to appear too eager for the conclusion of a pact, thereby reducing French leverage, he cautioned his ambassador to remain patient and to not make any offers until there was a formal British response to the French proposal. It was "not for us to remind them" of the French interest in the pact (DD, No. 28; see also Marks 1982). When Poincaré met Lloyd George in Boulogne, the prime minister raised the security issue at the beginning of the meeting, according to minutes. But the French premier deferred the question and never brought it up again, except to

[69]

express feigned regret that they might have discussed it "had there been time" (Cmd. 2169, No. 45). As the pressure grew on the French government, the premier did ask his ambassador to seek a formal reply from the British to his draft treaty (DD, Nos. 30, 32) and instructed him to reveal to the British how much the French would value an alliance (DD, No. 33). He asked the British to restart conversations (DD, Nos. 35, 46) but never made any further concessions to sweeten the deal.

Coercive diplomacy by both sides meant that negotiations were marked by a spirit of value claiming, making agreement more difficult. The Poincaré government rejected any linkage between completion of the treaty and the side payments that the British were connecting to the security arrangement (DD, Nos. 24, 31; CP 3961 (22); see also Cmd. 2169, No. 41). The French ambassador to Britain cautioned against the appearance of *marchandage*—that is, haggling or wrangling. This association of independent issues could create an impression of "an exchange of money." This was, of course, exactly the British intention. The side payments were not extremely costly to France. The exasperated French ambassador asked how the British could allow a problem such as Tangiers to be the cause of delay given that there was no comparison in terms of its importance. The treaty should not be subordinated to a "second rate question," he argued (DD, No. 31). Yet it was precisely the triviality of those other issues that should have made conceding easy for France had French decision makers been using a different diplomatic style.

The interactions were colored by emotion, not pragmatism. The French warned that the British coercive linkage could lead them to reject a treaty simply out of principle (DD, No. 31). Indeed, the French conservatives felt that Britain owed France, given the sacrifices France had made at Versailles in return for a security guarantee that had never materialized in 1919 (DD, No. 31).[2] At one point Poincaré said, "It would be the worst blunder to seem to be begging for friendship and to forget who we are, what we value, and that which we can do" (in Wolfers 1940: 92). Poincaré also engaged in a petty quarrel with British representatives. He felt insulted that they had not formally replied, and he would not revisit his offer until they did (DD, Nos. 28, 32; Cmd. 2169, No. 37).

For their part, the British conservatives reacted sharply to Poincaré's accusation that a British pledge to come to the aid of France was not sufficiently valuable. "It would be much better to trust to the honour of England," Lloyd George advised the French premier. "The important thing was Britain's pledge." France should "take the word of the British

---

2. France had wanted to occupy more German territory, even annex part of the Rhineland either for France or to place it in the hands of an international authority. It had relented only in exchange for an Anglo-U.S. security guarantee.

Empire, the value of which, and the strength behind it, she knew. . . . If the word of the British people was not sufficient for France, he feared that the Draft Treaty must be withdrawn." Lloyd George threatened that "if France was not satisfied with the promise of England to put all her forces at France's side, there was really no possible basis for a genuine accord between the two countries. . . . It only remained for M. Poincaré to communicate those views [officially]" (CP 3612 (22)). This emotionalism undermined the pragmatic diplomacy that might have facilitated a mutually beneficial agreement.

The British concluded that the French were uninterested in an agreement. Lloyd George told his cabinet colleagues, based on his experience at Boulogne, that Poincaré did not "put much stress on the conclusion of the Pact. . . . He could easily have discussed the matter at Boulogne had he so chosen" (CC 29 (22)). Marks writes that the French premier had "overplayed his air of indifference and convinced British leaders that he did not want a pact" (1982: 540). With Poincaré remaining steadfast, Curzon informed the French in June that there would be no pact because it hinged on the prior resolution of other issues. "The prospect of an early settlement of these questions is, I regret to say, far from hopeful, largely owing to the attitude of the French Government; and in these circumstances no useful purpose would be served by pursuing further, at present, the conversations on the subject of the treaty of alliance," he wrote. "I should be glad if your Excellency would take an early opportunity of impressing on M. Poincaré the unaltered determination of His Majesty's Government to clear up the outstanding questions at issue between our two countries before entering upon a renewed discussion of the treaty" (Cmd. 2169, No. 47).

Although the door had been left just slightly open by the British, Poincaré slammed it shut. Referring to the "declared indifference of the French Government," the conservative leader maintained his course and dealt the final blow to any prospect of a security treaty (DD, No. 42). He expressed the same view that he had earlier, that "in the form presented to him . . . he attached no importance whatever" to a pact. "France was absolutely indifferent as to whether there was a Pact or not" (Cmd. 2169, No. 48). He denigrated the value of any British commitment, stating that everyone "well knew that Great Britain would be found at her side if she . . . were again attacked by Germany, since in the future, even more than in 1914, any attack against the French frontier would directly imperil the equilibrium of the world and the safety of Great Britain herself. Above all, the Pact would have a moral effect on Germany. That result, though admittedly important, would not be of a nature to justify France in making any sacrifice of her essential interests" (Cmd. 2169, No. 49 (appendix)). The British and French did not take up the issue again until Poincaré had left power.

[71]

They had missed an opportunity. British and French decision makers both subsequently expressed the opinion that had it not been for the "upheaval in France," by which they meant the ideological shift in the French government, they would have successfully negotiated a treaty. Briand later referred to the "folly of the decision taken in Paris at that moment to render null the negotiations at Cannes" (CP 105 (25), minutes of the December 16, 1924, Committee of Imperial Defence (CID) meeting). Of course, the British were also partially responsible. Had they proposed to resolve the issues they linked to the security pact simultaneously at a conference such as the one in Cannes, reaching an agreement might have been easier. Value claiming made a win-win integrative deal impossible. Diplomacy had an effect on value, although in this case by subtraction, impeding what should have been a somewhat easy case for success.

THE NEAR SUCCESS: LEFTIST GOVERNMENTS AND THE GENEVA
PROTOCOL OF 1924

The period immediately following the collapse of negotiations was perhaps the nadir of interwar French relations, culminating in the Bloc National government's occupation of the Ruhr, over British objections, as a means of pressing Germany to pay its reparations. But by the time the pact issue was reopened, there had been significant changes in the governments of both countries, a shift from the right to the left in 1924. The Conservative government in Britain was defeated by the Labour Party, which formed a weak minority government relying on the parliamentary support of what was left of the Liberals. In France, a new electoral alliance composed of the center-left Radicals and the Socialists took over from the Bloc National. The two countries tried again to find common ground, this time with a very different diplomatic style.

The liberal diplomatic style of Labour was consistent with the overt prosocial motivation of the party in domestic and foreign affairs. Scholars of the Labour movement agree that the party advocated internationalism and nonviolence in foreign policy, the natural expression of its self-transcendence values and the moral foundations of avoiding harm and caring for others (Naylor 1969: chap. 1; Gordon 1969: chap. 1). Labour consciously sought to reform (indeed, create) international society in the same way and on the same principled basis as it was doing at home—through cooperation and justice (Gordon 1969: 6). Naylor writes of the party's "belief in human brotherhood" (1969: 9).

In its wartime blueprint for a postwar order, *Labour and the Peace Treaty*, the party lamented the prevailing view of international relations before the war, in which the security and prosperity of one was thought to mean the poverty and insecurity of the other (Labour Party 1919). The "Labour Party . . . took it for granted that national interests and international obligations coincided," writes Michael Gordon (1969: 17). Party members had a prosocial motivation that sought to maximize joint benefits. They rejected a zero-sum framing of international relations, adopting instead a win-win heuristic conductive to integrative negotiating. Gordon writes, "[I]t is necessary to try to get at Labour's understanding of discord and conflict in political life. . . . To put it simply, the party regarded conflict as unreal, illusory, mistaken." The party believed in a "profound truth about life: namely, when two or more individuals (or nations for that matter) fell out with one another, the resulting discord was unnecessary. It was a mistake—the disputants didn't really understand or appreciate each other's objectives" (Gordon 1969: 17).

Gordon directly fingers the liberal origins of the diplomatic style: The "heart of Labour's understanding—is that harmony (cooperation, accord) was alone natural. . . . The disputants had only to discover the common good which was at the same time their own highest good. . . . There was nothing new about this notion. Far from Labour inventing it, a doctrine postulating an ultimate harmony of interests was part and parcel of the whole Liberal metaphysic that sprang out of the . . . Enlightenment. . . . It is hardly surprising that Labour absorbed this doctrine, given its intellectual indebtedness to classical liberalism in so many areas of its thought" (1969: 40–41).

Labour also came into the government with very different foreign policy goals than the Conservatives. The party had long advocated the abolition of war as a means of resolving conflicts between states. Labour believed that the disarmament of Germany should be accompanied by universal disarmament (Labour Party 1919; Naylor 1969, chap. 1; Gordon 1969: 39–42; Winkler 1994: chap. 2). It called for the elimination of conscription and the private manufacture of arms. After the war, Labour also placed great stress on the League of Nations. Gordon writes, "Labour spokesmen continually referred to the League as the focus of an already existing 'community of nations.' Peace was indivisible, international cooperation was inevitable, world opinion was real and could be counted on" (1969: 16).[3]

---

3. Although the Labour Party had been cool to the League of Nations in the immediate aftermath of the war, seeing it as the continuation of the wartime alliance dedicated to preserving the status quo for the victors (Winkler 1994: 38; Naylor 1969: 7–8), it gradually warmed to the idea of making the League an "organ of international justice, inclusive of all free peoples" (Labour Party 1919; see also Winkler 1994: 55; Naylor 1969: 8; Gordon 1969: 16).

Just a few months after Labour came to power, the conservatives in France were also replaced, by a leftist coalition called the Cartel des Gauches.[4] The Cartel was originally led by Edouard Herriot, who took on the posts of both premier and foreign minister. The Radicals supplied all the ministers, and the Socialist Party merely provided the votes necessary for a majority in the French parliament (Keeton 1987: 11; BDFA, Part II, Series F, Vol. 17, No. 91: 381). Liberal republican values and socialist ideology were quite compatible, with differences mostly centering on whether change was best accomplished through participation within the normal political process (Unger 2005: 78, 98; 101–2, 181–84; Oudin 2004: 98–99, 120–26, 144–46).

France was more structurally constrained by material factors—the potential power of Germany and its proximity—than Britain. The left was just as terrified of a German *revanche* as the right was and therefore just as fixated on guaranteeing French security. All parties on the left but a small Socialist minority had supported the Ruhr invasion. Herriot told Ramsay MacDonald, who also held both the positions of prime minister and foreign minister, "My country has a dagger pointed at its breast, within an inch of its heart. . . . I think that I should not have done my duty towards my country if I did not place Germany in a condition to do no harm. . . . If there was a new war, France would be wiped off the map of the world. . . . One takes precautions against common criminals" (PRO 30/69/123, C 11976/70/18). Herriot continued at another meeting with the British:

> What Germany lacked at the actual moment was leaders. . . . If a new Bismarck appeared, there would be a good reason to fear that a war-like policy would instantly make its reappearance. . . . In ten years' time Germany would be faced with a terrible temptation. France would then be in a bad situation; firstly because the classes of military age would have few effectives—they would be the generation born during the war. . . . The danger was accordingly not one of the morrow. It was for ten years hence. That was what it was the duty of a French Government to think of. That was the peril against which it had to forearm itself. (DBFP I, Vol. 26, No. 508).

Briand said the same (Keeton 1987: 90); fear of Germany was hardly confined to the French right. British representatives reported back to London

---

4. It was composed of the Group du Parti radical et radical-socialiste (the Radical Socialists, sometimes simply known as the Radicals), the Groupe du Parti socialiste-unifié (the Socialists), and the much smaller Groupe du Parti républicaine-socialiste (the Radical Republicans) (BDFA, Part II, Series F, Vol. 17, No. 91: 381).

that "the security question would be as vital for the next French Government as for that of M. Poincaré. *Even the Socialists* made it a corner-stone of French foreign policy" (BDFA, Part II, Series F, Vol. 17, No. 91: 307, emphasis added).

The Cartel des Gauches had preferences identical to the Bloc National coalition. It insisted on strict German compliance with Versailles, including complete disarmament to the letter. There would be no early evacuation of the Rhineland. The French government hoped to secure the right to permanently monitor German compliance with its treaty obligations, particularly the demilitarization of the Rhineland, through League auspices after the withdrawal of the Interallied Military Control Commission (BDFA, Part II, Series F, Vol. 17, No. 91: 309). And, like the Bloc National, the Cartel des Gauches placed most value on an alliance with Britain. Herriot proclaimed after taking office, "It is necessary to choose between the reestablishment of the interallied entente and the maintenance of unilateral action" (in Wolfers 1940: 59). Briand said that a pact with Britain "ought to take precedence over all the other problems, because it is like the *sine qua non* of everything else" (in Keeton 1987: 108).

Herriot sought to obtain what Poincaré had not. Early on, he resuscitated the idea of a bilateral treaty, telling Prime Minister MacDonald that he aimed to "remain faithful to the ideas which the pact prepared at Cannes had endeavoured to crystallise" (DBFP I, Vol. 26, No. 508; see also PRO 30/69/123, C 11976/70/18; Stambrook 1968: 235). Given, however, the change in foreign policy goals that resulted from the ideological shift from right to left in Britain, the British were no longer interested in such an arrangement. British and French preferences were further apart than when the Tories and Bloc National governed. MacDonald would not countenance a traditional bilateral alliance or pact because it was inconsistent with the Labour program. The party had argued against an alliance with France since the end of the war as part of a general rejection of "partial" military arrangements that would perpetuate the pursuit of national armaments and the creation of hostile blocs. Labour had come out specifically against the Cannes proposals in 1922 (Winkler 1994: 86–87). MacDonald told Herriot that an alliance would provide only a "false security" (PRO 30/69/123, C 11976/70/18).

MacDonald instead suggested a more inclusive solution: "We wish to draw to our side the greatest possible number of friends," he explained. "When all that has been done, we shall be able to defy all the fomenters of trouble. This is, perhaps, a very vast conception of broad policy and continuous collaboration. . . . I am convinced that it is only in this way that we shall obtain the definite peace which we all desire" (PRO 30/69/123, C 11976/70/18). "Security for Great Britain did not mean hastening to the side of France if she was attacked," MacDonald believed. "The problem was vaster" (DBFP I, Vol. 26, No. 508).

MacDonald proposed as an alternative an arrangement constructed within the League of Nations. Noting that the two countries had failed to agree at Cannes, he concluded, "It was therefore useless to continue along a way which led nowhere. . . . Other means must be found. In that connection there was perhaps an issue; it was the League of Nations which supplied it. . . . Through the channel of the League of Nations on the one hand, through that of disarmament on the other, the solution of the problem would be attained, but if [the French] confined themselves within the actual limits and went on talking about a Franco-British Pact of Guarantee, they would only meet with a check" (DBFP I, Vol. 26, No. 508). MacDonald's notion was vague at the time, but he proposed that he and Herriot, while attending the upcoming League Council meeting in September, announce their desire "to create a system which would not be limited to two countries but which would include the other nations; for in contributing to the solution of the general problem each country would contribute to solve the problem for its own benefit" (DBFP I, Vol. 26, No. 508).

Therefore, it was on the basis of a strengthening of the League of Nations that there was a possible agreement between a leftist British government and a leftist French government (DBFP I, Vol. 26, No. 508). Nevertheless, their interests were still far apart. The French, even the right, saw the League differently than the British did, as the nucleus of what they sometimes called a "general alliance" that could bring in more help in the event of German aggression, thereby preserving the favorable status quo. (Wolfers 1940: 25, 31, 153, 162; Gordon 1969: 52, 58; Keeton 1987: 103). In keeping with this conception, the French sought to increase the coercive powers of the League, that is, the automaticity and the force of its sanctions provisions (Wolfers 1940: 153–58; BDFA, Part II, Series F, Vol. 17, No. 91: 308). In addition, the French still envisioned a bilateral alliance that would serve as a stopgap during "an intermediary period to be traversed, during which France would be unprotected . . . before arriving at this ideal state of affairs" (DBFP I, Vol. 26, No. 508). If there was to be an agreement, it would depend on interaction of the diplomatic styles of the two governments and the spirit of negotiations that emerged. Whereas their interests diverged, their liberal diplomatic styles were now aligned.

Bridging the Gap: Integrative Negotiation at the League of Nations

At the beginning of the Fifth Assembly of the League of Nations, MacDonald gave a rousing speech calling for a revision of the Covenant to require compulsory arbitration. As it then stood, members of the League were supposed to submit disputes that might lead to the outbreak of an armed conflict to some form of conflict resolution—judicial if they were matters of international law, arbitration through experts or the League Council consideration if they were solely political matters. Were the Council members[5] to find themselves unable to form a unanimous judgment about how the conflict should be resolved, however, war was legal under the terms of the Covenant. And even after a determination had been made through one of these mechanisms, war was still allowed following a three-month "cooling off" period. League members simply agreed not to materially help the state that did not comply with the decision.

MacDonald proposed to plug what was called the "gap" in the Covenant by requiring states to arbitrate all of their disputes, even if the Council could not agree. The prime minister was essentially attempting to outlaw war by institutionalizing liberal diplomacy—the impartial, deliberative, and reasoned resolution of political conflicts. He spoke of dispute settlement "not of a military kind but of a *rational* and judicial kind" (Marquand 1977: 353). MacDonald highlighted how such an approach would be based on the open and reasoned exposition of competing arguments between two sides. "The test is, Are you willing to arbitrate? The test is, Are you willing to explain? The test is, Will you come before us and tell us what your propose to do?" (in Marquand 1977: 353). The prime minister argued that by removing grievances in this way, nations would feel the security that made global disarmament, the other major Labour goal, possible (Walters 1952: 269).

The French found MacDonald's vision lacking. Herriot's speech placed emphasis on the sanctions that would follow any violation of the terms of the Covenant. Consistent with the French focus on security, Herriot proclaimed that arbitration was not enough and that France would "regard these three terms—arbitration, security and disarmament—as inseparable." If the League did not back its obligations with force, arbitration could become a "snare for peaceful nations" (in Marquand 1977: 353). The leftist coalition government was fine with compulsory dispute settlement, provided that League members also increased the sanctions in the Covenant for noncompliance (Walters 1952: 269).

Despite these very different positions, the two nations drafted a joint resolution embodying the points of both governments and calling for immediate negotiations to revise the Covenant in this direction. Two League committees, one dealing with sanctions and the other with

---

5. Under the Covenant, only those who were not party to the dispute were allowed to deliberate. The parties involved were forced to abstain.

arbitration, set to work at once to devise a new mechanism that would blend French and British interests. Indeed, these countries often took the lead in private meetings, and their common position was presented to the others. Britain was represented by Arthur Henderson and (Charles Cripps) Lord Parmoor, prominent Labour politicians; France was represented by Briand, the former premier, and Joseph Paul-Boncour, Socialist member of parliament. The delegates agreed to negotiate a voluntary supplement to the Covenant that could be signed, ratified, and applied by members of the League that consented. But they also would make a later effort to incorporate its provisions into the Covenant so that all members would eventually fall under its rules. The instrument became known as the Geneva Protocol.

The almost impromptu nature of the negotiations meant that the British and French representatives did not have approved negotiating platforms. The British delegation, for instance, was given almost complete discretion; it merely reported the minutes of the committee meetings. The Foreign Office and the prime minister's secretary limited their responses mostly to continual reminders that any draft agreement was subject to government review and eventually the approval of Parliament.[6]

The French and British delegations believed that negotiations in Geneva were marked by a value creating spirit based on joint liberal diplomacy. Paul-Boncour stated at the first meeting, "He desired to put before the committee the ideas of the French delegation, and he was not going to withhold any part of them. It was not part of the policy of the French delegation, as used to be the fashion in the old form of negotiations, to withhold something in order to have something to bargain with. The French delegation wanted to put all their cards on the table; their desire was to collaborate whole-heartedly in any modifications that the committee might wish to put forward and to see to arrive at some agreed text which would reconcile all views" (FO 371/10570, W8159/134/98). This

---

6. It was "premature to subject this draft to close criticism," wrote Foreign Office bureaucrats on September 24 (FO 371/10570/W8146). The Foreign Office "acted on the assumption that they were not required to offer any observations on the proceedings of the British delegation, and they have therefore taken no initiative." There was "nothing to be done until something complete and definite has emerged." "In the meantime, it has been made clear by the British delegates that anything they agree to is subject to the covering approval of His Majesty's Government" (FO 371/10570, W8281/134/98). Only when the navy objected to a pledge to submit to the compulsory jurisdiction of the Permanent Court on International Justice on questions of international law arising out of actions taken under League Covenant obligations did London intervene in the negotiations. The British delegation noted a reservation that would overcome this obstacle (FO 371/10570, W8281/134/98 and W8493/134/98).

might, of course, have been cheap talk, but it was seconded in private by Henderson, who paid tribute to the "spirit . . . amongst the members of this subcommittee" (FO 371/10570, W8146/134/98). Francis Walters, the foremost historian on the League and personal witness to many acrimonious sessions in Geneva, writes that "they worked with extraordinary concentration, with frankness, good temper, and a sincere desire to reach agreement. . . . They threw off the artificial courtesies of diplomatic usage: they were frequently to be seen in shirt-sleeves, and to be heard addressing one another by their surnames alone" (1952: 272). In short, reasoned dialogue prevailed.

One might argue that it was the alignment of the bargaining positions of the two sides that made negotiation easier, that diplomacy was epiphenomenal. But that had certainly not been enough two years before, and the French and British ideal points were now considerably further apart. MacDonald later recounted, "This was not a mere evolution of good will like the pentecostal peace that we read about in the Acts of the Apostles. Not at all. The greeting was cold and critical, but that changed" (*Hansard*, Series 5, Vol. 182: col. 345). He situated that description in a general understanding of relations with France that indicated a win-win heuristic characteristic of liberal diplomacy: "French interests are not always the same as ours. I have said so in public several times and in private very often. But France has got no interest so diverse from ours that France and ourselves, approaching the problem in a friendly spirit, cannot find agreement upon it. I am profoundly convinced of that. It may take us six months to find agreement. That does not matter. I am certain that agreement is there if the situation be properly handled on both sides" (*Hansard*, Series 5, Vol. 182: col. 345).

The two sides somewhat easily settled on a mechanism by which states were obligated to submit all disputes to some form of nonviolent resolution. Any issue not taken up by the Permanent Court of International Justice or through arbitration by independent experts was to be brought before the League Council. If the Council unanimously agreed on the measures to be taken, its decision was to be binding and no recourse to war would be allowed. And if the Council was divided, parties could not proceed to settle the question militarily, as was currently the case. Rather, they would be obligated to forward the question for arbitration. This ensured that all conflicts would be resolved rather than left open. And it provided a simple mechanism for establishing the aggressor in any situation, a problem that had vexed previous negotiations—it was the power that refused peaceful conflict resolution (Walters 1952: 268–75).

Differences between the two countries centered on the sanction for nonsubmission or noncompliance. For the French, a mere legal commitment

[79]

was "not enough by itself." Rather, they wanted to "make it certain that those who refused arbitration would have to face the full consequences of their act. . . . Those nations must become convinced that they would find all the other nations of the world prepared to compel them to accept the arbitration which they had refused" (FO 371/10570/W8159). The French wanted both nonsubmission and noncompliance to automatically lead to a total severing of economic and financial ties with the aggressor of the kind identified by Article 16 of the Covenant. This was to be the case even if the state not living up to its commitments had not yet used force. The French also wanted to more precisely specify the exact obligations for League members to add to the organization's deterrent effect. There was, the French explained, "danger in employing terms of a general nature. An aggressor State would be tempted to think that, if two great nations like France and Great Britain could not agree exactly on what action they were going to take against a breach of the peace, it was worth taking the risk of common action by the members of the League being prevented by disagreement on the actual mode of procedure. What the French Government wanted to do was to prevent the possibility of aggression" (FO 371/10570, W7877/134/98).

This was a common French position. The French left and right had very similar foreign policy goals. The Foreign Office noted that French views did not "differ in any important respect from those of previous French Governments which have been in power since the armistice" (FO 371/10571, W9571/134/98). British civil servant Alexander Cadogan wrote, "If anything emerged from the debate, it was only the rather familiar fact that the French require a measure of security satisfactory to themselves before they will consent to disarmament" (FO 371/10570, W7877/134/98).

The British, however, made significant concessions to the French on security in a way that the previous government under the Conservatives had not. Henderson admitted that "adequate sanctions should be provided for seeing that award or decision should be carried out." Indeed, he argued, "It was advisable, where possible that sanctions should come into operation *ipso facto* without the necessity of further confirmation" (FO 371/10570, W8159/134/98). In other words, the Council would not have to meet and unanimously agree to institute economic sanctions. Henderson was actually the first to point out a contradiction in the text that unintentionally implied an authorization session would be necessary, for which the French were grateful (FO 371/10570, W7877/134/98). Henderson supported the French desire to make it clear that Article 16 entailed automatic obligations. The British delegate did maintain that states in noncompliance with their obligations, either to consent to dispute resolution or comply with its outcome, would have to first use force

[80]

before being branded an aggressor subject to sanctions (FO 371/10570, W8897/134/98). Nevertheless, the protocol was still a remarkable extension of British obligations for ensuring European and even global security in that it multiplied the potential number of infractions that would call Article 16 into play for Britain.

The extent of British concessions on sanctions might have just as much to do with Henderson's personal views and foreign policy goals as it did with the liberal diplomacy my theory expects of a leftist government official. He was known, in contrast to MacDonald, to believe that obligations undertaken under the Covenant must be backed by force to be effective (Winkler 1994: 4–5, 16, 90). In contrast, the prime minister, more of an antimilitarist, thought that the very practice of arbitration, if given a chance, would become a "new habit of mind" (Gordon 1969: 2). But archival research reveals that even the prime minister had telegraphed acceptance of the compromise formula on sanctions reached with the French during the negotiations, subject to the understanding that it would depend on parliamentary ratification and therefore "stand or fall with the rest of the draft" (FO 371/10570, W7877/134/93).

Henderson was also accommodating on the issue of the status of alliances in relation to the new protocol. Always eager for certainty, the French wanted explicit permission in the Geneva Protocol for states to devote specific forces to be placed at the discretion of the League Council in case the League decided to use military sanctions. Only then, they argued, would they feel the security necessary for them to disarm. They also offered an amendment allowing states that were victims of aggression to put into place prearranged military plans among smaller groups of countries (FO 371/10570, W7992/134/98). Essentially the French wanted to add a loophole in the protocol allowing military alliances.

Henderson initially objected, consistent with the long-standing opposition of his party to military alliances. He expressed his "regret that the members of the committee have not seen their way clear to make this instrument an instrument where the League will act as a whole, instead of dividing up into regional alliances. . . . I think we should have rather taken the line at which I hinted yesterday afternoon and this morning, of trying to get rid, once and for all, and as soon as possible, of all sectional alliances. The League ought to stand solidly as a whole. . . . I regret that we cannot see our way to the League acting as a whole and to putting our faces like flint against anything like the old balance of power" (FO 371/10570, W7992/134/98). Henderson suggested an amendment stating that, because members could devote forces to the League, "no agreement shall in the future be concluded between States members of the League providing for military action to be taken by them." This would have effectively made military alliances illegal for parties to the protocol

(FO 371/10570, W8067/134/98). He quickly relented, however, and acquiesced to the French position. "I accept it in order to show that I am anxious to conciliate in this committee," he stated (FO 371/10570, W7992/134/98). A spirit of value creating was prevailing.

The French, in turn, conceded on an issue important to the British. Henderson was not eager for his country to assume new obligations to enforce the Geneva Protocol without the guarantee that others would agree to disarm, the primary British security goal. Lord Parmoor stressed the linkage among the three items of "arbitration, sanctions and disarmament." The first two were "a step towards what is the real subject we are upon—namely disarmament. . . . We must have disarmament as an inseparable link with arbitration and sanctions before anything becomes operative for the work we are now doing. If disarmament is not carried out, all our work comes to nothing." The British would not agree to take on a greater role in providing security if there were no concessions in this regard. Parmoor explained, "The States who agreed to the proposal were giving up part of their sovereignty by accepting arbitration, and were incurring very heavy obligations in regard to sanctions. . . . It was very difficult to give sanctions such as those envisaged in an armed Europe" (FO 371/10570, W8063/134/98). The British took the line that the Geneva Protocol should come into force only provided that members of the League successfully concluded the general disarmament agreement foreseen in the Covenant itself but that had not come to fruition. The British were suggesting a package deal that created value.

The French, not surprisingly, wanted the additional security provided by the new treaty (and, more specifically, Britain) as soon as possible and did not want it made conditional on disarmament negotiations that were likely to be thorny, difficult, and protracted. Without disarmament, however, there would be no win-win, value creating aspect of the Geneva Protocol. Henderson suggested a compromise. Preparations for a disarmament conference would begin immediately, the parties would assemble in only a few months, and Britain would ratify the protocol in the interim, giving France greater assurance of British intentions. But Britain would only deposit the treaty, thereby making it operational, in the event of a successful disarmament agreement. This limited, to some degree, French concerns about the British commitment.

This was not an extractive linkage but, rather, an integrative one. The British were not withholding something from the French that was not of value to them. And had the Labour representatives used coercive bargaining, they would have refused to discuss enhanced sanctions until disarmament was complete. But, rather than hold the security issue hostage to coerce France in particular to disarm, Britain revealed its private position on security, allowed negotiations on sanctions to proceed, and even made significant concessions before any disarmament program was in place. The French were appreciative and did not hold out for more. They accepted the British offer gracefully and even "rendered homage to the great effort of conciliation made by the British delegation." In response, the British representative, Lord Parmoor, expressed his gratitude for the conciliatory way in which Paul-Boncour "had received the suggestion" (FO 371/10570, W8063/134/98).

The results of these concessions by both sides was, in David Marquand's words, an "adroit, indeed a brilliant compromise between Herriot and MacDonald—between the French fear that they might be left alone with resurgent Germany, and the old U.D.C. [Union for Democratic Control][7] doctrine that military pacts led to war" (1977: 355). Walters calls it "highly ingenious" (1952: 272). "At a stroke, it hoped, in accord with socialist prescriptions, to satisfy the French yearning for security . . . and to boost internationalism by amending the Covenant and enhancing the League's authority," writes Gordon (1969: 49). In the terms of this book, the two sides created value through an integrative deal that had not been possible between the conservative Poincaré and Lloyd George governments. The two sides made significant concessions, trading issues of less importance for what they desired most. They had solved a puzzle through reasoned dialogue.

Special Agreements for Special Needs: The Tory Rejection of the Geneva Protocol

The fate of the Geneva Protocol was still very uncertain. Eager for greater security, the French signed the final draft of the protocol immediately. But given the unconventional way in which it had been negotiated, the British government had not subjected its provisions to a thorough dissection. Foreign Office bureaucrats indicated in their notes to one another in London during the conference that much of their understanding of its contents came from press reports (FO 371/10570, W8281/134/98). On the completion of the negotiations, the Foreign Office began to prepare for the review of the protocol, first by the Committee of Imperial Defence (CID) and then by Parliament (FO 371/10570, W8487/134/98).[8]

---

7. The Union for Democratic Control was an extraparliamentary pressure group advocating "liberal" positions on foreign policy, most notably democratic oversight of foreign policy. The organization was closely aligned with Labour after the war.

8. There were major objections on the part of the armed services, which feared greater international commitments to enforce the peace. Foreign Office bureaucrats opposed the radical departure of the protocol from traditional diplomacy. Nevertheless, MacDonald's

As Henderson and Parmoor negotiated in Geneva, however, early elections were called in Britain. When the latter sent a memorandum to MacDonald rebutting the objections of the navy to the proposed protocol in late October, the Foreign Office prepared a curt response: "Reply saying that next week we may be defeated" (Marquand 1977: 356). The Foreign Office understood the consequence of that outcome for the fate of the protocol. "We must wait and see what government will be in office after the election," they wrote in internal correspondence (FO 371/10571, W9571/134/98). The election returned a majority Conservative government under the leadership of Stanley Baldwin, which then had to complete the government review.

For the Conservatives, a detailed examination was hardly necessary. The Tories rejected the Geneva Protocol because of their substantial foreign policy differences with Labour rather than variation in diplomatic style. The Conservative government had no interest in any universal arrangement such as the protocol. This was the position taken in private and in public. Lord Curzon complained that it "cuts a slashing gash into the root of national sovereignty, that it involves a very serious loss of national independence, and that it does convert the League into the very thing we have always been trying to avoid, namely, into a sort of super-State" (CP 105 (25), minutes of December 4, 1924, CID meeting). The Conservatives preferred traditional alliances. Foreign Secretary Austen Chamberlain said that "the way to promote the peace . . . is by proceeding from the particular to the general. . . . The reason why the Covenant fails is because we undertake equal obligations in respect of matters in which we have a vital concern and matters in which we have no concern whatsoever, except as one society of nations" (CP 105 (25), minutes of February 13, 1925, CID meeting). He complained specifically that the protocol obligated Britain to help Eastern Europe "when those who support it say that it is impossible that we should undertake a similar guarantee for the Eastern frontiers of the countries bordering on the Channel" (CP 105 (25), minutes of December 16, 1924, CID meeting; see also DBFP I, Vol. 27, Nos. 180, 300).

---

biographer concludes that he would have probably accepted it, provided it was altered to meet the objections of the armed services and the dominions (Marquand 1977: 356). Indeed, following the Tory dismissal, MacDonald planned a major campaign in support of the protocol (ADAP A12, No. 162). The National Executive of the party and the General Council of the closely related Trades Union Congress proclaimed that they "should do everything in its power to obtain the acceptance of the principles of the Protocol" and "strongly oppose any suggestion of substituting for the Protocol any form of limited military alliance or guarantee" (Henderson 1925).

The Geneva Protocol, however, created a profound diplomatic problem for the Conservative government, which agreed that it needed an alternative lest it be blamed for shattering the world's hopes for security and peace. The meetings of the Committee of Imperial Defence were preoccupied not with the merits of the protocol, which it soundly rejected, but with the question of whether Chamberlain's formal refusal at the March 1925 meeting of the League Council should be accompanied by some sort of compromise alternative (CP 105 (25), minutes of December 4, 1924, and February 19, 1925, CID meetings).

Here Austen Chamberlain, the center-right and pragmatic foreign secretary, left his first mark on British diplomacy. He said that "to turn down the Protocol . . . is quite the easiest of the decisions that we have to take, and that act by itself, unaccompanied by anything else, would, in my opinion, be an absolute disaster" (CP 105 (25), minutes of December 16, 1924, CID meeting; see also DBFP I, Vol. 27, No. 180). The cabinet agreed, concluding "that the Geneva Protocol is open to grave and objection and cannot be accepted" but also that "a reply to the League in the form of a simple rejection of the Protocol, without any attempt to pave the way to some alternative plan in regard to the vital question of national security, is to be deprecated as calculated to prolong the present state of insecurity and tension in Europe which it is the aim of His Majesty's Government to allay" (CC 12 (25)). The British needed a "constructive policy," wrote Chamberlain (DBFP I, Vol. 27, No. 180).

The Conservative government settled on a general formula, announced by Chamberlain at the League, to supplement the Covenant with "special arrangements in order to meet special needs" (CP 136 (25); see also DBFP I, Vol. 27, No. 349; *Hansard*, Series 5, Vol. 185: cols. 1560–62). Countries should not be asked to undertake universal obligations. Instead, he proposed "knitting together the nations most immediately concerned" (CP 136 (25)). More specifically, although the British "could not accept an extension to every frontier of obligations of the most serious kind, they could properly undertake such obligations in that sphere with which British interests are more closely bound up, namely, the frontier between Germany and her western neighbors" (DBFP I, Vol. 27, No. 349).

Even though both of these cases ended in failure, they demonstrate how value creating differs from value claiming and how variations in social motivation lead to distinct diplomatic styles between the left and right in the same country. These were pronounced enough even to overcome the effects of the distribution of interests. The two cases also lay the groundwork for the next chapter, providing the historical context for the extremely domestically and diplomatically difficult position that the British found themselves in following the rejection of the protocol. The Conservative government needed an alternative to the Geneva Protocol consistent with its conception of British foreign policy interests. Help came from an unlikely place—the German government.

[4]

Setting the Table

GERMAN REASSURANCE, BRITISH BROKERING, AND FRENCH UNDERSTANDING

France in 1924 was still preoccupied with security and terrified of Germany. In the winter, at French insistence, the allies announced that they would not evacuate the first zone of the Rhineland occupation area, centered around Cologne, as scheduled in 1925. The Treaty of Versailles gave them the right to maintain their forces in German territory if Germany did not disarm completely. The allied decision demonstrated the depth of the problem posed by French insecurity. The German infractions were for the most part trivial. Given French fears and the allies' position of strength, German leaders fretted that foreign troops might remain on German soil indefinitely. In addition, the post of foreign secretary in Britain had been taken up by Austen Chamberlain, in the past a strong and consistent voice for a bilateral entente with France. The possibility of a Franco-British alliance threatened a further deterioration of the already prostrate German position (Jacobson 1972: 10–12; Gratwohl 1980: 62–63; Stresemann, Vol. 2: 97–113; Vermächtnis II: 73–80; Wright 2002: 303).

The German foreign minister, Gustav Stresemann, sought through diplomacy to reverse the declining fortunes of Germany and its persistent role as the "object' of international negotiations. He wanted Germany to be a subject, demonstrating its own agency (Jacobson 1972: 10–12; Gratwohl 1980: 62–63; Stresemann, Vol. 2: 97–113; Vermächtnis II: 73–80; Wright 2002: 303). Stresemann wrote of "fundamentally changing the situation" (Vol. 2: 88–95) and avoiding "passive purposelessness" (Vol. 2: 225). "German foreign policy need not be inactive," he wrote (Vermächtnis II: 171). To reassure France, and to block a Franco-British alliance, Stresemann proposed a multilateral security pact in which France and Germany would both legally renounce the use of force to change their

[87]

mutual border, backed by a British guarantee of both sides against aggression from the other.

The chances of success were slim. The French would have to enter an agreement with their most hated and feared adversary and face the prospect of armed military action against them by a German-British combination. The British would have to make a commitment on the continent they had so far been reluctant to give. And Franco-German relations were at a nadir. The failure by Germany to pay its reparations on time had led the conservative Poincaré government in 1923 to move French occupation forces deeper into Germany territory, seizing the industrial Ruhr area as compensation. German passive resistance, marked by the refusal of German workers to report to their jobs in factories held by the French, was bankrolled by printing money. This hyperinflation ruined the German middle class and further poisoned relations with the French. This type of animosity and mistrust made value creating very difficult.

Making things even more difficult, Germany had little to offer. To convey its vulnerability, the German foreign minister referred to his proposal as *das Kind* ("the child" or "the baby") (Stambrook 1968). How would Stresemann be able to keep his progeny alive long enough to develop and thrive? Stresemann was armed only with diplomacy.

Stresemann's proself motivation and high level of epistemic motivation, consistent with the ideology of his party, led him naturally toward a realist diplomatic approach. Stresemann was a center-right politician and leader of the DVP (German People's Party). Given the very weak German position, realism dictated that returning Germany to its former position as a great power required conciliation rather than confrontation. Stresemann's pragmatism allowed him to put himself in the French position and realize that French insecurity was the source of German problems. Only when France felt secure could it be led to withdraw its troops from the Rhineland and take a softer line on the longer-term ambitions of Germany, particularly to revise the territorial settlement in Eastern Europe and regain its former lands with large numbers of German inhabitants.

His proposal was an expression of pragmatic statecraft in which Germany would surrender something of value now for greater gains down the line. It was a costly signal of reassurance. The pact amounted to the de facto recognition of the loss of Alsace-Lorraine to France. And the German foreign minister also offered to conclude arbitration treaties with the eastern neighbors of Germany so that its efforts would not be seen as a ruse to tie France up legally while Germany turned its sights in the other direction. The foreign minister believed that, by making concessions,

Germany would create the rapprochement and trust that would allow France to ease and end the Rhineland occupation early. He was setting the table for future gains.

Rationalists might argue that Germany, given its weakened state, simply had no other options. Its conciliatory diplomacy of concessions was structurally determined. This is belied, however, by the opposition that Stresemann faced in cabinet from his coalition partners, the DNVP (German National People's Party). This far-right party, with a low epistemic and a proself motivation, embraced coercive diplomacy even though Germany had little leverage. Although Stresemann shared all the goals of the DNVP—unification with Austria, the rectification of eastern German borders, and the early end of the occupation—the nationalists wanted a resolution of all these issues quickly and without any significant German concessions, much less unilateral ones. Consequently, Stresemann found support from the centrist parties in his coalition and the socialist opposition in the legislature.[1] Diplomacy was not endogenous to structure.

The German gambit came at precisely the right moment for the British, who were struggling to articulate an alternative to the Geneva Protocol. Austen Chamberlain, center-right politician and British foreign secretary, was an ideological fellow traveler. He had a two-stage strategy of, first, reassuring France and, then, bringing Germany into a new Concert of Europe in which the three powers would institutionalize the quiet, private, and pragmatic diplomacy of the post-Napoleonic period. With the long-term perspective facilitated by a high level of epistemic motivation, Chamberlain believed the return of Germany to great power status was inevitable, so pragmatism dictated that its main concerns be addressed lest it turn violent. Britain would pay the present price of guaranteeing the European status quo for the future gain of European peace, which was in the British interest.

The right-wing members of the conservative British cabinet opposed a guarantee of French security at the current time. They shared Chamberlain's foreign policy goal of improving relations between France and Germany but did not share his diplomatic style. The more conservative Tories wanted to withhold British willingness to make such a commitment until later in the negotiation process to extract as much as possible from the French. Only the foreign secretary's threat of resignation led Britain to reveal its preferences and make such a commitment before formal negotiations began. By making such a pledge, British brokering

---

1. The Communists opposed any rapprochement with the West, seeing it through their Marxist lenses as the precursor to a capitalist alignment against the Soviet Union.

contributed to constructing a zone of possible agreement between the French and the Germans. The realist diplomacy of Britain was a necessary condition for successful agreement.

Value creating, however, requires reciprocation by others. Therefore, it was crucial that the French government still be led by the left-leaning and more prosocial Cartel des Gauches. Although distrustful of Germany, the coalition still engaged in liberal diplomacy, which led the Cartel to explore the German proposal rather than dismissing it outright. As coercive bargainers, the French right derided the significance of the German offer; it did not see the German offer as a costly signal. Had it been in government, the diplomatic style of French conservatives would have strangled Stresemann's baby in its cradle.

GERMAN REASSURANCE

Stresemann's Realism in Theory: Recognizing German Weakness

The origins of the German initiative cannot be understood without reference to the pragmatic statecraft of the German foreign minister, Gustav Stresemann. The man himself constantly described his approach as "sober realpolitik" (in Wright 2002: 285). Stresemann's realism is evident in his insistence on putting vital interests first, a careful "ordering of priorities" as Robert Gratwohl (1980: 120) puts it. In an indictment of coercive bargaining, the foreign minister cautioned that "a nation must not adopt the attitude of a child that writes a list of its wants on Christmas Eve, which contains everything that the child will need for the next fifteen years" (Stresemann, Vol. 2: 221; Wright 2002: 345). Good diplomacy "depends . . . on the actual restriction of these aims, and the consequent abandonment of a policy that attempts to advance in every direction at once" (Stresemann, Vol. 2: 159; Jacobson 1972: 116).

Separating vital interests from more peripheral ones was particularly important given the disarmed state of Germany (Vermächtnis II: 172). Realism required an objective view of German options that was "conscious of the limitations on our power" (Wright 2002: 298). "Power politics works to our disadvantage presently," Stresemann wrote. "It is necessary to draw the consequences from that in order to be able to move forward, as difficult as it is to admit" (Vol. 2: 88–95). Lacking military might, Germany needed to develop friendlier relations with other nations: "Progress within the sphere of these foreign-political aims is not dependent on warlike resources, which German lacks. But it does depend on co-operation and understanding with the Powers whose decision on these questions is essential for its attainment" (Stresemann,

Vol. 2: 159). Cooperation would bring greater gains than saber-rattling. He wrote that "abroad, we have at present neither political power nor influence. You can conduct successful policy only if you have one or the other or the first through the second. The only policy which can succeed is that which aims to become a worthwhile ally for other nations" (in Wright 2002: 285).

Stresemann was therefore carefully attuned to situational constraints. He was inspired by the example of Otto von Bismarck, as a "master of the art of the possible" (Wright 2002: 267). He admired the former chancellor's ability to adapt to circumstances and conditions, quoting him in public that "consistency in a politician must mean that he had only one idea" (in Wright 2002: 329). Stresemann himself was constantly adjusting: "I frankly declare that it is to-day not possible to lay out a programme of policy, because in certain circumstances events dash onward like a torrent, and in others, barely trickle forward at all" (Vol. 2: 225).

This was, of course, not a principled commitment to cooperation but, rather, an instrumental one: "The preservation of peace and the attempts to secure it are not weakness, are not timidity, they are the realistic recognition of our own national interest," Stresemann said (in Wright 2002: 472). In his famous letter to the crown prince, Stresemann wrote that his first priority was the "assurance of peace, which is an essential promise for the recovery of our strength" (Stresemann, Vol. 2: 503). Stresemann's diplomacy was thoroughly proself in its social motivation. Nations "are always egoists," he claimed, and cooperative relations with other states depended on "parallel interest" (in Wright 2002: 344). Under his leadership, Germany sought "understanding and peace because we need both" (in Wright 2002: 298). More specifically, but in a similar vein, he said: "If I am told that I pursue a policy friendly to England, I do not do so from any love of England, but because in this question German interests coincide with those of England, and because we must find someone who helps us" (Stresemann, Vol. 2: 225).

Although Stresemann was deeply discontented with the current circumstances of Germany, he recognized that changing them would be a long-term process (ADAP B1/2: 665–69; Wright 2002: 285). Expressing frustration with that long "Christmas list," Stresemann said, "In foreign politics I often have the feeling that I am being confronted with such a list, and that it is forgotten that history advances merely step by step, and by Nature not by leaps and bounds" (Stresemann, Vol. 2: 20).

The foreign minister recognized that not everyone in his country was similarly pragmatic and unemotional. It was "a difficult inner burden," as he put it, for many Germans to admit their current circumstances and to remain patient as Germany overcame its obstacles and achieved its objectives one by one. Stresemann cautioned that they had to objectively evaluate their situation, "which will not change any time soon" (Ver-mächtnis II: 73–80). Emotion was the enemy of pragmatism. "We are let-ting ourselves be led too much by our feelings," he wrote. "If our policy is driven by our feelings, then we have to reject diplomatic relations with the world. . . . That will not get us anywhere" (Vermächtnis II: 173–74). "One cannot make foreign policy or domestic policy with sentimental-ity," he advised his compatriots. "It is a question of adopting realpolitik" (in Wright 2002: 298). Stresemann preached sober and calm diplomacy. "It would be wrong to indulge in too much indignation," he wrote in his diary. "We should rather try to dispose of the matter on a common-sense basis, by negotiation" (Stresemann, Vol. 2: 21). In true pragmatic fashion, Stresemann thought the ends would justify the means, only in this case the means were cooperative. The foreign minister told German audi-ences: "Do not always worry about the [cooperative] methods so long as one is moving forward. For in the end success decides which methods are right" (ADAP B1/2: 665–69).

Statecraft required attentiveness to the interests of others. Strese-mann lamented previous German failures to do so, even when Ger-many was a great power. "We are not yet so great that we can ignore all this, and I believe that, in earlier days when we were great, we should have often held a different position in the world if we had paid more attention to this world atmosphere and other such considerations" (Stresemann, Vol. 2: 196–204).

The foreign minister was the architect of German foreign policy but throughout had the wholehearted backing of his parliamentary caucus, something that had not been true on domestic political issues at other points during Weimar Republic. Stresemann was the founder of the DVP, which occupied a center-right position in the party system and therefore combined a proself motivation in international affairs with a high degree of epistemic motivation that made it supportive of Strese-mann's realist diplomacy. As he saw it, the DVP, along with the centrist parties, would mediate between the far right and the left to allow "that great diagonal without which no *statesmanlike* policy can be conducted" (Wright 2002: 276, emphasis added). Before the December 1924 elec-tions, at the DVP conference, Stresemann opposed a right bloc or left bloc, instead backing a coalition of bourgeois parties united behind a foreign policy of "national realpolitik" (Wright 2002: 298).

Stresemann also had the consistent support of Hans Luther, the chan-cellor at the time. The head of the German government was also politi-cally of the center-right but refused party affiliation throughout his career, making him an ideal selection for coalitions ostensibly composed of experts rather than party officials. Consistent with his political ideol-ogy, he was a pragmatist. Luther disliked doctrinaire thinking, seeing it as an impediment to solving practical problems (Clingan 2010: 2, 4–5, 9, 19, 23, 32, 55). C. Edmund Clingan writes, "Luther lived a variety of lives, but there were consistent traits. The first trait was flexibility" (2010: 7).

Stresemann's Realism in Practice: Acknowledging French Fear

The most vital interest for Germany was regaining "the sovereignty of Germany on German soil" (Jacobson 1972: 8; ADAP B1/2: 665–69), the easing and eventual termination of the French occupation of the Rhineland, and the assurance that there would no future incursions into German territory such as the Ruhr invasion. Stresemann put it more colorfully before nationalist audiences. He called the Rhineland the "burning wound on the German body" (Vermächtnis II: 88–95). Stresemann wrote to the crown prince: "The most important thing . . . is the liberation of German territory from any occupying force. We must first get the stranglehold from our neck" (Stresemann, Vol. 2: 503–6; see also Jacobson 1972: 42). Only then could Germany turn toward longer-term German goals, particularly the revision of the eastern borders of Germany with Poland and the return of ethnically German majority areas to the Reich, aims that Stresemann shared with the nationalist right (Stresemann, Vol. 2: 503–6; Wright 2002: 268).

France was the primary obstacle to restoring Germany to its former great power status (Stresemann, Vol. 2: 158). Given the present weakened state of Germany, however, only a policy of reconciliation was possible. Stresemann advocated "reaching an understanding with France as the most stubborn opponent of international German renewal, thereby laying the foundation for German viability" (Vermächtnis II: 171).

Stresemann's high degree of epistemic motivation, which he shared with the German center-right and left, allowed him to see that, even in its current preeminent state, France required reassurance given its fear of an eventual German *revanche*. In his diary, Stresemann revealed that he personally thought that the French fears were irrational: "How far the madness has gone in France may be seen from the statement of a deputy in the French Chamber that Germany is to-day better equipped for a war than she was in 1914," he wrote. "We ourselves know that we have no weapons . . . so that the way stands open for a Polish march on Berlin. . . . Anyone who ventured on even a defensive war would be sending his men to certain death" (Stresemann, Vol. 2: 15). More irreverently, he wrote in a private letter: "The fact that in France the idea of security should still beset people's minds is comprehensible, though absurd" (Stresemann, Vol. 3: 421). He complained that the France maintained its troops in Cologne "because twenty thousand rifle-barrel castings have been found somewhere" (Stresemann, Vol. 2: 15).

[93]

Yet pragmatically Stresemann recognized that the Germans "shall do no good by ignoring this attitude. The other Allies will have to take it into account" (Stresemann, Vol. 2: 15). He set about trying to find some way of resolving French fears. "We must . . . ask ourselves whether the question of French security, this nightmare of a future German attack, all these modifications regarding the control of the Rhineland . . . whether all these obsessions could be abolished," he wrote (Stresemann, Vol. 2: 64; Jacobson 1972: 9). He had "security dilemma sensibility" (Booth and Wheeler 2008).

A more secure France would be less intransigent regarding the remaining disarmament questions that were postponing the evacuation of Cologne. Through diplomacy, Germany could avoid the strict interpretation of the Versailles Treaty and forestall the implementation of the permanent disarmament-monitoring regime that the French desired (Vermächtnis II: 88–95). It might also eventually allow for the alleviation of the stringent conditions under which the Rhine population lived, perhaps even an early end to the occupation in the other zones (Cohrs 2006: 228). In a memo to the German ambassador to France, Stresemann explained that the issues of the Rhineland and disarmament had to be understood as part of a general problem of security. The French would not leave the occupied areas unless "beforehand something in the general security question occurs" (ADAP A12, No. 22). Without security, the French would forever find reasons to drag their feet in leaving the Rhineland, perhaps, Stresemann and others feared, even staying beyond the date that was foreseen in the treaty (ADAP A12, No. 67). The French could always find some legal pretext for extending their stay (ADAP A12, No. 67).

A fearful France would also block any efforts by Germany to redraw its eastern borders. The settlement of the western situation was necessary for the resolution of the eastern (Cohrs 2006: 251; Wright 2002: 306). A peaceful transformation through diplomacy would be possible only "if [Germany] had previously effected a political understanding with all the world Powers who would have to decide the matter." France was the most important (Stresemann, Vol. 2: 215; see also Wright 2002: 342; Stresemann, Vol. 2: 73–80). Were he to successfully steward Germany toward better relations with Britain and France, it would have the "best and friendliest relations with those world powers" when it raised border questions down the line (Stresemann, Vol. 2: 73–80). France had established a system of alliances and agreements with the eastern neighbors of Germany, the Little Entente, as a second-rate replacement when the United States and the United Kingdom failed to provide the guarantee promised in 1919. Pragmatically, Stresemann explicitly thought in terms of a gradual progression of steps (Stresemann, Vol. 2: 503–6; Cohrs 2006;

[94]

Wright 2002: 327). He asked rhetorically, "But what stands in the way of a strengthening of Germany? What stands in the way of a recovery of German soil . . .? What stands in our way is the eternal anxiety that if this 60-million nation becomes a 70-million nation. . . . The moment the incessant threat of war on our western frontier ceases to exist, this argument is no longer valid" (Stresemann, Vol. 2: 221).

The Price of Realism: The Costly Signals in German Memoranda

In the deteriorating context sketched in the introduction, Stresemann proposed to bring about a rapprochement in Franco-German relations and open up opportunities for Germany to secure other longer-term interests by offering France a security pact. The two nations would pledge not to use force to alter their common border. France and Germany would also negotiate arbitration treaties establishing procedures to settle their bilateral disputes peacefully. Other interested parties, the most important being Great Britain, could be drawn in to guarantee, with force if necessary, the integrity of the present territorial status quo against any aggressor, whether it be France *or* Germany (DBFP I, Vol. 27, No. 189; ADAP A12, No. 64).

Recognizing that Great Britain was crucial to the success of such a project, the Germans ran the idea by Chamberlain first. Stresemann's first memorandum framed the issue as providing security for France. He began, "The present acute questions of disarmament and evacuation are frequently considered in France from the standpoint of security against possible aggressive intentions on the part of Germany. For that reason it would probably be easier to find a solution for them if they were combined with an agreement of a general nature, the object of which would be to secure peace between Germany and France." In an indication of his instrumental empathy, Stresemann wrote that "Germany is perfectly ready to take this [French] point of view into consideration. She is anxious to see the problems arising between her and France dealt with by no other method than that of friendly understanding" (DBFP I, Vol. 27, No. 189).

After sounding out the British, the Germans sent a similar memo to the French. When transmitting the document, Stresemann instructed his ambassador in Paris to describe it as a "sign of our goodwill," in spite of the very difficult and fraught relationship that prevailed currently between the two countries. Herriot had just recently given a sharp speech critical of Germany before the French parliament (ADAP A12, No. 67). In his conversation with the French premier, the German ambassador explicitly acknowledged French security concerns and pledged the willingness of Germany to begin open, fundamental, and discreet conversations to improve bilateral relations, perhaps even somehow making use of the preferred French vehicle, the Geneva Protocol (ADAP A14, No. 80; see also ADAP A12, No. 64). In his memo to the British, Stresemann wrote that, given the desire for peace of all involved, "a secure treaty foundation . . . cannot be difficult to find" (DBFP I, Vol. 27, No. 189). Rather than stressing, as one would using a coercive bargaining strategy, the great distance between the positions of each side, the Germans minimized the differences between the parties.

The German note contained two concessions meant as costly signals. First, the acceptance of the current territorial status quo between Germany and France amounted to a German "renunciation" of Alsace-Lorraine, the former German territory that many Germans still coveted and considered ethnically German (Gratwohl 1980: 78). The very offer by Germany of a security pact amounted to a concession of a long-standing German goal before any formal negotiations even began, one that would be particularly difficult for the nationalist right in the German governing coalition to accept. Rather than retaining all items as bargaining chips in a coercive diplomatic style, Stresemann let go of one without simultaneous reciprocity to demonstrate his cooperative intentions. The foreign minister used the German term for "renunciation," *Verzicht*, in his guidelines to his ambassador, although not in the written note presented to the British and Germans (ADAP A12, No. 67).

In a second costly signal in his memos, to alleviate French concerns that Germany was simply trying to neutralize the French militarily by treaty so that Germany could move with force against the east, Stresemann offered to negotiate arbitration treaties with any other states that desired them, a clear reference to the eastern neighbors of Germany (DBFP I, Vol. 27, No. 189; ADAP A12, Nos. 64, 67). Although these would not lock in the current territorial status quo, as the western agreement would (Stresemann, Vol. 2: 73–80, 88–95), this was nevertheless a concession, particularly given the special importance that nationalist Germans placed on the recovery of these territories, through force if necessary. It was meant again as a "sign of good faith" (ADAP A12, No. 99). German representatives were told to continually stress pacific German intentions in this regard (ADAP A12, Nos. 67, 99).

Honor and Dignity: German Nationalist Diplomacy and the Battle of the Proselfs

Might this simply have been the only way to respond to the particular structural circumstances of Germany? In other words, would a foreign minister or government of any ideological stripe have been forced to pursue such a policy? After all, what other options did such a weak country have? Rationalists and realists would emphasize these structural constraints in an explanation of German behavior, in which case diplomacy was simply endogenous to the distribution of power.

Had there been no room for agency, however, we would observe cross-party consensus on the course Germany should take, particularly among those who bore the responsibilities of governing. Yet a clear contrast in diplomatic style can be seen between Stresemann, his DVP, and his centrist allies, on the one hand, and their coalition partner, the highly conservative DNVP, on the other. The nationalists were the largest non-Socialist party in the German parliament and the most significant right-wing party in the country, dwarfing the only nascent Nazi movement.

As a rightist party, the DNVP shared the proself motivation of Stresemann and the DVP and their foreign policy goals—the restoration of Germany as a great power. They had identical foreign policy ends in mind—the most important being the return or incorporation of German-speaking populations in Eastern Europe and Austria, the revision of borders with Poland, and the pursuit of colonies. Yet the DNVP consistently opposed Stresemann's realist diplomacy. The nationalists preferred a coercive diplomatic style of direct confrontation with Britain and France and opposed Stresemann's pragmatic statecraft. Gratwohl writes, "It was the old story of catching bees: the Nationalists wanted to use vinegar; Stresemann preferred to use honey" (1980: 120). The nationalists wanted to "refight the war through the diplomacy of confrontation in order to assert Germany's rightful place in the sun" (Gratwohl 1980: 119).

The difference was epistemic motivation. Stresemann criticized the nationalists for their lack of pragmatism. They lacked objectivity, setting their immediate sights too high and not coming to terms with the weakened state of Germany. "That Germany is completely disarmed and cannot contend with other great powers at its current strength is only contested by a few fools hoping for a miracle," he wrote in an anonymous article (Vermächtnis II: 170–75). At a party conference, Stresemann spoke of a nationalist prayer, "Give us each day our daily illusion" (in Wright 2002: 380). He said, "Those who hope for a miracle can reject all constraints and dream of growing wings that will fly him again to the dawn. Those who think that we must have both feet on the ground will frame the question: 'What serves my ultimate goal and brings me forward'" (Stresemann, Vol. 2: 172).

With a high degree of cognitive closure, the nationalists were also overly short-sighted and emotional, thereby undermining their very own objectives. The nationalists believed Germany was unjustly persecuted. Even when the DNVP was in government and at its most restrained, Graf von Westarp, a powerful leader in the party, complained that Germany "stands under the pressure of force and injustice."

[97]

Germany had "right without power" and the allies "power without right." The nonevacuation of Cologne was one of the "most disgraceful days in world history." The DNVP had no empathy, instrumental or otherwise, for the position of France; French policies were driven not by fear but by the "1000 year old" desire to dominate (VDR 62: 1894–1903). And this was the DNVP at its most moderate, before the decisive turn further toward the right led by Alfred Hugenberg in 1929.

For Stresemann, pragmatic statecraft was the surest path back to power. "The honor and dignity of the German nation, about which so much is spoken, will be protected soonest, if the success of this step serves to secure the development of Germany's vital needs in a peaceful way" (Stresemann, Vol. 2: 175). He was following the example of Bismarck, unlike those "political philistines who put principle above everything" (in Wright 2002: 275). He contrasted their emotional diplomacy with his own pragmatic diplomacy of "rational understanding" (Wright 2002: 380).

Stresemann criticized the DNVP for not prioritizing their goals and setting out a long-term program of diplomacy. He noted, "there were of course people in Germany who attach importance to raising question of Polish frontier at once, but this was the view of irresponsible individuals" (DBFP I, Vol. 27, No. 264). Stresemann shared their goals, but any effort to raise all the concerns of Germany at once would backfire, raising the hackles of the French right in particular. "I am of the opinion that everything must now be done first to achieve the evacuation of the Rhineland. . . . When we have achieved that, then we must consider whether the eastern question is more important than the colonial question, and that further to be considered is whether and when it would be desirable and successful to tackle the Austrian question."

The foreign minister justified this plan by referring to how it would be perceived in France, demonstrating greater epistemic motivation. "For if in my speeches and statements and my appearances in Geneva I let it be known that I wanted all that, then [the French nationalists] would say to [French Foreign Minister] Briand: 'There we have it! If we evacuate the Rhine, then they attack Poland, then they want Austria and then they want to have colonies!' and then Poincaré would declare: 'That is German imperialism against which you poor French must defend yourselves.' Therefore I have concentrated on one thing and I believe that we must do things one after the other" (in Wright 2002: 405). The center-right had a longer-term horizon and an ability to see things through other eyes that the far right lacked. The DNVP "still operated with delusions of pre-1914 grandeur," writes Gratwohl (1980: 119).

We might argue that the far right in Germany simply had different preferences. In rationalist terms, perhaps they simply preferred continued deadlock to reconciliation with France, regardless of the terms. Perhaps they were preparing for the day when Germany could take back former German territories by force. But such an argument neglects the impatience of the nationalists. Stresemann was the patient one. Gordon Craig writes that Stresemann's goals "were objectives that most people in the rightist parties regarded as desirable. The trouble was that they wanted them to be proclaimed publicly and to be accomplished forthwith. . . . They would not understand that the realities of the European situation made patience, ambiguity and opportunism requirements of German foreign policy" (1978: 512). The difference was in the level of epistemic motivation. "Unconditional men with a proneness to over-simplification, they had no sympathy with a minister who was always as acutely aware as Bismarck had been of the limitations of foreign policy" (Craig 1978: 512). Indeed, had the far right been more pragmatic, it might have supported Stresemann's efforts as a way of lowering the French guard for a later German strike. Stresemann is often accused, unjustly, of pursuing just such a strategy (see chapter 9).

At the time that Stresemann made his proposal to the allies, Germany was somewhat fortuitously in the midst of a political crisis. The previous coalition had fallen, and the cabinet did not have the backing of parliament. Constitutionally, however, German ministers were still allowed in the interim to pursue policies in their areas of responsibility, provided that they stayed within the guidelines set by the chancellor, who supported Stresemann's bid. An untraditional government was eventually formed in late January 1925. Rather than having the formal support of a set of parties in the Reichstag that constituted a majority of legislators, ministers were "personalities" without the explicit backing of their parties in a vote of confidence. Nevertheless, they served as the conduits between their caucuses and the government and functioned essentially as a multiparty coalition cabinet (ADAP A12, No. 28; Wright 2002: 317; Stresemann, Vol. 2: 127–28).

Even after the German government was formed and the DNVP took its place at the cabinet table with the greatest number of cabinet positions (although not a majority), Stresemann did not brief the government about his plans, preferring instead to work out the overall framework with the French and British in private without domestic complications in either Germany *or* France. Stresemann knew the pact idea would be extremely controversial in France and Germany and wanted to give the notion room to germinate before it was smothered by nationalist outrage on both sides (ADAP A12, No. 67; also No. 81). Stresemann conceived of the process as first winning over the French government, then convincing the German cabinet, and then bracing for the "right-wing circle's storm" (Stresemann, Vol. 2: 90). The foreign minister was wise. Had he not acted when he did, he would have had to seek prior cabinet (i.e., DNVP) approval and his initiative might very well never have gotten off the ground (Wright 2002: 317; Gratwohl 1980: 67–69; Stresemann, Vol. 2: 62–71). But when word of the proposal leaked in the international press, Stresemann and the German chancellor were eventually forced to discuss and justify the proposal in meetings with Martin Schiele, the DNVP minister of the Interior and spokesperson for the party in the cabinet, as well as a number of rank-and-file DNVP parliamentarians.

When details about the proposed pact became known, the DNVP promised the Pan-German League and Fatherland societies, conservative and nationalist pressure groups that were key electoral constituencies for the party, that it would protect the "honor and dignity of our nation" and oppose the renunciation of German populations (Gratwohl 1980: 77). The DNVP addressed a formal letter to the Chancellor insisting that further negotiations be undertaken in closest consultation with the DNVP and asserting the right of the party to refuse any deal if foreign policy continued in "the present spirit." This provoked a mini-crisis that almost ended in the exit of the DNVP from the cabinet.[2]

Despite this, save the German communists, who considered any security pact a de facto Western alliance against the Soviets (Cohrs 2006: 215; DBFP I, Vol. 27, No. 234), the other German parties largely supported Stresemann. The SPD (German Social Democratic Party), according to Leon Blum, prominent French leftist, showed the "same abnegation that the French Socialists had shown when they urged M. Poincaré to enter into negotiations with Germany on . . . the Ruhr" (DBFP I, Vol. 27, No. 252). It had suggested a similar policy, along with the centrist DDP (German Democratic Party), the previous year (Gratwohl 1980: 59). The SPD leader, Rudolf Breitscheid, spoke warmly of the German initiative. In keeping with the prosocial motivation and preference for reasoned dialogue of the left, he hoped for a "system of European states . . . without thoughts of the past, only with thoughts of the future, to live equally" in contrast to the vision of the nationalist right (VDR 62: 1886–94).

2. Luther accused the party of indicting the entire trajectory of Stresemann's foreign policy. The chancellor agreed to a formal response in which he pledged to consult with the DNVP going forward, but only if the DNVP reframed its previous letter as objecting to the secretive style rather than the substance of the German proposals. This was, of course, not the case, but Schiele agreed to it to prevent a cabinet crisis (Kabinette Luther, Vol. 1, No. 55; see also Wright 2002: 306–7; Gratwohl 1980: 71–73; DBFP I, Vol. 27, No. 263; Stresemann, Vol. 2: 78). That buried the issue for the time being. The secretive beginnings of the German initiative allowed the DNVP to deny any prior knowledge of the policy and therefore preserve its credibility while simultaneously justifying its continued participation in the cabinet to shape future developments (Gratwohl 1980: 78, 83).

The centrist parties were not as enthusiastic, waiting to see the details. But they took a more realistic line than the DNVP, in keeping with their moderate position on the ideological spectrum. Ludwig Kaas spoke for the Center Party, noting the possibility for steady, if not revolutionary, progress in German relations with the western powers and the importance of reassuring the French as a step in that process (VDR 62: 1903–11). Johann Heinrich Graf von Bernstorff of the DDP was less charitable but embraced Stresemann's practical approach given the German dependence on others. As "laughable" as it was to think that France, "armed to the teeth," was afraid of Germany, Germany would be unable to free the occupied areas until France had security. There was no use in "putting their head in the sand" (VDR 62: 1930–34). Germany should see things objectively.

BRITISH BROKERING

Chamberlain as Castlereagh: British Realism and the New Concert of Europe

Stresemann, however, was only one piece of the puzzle. Whether the foreign minister's opening to the allies would produce anything tangible depended on how they received his signals of peaceful reassurance. The German gambit could not have come at a better time for the British. The new Tory government was set to reject the Geneva Protocol, but, as seen in chapter 3, it needed an alternative to avoid the opprobrium of the international community and prevent a deepening of the sense of crisis prevailing on the continent (Jacobson 1972: 15). Here the Conservatives disagreed due to differences on how to conduct diplomacy, opening up a divide between advocates of coercive bargaining and of pragmatic statecraft.

Chamberlain, the new foreign secretary, took it upon himself to find an alternative to the Geneva Protocol. As a moderate in his rightist party, he was inclined, as expected, toward realist diplomacy in a way not true of his more conservative predecessor at the Foreign Office. In an indication of his centrist ideological position, a few years earlier Chamberlain, as leader of the party, had sought a merger into a new "centre party" of the Tories and the Lloyd George Liberals, with whom the Conservatives had governed during and after the war. This would have amounted to a shift to the left, and Chamberlain's initiative led to an intraparty split along ideological lines. Chamberlain talked of a union of those with "progressive" views, whereas his opponents appealed to those "who still believe in their principles" (Lindsay and Harrington 1974: 35–36, 39).

Chamberlain ultimately failed, and the coalition parties split apart, leading the Conservatives to fight the election of 1922 as a separate party (Smith 1997: 77–78).

Chamberlain's proself and high epistemic motivations are seen clearly in a memorandum early in his tenure outlining his vision for British diplomacy. "A successful British foreign policy depends, first, on a clear appreciation of the facts of the situation with which we have to deal, and secondly, on an equally clear conception of British interests and of their relation to the facts," he wrote. Consistent with this realism was a preoccupation with the vital interests of Britain: "The only sound line of British policy is the path of British interests. The road is too dark for any altruism or digression; it is our own security which must remain the sole consideration" (DBFP I, Vol. 27, No. 205).

Chamberlain identified as vital those interests that no Conservative (or Labour or Liberal Party member, for that matter) would have objected to, such as the safety of sea communications with the British dominions (DBFP I, Vol. 27, No. 205). More relevant to the European situation, Chamberlain highlighted, again uncontroversially, the need to prevent any single power from occupying the channel and North Sea ports (CP 122 (25)). In light of changes in military technology such as the advent of air warfare, this required that Britain also prevent any aggression against France and the Low Countries: "The frontiers of France and the Low Countries now bear the same relation to the heart of the Empire as the Channel ports did 100 or 200 years ago." Chamberlain had Germany in mind: "A Germany established in the Low Countries and dominating France would hold the heart of the British Empire at its mercy" (CP 122 (25)).

Even though the foreign secretary admitted he was the most pro-French member of the cabinet and that he loved France "as a man loves a woman" (Grayson 1997: 32; Jacobson 1972: 16), his epistemic motivation is evident in his ability to objectively evaluate the situation in Europe and see the perspectives of both sides. Chamberlain diagnosed the problem on the continent as one of French fear and German hatred that created a cycle of acrimony and conflict, which could trigger war and draw Britain in. He wrote,

> The main psychological factors in every case are almost the same. All our late enemies continue full of resentment at what they have lost; all our late Allies are fearful of losing what they have won. One-half is dangerously angry; the other half of Europe is dangerously afraid. The friction between these inflamed emotions is incessant, and acts as some septic irritant, poisoning the wounds which are yet unhealed. Fear begets provocation, armaments, secret alliances, ill-treatment of minorities; these in their turn

beget a greater hatred and simulate a desire for revenge, whereby fear is intensified, and its consequences are enhanced. The vicious circle is thus established. (DBFP I, Vol. 27, No. 205; see also No. 180; CP 105 (25), December 16 CID meeting)

Chamberlain believed that both the German and French positions were emotionally driven, rather than based on sober realism. Chamberlain's perceptions of the French were similar to Stresemann's: "As the genuineness of the feeling, I have no doubt. . . . If you ask me whether the facts are such as to justify fear as to the immediate future, in my opinion they are not" (CP 105 (25), February 13, 1925, CID meeting).

The foreign secretary identified a worst-case scenario, in which Britain would be "dragged along, unwilling, impotent, protesting, in the wake of France towards the new Armageddon. For we cannot afford to see France crushed, to have Germany . . . supreme on the Continent, or to allow any great military power to dominate the Low Countries" (DBFP I, Vol. 27, No. 180). It was up to Britain, therefore, to provide security and interrupt the cycle, thus encouraging more pragmatic behavior on the part of others. "As long as Security is absent, Germany is tempted to prepare for the Revanche," he wrote. "'The Day' will still be the national toast and with far more reason, whilst French fears, goading France to every kind of irritating folly, will keep alive German hatred and lead us inevitably, sooner or later, to a new catastrophe" (DBFP I, Vol. 27, No. 180). He sought to prevent France from "committing suicide under the influence of her fears."

This aim was not altruistically or prosocially driven. Chamberlain wrote in a memorandum, "So far I have spoken of the uneasiness of Europe and of the feelings of Frenchmen. But the case for an agreement with France does not rest only or mainly upon these considerations. British interests are affected at every turn by the insecurity of the European situation. We live too close to its shores to escape being affected by the unrest of the Continent" (CP 122 (25)). Even for the Francophile Chamberlain, Britain was interested in the security of France because its interests were interdependent with those of his own country. He wrote to a like-minded friend: "Do not let you and me because of our strong French sympathies tie ourselves to the defence of all the vagaries of French policy or allow our reason to be quenched in her fears" (Grayson 1997: 45). His epistemic motivation made him conscious of his biases.

Because the problem was psychological and emotional, Chamberlain believed that the task was to preserve peace long enough for scars to heal. His diplomacy was far-sighted and oriented toward the long term: "The only hope for world peace is that the situation should be stabilized for long enough to allow new generations growing up who *can* accept

[103]

the *fait accompli* and *will* accept it rather than face again the horrors of war with no certain prospects of success" (DBFP I, Vol. 27, No. 180). In a letter to the king, he wrote, "I am working not for today or tomorrow but for some date like 1960 or 1970" (Grayson 1997: 41; see also CP 105 (25), February 13, 1925, CID meeting).

More specifically, Chamberlain's realist plan had two main components. In a memorandum, he wrote: "I believe that Great Britain has it in her power at this moment to bring peace to Europe. To achieve this two things are indispensable: 1) that we should remove or allay French fears. 2) That we should bring Germany back into the concert of Europe. Both are equally vital. Neither by itself will suffice & the first is needed to allow the second" (Grayson 1997: 45; see also Cohrs 2006: 212). The foreign secretary proposed that Britain should first offer France and Belgium a security guarantee that would allow them to adopt a more pragmatic, conciliatory policy toward Germany. Had such an entente been in place before 1914, Chamberlain believed, the Great War would have never broken out. The foreign secretary imagined that Germany would be admitted into the security arrangement later, after French fears had softened due to the British commitment to their security (DBFP I, Vol. 27, No. 205).

The second, longer-term aspect of Chamberlain's plan was to bring Germany back into the community of nations as a great power. He did not want to "hold Germany down in a position of abject inferiority and subjection." The foreign secretary proposed to "close the war chapter and start Europe afresh as a society in which Germany would take her place as an equal with the great nations" (Jacobson 1972: 24). This was not, as Jon Jacobson correctly notes, the expression of an "internationalist" frame of mind like that of Labour, in which Chamberlain sympathized with the German plight (1972: 215) but, rather, based on a far-sighted and pragmatic conception of British interests. The return of Germany to great power status would occur "sooner or later," however objectionable. Chamberlain believed that "no power on earth can keep Germany disarmed indefinitely" (Wright 2002: 383). And when Germany became a military factor again, it would inevitably set out to fix the "two most objectionable provisions" of the Versailles order: the Polish corridor and the partition of Silesia (DBFP I, Vol. 27, No. 205). Chamberlain wanted to lock in a favorable status quo before the structural environment and the distribution of power shifted in favor of Germany. If Germany were not accommodated beforehand, it would challenge the status quo by force (Cohrs 2006: 214).

Chamberlain shared this thought with Herriot, the French premier. The allies "could not hold Germany down forever, and our object ought to be to bring about such a change in the situation that by the time that

Germany might really have become dangerous again she should enjoy sufficient well-being and have travelled too far away from the bitter thoughts of today to care to risk what she then possessed on the chance that she might recover what she had lost in 1914" (DBFP I, Vol. 27, No. 225). He wanted to make "the position of German tolerable, so that she may lose something of her bitterness and forget something of her humiliation" (CP 105 (25), February 19 CID meeting).

Chamberlain conceived of a re-creation of the Concert of Europe, in which Germany would take its rightful place. Points of friction would be resolved through pragmatic, unemotional, and far-sighted diplomacy. "If the concert of Europe can thus gradually be recreated, saner councils will prevail," he believed. He drew a direct analogy with the situation after the Napoleonic Wars, where the position of France was that now occupied by Germany. He was the new Robert Stewart, Lord Castlereagh: "That policy was in principle the same as I was pursuing today: first to secure the Allies against a possible attempt by France to reverse the settlement of 1815, and, having secured their own safety, to bring France into the comity of nations" (DBFP I, Vol. 27, No. 326; see also Jacobson 1972: 217). Chamberlain envisioned the League of Nations Council as providing the forum (Grayson 1997). Although he made this idea his own, it was a common British conception of the League of Nations, even at the inception of the organization (Rathbun 2012; also CP 105 (25), February 19, 1925). Chamberlain's concert strategy contrasted sharply, of course, with the Labour view of the League of Nations (seen in chapter 3). Whereas the Labour Party, based on its diplomatic style, wanted to institutionalize reasoned dialogue through a legalistic process of compulsory arbitration under League auspices, Tory pragmatists such as Chamberlain sought to institutionalize realist diplomacy.

When it became clear that he would not obtain his first option of proceeding step by step, first through a bilateral agreement with France, Chamberlain backed Stresemann in earnest. He sought to make the German initiative a vehicle for his Castlereaghian strategy, proposing "to found upon the German proposals a restoration of the concert of the Great Powers in Europe and a lasting peace for our countries" (DBFP I, Vol. 27, No. 259). Chamberlain recognized the importance of the German memorandum, calling it the "most hopeful sign yet" from Germany (DBFP I, Vol. 27, No. 200; Cohrs 2006: 210).

Chamberlain was impressed by the German concessions. It "appeared to me an incident of the utmost importance, which might be of vital consequence to the Allies and have a determining influence upon the whole question of our future security. As I understood the German proposal, it was in the first place a voluntary acceptance of the present western frontiers of Germany. These frontiers Germany had accepted under

[105]

compulsion at the time of the signature of the Treaty of Versailles. Now they not only for the first time accepted them voluntarily, but they offered their guarantee" (DBFP I, Vol. 27, No. 212; see also No. 269).

He also noted the German pledge to resolve eastern border changes peacefully: "I took their reference to the eastern boundaries as a fact of great importance and as an earnest of their good faith and their pacific intentions" (DBFP I, Vol. 27, No. 283). The memo was particularly important given the high cost that the government would pay in domestic politics. This was indicative, to Chamberlain and others, of "courage and statesmanship" (DBFP I, Vol. 27, No. 395). The British ambassador to Germany, Edgar Vincent, Viscount D'Abernon, expected that "when text of this communication becomes public there will be general surprise at boldness of policy indicated—a surprise which in many circles [in Germany] will be accompanied by resentment" (DBFP I, Vol. 27, No. 218).

As Stresemann had hoped, Chamberlain also appreciated what Germany did *not* ask for. He attached "immense importance to this new move on the part of the Luther Government" precisely because it was not made conditional on a shortening of occupation (DBFP I, Vol. 27, No. 200). He spoke of Germany's "reasonable representations" (DBFP I, Vol. 27, No. 212). The foreign secretary also noticed the German consideration of French needs. Chamberlain wrote that he "welcomed the evidence afforded by this communication that the German Government appreciated the reality of French fears and were spontaneously considering what Germany could do to allay them" (DBFP I, Vol. 27, No. 195).

Chamberlain's reaction indicates a high level of epistemic motivation, particularly because Chamberlain and his colleagues frequently expressed negative and essentialist views about the Germans as a whole, even during this process. Yet they did not let this blind them, which facilitated productive discussions (cf. DBFP I, Vol. 27, Nos. 409, 493; Grayson 1997; DBFP IA, Vol. 1, No. 53).

Conservative Coercion: The Distributive Style of the British Right

As with Stresemann and Germany, it might be argued by rationalists that any foreign minister would have taken Chamberlain's position. Was his strategy simply the "rational response of an overcommitted world power seeking peace" (Jacobson 2004: 14)? In other words, was the foreign secretary's realist diplomacy endogenous to Britain's structural position? Again, the fact that that there were very different approaches within the government suggests otherwise. A significant number of "conservative imperialists" within the cabinet opposed Chamberlain's proposal to immediately offer France a security guarantee as a first stage toward European pacification. Leo Amery, Lord Curzon, and Frederick

Smith (Lord Birkenhead) all spoke out against it (Jacobson 1972: 19; Jacobson 2004: 23). Curzon, the former foreign secretary, was the fiercest opponent (Jacobson 2004: 23), but Winston Churchill, the chancellor of the Exchequer, was the most articulate spokesman of the group. His precise ideology is hard to identify, but his followers in the British cabinet were primarily drawn from the right of the party (Cohrs 2006: 208; Jacobson 1972: 18) and Churchill's views on foreign affairs have been identified by others as lacking in epistemic motivation (Tetlock and Tyler 1996). As expected, ideological divides corresponded with differences between the coercive bargainers and pragmatic realists.

Churchill and his counterparts had a similar diagnosis of the continental situation and British interests, especially that Franco-German rivalry and friction threatened to draw Britain into a conflict that it would prefer to avoid. In his memorandum for the cabinet meeting at which Chamberlain's alliance idea was also presented, Churchill echoed Chamberlain: "What is the cause which brings this dreaded possibility and choice before our minds? It is the quarrel between France and Germany. This antagonism, which has lasted through centuries, is unappeased. All the minor feuds of Europe group themselves around it. Everyone fears that it may lead to another World conflict. No one at any rate feels any assurance that it will not. We feel that we are deeply involved in this quarrel. Though we do not share its hatreds, though we cannot control its occasions, though all our interests and desires are to avoid it, we may irresistibly be drawn in" (CP 118 (25)). Nor did the groups differ on foreign policy goals. Churchill also believed that "Our interest in the ports of the Channel and North Sea is vital. . . . This necessity has given to the foreign policy of this country in European affairs whatever consistency it has possessed. The creation of the British Empire may almost be said to be a by-product of its execution" (CP 122 (25)).

The British advocates of coercive bargaining were even warm to the idea of a trilateral pact. Curzon urged Chamberlain to "seize this favourable opportunity" (CP 105 (25), February 13, 1925). Churchill had earlier expressed his willingness for Britain to act as a guarantor of a pact between France and Germany (CP 105 (25), February 13, 1925). Stresemann's note could attract the support of all conservatives such as Churchill because it was less universal in character than the Geneva Protocol (CP 118 (25)). It application was limited to where Britain had vital strategic interests—in Western Europe (Jacobson 1972: 23, 37; Grayson 1997: 36; DBFP I, Vol. 27, Nos. 300, 349; CP 105 (25), February 19, 1925).

The difference lay in diplomatic style. Whereas Chamberlain and the British realists were willing to make this short-term concession now as a long-term investment in British security, the coercive bargainers proposed withholding a British commitment for the time being in hopes of

[107]

inducing more conciliatory French behavior vis-à-vis Germany. Churchill believed that "increasing French anxiety will make them all the more desirous of obtaining our assistance. We may be in a position at a later date to procure from the French concessions to Germany of a far more sweeping character than any they contemplate at the present time" (CP 105 (25), February 19, 1925). He argued, "It is by standing aloof and not by offering ourselves that we shall ascertain the degree of importance which France really attaches to our troth" (CP 118 (25)). He suggested a message for France: "These are the years in which you have the opportunity of establishing much better relations with Germany, and so rendering a renewal of war less likely. We will do everything in our power to promote these improved relations. The better friends you are with Germany, the better friends we shall be with you" (CP 118 (25)). Cabinet members Amery, Arthur James Balfour, Birkenhead, and Curzon agreed (Grayson 1997: 49; Jacobson 1972: 15; Cohrs 2006: 209). They advocated postponing discussions on security until France was ready to end the military occupation and discuss a change to the eastern borders of Germany. Chamberlain, they thought, was too willing to concede a British commitment without appropriate compensation (Jacobson 2004: 25).

For these advocates of coercive bargaining, French conciliation was not something to be expected as a consequence of reassurance. It was a price to be paid in advance for British security. Were Britain to make such a commitment prior to French concessions, it would lose its leverage and encourage French provocation. Churchill told his colleagues that "there is a tremendous risk in our being involved in that way in a policy which will simply keep alive this antagonism between Germany and France. France, with us, would feel strong enough to keep that antagonism alive" (CP 105 (25), February 13, 1925).

This group lacked the instrumental empathy for France that accompanied pragmatic statecraft. Curzon asked rhetorically, "Is there any ground for that feeling [of insecurity] existing in an aggravated form now? . . . There is no defenceless condition there. France is the most powerful military country in Europe." He suspected that the French were overstating their fear to exploit British sympathy: "For the moment, surely, there is no danger at all and when we hear about the French government and the French nation being obsessed with their own helplessness and insecurity, is not that done to a large extent to put pressure on us?" (CP 105 (25), February 13, 1925, CID meeting). Balfour remarked, exasperated, on how the French "are so dreadfully afraid of being swallowed up by the tiger, but they spend all their time poking it." Curzon replied pithily: "And the tiger is not a tiger for the moment" (CP 105 (25), February 13, 1925, CID meeting). Balfour complained of being asked to do things "which we should never do if [the French] were not rather insane" (CP 105 (25), February 13, 1925, CID meeting). Birkenhead agreed.

With other cabinet members backing Chamberlain's realist diplomacy and diagnosis of the situation (CP 116 (25)), the government was sharply split. "I am frankly at a loss," lamented Chamberlain in early January 1925 (DBFP I, Vol. 27, No. 180). The British cabinet, in meetings in early March, first endorsed the position that Britain "do[es] not feel able to enter into a dual pact with France" but that a "quadrilateral[3] agreement . . . for mutual security and for guaranteeing each other's frontiers in the West of Europe, stands on a different footing and might become a great assurance to the peace of Europe" (CC 12 (25)). Chamberlain, who was soon to travel to meet the French foreign minister in Paris on his way back from rejecting the Geneva Protocol at the League offices, was authorized to tell Herriot that the government "attached the highest importance to Germany's overture" as the "best chance for giving security to France and peace to the world." The British hoped that "the proposals would be most carefully considered" and pledged that they "would also do their utmost to contribute to the successful development of this most hopeful episode" (CC 12 (25)).

Then, due to pressure from conservative imperialists, the cabinet walked back from a decision to give a definitive pledge to participate, hoping to extract more concessions from France first. "So extensive a commitment," it was represented in the cabinet conclusions, "went considerably beyond what public opinion whether at home or in the Dominions would be willing to accept, *at any rate at this stage of the negotiations*, and the Cabinet were not prepared to sanction any step in that direction which it might afterwards be difficult to retrace" (CC 14 (25), emphasis added). In other words, the Tory right wanted to take a hard line and concede only gradually. It was only through threat of resignation that Chamberlain was able to force the cabinet to make a firm statement of British willingness to participate in a pact. In his meeting with Herriot, the foreign secretary blamed the conservative imperialists for the British indecisiveness (Jacobson 1972: 20; DBFP I, Vol. 27, Nos. 224–25).

FRENCH UNDERSTANDING

It cannot be contested that the structural position of France, particularly its geography, made it more vulnerable to a German *revanche*. This

---

3. Including, perhaps, Belgium.

made it difficult for any French government, regardless of its ideology, to ponder rapprochement with its former adversary. As discussed in chapter 3, the leaders of the Cartel des Gauches demonstrated as much distrust of Germany as those of the Bloc National. Herriot confessed his fears privately to British officials. Citing the recovering German economy, which contrasted positively with lagging French fortunes, the foreign minister said, "From my heart . . . I tell you I look forward with terror to her making war upon us again in ten years" (DBFP I, Vol. 27, No. 224). He called the Rhine the "last condition of our security" (Jacobson 1972: 19). Chamberlain remarked that, when he spoke with Herriot, the French premier said that the only word that properly described the French attitude toward security was "obsession" (CP 105 (25), February 13, 1925, CID meeting). "We cannot have too many securities," the French premier stated (DBFP I, Vol. 27, No. 186).

Herriot's public position was hardly suggestive of, or conductive to, a security arrangement that included Germany. His speech before the French parliament in late January 1925, before he received the German note, was truculent. The foreign minister defended the continued occupation of the Cologne area, citing a litany of failures by Germany to comply with its disarmament obligations. He even suggested an indefinite occupation of Germany beyond the term specified in the Versailles Treaty (DBFP I, Vol. 27, No. 193; Grayson 1997: 51). The British ambassador reported that the "speech was acclaimed by the entire Chamber, most of the deputies rising to their feet. [Herriot] was throughout listened to in almost religious silence, save for occasional outbursts and spontaneous and unanimous applause in which the right took a prominent part." Indeed, wrote the ambassador, many passages might "have been made by M. Poincaré himself" (DBFP I, Vol. 27, No. 193). Foreign policy under the left was not weak or neglectful of French interests, despite the prosocial motivation of the Socialists and Radicals. There was unanimity on foreign policy goals and beliefs in a way that was not true in Britain at the time.

The British move was therefore decisive. As seen in chapter 3, the French valued a British security guarantee of some form more than anything else. Briand, who became foreign minister in April 1925 after Herriot's cabinet collapsed, declared that "the best security for France is to remain always in close contact with her allies and to do nothing save in agreement with them" (DBFP I, Vol. 27, No. 294). The British offer had the effect of transforming a distributive game vis-à-vis Germany into a potentially positive-sum one. Without British assistance, French security from Germany depended mostly on the occupation and demilitarization of the Rhineland (Jacobson 1972: 19), but ridding the area of French troops was Stresemann's top priority. A British guarantee allowed the possibility of providing France enough security to allow it to restore

German sovereignty. British realist diplomacy had real value in solving the European crisis of the 1920s. Herriot stated that without Britain a pact was a nonstarter, given "sentimental distrust of any German promise" (DBFP I, Vol. 27, No. 216). Chamberlain was not modest, taking the credit (DBFP I, Vol. 27, No. 283).

Reserving the Right: The Exploration of Stresemann's Proposals by the French Left

British diplomacy was not sufficient, however. Britain had, after all, been willing to make such a pledge in 1922 as well, but the conservative Bloc National government under Poincaré had refused a bilateral security guarantee on British terms. The French left was somewhat suspicious when first hearing about the plan from the British. They were concerned initially that the German proposal would be coupled with a demand for a reduction in the length of the occupation and might also be intended to split the allies (DBFP I, No. 27, No. 224; Jacobson 1972: 13; Cohrs 2006: 210; Wright 2002: 304). Herriot confessed that, the more the Germans stressed their desire for peace in the west, the more he feared war in the east (DBFP I, Vol. 27, No. 225).

Yet Herriot was very receptive to the German proposal when it was actually delivered by the German ambassador. The French premier expressed the "greatest interest" in the German memorandum (ADAP A12, No. 99) and promised to bring it to the attention of the French President Gaston Doumergue that very evening (ADAP A12, No. 81). Herriot subsequently sought him out at the opera house (ADAP A12, No. 107). The German ambassador reported to Stresemann that his impression of his meetings with Herriot were "favorable beyond expectations" (ADAP A12, No. 99), even the first time he broached the subject (ADAP A12, No. 81). The British also reported that Herriot "received the memorandum rather favourably" (DBFP I, Vol. 27, No. 197) and that he had no objection to the inclusion of Germany in a security pact (DBFP I, Vol. 27, No. 198; Jacobson 1927: 27).

What explains the favorable reaction of the French? The prosocial motivation of the coalition and its preference for reasoned dialogue made the French government more likely to engage the German government in a way that a conservative government could and would not have done. Had the left not been in government, the German plan would have been stillborn. Chamberlain's realism was a necessary but not sufficient condition for the pact idea to survive its infancy.

The French were seeking a mutually beneficial solution consistent with their prosocial motivation. The French left indicated empathy and consideration for the German position. Herriot told the German ambassador that he understood that Germany also wanted and needed security, that any bilateral alliance would jeopardize the prospects for the German proposal, and that this was not his intention (ADAP A12, No. 99). Similarly, he told the British that "He recognized completely that, if France is guaranteed against German aggression, Germany has an equal right to be similarly guaranteed against any attack by France. He said this . . . with no sort of *arrière pensée* ["ulterior motive"]" (DBFP I, Vol. 27, No. 198). Briand expressed understanding when the German ambassador stressed that little could be accomplished on the diplomatic front unless Cologne were evacuated (ADAP A12, No. 263). Herriot even told the British in private that "it must be admitted that there was much in the present arrangement of the map in the east which lent itself to serious criticism" and that it should be possible to work out deal between Poland and Germany peacefully (DBFP I, Vol. 27, No. 232). Briand recognized that French behavior was also part of the solution: "We must take all precautions, but we must also take precautions in order that we do not uselessly disturb people's minds" (DBFP I, Vol. 27, No. 294).

Herriot was replaced shortly afterward by Briand, who continued the same path. The British attributed the diplomacy of France to its foreign minister's liberalism, implicitly evoking his epistemic and prosocial motivations. Chamberlain described Briand as "a man of supple & ingenious mind, capable of admitting disagreeable truths & forming broad & liberal views" (Grayson 1997: 57). He remarked on the liberal diplomacy of France and Briand's belief that the creation of the right character of diplomatic interactions could transform European relations. "What struck me most about Briand was . . . the conviction which he holds, and which appeared again and again in the course of the conversation, that if we can bring these negotiations to a successful conclusion, our success will change the whole situation, and many problems which are now of great difficulty will solve themselves" (DBFP I Vol. 27, No. 364). The foreign minister was actively trying to create a new spirit that could make agreement easier.

The French left, therefore, appreciated the concessions embedded in the German memorandum rather than denigrating their importance. Briand admired Germany for how it had "acted courageously" in sending its memorandum (DBFP I, Vol. 27, No. 516). Herriot called Stresemann "well intentioned and honorable" (DBFP I, Vol. 27, No. 198). He publicly empathized with Stresemann's domestic situation, noting that the German foreign minister had to reckon with his own public opinion and pointed out that the conciliatory attitude of the German government persisted even in the wake of the recent election of the nationalist Paul von Hindenburg as president, which had so unsettled France. Referring to Stresemann's recent speeches, he said, "One must think of the intention of his words. I was not able to find in what he said the brutal *non possumus*[4] that might have been expected after a certain election." Stresemann picked up on the significance of this statement (DBFP I, Vol. 27, No. 346; Stresemann, Vol. 2: 84). Rather than engaging in reactive devaluation and ego defensiveness, Briand noted the "many Germans who were genuinely anxious to reach a pacific solution" (DBFP I, Vol. 27, No. 353). The approach of his government became known as the policy of "understanding," conveying both the epistemic and social motivation that drove it.

The Reservations of the Right: Conservative Opposition to Stresemann's Proposals

Rationalists might argue that a French government of any ideological make-up, given the vulnerable position of France, would have been receptive to a German proposal that offered the prospect of a British guarantee, particularly given the recent and painful failures to commit the British to French defense. France had failed in its efforts to handle Germany unilaterally, evident most clearly in the Ruhr crisis. From this perspective the French had overplayed their previous hand and returned to a conciliatory diplomacy that more closely reflected their structural bargaining position.

But this potential argument is belied by the fact that the French right did not greet the pact idea with enthusiasm. When news of the pact began to leak, Herriot felt pressured to put the record straight in a private session before the Foreign Affairs Committee of the French parliament. Poincaré, a member of the committee, dismissed the German idea as a mere retread of proposals made a few years before by the Wilhelm Cuno government in Germany that he had rejected when premier. Even before the security pact had developed a specific form, Poincaré was opposed and saw little need to negotiate. In keeping with his preference for reasoned dialogue, Herriot responded that the French should keep an open mind to see how discussions developed (DBFP I, Vol. 27, No. 134).

After the German memo became public knowledge, the conservative former prime minister made public statements against it. In an indication of his coercive style of diplomacy, he dismissed both the value of the concessions made by the Germans and the worth of a pact from Britain. Costly signals did not speak for themselves. He pleaded of Marianne: "Let her not be asked to exchange those means of protection for the

---

4. Latin for "We cannot," shorthand for an intransigent and uncompromising attitude.

semblance of guarantees or the mirage of security. In the diplomatic negotiations now going on France must not sacrifice the substance for the shadow" (DBFP I, Vol. 27, No. 277). He engaged in reactive devaluation: "In exchange for a few concessions, we are obtaining a commitment from the Reich worth only what the reigning mood in Germany is worth" (Keiger 2004: 103).

Poincaré's views were shared by prominent figures on the French right (DBFP I, Vol. 27, No. 266). French conservatives accused Herriot, by engaging in an exploration of conciliation, of "naïve idealism" and believed that his government's "policy of understanding" would lead to a "fiasco" according to German reports (ADAP A12, No. 48). The leftist coalition had difficulties with the French military as well, which was conservative and nationalistic. Particularly problematic was the French war hero, Marshal Ferdinand Foch. A British diplomat described him as low in epistemic motivation. He was "impervious to arguments of any kind. . . . He certainly represents one of those solid breakwaters of obstinacy on which the waves of M. Herriot's eloquence and good intentions must dash themselves in vain" (DBFP I, Vol. 27, No. 238). The French right might have given up on the use of force to realize French objectives; however, the experience of the Ruhr did not convince conservatives to change their style of diplomacy. The Cartel des Gauches did manage to elicit the support from some center-right politicians, but given the lack of cohesiveness of French political parties in general, this meant less than it did in Germany (Keeton 1987). This pragmatist group was not well organized.

The hostility of the right presented a significant challenge for the Cartel des Gauches, which did not have a secure majority and was recognized as fragile both at home and abroad (Stresemann, Vol. 1: 75; Wright 2002: 287). This necessitated a difficult balancing act between domestic and international politics. Herriot explained to the British that if too cool a reception were given to the German proposals, the DNVP would be strengthened and encouraged. And if the proposals were greeted too warmly, it would stimulate opposition in France and perhaps put the rightist Bloc National in power (DBFP I, Vol. 27, No. 266). After taking over as foreign minister, Briand told Stresemann, "You are not to imagine, however, that you have a monopoly of [nationalist opponents]. . . . They are to be found everywhere. . . . There are people in my country who gaze into the past and remember that we once held the Palatinate, that Mainz was once French, and that the Rhine policy was once the historic policy of France; and I must fight against these people in France just as you have to contend against such moods in Germany" (Stresemann, Vol. 1 224–25). The French asked for patience from the Germans, time to make palatable the idea of a security pact "step by step" (ADAP A12,

No. 134). Briand reminded the Germans that they did "not have a monopoly of insanity" (Unger 2005: 494; Stresemann, Vol. 2: 180–81). He explained his need to reassure public opinion as they embarked on a "new way of reaching mutual agreements between former war adversaries" (ADAP A13, No. 219).

Both the British and Germans believed the French, recognizing that the French left would be more receptive to Stresemann's ideas than the right, given variations in diplomatic style. Of the French, a British diplomat wrote, "What a relief it is to have Briand to talk to after the sinister Poincaré" (DBFP I, Vol. 27, No. 354). The British understood the value of diplomacy. A memorandum cautioned that "if the spirit of France becomes again the spirit of Poincaré, the negotiations will break down" (DBFP I, Vol. 27, No. 255). British officials in Paris urged their home government to be more forthcoming to make the job of the French government easier: "Unless [Herriot] can allay feeling on the [security] subject, he may be swept away and replaced by an administration of more Nationalist temper" (DBFP I, Vol. 27, No. 198). Referring to the Poincaré government, Chamberlain noted that the German memorandum, though brave, "met with a far more friendly reception from the French Government that would have been possible a little time ago" (DBFP I, Vol. 27, No. 395). The Germans recognized Briand's "goodwill" (ADAP A12, No. 263).

The British and Germans understood the French government to be well intentioned but forced by domestic circumstances to behave somewhat differently, precisely because of their political stripes. Stresemann wrote pessimistically, "[Herriot] is a Democrat and a Pacifist, and for that very reason he cannot give way to any weakness on the question. Against the attacks of the Right we must prove that he is guarding the rights of France and not sacrificing the security of France. . . . In any event there can be no doubt that Herriot's standpoint being what it is, we have nothing to expect from him. He will, in this connection, roar with the lion, and we have to reckon on determined opposition from France to the evacuation, for these reasons, which may be regarded as originating in home politics" (Stresemann, Vol. 1: 17–18; see also ADAP A12, No. 22). Stresemann expected the French to engage in coercive bargaining. The German foreign minister compared this dilemma to his own position at home (Grayson 1997: 58) and attributed the failure to evacuate Cologne to these pressures rather than to a lack of good faith on the part of the Cartel des Gauches (Stresemann, Vol. 1: 30). The German ambassador gave his impressions of early meetings with Herriot: "I became convinced of the unconditional honest and personal intentions of the minister, who is under great pressure due to the security the problem and is honestly striving to find an exit" (ADAP A12, No. 99). Similarly, a British memorandum described how Herriot was often overcome by military resistance to his plans: "M. Herriot may enter the marshal's [Foch's] presence an *homme de gauche* ["man of the left"]. . . . He must always leave it so transformed as to be indistinguishable . . . from M. Poincaré" (DBFP I, Vol. 27, No. 238).

The situation in early 1925, therefore, presented a potentially favorable window of opportunity for consolidation of peace in Western Europe due to the conjunction of domestic political developments and diplomatic styles in these three countries. The British, in particular, recognized the importance of the ideological character of the governments and the change in diplomatic styles that accompanied them. Chamberlain told his colleagues, "You have a Government in Germany which can settle some of these questions, and certainly I do not think you are likely to have a more pacific Government or one more anxious to find a reasonable solution than exists at present in Paris" (CP 105 (25), February 19, 1925). Others agreed. Curzon noted, "It gives us a chance which we have never had before. You have got a friendly minister in France; you have for the first time a reasonable minister in Germany. It is an extraordinary combination" (CP 105 (25), February 13, 1925). British pragmatists saw the possibility of value creating negotiation in the Baptist-bootlegger combination of the French left and the German center-right. The various parties had set the table for the tough diplomatic work that would follow, which is the subject of the next two chapters.

[5]

Getting to the Table

THE DIPLOMATIC PERILS OF THE EXCHANGE OF NOTES

An agreement on a deal that created value for both France and Germany, even with the British lending a hand, was hardly foreordained. Simply getting to the table posed its own problems. The French and German governments, both dealing with domestic constraints, exchanged a number of formal notes whose contents could have broken off negotiations. Under pressure from the French right to engage in coercive bargaining, the Cartel des Gauches government reimagined the German proposal somewhat dramatically in a way that suited French interests. It wanted infractions of the Versailles Treaty to call in the British security guarantee and for France to be able to protect the eastern neighbors of Germany against any German violation of their arbitration treaties with Germany.

Yet diplomacy was again of great value. Even though the French left put forward the same demands that the French right had earlier in terms of the scope of a British guarantee, the former did not hold out in hopes of greater gains, instead expressing understanding and appreciation of the British point of view. And even as they filled in Stresemann's skeletal sketch of a pact in a way that tilted it heavily in France's favor, the French refused to draw any lines in the sand that would make agreement difficult to find. They expressed their optimism about the possibility of success as opposed to the instrumental skepticism that would have marked a purely coercive bargaining style. And the French expressed an appreciation for the concessions that the Germans had made. These behaviors are all indicative of the liberal diplomacy expected from a government with prosocial motivations.

Had the French responded differently, it would probably have triggered enough conservative opposition in the German cabinet to sink the negotiations. As it was, the nationalists regarded the French proposal, incorrectly, as set in stone and indicative of a wide gulf between the two parties. The DNVP wanted Stresemann to break off negotiations. Only with great difficulty did Stresemann and his realist allies manage to keep the possibility of a deal open in the face of the premature conclusions drawn by those with lower epistemic motivation.

As a pragmatist, Stresemann took a tough line on matters of vital interest to Germany, such as the French guarantee of the eastern treaties, but made concessions on other, less important issues. He also had long-term gains in mind. The German foreign minister believed that, by not linking the conclusion of a security pact to the occupation of the Rhineland, Germany could better signal its cooperative intentions, thereby making the securing of such goals easier in the future. More instrumentally empathetic, he thought such demands would imperil a deal with the French.

Stresemann's far right adversaries in the German cabinet, however, insisted that the German response to the French notes formally refuse its war guilt and forced Stresemann to explicitly link any approval of the security pact to alleviations in the Rhineland occupation and the evacuation of the Cologne zone. This could have easily derailed the negotiations. Briand, however, disregarded the German notes as harmless blustering in a way that his rightist counterparts would not have, given their different diplomatic styles. In something of a role reversal, he responded with more equanimity than even the pragmatic British, indicating the importance, again, of the liberal diplomatic style. French diplomacy was an iron glove over a silken fist.

The role of Britain in the run-up to the negotiations was to urge the two sides to avoid coercive bargaining statements and to keep their exchanges short on the demands that would prevent them from sitting down to resolve their difference privately and calmly in the pragmatic fashion favored by the realist foreign secretary, Austen Chamberlain. As an honest broker, the British defended the Germans to the French and the Germans to the French, regardless of how they actually felt about their respective positions. They continually stressed that the two countries should consider the practical benefits of an agreement and eventually succeeded in getting all the parties to the table.

LEANING LIBERAL: THE FRENCH RESPONSE TO
THE GERMAN MEMORANDUM

As seen in chapter 4, the Cartel des Gauches government was open to German overtures, given its diplomatic style of reasoned dialogue. Nevertheless, even though Stresemann's memorandum marked a significant and promising departure for German foreign policy, a turn-over in the French government did not lead simply to a rapprochement between the two countries and an integrative deal on a security pact. There was significant distrust of Germany, even on the French left. And the position of the coalition in French domestic politics was precarious, making it impossible to ignore the objections of French nationalists on the right. Briand explained, through his ambassador, the square he was trying to circle domestically: "He must not rouse French Nationalist opinion by appearing to yield too much or too readily, nor, on the other hand, must he antagonize Socialist opinion by an unsympathetic or harsh reply" (DBFP I, Vol. 27, No. 322). In other words, Briand had to balance a reasonable and liberal diplomatic approach with a coercive and distributive one.

In their formal response to the first German note, whose drafting was supervised by Aristide Briand, the new foreign minister, the French took a position considerably different from that of Germany (and Britain). Their diplomacy, although liberal, was not one of capitulation. Like the Germans, the French envisioned a legal commitment by the parties to the pact to refrain from the use of force against one another to revise borders and also, in the event of the violation of that pledge, an obligation by Britain to come to the aid of the party attacked. Beyond this, however, the French added elements seen before in their bilateral negotiations with the British, when the French conservatives were in power. The British guarantee was also to apply to violations of the Versailles Treaty. The French also wanted a far-reaching compulsory arbitration agreement be-tween the French and the Germans on matters both juridical and political in nature (DBFP I, Vol. 27, Nos. 318, 349). A simple refusal to submit to arbitration, even if the party that declined to do so did not subsequently use force, would require coercive action by the guarantors of the pact (CP 268 (25)). The French, however, excluded any interpretation of the Ver-sailles Treaty from the arbitration process (CP 256 (25). In essence, the meaning of the treaty would be judged solely by the French and British, allowing France to intervene forcefully against the Germans without submitting to a conflict-resolution process in ambiguous cases. The French also stressed that the new agreement would not be accompanied by any easing of German obligations under the Versailles Treaty (DBFP I, Vol. 27, Nos. 318, 349).

Most controversially, the French took up Stresemann's willingness to conclude treaties of arbitration with the eastern neighbors of Germany but recrafted his proposal so that these agreements would have a form similar to those concluded with France and Belgium. Although these eastern treaties would not require a recognition of the territorial status quo, they would obligate their parties to negotiate all types of disputes peacefully. Any power associated with the western pact would also have the legal right to protect the victims of an attack in the east (DBFP I, Vol. 27, Nos. 318, 349; CP 268 (25)). France was essentially trying to bring its alliances with the Little Entente under the same umbrella as the proposed security pact and to commit the Germans to peaceful revision. The French feared that, otherwise, the Germans might use the western pact as a legal shield to prevent French intervention in Eastern Europe (CP 268 (25); DBFP I, Vol. 27, No. 389). Without this, if Germany did not move against France and the east simultaneously, France would be faced with the unpalatable choice of standing by or risking the intervention of Britain against it if France moved into Germany.

Therefore, the effect of the liberal diplomacy of the French government was not to make immediate concessions but, rather, to facilitate an open exchange of views that might reveal a basis for an agreement in the interest of both sides. The difference with the conservatives was stylistic, not substantive. For instance, the French did not draw any red lines in their memorandum. The French response was presented as a kind of brainstorming document that filled in the sketch provided by Stresemann. Briand explained that it "was not his intention to make exactly formal conditions. . . . He had no intention of dictating the sense of the Germany reply. He wished to give them full freedom as to the character of their answer, and not in any way to appear to force upon them a Yes or a No" (DBFP I, Vol. 27, No. 322). He told the British the same as they coordinated their policy: "M. Briand particularly emphasized the importance of avoiding any appearance of confronting the Germans with a cut and dried scheme which they would have to accept or reject as it stood." Rather, the French note would be a "basis for free discussion" (DBFP I, Vol. 27, No. 443).

Under the leadership of the Cartel des Gauches, the French also did not denigrate the offer made by Germany. Their reply stated that the "French Government do not fail to appreciate the value to the cause of peace . . . of a solemn repudiation of all idea of war." The French recognized "with satisfaction" Germany's willingness to negotiate arbitration treaties with its eastern neighbors. It hoped for a response that would allow the countries to enter into negotiations of a treaty (DBFP I, Vol. 27, No. 349; Locarno-Konferenz, No. 14). As Briand described it, "His object had been to show that he accepted the German overtures as made in good faith" (DBFP I, Vol. 27, No. 322). These, of course, might be regarded as purely cheap talk, but it should be recognized that even this costless type of signal had not been offered by the rightist coalition under Poincaré. Briand's foreign ministry wanted to encourage Germany to engage in reasoned dialogue.

The note was also quickly followed by the announcement that France would, earlier than scheduled, withdraw its troops from the Ruhr, which

had been occupied by France in 1923 to coerce Germany to pay its reparations. The Germans recognized this more costly unilateral concession as a
sign of "goodwill" (Stresemann, Vol. 2: 145). The British noted that it eased
the domestic political pressure on Stresemann considerably (DBFP I,
Vol. 27, No. 417).

Briand's government transmitted its note to Germany on June 16,
1925, and was very pleased with the domestic reception of the memo.
The reaction of the press and politicians in all circles was positive. A leading British diplomat reported that the general opinion in France was that
"French essential interests have been adequately and successfully safe-
guarded by M. Briand" but also that the memo was a "work of goodwill
and good faith, a sincere effort at conciliation and realization of the desire to safeguard treaty rights" (DBFP I, Vol. 27, No. 389). Briand used the
same argument on Germany that its representatives had used on him.
He noted to the German ambassador that circles that had been skeptical
of reconciliation were supportive of his conception of the pact and that
Germany should grasp this opportunity at peace (ADAP, A13, No. 88).
Briand had squared his domestic circle.

Bringing Something to the Table: Bilateral Franco-British Negotiations on the Guarantee

The difficult question for the British cabinet was determining the extent of the security guarantee it was willing to offer (CC 26 (25)). The
foreign secretary suspected correctly that France would seek greater British involvement, "involving us in obligations that we have hitherto refused to assume" (CC 26 (25)). British officials wanted to limit the
commitment to the continent to situations that directly threatened the
interests of Britain. The cabinet authorized Chamberlain to endorse in
the House of Commons only a pledge to safeguard the frontiers of the
Rhineland countries (CC 17 (25).

At the same time as the French were drafting their response to Germany, they were working on a draft security treaty with Britain. Chamberlain insisted that the guarantee would be called into effect only if armed
force were used and the actual peace broken (DBFP I, Vol. 27, No. 343). The
French position that parties would commit to an automatic use of coercive
force in case of an infringement of the Versailles Treaty, without recourse
to arbitration and even if a party did not actually resort to armed hostilities, threatened to draw Britain into smaller conflicts that did not threaten
its interests (DBFP I, Vol. 27, No. 424). The British therefore amended
French plans to give the League a larger role (DBFP I, Vol. 27, No. 349). In
their exchanges over a draft security pact, the British drafts envisioned the

[121]

League Council, and not just the allies, determining whether a violation of the Versailles Treaty had actually occurred and recommending the appropriate response. The British wanted to "make it clear that the Council of the League has a *locus standi* to intervene" (DBFP I, Vol. 27, No. 424). The League Council would also take up issues of nonsubmission of disputes to arbitration and noncompliance in which force was not used (CP 312 (25); CP 318 (25); DBFP I, Vol. 27, Nos. 316, 317, 384, 405). This conception limited British commitments while simultaneously promoting the League venue as a new Concert of Europe.

Britain, of course, had the most bargaining leverage in this situation. We might argue that it is therefore unsurprising that its view on the scope of the security guarantee prevailed. But, as we have seen, the French under the conservatives had refused better offers, holding out for greater gains. Chamberlain warned against doing so again. He wrote the French, "I was apprehensive lest the French, in seeking to fill every gap and to provide against unimportant contingencies such as some slight infraction of the demilitarization clause, should so confuse and alarm public opinion that the real guarantee of security which was within their grasp might escape from their hands" (DBFP I, Vol. 27, No. 424). Even as they had similar goals, however, the French left and right had different diplomatic styles, allowing the Cartel des Gauches to achieve what the Bloc National had not. The British were impressed with Briand's liberal diplomatic style, particularly his regard for British interests. He had "showed himself fully alive to the need of distinguishing between flagrant violations and purely technical infractions" and "admitted frankly that Great Britain could not be expected to give a guarantee which might involve her in a war as a result of a trivial incident" (DBFP I, Vol. 27, No. 443). The two sides agreed that only gross breaches of the treaty, such as an assembly of troops in the demilitarized zone, would call into play the security guarantee (DBFP I, Vol. 27, No. 412).

The liberal-led French coalition government and the realist-led British government were in total agreement that Germany must join the League as a part of the conclusion of the pact. Chamberlain identified German membership in the League as "the basis of our whole conception of the pact" (DBFP I, Vol. 27, No. 340; see also No. 231). German entry was the "essential condition of the new settlement (DBFP I, Vol. 27, No. 426). The French also wanted Germany to join the League of Nations on the basis of the conditions affirmed in a note by the League of Nations from March of that year, in which it was implied that the disarmed condition of Germany did not give it a waiver from participating in economic or military sanctions organized by the League against an aggressor (DBFP I, Vol. 27, Nos. 261, 322; CP 256 (25)). The Germans had not proposed joining the institution at all in their earlier memoranda (Locarno-Konferenz No. 14).

PRESSURE ON PRAGMATISM: THE GERMAN NATIONAL PEOPLE'S
PARTY AND THE GERMAN REPLY TO THE REPLY

In his proposal, Stresemann did not link the pact to other concessions that Germany desired, in an attempt to extract greater gains (ADAP A12, No. 40). Rather than making the German renunciation of the Alsace-Lorraine contingent on French reciprocity in the areas of disarmament, the evacuation of Cologne or the alleviation of the occupation, Stresemann explicitly advised German representatives to separate these questions to indicate that Germany was not using the security pact to try to wiggle out of any remaining disarmament obligations (ADAP A12, Nos. 67, 81). He suggested language to his ambassador in Paris: "We believe that it would contribute to the relaxation of the situation and would be completely in the interests of a reasonable development of general policy if security policy were simply discussed openly and intimately with the participation of Germany separate from the disarmament question" (ADAP A12, No. 67). He stressed to the British that his proposal "must not be confounded or confused with the controversies respecting disarmament and the evacuation of the Cologne area. From these they are distinguished by being of a different order of magnitude" (DBFP I, Vol. 27, No. 189).

The questions were, of course, connected in Stresemann's mind. The foreign minister did hope that the Cologne situation and the remaining disarmament squabbles could be folded into a security pact deal, but he intentionally did not link them explicitly at the beginning (Cohrs 2006: 228), as the British duly noted (DBFP I, Vol. 27, No. 263). Stresemann believed that the importance of the German step would be deprecated if it were connected to the shortening of occupation since this would suggest an ulterior motive (Stresemann, Vol. 2: 73–80). The foreign minister, instead, counted on the fact that his offer would create trust that would allow the later solution of the remaining difficulties (ADAP A12, Nos. 40, 67). If the proposal were to be successful, a new "atmosphere" would be created (ADAP A12, No. 81). Stresemann talked and thought in terms not of bargaining quid pro quos but of natural and logical "ramifications" or "consequences" that would follow an ease in tensions. In German, the term is *Rückwirkungen*, and in later chapters I show the importance the foreign minister attached to them. He wrote privately, "It goes without saying that the conclusion of such a treaty, in which the chief powers of Europe proclaim that the security of Europe has thereby been established, involves the corollary that an absolute security no longer needs to be strengthened by a ten years' occupation of the Rhineland. The period of occupation would thus be shortened" (Stresemann, Vol. 2: 67). The Rhineland issue would arise naturally over time as the "logical conclusion of a security pact" (Kabinette Luther, Vol. 1, No. 62; see also Gratwohl 1980: 73–75; Stresemann, Vol. 2: 79).

Seeing things from the French point of view, a part of pragmatic state-craft, helped in this regard. He did not make any demands about early evacuation, for instance, "because I said to myself that we ourselves should not do anything of the sort if we were in the position of the other side, and because I always tell myself that policy is the art of what is possible" (Stresemann, Vol. 2: 222). For the time being, "there must be no attempt to make a condition of these matters beforehand. It is of course merely Utopian to try to put forward claims that, for those in responsible positions, do not come into question" (Stresemann, Vol. 2: 135–36).

Stresemann's DNVP coalition partners preferred a more confrontational diplomacy of coercive bargaining, consistent with the proself and low epistemic motivations typical of the far right. With a distributive mind-set, they denigrated the French proposal as not offering enough for Germany. Schiele believed that the Germans had made too many concessions in their note and "found missing guarantees for us" (Kabinette Luther, Vol. 1, No. 50). D'Abernon, the British ambassador to Germany, explained to London that the DNVP did not understand why its government was giving something away for nothing (DBFP I, Vol. 27, No. 266). Schiele, the liaison between the DNVP parliamentary party caucus and the cabinet, argued that, by surrendering a concession without a counter-concession, Germany had "thrown a net over its own head" and proposed rescinding the offer of fixing the mutual borders of the countries (Kabinette Luther, Vol. 1, No. 123).

The DNVP demanded concessions prior to any negotiations. In the full cabinet, Berndt asked what the Germans would receive as a reward for their very willingness to negotiate (Kabinette Luther, Vol. 1, No. 62; see also Stresemann, Vol. 2: 79). In the first party statement concerning the pact idea in the parliament, Kuno Graf von Westarp noted that France wanted Germany to first completely disarm, enter the League, and negotiate a security pact; only after that would France leave Cologne. For the DNVP, he argued, the order should be the reverse (VDR 62: 1894–1903). This was a staging concern typical of coercive diplomacy. The nationalists opposed giving away Alsace-Lorraine without significant compensation. DNVP members outside the cabinet called on their government to make the inflated goal of a complete evacuation of the Rhineland the basis for negotiations (Kabinette Luther, Vol. 1, No. 62; see also Stresemann, Vol. 2: 79).

Given the great divide between France and Germany on a number of issues and the presence of the DNVP in the German government, it is not surprising that Stresemann and the German cabinet received the French note unfavorably. The foreign minister complained that it "twisted the original German offer out of all recognition" and linked it to issues that for Germany were separate, most notably German entry into the League (DBFP I, Vol. 27, No. 401; see also ADAP A13, No. 136). The Germans had warned the allies against this earlier (ADAP A13, No. 263). Stresemann emphasized that he had proposed treaties with the eastern neighbors of Germany precisely because he had not contemplated entering the League, which was a very contentious issue for his country, given its symbolic connection to the Treaty of Versailles (ADAP A13, No. 136; Stresemann, Vol. 2: 97–113; DBFP I, Vol. 27, No. 211). The League had its own provisions for political reconciliation that would make arbitration treaties superfluous. The scope of arbitration was also too broad. The Germans had in mind a process in which only decisions on juridical questions would be binding, whereas political arbitration would only be advisory, even with France (ADAP A13, No. 136; DBFP I, Vol. 27, No. 401). Stresemann also found the French hypocritical. They stressed the importance of the League and yet shielded any alleged violation of the Versailles Treaty on their part from the consideration of the League Council (ADAP A13, No. 136; Stresemann, Vol. 2: 89–91, 97–113; DBFP I, Vol. 27, No. 401). The Germans pointed out that any French invasion of Germany short of self-defense would violate the terms of an agreement reached in London the year before (ADAP A13, No. 136; DBFP I, Vol. 27, No. 401).

The two main points for Stresemann, however, were the effort by France to force Germany into signing nonaggression pacts with its eastern neighbors that France would itself guarantee and the conditions under which Germany would enter the League. These were the issues of most vital interest to Germany (Stresemann, Vol. 2: 97–113; ADAP A13, No. 136). Even as the Germans expressed their desire to resolve conflicts with their eastern neighbors peacefully, they had honestly admitted from the beginning that they were not willing to make formal commitments officially foreclosing the use of military force to rectify German borders. This would have been impossible domestically (ADAP A12, Nos. 201–2; DBFP I, Vol. 27, No. 254). The German offer of arbitration treaties was "an indication of our desire to settle any matters in dispute by peaceful methods" (Stresemann, Vol. 2: 67). These would de facto exclude force, the Germans explained privately (ADAP A12, No. 201). Germany would declare formally in a private letter only that the "German Government renounce any idea of bringing about by warlike measures an alteration in the present German-Polish frontier" (DBFP I, Vol. 27, No. 392; see also DBFP I, Vol. 27, No. 274; ADAP A12, No. 213). This "solemn engagement" (DBFP I, Vol. 27, Nos. 216, 220), however, could not be published (DBFP I, Vol. 27, No. 212). Publicly, Stresemann would declare in the Reichstag only that "to bring about a forcible alteration to the eastern frontiers Germany has neither the strength nor the will" (DBFP I, Vol. 27, No. 392; see also Stresemann, Vol. 2: 84).

Also at issue was whether Germany in its disarmed state could be obligated as a League of Nations member under Article 16 to participate in a mandatory economic boycott of states deemed aggressors by the League Council. There had been ongoing negotiations previously between the League of Nations and Germany over the terms of its potential membership, and the international body had insisted that Germany take on all the same obligations as other members. Germany was particularly worried about the devastating possibility of being drawn into a war with the Soviet Union. In addition to its inability to defend itself against a Soviet invasion, any such conflict would probably incite a civil war in Germany between communist and nationalist militias. "No obligations can be laid upon us which may involve Germany in the risk of a declaration of war upon her by another Power," said Stresemann (Vol. 2: 97–113). The pragmatic diplomat was, however, willing to accept an informal, de facto release from its treaty obligations rather than a formal exception (Stresemann, Vol. 2: 135).[1]

When the German cabinet met to discuss the French note and the German reply, Stresemann identified these two items as the major sticking points (Kabinette Luther, Vol. 1, No. 110). Nevertheless, the foreign minister, given his realist diplomatic style, believed that the German response should be general and conciliatory. He wanted to make sure that the note "should not be packed with demands"; he cautioned not to "burden the [discussions] with conditions, or with questions that will be dealt with as a matter of course during the negotiations" (Stresemann, Vol. 2: 135). Germany should let negotiations proceed to see if something of value might be gained, even though in light of the French response it might seem doubtful. The best way to proceed was by raising the questions together in a diplomatic conference rather than laying out firm negotiating red lines in an exchange of diplomatic notes (Kabinette

1. At no time did Stresemann attempt to extract more from the allies by dangling the prospect of developing closer relations with the Soviet Union, a coercive diplomatic move that many nationalists advocated. He refused to play the "Rapallo bluff." As a realist, Stresemann saw the need to cultivate good relations with both sides given the currently weakened state of Germany. Stresemann emphasized that Germany was not under the "tutelage of any power or group of powers." He balanced his negotiations with the West by opening discussions with the Russians on commercial matters and eventually concluding the Treaty of Berlin in 1926, a limited neutrality agreement with the Soviet Union to be superseded by German obligations under the League of Nations Covenant (Wright 2002: 310–12, 322–24, 354–59; Jacobson 1972: 81–82, 367–71). "In his effort to win agreement and support in the West, the Russian connection was of no real disadvantage or advantage to Stresemann," writes Jacobson (1972: 369).

Luther, Vol. 1, No. 62; see also Gratwohl 1980: 73–75; Stresemann, Vol. 2: 79). This pragmatism reflected his greater epistemic motivation, which contrasted with the right-wing need for closure. The British noted how this was a departure from the coercive diplomatic style that Germany had employed historically (DBFP I, Vol. 27, No. 409).

Domestic politics, however, particularly the position of the DNVP, made a simple reply of that kind impossible. Whereas Stresemann's early diplomatic initiatives had taken place without cabinet scrutiny, the formal German response to France required cabinet agreement. The sessions were acrimonious (Stresemann, Vol. 2: 96). Despite French efforts, DNVP ministers treated the French demands as a fixed and unalterable ultimatum rather than an opening offer in a negotiation process. It indicated their perception of the negotiations as zero-sum in nature, in which Germany faced an intractable and unyielding French adversary. Lacking epistemic motivation, they were unreceptive to the signals of the French openness to discussion. Instead, the nationalists saw the French note as an accurate reflection of an unacceptable French position that made talks pointless (Kabinette Luther, Vol. 1, No. 110; Wright 2002: 316–17; Gratwohl 1980: 86–88; Jacobson 1972: 53). To proceed would amount to a formal recognition of the points of the French note. Their position was highly emotional. Any discussion based on the French note was for the nationalists a "difficult sacrifice" and a "humiliation" of Germany (Kabinette Luther, Vol. 1, No. 123). Privately Graf von Westarp estimated "with 99% probability that the minimum demands for the protection of honor and interests would not be met by the allies" (Gratwohl 1980: 106).

DNVP cabinet members demanded that the government call off negotiations. If they were to consent to allow them to move forward, it was only with the explicit hope that they would fail. Albert Neuhaus said it would be a "gift from God" if nothing ever came of the German memorandum as he saw no advantage (Kabinette Luther, Vol. 1, No. 110; Wright 2002: 316–17; Gratwohl 1980: 86–88; Jacobson 1972: 53). Had it been up to the nationalists, Stresemann's ideas would have been abandoned. Schiele advocated abandoning the terms of the original German memorandum and walking back from any pledge on the western borders (Kabinette Luther, Vol. 1, No. 123).

In contrast, the center-right pragmatists proved more open to recognizing the liberal elements of French diplomatic style. Before the Foreign Affairs Committee, Stresemann stated, "We are convinced that we are not here confronted with an ultimatum" (Stresemann, Vol. 2: 110). Stresemann and Luther were supported by the centrist parties, which all favored the continuation of negotiations without prejudging the results

(Kabinette Luther, Vol. 1, No. 110; Wright 2002: 316–17; Gratwohl 1980: 86–88; Jacobson 1972: 53).[2]

Stresemann tried to make the pragmatic case to the DNVP. The foreign minister denigrated the cost of German concessions, arguing that the recognition of the status quo of Franco-German borders was of no consequence given that Germany, currently weak, was in no position to change them (Stresemann, Vol. 2: 67–69, 88–95). There was "no question of a moral renunciation [of the Alsace-Lorraine] but merely a recognition of the fact, which every sensible person would admit, that it would to-day be madness to play with the idea of a war with France" (Stresemann, Vol. 2: 215–25). It was only of a "theoretic character, as there is no possibility of a war against France" (Stresemann, Vol. 2: 503–6). In short, Germany was gaining more and giving up less than the DNVP claimed. "It was not we who were the givers," he said to them (Stresemann, Vol. 2: 100).

The conservatives were not convinced by this pragmatic logic. Outside the government, the DNVP launched a vigorous attack against Stresemann to force him to resign. Fifty-one of 111 nationalist delegates to the Reichstag signed a protest demanding that he step down (Stresemann, Vol. 2: 91; Gratwohl 1980: 90; Kabinette Luther, Vol. 1, No. 116). Although they failed, Stresemann described the episode as among "the severest fights of his career" (DBFP I, Vol. 27, No. 399). And the party pressure clearly affected the German response to the French note. Stresemann's challenge was to craft a formal reply that alienated neither the allies nor his nationalist coalition partners. In his instructions to the German ambassador in France upon transmitting the final draft, he told him of his dilemma in answering generally while not giving the impression of conceding specific French points and drawing right-wing ire (ADAP A13, No. 182).

The influence of the DNVP can be seen in Stresemann's linkage of the security pact to the occupation. Germany, for the first time, made reference to the alleviation of the occupation's conditions in the other two zones as a "ramification" of the conclusion of an agreement. The "security pact would be such an important improvement that it could not be without consequences for the arrangements in the occupied zones and the whole question of the occupation," read the German reply (Locarno-Konferenz, No. 16; Stresemann, Vol. 2: 143; Jacobson 1972: 55–56). This question of *Rückwirkungen* had been part of Stresemann's thinking all along, of course, but he had wanted to wait and raise it afterward. The

2. See contributions by Heinrich Brauns, Otto Gessler, and Rudolf Krohne. The only exception to this pattern was Josef Frenken, the Center Party minister. He, however, also served as minister for the occupied territories and took a strident position, in keeping with his portfolio (Kabinette Luther, Vol. 1, No. 110).

foreign minister told his diplomatic emissaries abroad to stress that this was not a formal condition for agreement on a pact (ADAP A13, No. 211). Stresemann did, however, explicitly link the belated evacuation of Cologne with the conclusion of a security treaty (ADAP A13, No. 211; Kabinette Luther, Vol. 1, No. 116). Heretofore he had refrained from doing so formally while promising such a result to the cabinet (Jacobson 1972: 53–54; Gratwohl 1980: 95; Stresemann, Vol. 2: 113, 134). Now, although it was not in the official note, Stresemann was laying down this condition. Under pressure from the right, Stresemann was departing from his preferred pragmatic statecraft for the first time and using extractive linkages.

The moderate parties had a different type of influence. To the extent that moderate party members added to the debate, it was to urge Stresemann to add "warmth." The draft was not "kind" enough (Kabinette Luther, Vol. 1, No. 123). Stresemann's DVP was more concerned about overstating its objections to the eastern arbitration treaties than it was about listing its preconditions for an agreement (Kabinette Luther, Vol. 1, No. 123). Cabinet transcripts show the center of the political spectrum shared the goals of the German right but differed in diplomatic style.

Like the French, the Germans directly stated their position on the issues that mattered most to them, most notably the French guarantee of the eastern arbitration treaties and the right of the League to play a role in settling differences over the interpretation of the Versailles Treaty. Germany conceded to joining the League of Nations but stressed that a solution must be found to the question of Article 16 that took into account the special geographic and military position of the country (Locarno-Konferenz, No. 16; see also ADAP A13, No. 211; Stresemann, Vol. 2: 143; Cohrs 2006: 251–52; Gratwohl 1980: 99).

Rather than remaining aloof and skeptical about the potential for agreement, as when coercive diplomacy is used, the note stressed the openness of Germany to negotiation, its goodwill in working toward an agreement of mutual benefit, and its optimism about the eventual outcome. As the French had done, the note began by stating the German "satisfaction" that the allies were "ready to consolidate peace together with the German government" and "enter into a mutual exchange of opinions" (Locarno-Konferenz, No. 16). The note ended in a conciliatory way as well, stressing that, despite concerns about specific points, Germany observed a "convergence" of the positions of both sides that were "fundamentally united in their genuine desire to settle the security question through the security pact suggested by Germany as well as the expansion of the system of arbitration treaties." The memo advocated far-sighted realist diplomacy that did not lose sight of the big picture. "Specifics" on which there were still "doubts and differences of opinion would be overcome if the governments kept in view their goal." For its part, "the German government" hoped "that further discussions will lead to a positive result" (Locarno-Konferenz, No. 16). This had been Stresemann's position vis-à-vis the French since the receipt of the French note (ADAP A13, No. 136).

When the allies, following a preparatory conference of the judicial experts of the three countries, formally invited Germany to a conference in Locarno to conclude a security pact, the same process was repeated. The German nationalists again proved to be a stumbling block, demanding that any acceptance be accompanied by a long list of German demands. They wanted to make resolution of the Cologne-evacuation issue a precondition for any conference rather than an object of negotiations—Germany should claim all it could before it went to Locarno rather than having to pay for this concession in Switzerland. More controversially, however, they insisted on an official denial by Germany of its war guilt, even though previous German governments had already made several such declarations. Although it was not directly relevant to the negotiations, the DNVP claimed that, by agreeing to join the League, Germany would be symbolically and tacitly affirming its guilt were it not otherwise stated (Kabinette Luther, Vol. 1, Nos. 158, 159, 160, 161). The DNVP insisted on a public and formal statement against the "great injustice" of the war-guilt clause (Kabinette Luther, Vol. 1, No. 158) to be announced not only to the allies but to all the members of the League (Kabinette Luther, Vol. 1, No. 159).

Stresemann, again, opposed a long list of demands and favored a written response of only a "few words," accompanied by an informal, private, and oral explanation of the German positions on Cologne and war guilt (Kabinette Luther, Vol. 1, No. 158). He believed that proceeding otherwise, particularly in regards to the morally charged war-guilt question, would ignite a conflagration that could lead the allies to break off the talks (Kabinette Luther, Vol. 1, No. 160). As a pragmatist, he believed that Germany had to keep its eyes on its main political goals and not be distracted by largely symbolic issues that did not confer distinct political benefits (Kabinette Luther, Vol. 1, No. 161). The moderate centrist members of the cabinet agreed (Kabinette Luther, Vol. 1, No. 158). When the nationalists refused, Stresemann suggested the compromise of an oblique reference to a previous document that had refused German war guilt without direct quotation (Kabinette Luther, Vol. 1, No. 159).

The allies, however, told Germany that they would not accept the receipt of such a document, threatening to derail the conference before it had even begun. In the end, the German reply to the invitation was, instead, accompanied by a written declaration stating that, if Germany were to enter the League, it should not be understood that it was taking

[130]

on any "moral charge" against the German people. The reply also stated that any effort toward reconciliation would be prejudiced if there were no settlement of the remaining points concerning the disarmament necessary for the evacuation of the Cologne zone (Stresemann, Vol. 2: 168; Locarno-Konferenz, No. 22; DBFP I, Vol. 27, No. 493; Jacobson 1972: 57). The Germans linked these issues to a successful conclusion of a treaty, although they refrained from making them a precondition for negotiations to begin. Thus, the DNVP had an impact on the German diplomatic style.

PUSHING PRAGMATISM: BRITISH BROKERING AND
FRENCH NONCHALANCE

An important part of Chamberlain's realist diplomacy was facilitating an agreement between the French and Germans, acting as an "honest broker" in the foreign secretary's words (Jacobson 1972: 23; Grayson 1997: 59). Early on, he told both countries it "would be a great mistake for the Germans to withdraw [their plan] or for the French not to consider it with the serious and even appreciative attention which it demands" (DBFP I, Vol. 27, No. 216). Chamberlain urged both sides to negotiate in a pragmatic and far-sighted rather than a short-sighted and coercive fashion. The foreign secretary continually cautioned both sides to focus on their most vital of interests. He stressed that they "must have patience in dealing with immediate difficulties so that the larger hopes which seemed to be within our reach might not be shipwrecked on some smaller point before we could bring them into port" (DBFP I, Vol. 27, No. 259). He told the French, "Whether we can do something for France depends on French behavior. . . . An attitude . . . which showed a sincere desire gradually to improve the relations between the two countries and to reconcile Germany to the conditions of the Peace of Versailles would do a great deal to remove one of the difficulties in our path. On the other hand, an attitude of unreasonable insistence on small points or a constant succession of irritating incidents would . . . only keep alive the hostility of Germany and accent the danger to French security with which France was already oppressed" (DBFP I, Vol. 27, No. 188). At one point, Chamberlain said that he was "not unhopeful that in spite of . . . all the *unreason*, whether in Berlin or in Paris, we have made some progress" (DBFP I, Vol. 27, No. 255 emphasis added).

Britain pushed France toward Germany and Germany toward France, encouraging them to seize the window of opportunity to remake Franco-German relations. On remaining issues of disarmament preventing the evacuation of Cologne, he wanted to show "consideration for German feeling" and to "honestly try to meet their point of view," focusing on "big questions" rather than "trifling matters of no military consequence" (Jacobson 1972: 49). He asked the French to "stretch a point here and there in favor of Germany, provided she shows a reasonable spirit" (Cohrs 2006: 245). At times, he called French policy "frivolous" (Cohrs 2006: 215). But Chamberlain simultaneously reminded the Germans of Briand's domestic political difficulties with the French right.

During the initial exchange of notes, the British stressed to both the French and Germans that their notes should be conciliatory in nature and general in substance (DBFP I, Vol. 27, No. 388). He saw the formal exchange of notes laden with preconditions and demands—in other words, coercive diplomacy—as inhibiting the negotiation of deals of mutual benefit. Chamberlain characterized the French and German notes as conciliatory whether this was true or not. When the French sent their formal reply to Germany, he asked his ambassador to make sure the Germans saw it "as a not unfriendly response" (DBFP I, Vol. 27, No. 283). When the French formally responded on June 16, he told Luther, "The Briand note was as favourable an answer to Germany as could be expected in view . . . [of the] necessity of protecting . . . against nationalist attack" (DBFP I, Vol. 27, No. 409). He then urged the Germans to respond in kind: "I most sincerely trust that German government are not going to be misled into making quibbling difficulties over French note of June 16th. It was drafted by the French government in markedly conciliatory terms. . . . It is surely inconceivable that they will throw away such an opportunity. To my mind the proper course for the German government is to express acknowledgement of the spirit of conciliation which so obviously inspired the French note, to avoid all petty discussion of detail, and to accept without cavil the broad general principles which it enumerates" (DBFP I, Vol. 27, No. 388). Chamberlain promised to "to use his whole influence with the German Government to induce them to send a reply of an equally conciliatory character, to refrain from offering meticulous criticisms and to get to practical negotiations as early as possible" (DBFP I, Vol. 27, No. 410).

By July 1925, Chamberlain wanted both parties for stop their exchange of notes and begin private negotiations that would facilitate value creating negotiation. "It seems to me impossible to continue indefinitely a written and public exchange of views in which it must be clear that neither side will be willing, or indeed able, to commit itself beyond a certain limit. . . . It is clear that personal meetings and informal conversations will be necessary before complete harmony of views can be obtained" (DBFP I, Vol. 27, No. 426; see also No. 429). Getting to the table, however, was not easy because of the diplomatic style of the German nationalists.

Chamberlain's response to the German note is worth quoting at length because it so trenchantly analyzes the distinction between pragmatic and coercive diplomacy and shows how poorly British realists received coercive bargaining. The British foreign secretary maintained that Germany was in danger of sinking the entire negotiation through its diplomatic style. He complained that "Germany having opened to her a prospect which would have seemed impossible a few months ago now shows a disposition to delay and haggle which would justify every suspicion of her good faith and would not only deprive us of all power to help her but must make us feel that it is not only useless but dangerous to attempt it" (DBFP I, Vol. 27, No. 400). This stood in contrast to its earlier, more pragmatic diplomacy. He also wrote,

> It cannot be too strongly insisted that the problem which faces us is psychological. Security is a state of mind rather than a physical fact. It can only exist in stable conditions and when there is confidence that stability will continue. The German offer of the 9th February was valuable because it tended to produce stability and confidence, and therefore, in the end, security. It diagnosed the situation correctly and proposed the proper remedy. . . . The German note of the 20th July, on the other hand, appears to have been based on a different principle and wears a wholly different aspect. The German Government no longer appear in the role of a far-seeing contributor to the general cause of peace, but rather in that of a somewhat unwilling participant, who acquiesces in a scheme, not because of its intrinsic merits, but merely in the hope that consent will enable him to drive a bargain in other directions. (DBFP I, Vol. 27, No. 429)

Chamberlain emphasized how coercive bargaining could raise suspicions about German intentions and undermine the efforts of Germany to reach a mutually beneficial deal. "In a word, the German note raises again those doubts as to Germany's real intentions, which had in a large measure been allayed, and which must be cleared up if a lasting settlement is to be reached" (DBFP I, Vol. 27, No. 429). He excoriated Germany for its lack of regard for others' interests. He complained, "Thinking only of the party position in Germany they published an election manifesto and addressed it to the French government" (DBFP I, Vol. 27, No. 431). Due to this shift in diplomacy, Germany was in danger of missing an important window of opportunity offered by the reasoned dialogue of France and the pragmatic statecraft of Britain. "Never was France so set on peace or her government so liberally inclined. Never since the war has the British government so definitely marked its desire for better relations with Germany or spoken with such generous appreciation of the attitude of the German government. What is the result? As we advance, Germany recedes" (DBFP I, Vol. 27, No. 400).

Specifically, Chamberlain chastised the Germans for making an explicit link between the pact and the easing of the occupation, which of course Stresemann had done to pacify nationalist opposition at home. Consistent with his diplomatic style, Chamberlain did not begrudge the Germans for their "very pertinent criticisms" and goals but, rather, their clumsy and unpragmatic diplomacy. "Quite apart from its relation to their previous assurances, it is permissible to question the wisdom of the German Government's attitude. Even if it be true that the condition of a security pact 'could not but react on the conditions in the occupied territories and the question of occupation in general', the *manner and moment* chosen by the German Government for its assertion are such as merely to invite rebuff" (DBFP I, Vol. 27, No. 429, emphasis added). He objected to the diplomatic style of Germany, not its foreign policy. He continued, "It was only to be expected that the German Government would advance them at some stage. I had hoped, however, that they would have found means of reserving such questions of detail for later verbal discussion" (DBFP I, Vol. 27, No. 429). This, of course, had been Stresemann's preference, but he was overcome by the DNVP.

When the second German note raised the issue of war guilt, the British were again outraged because this indelicate act of diplomacy undermined their attempts at honest brokering. As a pragmatist, Chamberlain objected not to the German position but to the obstacle it placed in the way of beginning negotiations on more important and tangible issues. "All that the German government are asked to decide is whether or not they will take part in a conference where they will have full opportunity of making such declarations as seem good to them. . . . It is unnecessary to make specific reservations which can only be regarded as conditions and will thus introduce precisely that controversial element which it is essential to avoid at this stage" (DBFP I, Vol. 27, No. 488).[3] This was particularly galling because the allies had not made any recognition of war guilt a condition of a pact. Germany was very unpragmatically creating problems that did not exist. "As far as my memory served me, not one word had passed between the German and the British Governments on the subject of war guilt since the Pact negotiations opened. Why on earth did the German Government raise the question now? What possible useful

---

3. In response, "The German ambassador sheepishly stated that he did not expect Chamberlain to confirm or respond in any way. He simply had to deliver this message." It was "not his intention to make any conditions" (DBFP I, Vol. 27, No. 493). This was not something that Stresemann cared about, but it was needed to get the Germans to the table.

purpose could be served by their so doing? . . . Nobody asked the German Government to repeat [their war guilt]" (DBFP I, Vol. 27, No. 493).

Yet, as he had done for the French note, Chamberlain defended the Germans to the French. He emphasized that the German note accepted membership in the League. The Germans indicated no desire to modify existing treaties, in particular provisions regarding the occupation. "A careful examination of the German reply shows on the whole a closer approximation of views than might have been expected," he wrote. As he had for the French note, he stressed the difficult domestic circumstances the government was facing (DBFP I, Vol. 27, No. 426). Privately, however, Chamberlain was vexed by the coercive style of the German response. He told D'Abernon he was putting "the most favourable construction possible upon the note" (DBFP I, Vol. 27, No. 429).

As much as Britain acted as mediator between the two sides, Germany and France would have never gotten to the table were it not for what Chamberlain called Briand's "liberality." Although under more pressure at home than the British foreign secretary, the French foreign minister was not particularly annoyed by the first German note. Briand said it was necessary to read between the lines of the German reply (Unger 2005: 491). Unlike Chamberlain, who was irritated that Germany had raised the question of the occupation, Briand was reassured by the German promise not to make this an issue during the formal pact negotiations. On the eastern treaty question, Briand stressed his simple desire to prevent the possibility that governments might use arbitration treaties as a way to prevent self-defense in situations of obvious aggression. In other, more ambiguous situations, another mechanism could be used, and he stressed his belief that a solution could be found. In an expression of empathy, Briand even went as far as to say that he would have taken the same position had he been in the Germans' shoes. The German ambassador to Paris, after meeting Briand, reported that his meeting "went as well as one could have hoped. . . . The understanding he has for our position even surprises me somewhat" (ADAP A13, No. 219).

Whether proceeding to face-to-face negotiations was possible depended on how the French received the second German note. Stresemann was not optimistic. He believed that it would lead "French public opinion . . . [to] boil over" (Stresemann, Vol. 2: 135). The foreign minister wrote, "It is so unfavourable to the Briand Note that I should not be surprised if the whole matter dropped. Much diplomacy will be needed to get the matter through at all" (Stresemann, Vol. 2: 141). Yet the French treated even the war-guilt issue with more equanimity than did the British, again showing the importance of liberal diplomacy in facilitating an agreement. The French response simply stated matter-of-factly that the issue of war guilt had been settled and was not a question for upcoming negotiations (DBFP I, Vol. 27, No. 499; Locarno-Konferenz, No. 23). Other than that, the French were pleased that the Germans would come to Locarno. The French did not rise to the bait of the German nationalists, allowing negotiations to proceed. The reasoned dialogue of the leftist coalition allowed discussions to continue, whereas previously they might have broken down due to conclusions about German intentions drawn from the German coercive bargaining style.

During this entire period, members of the French and German right who opposed diplomatic rapprochement were working against, rather than with, the core economic interests of their constituencies. French and German business interests had an acute interest in securing credit from U.S. investors, who had been largely scared off from placing their capital in Europe given the instability of security relations between the two countries (Jacobson 1972: 5; Wright 2002: 342, Cohrs 2004: 250; Keeton 1987). The agricultural and business interests that supported the DNVP were particularly in need of a cash infusion and upset with the line that their party was taking (Wright 2002: 279; Stresemann, Vol. 2: 140, 205, 233; Gratwohl 1980: 145). Yet it was the French left and German center-right that pushed this financial and economic argument. This was not a case of political economic determinism, however. Stresemann and Briand were the drivers of the policy. Their motivations were primarily political, and they mobilized business interests behind them to place pressure on those in their countries who were reluctant (Wright 2002: 287, 319; Cohrs 2004: 250; Gratwohl 1980: 87). Even Edward Keeton (1987), who more than any other scholar stresses the role of political economy in 1920s diplomacy, claims only that business did not act as an encumbrance on their efforts.

Crass electoral party politics also seemed to not have influenced the process in any meaningful way. Genuine policy-seeking motivations, rather than office-seeking motivations, drove Stresemann (Rathbun 2004). The foreign minister's considerations about the constellation of German party coalitions were based on what he felt gave him the best chance of bringing his pragmatic statecraft to fruition. It had been largely at Stresemann's insistence that the DNVP was brought into government. The foreign minister, largely on the basis of his experience with the nationalists' parliamentary intransigence during the reparations negotiations over the Dawes Plan, concluded that his policy of rapprochement with the western allies would be easier to accomplish if the DNVP were in government rather than criticizing it from outside. Stresemann believed that the "responsibility" of governing would have the effect of inducing a greater recognition of "realist political necessities" on the part of the DNVP (ADAP A12, No. 28; see also Wright 2002: 196, 279; Stresemann, Vol. 2: 26). He was overly optimistic.

[6]

Cards on the Table

THE TREATY OF MUTUAL GUARANTEE AND
THE "SPIRIT OF LOCARNO"

Having persevered during the difficult prenegotiation phase, the three powers met in Locarno, Switzerland, in October 1925, where they drafted the Treaty of Mutual Guarantee as well as bilateral treaties of arbitration between Germany and its eastern neighbors.[1] The final product heavily favored Britain and Germany. Unlike Poincaré, Briand readily conceded to British demands that restricted the scope of the British guarantee to flagrant violations of the Versailles Treaty amounting to precursors to the use of armed force. More surprisingly, Germany avoided a French guarantee of its eastern arbitration treaties with Poland and Czechoslovakia and also secured a note indicating that, when it joined the League of Nations, consideration would be given to its weakened military and economic position if the League implemented sanctions against an aggressor.

We are tempted to work backward from the results of the treaty and to infer that Germany had more negotiating leverage, possibly as a consequence of its more precarious domestic political situation. Or perhaps German preferences on both issues were simply more intense, allowing it to engage in more credible coercive bargaining. In reality, this is not how diplomacy proceeded around the table at Locarno. Accounts of the meeting universally indicate an absence of value claiming. Instead value creating prevailed. Despite the incentives present in all negotiating situations to retain private information and not reveal bottom lines, the Locarno discussions were remarkable for their good faith. All sides laid their cards on the table, revealing their negotiating positions openly

---

1. Italy, Belgium, Czechoslovakia, and Poland also sent representatives.

and honestly. Transcripts reveal that the French and Germans did not resort to threats, positional commitments, or inflation of demands. They argued their positions and tried to convince others of their point of view. Indeed, participants noted how distinct the talks were from prior interactions among the parties. Negotiators spoke later of the "spirit of Locarno."

This value creating was made possible by the combination of German and British pragmatic statecraft, on the one hand, and French reasoned dialogue, on the other. Consistent with the psychological argument I have made, it was the most liberal of the three governments, the French, that seemed to respond most to argumentation. France ceded on most issues to Germany, even though its initial position had British support. The outcome was not epiphenomenal to the distribution of power and interests.

Even as the nations agreed on the terms of the Treaty of Mutual Guarantee, Germany placed other issues on the table. Stresemann's realist diplomacy originally foresaw that Germany would first reassure the French and British by negotiating the treaty and only then bring up the issue of the Rhineland in a new climate of trust. His conservative cabinet colleagues opposed this strategy, however, demanding, in essence, payment on the spot. Over their objections, and despite the weakness of Germany, the DNVP pressured Stresemann and Luther to demand certain concessions on the Rhineland as part of the formal negotiation requirements of the delegation sent to Locarno. The nationalists were again pushing the foreign minister and chancellor away from their preferred pragmatic style toward a more coercive and distributive one.

Stresemann raised the issue at the conference in its final days but received only a promise from France and Britain that they would work quickly to create a package of Rhineland alleviations. Nevertheless, in mid-November, the allies came through with an extensive list of ameliorations of the occupation, resulting in the ratification of the Locarno treaty by a sizable margin in the Reichstag. A rationalist account might claim that Germany, given the hostile reception of the draft treaty on Stresemann's return to Berlin, was able to force these concessions because domestic opposition strengthened its leverage and credibility—what the allies were not initially willing to provide, the Germans were able to extract through coercive bargaining.

But a review of the documents shows that France and Britain did not grant these concessions on the occupation in response to German pressure. The allies intended to make these allowances to Germany as a gesture of reciprocity for Stresemann's realist policy of reassurance. These concessions were the continuation of value creating. All parties spoke of the new spirit of Locarno that would make agreement on previously contentious issues much easier. These *Rückwirkungen* might have indeed been necessary for German ratification, but this is not what motivated Britain and France.

At the end of this period of negotiations, all had received what they valued most. The French received security, the Germans greater sovereignty, and the British conciliation on the continent. Franco-German relations had been completely altered. In less than a year, with help from British realists and French liberals, Stresemann had transformed Germany from the object of negotiations to an equal participant, despite his complete lack of bargaining leverage. The overall result was not, however, a foreordained exchange of benefits based simply on a favorable distribution of interests. The German foreign minister recognized, and the French and British confirmed, that had the Germans first come to them with a package deal of the kind eventually agreed on—alleviations of the occupation in exchange for a pledge of nonaggression—the proposal would have failed. Structure allowed but did not determine events. Diplomacy added value.

AROUND THE TABLE: THE LOCARNO CONFERENCE

Diplomacy in Locarno proceeded through an exchange of arguments rather than demands, threats, and counterdemands. The parties practiced value creating rather than value claiming negotiation. Indeed, we can say that in some ways the representatives of the three countries went beyond value creating, engaging in communicative action in which all sides remained open to being persuaded to rethink their positions. As the representatives of the three countries (as well as Italy, Belgium, Czechoslovakia, and Poland) met in Locarno in October 1925, there were two major issues of contention, both of which had occupied a prominent place in the earlier exchange of notes: the sanctions obligations of Germany when it became a member of the League of Nations and whether France would guarantee the treaties of arbitration that Germany would sign with its eastern neighbors. Briand playfully referred to these as the "rheumatism points" (DBFP I, Vol. 27, app. 1; Locarno-Konferenz, No. 25).

On the question of the eastern treaties, France framed its guarantee of the German arrangements with its eastern neighbors as different from a traditional alliance. Whereas the aborted 1919 treaty had been directed against Germany, the treaty that now was imagined in both the east and the west was reciprocal in nature. France would be guaranteeing Germany against Polish aggression as well. Briand stated that he did not believe in old-fashioned alliances but, rather, looked for pacts along the multilateral lines of the League (DBFP I, Vol. 27, app. 5; Locarno-Konferenz: 149–54; ADAP A14, No. 123; Kabinette Luther, Vol. 2, No. 174). The French foreign minister also argued that if Germany indeed had peaceful intentions and was indeed serious about not resorting to force to change the eastern borders, then it should have no problem with a French guarantee. There was "no reason why the principles applied to one frontier should not be applied to the other" (DBFP I, Vol. 27, app. 5; see also Locarno-Konferenz: 149–54). Stresemann had his own counterargument. He questioned whether it was possible for a state to objectively guarantee a treaty in which an ally was involved. France could not credibly claim it would go to war against Poland if its ally attacked Germany or judge Poland, rather than Germany, to be at fault in an ambiguous case.

On the issue of Germany's obligations under Article 16 of the League Covenant, Stresemann used two arguments. First, he claimed that it was not fair to ask Germany to contribute to military or economic sanctions on behalf of the League in its currently disarmed state, one that Germany had not asked for but which had been imposed as part of the Versailles peace terms. This was not "willful inequality." In its "exceptional position," Germany "did not ask for privileges, but only for special treatment during a transitional period." Germany would be able to take on the same obligations as other countries when, as foreseen in the League Covenant, global disarmament took place (DBFP I, Vol. 27, app. 8; see also Stresemann, Vol. 2: 176–78; Locarno-Konferenz: 161–72). Second, he noted that Britain and France, and the League in general, had already, during negotiations over the failed Treaty of Mutual Assistance, conceded the point that obligations to the League might take into account the different geographical positions and military power of the countries (DBFP I, Vol. 27, No. 522 and app. 8; Locarno-Konferenz: 161–72). The Germans were simply asking for an affirmation of this established principle.[2]

The French responded that the League of Nations was the "pivot" for the entire pact and was based on equal obligations that applied to all. For Briand, the League was "one and indivisible. It was not compatible with choosing what was pleasant and rejecting that which was unpleasant. All

---

2. The allies suggested that that Germany simply rely on its veto power as a future permanent member of the League Council to prevent the organization from implementing any undesirable sanctions. Luther and Stresemann protested that doing so would leave Germany in an unacceptable position of "moral isolation" in the event it blocked action against a wanton act of aggression by another state. They did not want to be under any ethical obligation to participate when it might prove practically impossible for Germany to do so (Kabinette Luther, Vol. 2, No. 175; DBFP I, Vol. 27, app. 8 and No. 523; Locarno-Konferenz: 161–72).

members must all take on the same obligations or the spirit of association would be broken." The German position was the "point of view of the individual and not the whole body" (DBFP I, Vol. 27, app. 8; Locarno-Konferenz: 161–72).

The British made different, more pragmatic arguments. The foreign secretary urged the Germans to consider the practical effect of a French guarantee of the eastern treaties "apart from the objections of sentiment." Chamberlain pointed out that France already had alliances with the Eastern European neighbors of Germany, so any new guarantee changed little for Germany. Indeed, the treaty might limit the operation of this alliance if the League was obliged to take up any violations of the arbitration pact before France took action (DBFP I, Vol. 27, No. 518). German representatives responded that the symbolic recognition of this Little Entente was impossible for Germany (ADAP A14, No. 123). Luther described the German public's objections on the issue as "emotional" yet very real (Kabinette Luther, Vol. 2, No. 174).

On Article 16, Chamberlain's realism made him sympathetic to the points made by Germany about the uniqueness of its position, particularly its vulnerability vis-à-vis the Soviet Union: "If he had been a German, Mr. Chamberlain said he would no doubt have the same ideas as the German Government and would have sought to do what they were doing. All the same, it was certain that it would not be possible to get the League of Nations to accept the German view" (DBFP I, Vol. 27, app. 8; No. 522). To ease German fears, the British urged the Germans to think of Article 16 as they did and to take advantage of its ambiguity. The League Covenant obligated some action to be taken by all states, particularly in regards to economic sanctions, in the case of aggression. It did not, however, specify any particular measures (DBFP I, Vol. 27, app. 8). There was already a "certain liberty left to the Powers as regards the extent and even the times of their co-operation" (DBFP I, Vol. 27, No. 522). He even suggested that the Germans join the League and work to dilute Article 16 with the British from within. Given its extensive global economic ties, Britain would suffer the most from cutting off international commerce. And it was more important than any other country, given its navy, in implementing any blockade (DBFP I, Vol. 27, No. 533). When Luther expressed his admiration for Chamberlain's "practical idealism," the British foreign secretary reported, "I believe I blushed" (DBFP I, Vol. 27, No. 528). Pragmatism was the greatest compliment such a realist could receive.

All parties remarked on the value creating that prevailed at the conference. The delegates were impressed by the skilled exposition of competing arguments. Miles Lampson wrote, "I claim to be as phlegmatic and unemotional as most of my countrymen: but I admit having been thrilled to the bone once or twice by the eloquence and obvious sincerity of both Briand and Stresemann. . . . My pen has somewhat taken charge and you may well think that I am overdoing it as regards enthusiasm. Optimism is a catching complaint, and perhaps it blinds my vision; but I do not wittingly exaggerate (DBFP I, Vol. 27, No. 529). Stresemann wrote in his diary, "In the evening Chamberlain said that never in his life had he been present at a more interesting debate. [Oswald] Hesnard observed that the debate had touched the limit of what was politically possible, but had been conducted in such a dignified manner that Briand himself had spoken with great appreciation of the argument, though my observations were naturally not much to his liking" (Stresemann, Vol. 2: 178). Lampson reported back home, "Yesterday, over the question of Germany's entry into the League, they were both at their best and I have never before had the good fortune to hear a discussion conducted on so high a plane" (DBFP I, Vol. 27, No. 529). A German memo noted that Briand spoke with "excellent rhetoric" and Stresemann with "the most effective execution" (ADAP A14, No. 127).

Germany ultimately prevailed on both issues despite its lack of bargaining leverage. The parties moved beyond even integrative negotiation toward something resembling Habermasian communicative action. Each of the "rheumatism points" was discussed separately and resolved on its own merits rather than linked to concessions on a different point. The nations agreed that they could act against another pact member in defense of countries in Eastern Europe only if the League Council approved it. If the League Council could not come to an agreement about the measures to be taken, the parties could act only against the country that was the first to attack (DBFP I, Vol. 27, app. 12). The French then signed a treaty with the Polish, making such a commitment should the Germans be the first to strike, but this was not part of the official conference deliberations or protocol. By claiming they had reaffirmed their alliance, the French saved some face. As a result of the pact, however, France was in less of a legal position to defend its eastern allies than it had been before the treaty. On Article 16, the allies formally stated that their understanding of that particular clause of the League of Nations Covenant was that members would take action compatible with their geographical and military situation (DBFP, Vol. 27, No. 532, app. 10; Locarno-Konferenz, No. 182). This was effectively an informal exemption for Germany.

We may be tempted to simply reduce the German victory on these two conference issues, after the fact, to the bargaining leverage conveyed by their smaller "win set" domestically, the international strength conferred by domestic weakness (Putnam 1988). Stresemann declared that Germany was "absolutely unable to accept" a French guarantee of the east (DBFP, Vol. 27, No. 516; see also app. 1). Luther said the issue posed an "almost insuperable difficulty" (DBFP, Vol. 27, No. 518). A guarantee was "impossible of acceptance by any representatives of Germany" (DBFP, Vol. 27, No. 518; see also Kabinette Luther, Vol. 2, No. 174). Did German threats coerce the allies into concessions? Was the outcome the reflection of the distribution of interests and power?

But this is not at all how the negotiations proceeded. Germany indeed stressed its domestic difficulties; however, the French did also. Briand noted that France had its own "nationalist hotheads" to convince. He reminded Stresemann and Luther that Germany was not the only country with a problem of domestic public opinion (Locarno-Konferenz: 149–54; DBFP I, Vol. 27, app. 5). And each side did so not to coerce but to evoke understanding from the other. Lampson wrote, "Briand, Stresemann and Luther sit opposite to one another in the Conference Room and discuss with the utmost discretion and good humour their various difficulties. Each goes out of his way to show that he realizes those of the other; each is obviously genuinely desirous of helping the other out so far as he possibly can consistent with his own national interests. In short, there is a complete absence of bitterness or back biting. . . . This strikes me as really the most significant feature of the whole conference" (DBFP I, Vol. 27, No. 529). At Locarno, both the French and Germans were open and honest about their domestic constraints and believed the statements of the other even though each had incentives to bluff and to dismiss the claims of the other side. Extensive value claiming did not occur.

All observers at the conference commented on the spirit of good faith and goodwill that prevailed. Even on the very first day, Chamberlain offered the "general comment" that the "most striking atmosphere of helpful goodwill prevailed throughout. M. Briand and Dr. Luther went out of their way to emphasize their determination not only to bring Pact to a successful conclusion but also to eliminate once and for all division of Europe into rival camps of victor and vanquished." He described the interactions as "easy, frank and loyal" (DBFP I, Vol. 27, No. 516), with a "noteworthy absence of any spirit of bargaining" (DBFP I, Vol. 27, No. 547). The Germans agreed. Luther reported to the German cabinet, "The goodwill of the English, French and Belgians to reach a positive outcome that is also acceptable to Germany cannot be doubted based on all that we see. The type of cooperation and the mutual dealings have been completely irreproachable" (Kabinette Luther, Vol. 2, No. 180). The Germans praised Briand's "courage" in making the concessions he did (ADAP A14, No. 157). On this good faith, Lampson wrote, "Frankly I am amazed—I think everyone must be—by the absence of all chicanery. All parties come to the table and explain their particular difficulties in the simplest and most straightforward language" (DBFP I, Vol. 27, No. 529).

[143]

In other words, the countries were putting their cards on the table. The foreign secretary wrote,

> Something which the Chancellor had said led me to observe that if an inhabitant of Mars suddenly visited the Conference room, knowing nothing of the history of the last few years, he would certainly get no idea that those who were sitting round the table were lately bitter enemies: he would think, rather, that they were good friends who had indeed differences of opinion upon serious matters, but were bent upon settling them in the most amicable spirit. . . . Who would have dreamed a few months ago that a discussion of that kind, so frank, so open, so conciliatory on both sides, would have been possible? (DBFP I, Vol. 27, No. 528; see also *Hansard* Series 5, Vol. 188: col. 421)

The discussion proceeded on the basis of the equality that facilitates value creating. Lampson, the veteran British civil servant familiar with past efforts at conference diplomacy, claimed there was "all the difference in the world" between the Locarno negotiations and those of previous meetings:

> However much in theory we may have met in London[3] on a footing of complete equality, in practice we certainly did not: we, the allies, decided what we wanted; we, the allies, persuaded the Germans to accept our proposals after, it is true, thorough and perfectly fair discussion: so that it was in fact a division into two groups. What is the position here? Strikingly different. No groupings of parties, no division into allies on one side and Germans on the other. . . . For the first time since the war the French and the Germans meet as man to man, one might almost say as friend to friend. There is complete equality; there is no longer a division into groups; all that is past and gone. (DBFP I, Vol. 27, No. 529)

Briand claimed that he would not have found himself in Locarno if he had wanted the division between the allies and Germany to persist. He wanted complete equality. Chamberlain agreed. If this split persisted after Locarno, then the countries would not have achieved anything, he asserted (DBFP I, Vol. 27, No. 516 and app. 1; Locarno-Konferenz, No. 25).

Nor was this atmosphere simply endogenous to prior agreements on the issues being discussed or a glow that emerged after a successful compromise. "Fundamental divergencies of view of course there are: but in no single instance have they been expounded in such a way as to cause

---

3. The reparations conference of 1924.

the slightest umbrage to the other party," Lampson wrote (DBFP I, Vol. 27, No. 529). At another point, the British described a "prolonged interchange of views and arguments between Herr Stresemann and Herr Luther and M. Briand conducted with excellent temper on both sides but not disclosing any possible basis for agreement. M. Briand insisted that the principle was fundamental but offered to consider any alternative form of its application" (DBFP I, Vol. 27, No. 517).

In their role as honest broker and facilitator of a pragmatic compromise, the British were intentionally trying to create such an atmosphere. Although he had been asked to chair the discussions, Chamberlain proposed, instead, at the first meeting to forgo any formal chairmanship so that the negotiations should have the "character of 'conversations'" (DBFP I, Vol. 27, No. 516) that were "as free and as informal as possible" with "complete frankness" (DBFP I, Vol. 27, app. 1). The parties should proceed on the basis of "perfect equality" (DBFP I, Vol. 27, app. 1).

Nevertheless, it was the French who were most responsible for the value creating that prevailed at Locarno. The French foreign minister came to the conference with an integrative mind-set characteristic of liberal diplomacy. Of their meetings to draw up a draft treaty in August before departing to Locarno, Chamberlain wrote, "Briand was the first to insist . . . that we must prepare for a real discussion with the Germans so as to arrive at a mutual agreement, and not another treaty imposed by the Allies upon Germany" (DBFP I, Vol. 27, No. 439). At the conference, the Germans described Briand as "conciliatory on even the most difficult questions" (ADAP A14, No. 163).

Sitting with Luther early in the conference, Briand revealed his prosocial motivation: "You are a German, and I am a Frenchman. But I can be French and a good European. And you can be German and a good European. Two good Europeans should be able to understand one another" (in Unger 2005: 495). Stresemann put his finger on the essence of French liberal diplomacy as well. He praised France's effort to balance the national interest with that of the collective. Paying tribute to Briand, the foreign minister said, "You started from the idea that everyone of us belongs in the first instance to his own country . . . but that everyone also is a citizen of Europe, pledged to the great cultural idea that finds expression in the concept of our continent. We have a right to speak of a European idea" (Stresemann, Vol. 2: 239–40). Chamberlain had also commented on how Briand "has, in truth . . . a European mind" (DBFP I, Vol. 27, No. 364).

Briand was perpetually optimistic rather than instrumentally pessimistic. He told the delegates in his opening statements that "He himself had long reflected on the consequences resulting from that act by Germany. . . . He wished to assure Dr. Luther that he had come to Locarno

[145]

without arrière-pensée, and with a real desire to settle this question of security so that it would not arise again." He wanted "to arrive at a balance" (DBFP I, Vol. 27, No. 516). Even as he laid out his arguments in favor of a French guarantee of the eastern treaties, Briand stressed that the solution was largely a question of doing the "same thing in another way in order to satisfy German public opinion" (DBFP I, Vol. 27, app. 5). It was a matter of finding a "formula" (ADAP A14, No. 123; Kabinette Luther, Vol. 2, No. 174). He was "sure that each side would use its ingenuity to seek another solution" (DBFP I, Vol. 27, app. 5). Chamberlain wrote that Briand "has almost taken my breath away with his liberality" (Grayson 1997: 57).

The French foreign minister also disclosed private information. When Luther asked him if France envisioned a guarantee of Poland and Czechoslovakia in which France would be able to act immediately without waiting for League deliberation, he revealed that this was negotiable (DBFP I, Vol. 27, app. 5). He even proclaimed himself "naïve enough to admit that he had proposals for a compromise to put before the conference" (Stresemann, Vol. 2: 175). Briand had in mind identifying a set of trustees that would act on behalf of the League to guarantee the treaty. He had told the British in August that he hoped this would meet the German concern about impartiality without diminishing the effectiveness of the guarantee, suggesting he recognized the power of their argument (CC 42 (25)). His eventual concessions went even beyond this.

The French concessions were not driven by British pressure. Given the importance of the security guarantee of Britain to France, the British could have exercised considerable leverage on the French to make concessions to the Germans. But they did not do so. Even though the British were relatively uninterested in the east, they sided with the French on the issue of the French guarantee of the eastern treaties. And the British were insistent that the Germans be under some obligation to participate in League economic sanctions, even if the precise form were decided on a case-by-case basis (DBFP I, Vol. 27, app. 5). This was true during the entire course of negotiations, even before the conference (DBFP I, Vol. 27, Nos. 249, 321, 363, 405); CP 245 (25); CP 312 (25); CP 318 (25)).

Chamberlain's credited the success of the conference to diplomatic style, which he attributed to the characteristics of the German and French diplomats. On the first day he had observed that "Chancellor [Luther] seemed to me to show just the qualities which, joined with M. Briand's, are needed for success" (DBFP I, Vol. 27, No. 516). Later in parliament, Chamberlain declared, "I think I am not saying too much when I say that the success of the Locarno Conference was essentially due to the character of the representatives of Germany and the representatives of France at that Conference" (*Hansard* Series 5, Vol. 188: col. 421). Agency was necessary to deliver the Treaty of Mutual Guarantee. He gave particular credit to France. "I was particularly fortunate in the character of the great Frenchman who represented his country there. M. Briand is a man of singular courage, of great clearness of vision and of a wide and generous liberality of thought. When he sets to work to make peace, he does it in the largest spirit" (*Hansard* Series 5, Vol. 188: col. 421).

CLEARING THE TABLE: THE RAMIFICATIONS OF THE SPIRIT OF LOCARNO

Primate Diplomacy: New German Demands at Locarno

Stresemann's realist diplomacy was based on the idea that Germany would first secure a rapprochement with the allied powers through a security pact and then begin to push for the easing of the occupation and, eventually, the complete evacuation of foreign troops from German soil before the year stipulated in the Versailles Treaty—1935. From the beginning, the foreign minister told his cabinet colleagues that Germany would insist on an assurance that at least the Cologne zone would be evacuated after the conclusion of a pact. He believed that it would be too much to ask for any further alleviations for the Rhineland at the present moment (Kabinette Luther, Vol. 1, Nos. 49, 116, 123, 153; Gratwohl 1980: 71, 110–11). Full evacuation would not result from a treaty, but it was the "logical consequence" of a pact (Stresemann, Vol. 2: 79; Gratwohl 1980: 73). This was the official position of Stresemann's DVP as well (Kabinette Luther, Vol. 1, No. 116). In a Reichstag address in July, Stresemann merely stated that he "expected some alleviations, notably of the burden of occupation if the pact came into being" but not as a condition for its successful conclusion (DBFP I, Vol. 27, No. 422). Stresemann was restraining his demands to better reassure the French and British of Germany's peaceful and cooperative intentions.

This was not sufficient for the DNVP, as mentioned in chapter 5. Kuno Graf von Westarp, the leader of the nationalist parliamentary caucus and a strong conservative, identified not only the amelioration but also the reduction of the length of occupation as part of any acceptable deal (Gratwohl 1980: 98). This was the party official position (Gratwohl 1980: 84). In the cabinet, Schiele of the DNVP had more moderate aims but, at least in the short term, they were still markedly more inflated than Stresemann's. In the cabinet, he called for a revision of the occupation regime as part of any deal on the security pact and an evacuation of the Cologne zone before the conference took place so that it would not become an "object" of the negotiations, a bargaining chip that the allies could use to pressure Germany to accept other terms (Gratwohl 1980: 110–11;

Kabinette Luther, Vol. 1, No. 158). As part of coercive diplomacy, the right-wing politician was attempting to remove a source of leverage from the allies by claiming as much value as possible now.

This nationalist pressure from inside the coalition forced Stresemann to shift in the direction of coercive bargaining. The official guidelines for the delegation to Locarno required that Germany secure both the settlement of the remaining disarmament questions and the evacuation of Cologne, as well as an assurance that the conditions of the occupation would be made less burdensome. The representatives to Locarno were also to "strive" for a reduction in the length of occupation, although this was not a precondition for acceptance (Gratwohl 1980: 113–22; Kabinette Luther, Vol. 1, No. 170). Stresemann was obliged to bring home something tangible in terms of the occupation.

Feeling this pressure, the Germans began to broach the topic of ramifications for the Rhineland with the allies even before the conference (Stresemann, Vol. 2: 151–53). The allies noticed the change in the German diplomatic style. Chamberlain complained that, although the German government obviously wanted to secure a deal on the security pact, he had "to confess that they hold at times a language incompatible with their earlier statements and assurances and their attitude may present unexpected difficulties" (DBFP I, Vol. 27, No. 509). The Germans then attempted to raise the subject of ramifications early in Locarno (ADAP A14, Nos. 127, 132; Kabinette Luther, Vol. 2, No. 174) but were told to hold off until the pact was settled (Kabinette Luther, Vol. 2, No. 174; ADAP A14, No. 137). It was only after the deal on Article 16 and the eastern arbitration treaties had taken shape that the British and French were willing to engage the subject, and then only on the perimeter of the conference in a private meeting that was to be "absolutely informal" and "non-official" (DBFP I, Vol. 27, app. 11).

Stresemann began with a long list of concessions that the German delegation "wished to obtain to order to render their position in Germany easier." In addition to holding firm on a few issues of disarmament that had blocked the evacuation of Cologne, the foreign minister asked for a reduction in the number of foreign troops in the Rhineland to the level of German troops that had been stationed in the Rhineland before the war. He requested the creation of a mixed commission, including German representatives, that would reduce the number of ordinances in the occupied zones that had created de facto martial law in the Rhineland. Stresemann called for an assurance that there would be no permanent inspection of German disarmament, an assurance of the right of Germany to develop civilian aviation, the immediate withdrawal of all black allied troops, and even the shortening of the length of occupation (DBFP I, Vol. 27, app. 11;

ADAP A14, No. 138; Stresemann, Vol. 2: 179–80). The Germans did not make a positional commitment. They stressed that this was simply a list of desires, not demands. But something "concrete," in Luther's words, on the Rhineland was necessary to avoid the impression that they had returned "empty-handed" (DBFP I, Vol. 27, app. 11). Stresemann explained that "it was necessary to have something beyond mere words to satisfy that anxiety" (DBFP I, Vol. 27, app. 11; see also ADAP A14, No. 138). Stresemann's right-hand man, Carl von Schubert, later almost apologized in a private meeting with Chamberlain for the coercive bargaining. Nationalist pressure, he disclosed, was forcing Germany to engage in "primate diplomacy." Germany could not operate with "diplomatic subtleties" but, rather, had to present "our wishes and demands very openly and baldly" (ADAP A14, No. 141).

A deal was reached on Cologne and disarmament on the basis of a British compromise proposal.[4] The first zone was finally to be freed. As for the other German demands, Stresemann wrote later that "Briand had almost fallen off the sofa. . . . He was astonished at my boldness, which indeed he thought had gone too far. If my views were to be accepted, the Treaty of Versailles might as well cease to exist" (Stresemann, Vol. 2: 180–81, 185–88). Briand joked that all these issues would require their own conference. It bordered on "foolhardiness" (ADAP A14, No. 138).

Yet, in keeping with his liberal diplomatic style of reasoned dialogue, Briand did not reject the German demands outright but, rather, was conciliatory and empathetic. It was "natural" that after the pact was signed that they "should consider everything for the realization for which we hoped" (DBFP I, Vol. 27, app. 11). German desires were "completely normal" (ADAP A14, No. 138). He recognized that the Germany "could not be satisfied with mere expressions of hope otherwise they would be called illusionists" (DBFP I, Vol. 27, app. 11). Briand even expressed optimism. "In a general way, Dr. Stresemann's list did not *a priori* seem

---

4. As he had before, Chamberlain took it upon himself to broker a deal on the remaining points of disarmament so that Cologne might be evacuated quickly, thereby helping to clear the path for German ratification. He devised a solution in which Germany would address a note to the Conference of Ambassadors on those issues that remained unsettled and pledge that it would make an effort to resolve them as soon as possible with the allies. The allies would take the Germans at their word and formally set a date for evacuation. The realist foreign secretary saw the remaining points of disagreement as trivial and wanted to remove them as an obstacle to a much more important goal—the conclusion of a security pact. Chamberlain applied pressure on his military representatives to move quickly and to stop quibbling about small points, such as how many German troops were allowed to be stationed in barracks or the title given to the German police (DBFP I, Vol. 27, app. 11 and No. 541; ADAP A14, No. 149; Stresemann, Vol. 2: 186–88; Kabinette Luther, Vol. 2, Nos. 195b, 195a).

impossible of realization. Quite the contrary. He would say for himself that he could even conceive further points which might be considered" (DBFP I, Vol. 27, app. 11). Briand even used Stresemann's terms. The pact must have "important repercussions" (Stresemann, Vol. 2: 186). This was not simply cheap talk. Briand expressed the same sentiments to the British privately before the Germans raised these issues.[5]

Briand was willing to consider the German proposals because of Stresemann's pragmatic statecraft. At Locarno, the French foreign minister stated that, as a consequence of Stresemann's overtures, France had had its "anxieties allayed as regards her own frontiers" (DBFP I, Vol. 27, app. 5). He said, "If there was general security we could make certain allowances" (DBFP I, Vol. 27, app. 11; also Stresemann, Vol. 2: 180–81).

Briand did not grant these concessions immediately at the conference for two reasons. First, he did not have any backing yet from his government. Stresemann had inserted issues on the agenda on which the French government had not formulated an official position.[6] Second, domestic opposition to his diplomacy also meant that it "must not appear that there had been any sort of bargain about the Pact behind the scenes" (DBFP I, Vol. 27, app. 11; see also ADAP A14, No. 138). In essence, any additional concessions would raise questions about the genuineness of German intentions at home in France (ADAP A14, No. 138). This had been the German foreign minister's own concern. Briand stressed he "had no objection to the treaties working out in this sense. Still we could not expect all this to happen at once. . . . He, too, had many enemies in France. *Unreasonable* persons were not a monopoly of Germany. He was attacked in Paris for exchanging a sound system of defence for a security system. He, too, had been called a traitor" (Stresemann, Vol. 2: 180–81, emphasis added). The French military was a particularly formidable obstacle (Kabinette Luther, Vol. 2, No. 195a).

Briand was not using the French right as an excuse for inaction, however. The foreign minister told the Germans that "it would be his first task to press this on the French Cabinet on his return to Paris" and even promised to resign if it did not bear fruit. He promised that the "facts which

5. The British wrote, "For example, he proposed that we should adjourn the question of military control after evacuation of the Rhineland, which appears on the agenda of the Council, remarking that, if our pact negotiations went through this would be easy to arrange. Many matters which would now present great difficulty would become of little or no importance" after conclusion of the pact (DBFP I, Vol. 27, No. 364).

6. The French foreign minister stated that "this was not the moment. He had not the mandate and his position would be untenable." It was "outside the notes which had been exchanged" (DBFP I, Vol. 27, app. 11).

would follow on the Pact would be sufficient proof" that the original memorandum had led to decisive gains for Germany (DBFP I, Vol. 27, app. 15; see also Kabinette Luther, Vol. 2, Nos. 184, 195b). Briand hoped to reduce the number of troops and ordinances. The French minister even promised the Germans that they could "enlarge on the effects of the general reaction on all sorts of things, with the practical certainty that it would have these concrete results" that would "follow very quickly, more quickly indeed than the German public could at present anticipate" (DBFP I, Vol. 27, app. 11; also ADAP A14, No. 138). Rather than dismissing German desires as being impossible to realize, as one would do when engaged in coercive bargaining, Briand went so far as to ask the German government for an official memorandum identifying a wish list on the occupation (ADAP A14, No. 140; see also No. 149). He said he would think it dishonest to not follow through and bring about a decisive change in the occupation regime (Kabinette Luther, Vol. 2, No. 184).

The Germans trusted Briand. Stresemann described a remarkable exchange at the conference. "After his speech on Friday evening, Briand came to me and stretched out both his hands to me. I took his right hand and said that I was grateful to him from my heart for the words that he had spoken, to which he replied: 'No, don't speak of words. I shall prove to you that they are not merely words, but deeds'" (Stresemann, Vol. 2: 188; see also Kabinette Luther, Vol. 2, No. 184). The British recognized this explicitly as liberal diplomacy. Chamberlain wrote home of the "noble reply of M. Briand, breathing the true spirit of Liberal France. With his mandate exhausted and no longer able to speak in the name of his Government, he yet pledges himself on his return to France to endeavor to give the largest possible satisfaction to the unspoken wishes of the German delegation. None of us who had witnessed that scene would ever forget it" (DBFP IA, Vol. 1, No. 6).

Chamberlain responded differently, consistent with his pragmatic diplomatic style. He urged Germany to moderate its demands given the realities of the present circumstances (ADAP A14, No. 141; DBFP I, Vol. 27, app. 11). The foreign secretary told its representatives, "She [Germany] would always find the other members of the Council sensible of what had passed at Locarno. We were just as anxious as they were that the new spirit engendered at Locarno should continue and bear fruit" but "there were concessions which were not in the [domain] of *practical* politics" (DBFP I, Vol. 27, app. 14, emphasis added). Whereas Briand, as a liberal, expressed genuine empathy for the position of Germany, Chamberlain, as a more instrumental pragmatist, complained privately about German primate diplomacy (DBFP I, Vol. 27, No. 547). Even though the French should have been most opposed to the new German demands given their greater vulnerability and insecurity, the British were actually the ones who objected the most. Nevertheless, Chamberlain promised the Germans that he would travel through Paris on the way home to impress on the French prime minister and other key officials the British support for Briand's concessions in this area (DBFP I, Vol. 27, No. 541).

The parties agreed to initial the final results in the form of a draft treaty to convey an official approval of the treaty proceedings while also allowing the German delegation to bring the instrument home to discuss with its cabinet. The success of the treaty hinged on the issue that had driven Stresemann to write his memorandum in the first place—steps toward returning Germany sovereignty in the western occupation zones.

Amputee Diplomacy: Stresemann Returns and the German Nationalists Depart

Stresemann returned home to an angry German cabinet. The members had been briefed during Locarno on the progress of negotiations, and the now familiar divide had opened up between the centrist and conservative elements. The nationalists complained that the Article 16 arrangement was not comprehensive and binding enough.[7] Outside the cabinet, in the Reichstag Graf von Westarp denigrated "gentlemen's agreements" on issues such as Article 16 (Gratwohl 1980: 128, 138). Schiele insisted that definitive concessions be brought home on the Rhineland occupation now so that they did not become objects of negotiation later (Kabinette Luther, Vol. 2, No. 197). He also wanted a specific commitment to reduce the length of occupation for the remaining zones (Kabinette Luther, Vol. 2, No. 201). Hindenburg responded emotionally, complaining that the treaty amounted to a "perpetual genuflection" for the Germans (Kabinette Luther, Vol. 2, No. 214).[8]

---

7. Hindenburg called the note on Article 16 that Stresemann had secured a "noose around the neck" (Kabinette Luther, Vol. 2, No. 183). Han von Seeckt complained that Germany must secure a categorical exception from any obligations, rather than merely the right to participate to the extent that it sought fit (Kabinette Luther, Vol. 2, No. 187). Schiele complained of its non-binding nature and demanded a League Council resolution absolving Germany of its responsibilities (Kabinette Luther, Vol. 2, No. 190). He and Otto von Schlieben, DNVP member, also insisted on an explicit assertion that Germany had no obligation to participate in economic sanctions either (Kabinette Luther, Vol. 2, Nos. 183, 190).

8. He insisted on a clarification that Germany had not permanently renounced the Alsace-Lorraine (only a settlement through force), a "more precise" statement on war guilt, a complete exemption from any Article 16 negotiations, more binding commitments beyond simple promises to ease the occupation, and absolute flexibility in exiting the pact.

The DNVP caucus in parliament issued a communique denigrating the achievement and betraying their zero-sum heuristic: "The German Nationalist Reichstag delegation is not able to see in the results of the negotiations in Locarno the fulfillment of the demands justified by the vital necessities of the German people. The delegation also fails to find the fulfillment of the prerequisites to the conclusion of a treaty, as well as the compensations by the other participating powers commensurate with the sacrifices to be assumed by Germany" (Gratwohl 1980: 137; see also Stresemann, Vol. 2: 193).[9]

The German delegation had been informed of nationalist feeling while in Locarno. Hermann Pünder, the foreign office representative briefing the cabinet, had telegraphed the negotiating party to report the very serious opposition at home (Kabinette Luther, Vol. 2, No. 183).[10] The nationalist opposition was so strong that Heinrich Brauns, as acting chair of the cabinet, could not secure cabinet approval for Stresemann and Luther to initial the draft treaty. The cabinet sent word forbidding them from doing so (Kabinette Luther, Vol. 2, No. 197). Upon receiving the message, Luther, who was sitting with his British interlocutors, stated in colloquial English, "Tell him to 'kiss my ass.' I mean to sign" (in Gratwohl 1980: 130; Wright 2002: 338).

In his briefing to the cabinet on his return and in a meeting with Graf von Westarp, Stresemann made the pragmatic case for the treaty. He persistently emphasized that Germany had realized "100%" of its main negotiating goals (Kabinette Luther, Vol. 2, 201; see also ADAP A14, No. 160). This was not just grandstanding; Stresemann wrote the same in his diary (Stresemann, Vol. 2: 232–34). In recounting his successes, the foreign minister noted that his achievements came despite the structural weakness of Germany: "Never had a delegation had such a success. We had been a nation of helots, and to-day we were a State of world importance" (Stresemann, Vol. 2: 191–92).

The difference between the centrists and the nationalists lay not in their goals but in their diplomatic styles. The right was unpragmatically

---

9. Beyond the issue of ramifications, the DNVP found fault with the fundamental premise of Stresemann's original memo, the legal rejection of using force to recover Alsace-Lorraine. The DNVP caucus vowed that "it will not approve any treaty . . . that does not exclude any renunciation of German land and peoples" (Stresemann, Vol. 2: 193).

10. Graf von Westarp wrote Luther demanding that he put the war-guilt question at the center of discussions (Kabinette Luther, Vol. 2, No. 171). Schiele telegraphed Stresemann once to complain of his "serious misgivings" (Stresemann, Vol. 2: 184) and then again, on behalf of all the DNVP cabinet members, to castigate the delegation for the abandonment of Alsace-Lorraine (ADAP A14, No. 154).

making the perfect the enemy of the good. Stresemann complained, "The Peace of Versailles has but one pattern in the history of the world; that is the peace that Rome imposed on Carthage after the second Punic War. I don't know if there was a single supporter of Hannibal in the Carthaginian Senate who would not gladly have agreed to an armistice of the kind indicated by Locarno. I see in Locarno the preservation of the Rhineland, and the possibility of the recovery of German territory in the East. I may be wrong. But hitherto no one has shown me the slightest sign of any other way that might lead to the same goal" (Vol. 2: 231). The nationalists were being unrealistic. "Politics is the art of the possible," he stated again (in Jacobson 1972: 65). For instance, it was pointless to insist on an allied statement against war guilt because the allies would never grant it (Kabinette Luther, Vol. 2, No. 215; see also No. 223). "Everything that could be done" on war guilt "has been done. . . . The idea that the Allies may on their side allow the Article to drop, I regard as purely Utopian" (Stresemann, Vol. 2: 196–204).

Stresemann explained to his colleagues that the pact was the cornerstone for a longer-term and pragmatic strategy of emancipating Germany and preventing "the plan of Poincaré to remain on the Rhine. That was the most important element" (Kabinette Luther, Vol. 2, No. 233). A Foreign Office memorandum emphasized the importance of thinking step by step "for a long future" and recognizing the current constraints of Germany. This was not a "genuflection" but, rather, a step forward in a long-term process of restoring German "freedom" (Kabinette Luther, Vol. 2, No. 215; see also No. 223). Luther spoke of "laying tracks for tireless work to hollow out the [Versailles] treaty." This would take considerable time, and there would be setbacks (Kabinette Luther, Vol. 2, No. 233). The "main point is the political effect," Stresemann emphasized (Vol. 2: 196–204). The spirit of Locarno would make it easier for Germany to overcome Versailles over time (Wright 2002: 343).

As pragmatists, Luther and Stresemann were more attuned to the opportunities offered by particular structural circumstances but also the necessity of exercising agency to seize them. Locarno was "like the hem of the garment in the story, to be grasped when opportunity offers," wrote the foreign minister (Stresemann Vol. 2: 304). Both recognized the deteriorating German status quo. Luther warned that "politics does not stand still" and that "such a passive approach is in the long run completely impossible." If Germany did not proceed, the possibility that it might find itself the target of a Franco-British alliance was "no fantasy" (Kabinette Luther, Vol. 1, No. 110; Wright 2002: 316–17; Gratwohl 1980: 86–88; Jacobson 1972: 53).

The more moderate elements in the German cabinet, those with greater epistemic motivation than the nationalists, endorsed Stresemann's statecraft. Heinrich Brauns, Center Party member, and Otto Karl Gessler, Democratic Party member, defended the results of the conference.[11] Expressing a similar realist style of diplomacy, Brauns praised the foreign minister for making an important step forward in what must be a long-term process. Rudolf Krohne of the DVP agreed that Germany had achieved much and would achieve more in the future. Not everything must be accomplished at once. Gessler likened Hindenburg's position to a "person missing both legs who threatens not to dance." He advised the former general, "We have to learn again to act in the spirit of Bismarck" (Kabinette Luther, Vol. 2, No. 233). The pragmatic moderates had a better understanding of the weak German position.

The precarious domestic situation again put pressure on Stresemann to engage in coercive diplomacy vis-à-vis the allies on the issue of the ramifications. Even though he was personally very pleased with the outcome for Germany at Locarno, he instructed his representatives abroad to downplay the extent of the German gains. This would enable Germany to extract more concessions before the treaty came before the Reichstag, thereby putting the government in a better position to sign and ratify the treaty (ADAP A14, No. 163).

Germany had to walk a fine line, however. It did not want to give the impression that it valued these "specific advantages" more than the peace pact itself. Yet these were matters of such "vital interest" that they had to be secured before ratification (ADAP A14, No. 160). If Germany denigrated the agreement to date, it would be accused of ill will, which might threaten the treaty ratification abroad. If, however, Germany seemed too pleased, the allies would feel under no further "obligation," endangering the treaty's prospects at home (Kabinette Luther, Vol. 2, No. 201). Luther agreed (Kabinette Luther, Vol. 2, No. 200).

Stresemann's realism softened the coercive diplomacy. The Germans never gave the allies an ultimatum with specific demands that had to be realized for legislative approval. The foreign minister simply wrote, diplomatically, "I take it for granted that friendly assurances given in Locarno will materialize in a practical form without undue delay" (DBFP IA, Vol. 1, No. 43). German representatives abroad were instructed to stress the difficulties Germany would face in the coming weeks (ADAP A14, No. 163; DBFP IA, Vol. 1, Nos. 28, 36). Stresemann told the allies that it was up to them to choose their concessions themselves so that these

---

11. They saw the note on Article 16 as binding and clearly in line with the German negotiating guidelines (Kabinette Luther, Vol. 2, Nos. 183, 187, 190). And the moderates lauded the delegation for its success on the eastern question (Kabinette Luther, Vol. 2, Nos. 190, 197).

would not be regarded as a price paid for German acquiescence (ADAP A14, Nos. 160, 195). The Germans framed the issue not in coercive terms, as the minimum side payment required for them to ratify the treaty, but, rather, as proof of the new spirit of Locarno that had arisen as a consequence of the conference (ADAP A14, No. 187; see also No. 212).

Ratification and the *Rückwirkungen*: German Ransom or Reward for Reassurance?

In mid-November, the allies sent a note to Germany listing their envisioned alleviations of the Rhineland occupation, including the removal of most ordinances governing civilian life, the reduction of the size of foreign garrisons, the abolition of the hated delegates who served as liaisons between the German local government and foreign troops, and the full evacuation of Cologne by December 1 (Jacobson 1972: 64; Wright 2002: 347; Kabinette Luther, Vol. 2, No. 223; DBFP IA, Vol. 1, No. 69; Stresemann, Vol. 2: 211). This was a dramatic series of alleviations. Even Stresemann, despite his vow to maintain unimpressed, later confessed that they were "much more considerable than any of us could have imagined" (Stresemann, Vol. 2: 232–34).

This outcome might appear on the surface to be the result of subtle coercive bargaining by Germany. Rationalists would point out the advantage conferred on Germany by the hostility to the pact within the cabinet. It restricted the win set of Germany and increased its leverage. But this was not what moved the allies. Rather, the concessions were the joint product of French liberal diplomacy and British realism. Chamberlain and Briand had always had every intention of making concessions to Germany following the conclusion of the pact. Germany did not need to coerce Britain and France. It was pushing on an open door.

The concessions to Germany by France and Britain were meant as a post-treaty reward for the new cooperative diplomacy practiced by Germany. They were the continued manifestation of the value creating that prevailed at Locarno. In transmitting their note to Germany, the allies wrote, "In the same spirit of confidence, good faith and good will, the Powers concerned in the occupation of the Rhineland have decided in regard to this occupation to introduce all the modifications compatible with the Treaty of Versailles" (in Stresemann, Vol. 2: 214–15).

That the allies had every intention of keeping their promise at Locarno was evident in British behavior immediately following the conference, well before Germany began to press. Before Chamberlain even returned to London, he wrote of the "*détente* which should inevitably follow entry into force of Pact and reaction which it should have not only upon question of evacuation of Cologne but also in direction of a general alleviation of conditions in Rhineland." He referred to the "inevitable and most desirable effect on conclusion of pact" and promised "that anything in the nature of mollification in the Rhineland to which French are ready to agree will have my strongest support" (DBFP IA, Vol. 1, No. 2).

The foreign secretary immediately instructed the British commissioner in charge of British forces in the Rhineland to cancel all ordinances not necessary for the safety of allied armies, with a particular focus on those that would be the most striking to public opinion in the Rhineland (DBFP IA, Vol. 1, No. 47). In keeping with the British role as honest broker, Chamberlain pushed the French for an evacuation of Cologne to begin on December 1, 1925, the day that that pact was to be signed (DBFP IA, Vol. 1, Nos. 50, 59). In British eyes, this was to be a "first gift" to Germany (ADAP A14, No. 49), not a quid pro quo brought about by the application of German leverage. The British felt that ramifications, in Chamberlain's words, "were not a bargain nor the purchase price of German assent" but, rather, "were to proceed from our own initiative because we felt that they were the natural results of the treaty of Locarno" (DBFP IA, Vol. 1, No. 73).

Because Britain had every intention of working earnestly on alleviations in the Rhineland, Chamberlain was irritated when Germany began to pressure the allies. He chastised the Germans again for shifting from pragmatic to coercive diplomacy. He wrote, "Since the return of the German delegates, the Nationalists have repudiated the treaty . . . and the German Ministers in this difficult situation open their mouths wider and wider, demanding the impossible, whilst more and more they and the supporters of the pact use language incompatible with the spirit of Locarno, create the appearance of a *marchandage* and give the impression of a condition or even an ultimatum to the doing of things *which were conceived and intended as a free act of appeasement and goodwill*" (DBFP IA, Vol. 1, No. 73, emphasis added). Chamberlain reacted particularly strongly to Stresemann's request after Locarno that the British consider a shortening the occupation. The Germans "must not make the mistake of asking the impossible, such as an assurance that the period of occupation of the remaining zones would be shortened, nor the equally grave mistake of treating concessions which would have appeared impossible to them a month ago, and which they now saw within their grasp, as valueless from the moment that they were offered, or of allowing themselves and their public to think that nothing was of any value except that which was refused" (DBFP IA, Vol. 1, No. 64).

If anything, the shift in German diplomatic style endangered rather than improved the prospects for ramifications. When the Germans began to press, the foreign secretary wrote to his ambassador in Berlin, "There is a limit beyond which we cannot go, and there is a risk that the German government, in trying to push us too far, may end by defeating the very object they have in view. In short they are in grave danger of falling into their usual error of opening their mouths too wide. Time is on their side if they play their cards even moderately well. Can you not make them realize this?" (DBFP IA, Vol. 1, No. 53). At another point, Chamberlain wrote, "I do not for a moment question the good faith of the Chancellor or Stresemann but this course is *full of danger.* . . . The Germans ask a great deal too much. The attitude of their Nationalists *make more difficult* the grant of the concessions *for which we were prepared* nor are we in any way helped by the attitude of the other parties" (DBFP IA, Vol. 1, No. 73, emphasis added). Stresemann had a greater chance of securing concessions by maintaining his realist course.

Briand also consistently demonstrated a desire to grant Germany concessions unilaterally, independent of any German pressure. The British noted that while in Locarno Briand "had practically pledged his government to undertake some modifications in the occupied territories" (DBFP IA, Vol. 1, No. 18), and when the French foreign minister returned to Paris, he set about trying to make these a reality. The liberal politician encountered great resistance on the part of the military, particularly in regards to the reduction in the number of French forces (DBFP IA, Vol. 1, Nos. 28, 33; ADAP A14, No. 176). The British thought that the French military resistance would ultimately stymie his efforts (DBFP IA, Vol. 1, No. 33). Marshal Foch demanded more time even on the issue of the Cologne evacuation. Briand and his leftist allies countered that a quick reply was necessary so as to maintain the "spirit of the Locarno Conference" (DBFP IA, Vol. 1, No. 33). In response to anxious inquiries, Briand told one of his representatives in Germany, "Tell your friends in Berlin that I am thinking of them, always thinking of them, and that I am working on it" (Kabinette Luther, Vol. 2, No. 210). The Germans themselves reported that Briand demonstrated "far-sightedness without narrow-mindedness" and always had the "best intentions" (ADAP A14, No. 212; see also No. 176). His diplomacy was marked by good faith and goodwill.

Despite their greater degree of vulnerability to German aggression compared to the British, the French were the ones who were willing to give more. In reporting on the Franco-British deliberations over the extent of alleviations, the Germans expressed their astonishment that Briand, even with his reluctant military, was willing to make more concessions than even the British War Ministry thought wise (ADAP A14, No. 254). For the first time, the German ambassador to France noted, Germany had been successful in direct negotiations with the French and even created a common front against others. He advised they "should not overlook the progress in relations with the French and should be pleased with the great change in Franco-German relations since the days of Poincaré" (ADAP A14, No. 25).

There is a second reason to believe that the limited coercive German diplomacy did not induce the allies to grant Stresemann's request for ramifications. The leverage of the German government came from the significant opposition of the DNVP in the cabinet. But the DNVP withdrew from the government several weeks before the allies sent their note on concessions. The nationalist cabinet ministers and even many of their parliamentary colleagues wanted to remain part of the government to be in a better position to shape negotiations. A meeting of provincial delegates and the executive committee of the DNVP, however, rejected the draft treaty as it currently stood and demanded the removal of the DNVP cabinet members, who subsequently resigned (Wright 2002: 304; Kabinette Luther, Vol. 2, No. 207). Differences over diplomacy broke apart the German coalition.

This removed much of Stresemann's bargaining leverage because it was, correctly, assumed that other parties were more favorably disposed to the treaty. The Germans recognized as much (Kabinette Luther, Vol. 2, No. 216; Stresemann, Vol. 2: 195) And, as Chamberlain told the Germans, the departure of the DNVP reduced the gains for the allies because a treaty approved by the DNVP would have been of greater value than one to which the party remained hostile (Stresemann, Vol. 2: 20; Kabinette Luther, Vol. 2, No. 216). Chamberlain wanted to court "every moderate and reasonable element in Germany" so that the treaty had the "widest obtainable support" in the country (DBFP IA, Vol. 1, No. 5). "A Pact endorsed by a Government supported by the Right is worth ten Pacts carried in the Reichstag against the votes of the Right," calculated the British ambassador to Germany (DBFP I, Vol. 27, No. 263). The Germans themselves had made this one of their selling points (ADAP A12, Nos. 28, 40, 81; Gratwohl 1980: 65). The resignation of the DNVP should therefore have, under rationalist bargaining logic, made the allies less likely to yield. Yet they persisted on the course of giving significant concessions. Briand was particularly unmoved by the change, showing again his more reasonable liberal diplomacy. Noting the difference between Britain and France on this issue, Stresemann correctly diagnosed that this was "because [Briand] . . . stands on the Left" (Stresemann, Vol. 2: 206).

Stresemann made up for the lack of DNVP support by relying on the votes of the SPD, which had consistently backed his diplomatic efforts and on whose support he had always counted, even though the Socialists had a political incentive to withhold support to see the government fall (DBFP IA, Vol. 1, Nos. 43, 64; ADAP A14, No. 195). Unlike the nationalists, the SPD appreciated the significance of the allied concessions. The alleviations were to them a "triumph of the spirit of peace" (DBFP IA,

Vol. 1, No. 107). With the final statement on ramifications in hand, the German government was now in a position to take a stand on the treaty. The unusual nature of the cabinet, as a collection of personalities representing the views of their parties but without the formal confirmation of the German parliament, meant that it could continue on in office despite the resignation of the DNVP ministers. Stresemann and Luther announced that they would continue the business of pushing the pact to a vote, after which the president would be given the task of forming a new government. This allowed the SPD members to vote their conscience without ruling out the possibility that they might take up the reins of government (ADAP A14, No. 187; DBFP IA, Vol. 1, No. 43, 49). The cabinet sent the document with its endorsement to the Reichstag, where the treaty passed by a vote of 291 to 174, although without any of the DNVP votes that both the allies and Stresemann had hoped for (Gratwohl 1980: 155).

Even if coercive diplomacy was not necessary to bring the allies to make the concessions on the Rhineland occupation that they had promised at Locarno, the outcome might be regarded as a simple package deal reflecting the distribution of interests. Rationalists expect that, in such instances of asymmetric preferences, parties create package deals in which each side trades off the issues it cares less about in exchange for concessions on those items it values most. Germany received its first priority, an improvement of conditions in the Rhineland and the return of a substantial amount of German sovereignty in the region, in exchange for a legal pledge of peaceful relations with the allies. France secured a British security guarantee. Britain obtained peace on the continent. In this view, diplomacy per se is not really important. It is epiphenomenal to the structure of interests.

But such an account neglects that the allies needed prior reassurance before they were willing to make such concessions at all. And only a specific type of pragmatic or liberal statesman (in this case, Stresemann) would have done this. Germany was only in the position to ask for ramifications because of its previous realist diplomacy. Indeed, had Stresemann's initial memorandum proposed such a package deal in January, the allies would certainly have turned him down. As seen in chapters 3 and 4, one of the most reassuring aspect of the initial offer of Germany was that it was not made conditional on any changes to the occupation. Earlier Chamberlain had written, "The German offer of the 9th February was valuable because it tended to produce stability and confidence, and therefore, in the end, security" (DBFP I, Vol. 27, No. 429). The pragmatic statecraft of Germany transformed European relations, according to the British foreign secretary:

My general feeling upon the whole question of German disarmament is that its importance has been fundamentally modified by the initialing of the Locarno treaties. . . . In brief, the policy of the allies was to safeguard the peace of Europe by insisting upon Germany's scrupulous execution of her outstanding disarmament obligations. The initialing of the Locarno treaties, however, has introduced a wholly new spirit into the relations between Germany and the Allies, which . . . is reflected in the view that the peace of Europe will be better guaranteed by the exhibition of a conciliatory spirit on both sides. (DBFP IA, Vol. 1, No. 50)

Now he vowed "to do everything that can be done to mark at once that our relations with Germany are now on an entirely new footing and that confidence established between us enables concessions to be made *which would have been unthinkable earlier*" (DBFP IA, Vol. 1, No. 2, emphasis added). Diplomacy had made the unthinkable thinkable.

[7]

Turning the Tables

REPARATIONS, EARLY EVACUATION, AND
THE HAGUE CONFERENCE

The French and Germans found it difficult to capitalize on the new spirit of Locarno following the return to power of the French right. Briand's leftist coalition was replaced in July 1926 by a conservative government. Briand remained on as foreign minister, but Poincaré returned as premier. The value creating that had prevailed between the two countries gave way to value claiming, making the pursuit of mutual gains much more difficult. The dynamics among the three countries from 1926 to 1929 show that the continuation of good relations marked by new achievements was contingent on diplomatic style and that coercive bargaining by any one side can undermine the potential for mutually beneficial agreement.

The preference of the French right for coercive bargaining undermined efforts by Briand to clear the table of all remaining grievances, which he called a "final liquidation of the war." In late 1926, he met privately with Stresemann in Thoiry, Switzerland, where the French foreign minister proposed a package deal covering the issues of reparations, the occupation, the return of the Saar, and the monitoring of German obligations under the Versailles Treaty after the removal of allied forces. In an indication of a liberal diplomatic style, he made concessions before Germany even asked for them and bluntly revealed the extent of the financial weakness of France, which had driven him to the table. When he returned home to Paris, however, Briand was forced to publicly disclaim the idea of an early evacuation from the Rhineland. The French right had turned the tables on the foreign minister.

There was still a simple package deal to be reached by linking reparations to the Rhineland, a win-win outcome for both sides, particularly because the occupation was of less and less value to France. As the deadline for total evacuation in the Treaty of Versailles drew closer, less could be extracted from Germany in exchange for early withdrawal. And with the construction of the Maginot Line, Poincaré and his colleagues thought the occupation was unnecessary for French security. At the same time, the Dawes Plan on reparations was provisional in nature. It did not even identify a precise final sum that Germany would pay the allies. The German payments were also set to balloon, raising questions about its capacity to pay, creating an incentive for both France and Germany to revisit the issue. And Germany desperately wanted French troops out of the Rhineland.

Nevertheless, the two countries struggled to link the issues, much less to identify a mutually beneficial outcome, given the coercive diplomatic style of France. Even though it was of little value to him, Poincaré insisted on holding the occupation as a pawn to extract the greatest possible concessions from Germany. He offered to only gradually withdraw German troops as Germany steadily made payments. The Rhineland was to be held as a deposit to coerce the Germans.

The coercive bargaining of the French right induced distributive negotiating by the Germans. As hypothesized, coercive bargaining by one side induces coercive bargaining by the other. Stresemann adjusted to the new situation brought about by the French shift in diplomatic style by abandoning integrative negotiation. In early 1928, Stresemann embarked on a public offensive, demanding unilateral French withdrawal from the two remaining zones of occupation. The Germans turned the tables on the French. Stresemann and his colleagues refused any link between reparations and the evacuation, knowing that the French could use the former to stall the latter and the latter as leverage for a better deal on the former. The Germans knew that the two issues were effectively linked given France's greater bargaining strength and that they would eventually have to settle. They decided to use distributive tactics in which they misrepresented their private position with a high opening offer and an inflated reservation price. As had been the case between Britain and France in 1922, value claiming inhibited the trade-offs and information sharing that would have benefitted both sides more. A favorable distribution of interests was not sufficient.

The countries agreed only to convene technically separate but parallel talks on reparations and evacuation, which culminated in a conference in The Hague in August 1929. There the French refused to negotiate, holding the Rhineland issue hostage as leverage in the stalled reparations negotiations. In the end, British intervention was necessary to bring about an agreement. In the face of French intransigence, the leftist British Labour government also shifted to distributive bargaining, announcing that it would begin to remove British troops from the Rhineland in just a

[163]

few weeks, thereby leaving France alone with Belgium. The British turned the tables on the French.

Rather than bringing the Germans and French together by providing a significant concession, as they had in the Locarno negotiations, the British facilitated an agreement through coercion. Only following the British ultimatum did the French begin to negotiate the dates and conditions of the end of the occupation. Due to distributive bargaining on both sides, the negotiations could have easily failed had it not been for British intervention. Even so, in stark contrast to the Locarno negotiations, both the French and Germans engaged in brinksmanship negotiation until finally settling on a termination date for the occupation of June 30, 1930. And given the lowest-common-denominator aspect of Franco-German interaction, this time the outcome was more skewed toward French preferences because France held the better cards. Although the agreement reflected the distribution of power, this was true only because both parties engaged in distributive bargaining. Diplomacy is a necessary factor to explain this triumph of structure.

Tea for Two: Consolidating Franco-German Rapprochement in Thoiry

For their efforts at Locarno, all three foreign ministers were awarded the Nobel Prize. Briand gave a riveting speech upon the entrance of Germany into the League of Nations, calling on nations to do away with their cannons and machine guns and make way for peace. The question was whether the three countries could consolidate their gains. At the time of the signing of the Locarno treaty, all three foreign ministers had made reference to the new spirit that animated their relations and that would propel them toward further reconciliation. Stresemann called this the "imponderable effect" of the treaty, that sense of good faith and goodwill that would contribute to better relations between the countries in a way that was hard to measure or pin down (Stresemann, Vol. 2: 88–95, see also 196–204). Briand stated, "If we had done nothing here but negotiate the terms of a treaty, and if we were then to return each to his own country, trusting to the hazards of fortune to realize the promises which it contains, we should have done nothing but make a futile gesture. If this gesture does not correspond to the new spirit, if it does not mark the beginning of an era of confidence and collaboration, it will not produce the great effects which we expect of it" (DBFP I, Vol. 27, app. 15). Chamberlain emphasized that "Locarno is a beginning, not a conclusion. It is not merely the written treaty, it is the spirit of Locarno that the world needs" (Stresemann, Vol. 2: 211). The mood in Europe was euphoric.

Stresemann and Briand each estimated that he had the support of three-quarters of his population (ADAP B1/2, Nos. 94, 173).

At the signing ceremony, Stresemann credited Chamberlain with making the conference "informal," thereby creating "the atmosphere of personal confidence that may be regarded as part of what is meant by the spirit of Locarno" (Stresemann, Vol. 2: 239–40). "It was not a relationship in which the three men consistently duped, tricked, or deluded each other," writes Jacobson (1972: 68–76). Value creating prevailed. And after Germany joined the League of Nations, the League Council meetings provided, as Chamberlain had envisaged, convenient opportunities for Briand, Stresemann, and Chamberlain to confer privately and informally to capitalize on the spirit of Locarno. Their face-to-face meetings became known as "Geneva tea parties."

It was at one of these Council meetings that Briand and Stresemann arranged to escape from the prying eyes of the press in Geneva and rendezvous in a tiny Swiss town called Thoiry in October 1926. They used subterfuge, each switching modes of transportation en route and travelling separately, so that they could arrive unseen and speak completely frankly. Briand had initiated the idea of discussing a "general settlement," a massive package deal that would clear the table of all of the remaining security issues between the two countries. He proposed the complete evacuation of the Rhineland within a year, the return of the Saar to German control, and the termination of the allied inspection of German disarmament. All he asked in return was an advance reparations payment by Germany, to be financed through the public sale of bonds that Germany had deposited with the Reparations Commission as security against default, for which the German railways served as collateral (ADAP B1/2, Nos. 94, 88; Kabinette Marx, Vol. 1, No. 83; Wright 2002: 374–80; Jacobson 1972: 87–90). As Briand conceived it, those bonds would be sold by Germany to private bondholders, mostly in the United States, and the proceeds would be given to France. This was, as Wright writes, a "bold proposal for a French foreign minister," and Stresemann recognized it as such (2002: 374). He understated when he told Briand that a "great gesture like the evacuation of the Rhineland would correspondingly strengthen the spirit of Locarno" (Wright 2002: 374; ADAP B1/2, Nos. 88, 94). The Thoiry scheme would, in one step, secure for Stresemann all the goals he had envisaged for the first stage of his long-term program of returning Germany to great power status.

Briand's immediate interest in a financial settlement lay in the deteriorating finances of France, which had precipitated a crisis in the value of the franc in July 1926 (Keeton 1987). Although this had added to the urgency, the French foreign minister had consistently supported such a deal long before the financial situation had become acute, indeed since immediately after Locarno (Jacobson 1972: 86; Keeton 1987: 211–15).[1] A discussion of Briand's ideas was postponed due to the fall of the German government, which saw Luther replaced as chancellor by Wilhelm Marx in a minority government of the centrist parties. The discussion was then delayed further until Germany joined the League on account of a controversy over the admission of other permanent members to the League Council. The acute nature of the economic crisis surely added to Stresemann's leverage. Nevertheless, Briand's concessions seem to have gone beyond what we might have expected given the structural position of France.

More significant was Briand's diplomatic style, again liberal rather than coercive. At the beginning of the meeting, Briand promised "to completely and openly lay the cards on the table" and tell Stresemann the true French position (ADAP B1/2, No. 94). In a violation of the coercive bargaining style, Briand confessed that France's financial needs were acute. He wanted to see a "general agreement" on all outstanding points between the countries because negotiating issues individually would simply make it more difficult. It amounted to a series of never-ending "pin pricks," he explained (Kabinette Marx, Vol. 1, No. 83). Briand was trying to cultivate goodwill by making concessions and openly stating the French position rather than maintaining private information to hold out for a better deal.

Indeed, Briand offered Stresemann significant concessions before the German foreign minister even had a chance to ask for them rather than retaining them as bargaining chips. When Stresemann asked about the existing plans to hold a referendum to determine the status of the Saar before it was returned to Germany, Briand waved him off, saying that he "hasn't the slightest wish" to hold a plebiscite (ADAP B1/2, No. 94); it was "completely unnecessary" (Kabinette Marx, Vol. 1, No. 83). Briand dismissed the concerns of the French military about the good faith of Germany in meeting its disarmament obligations, another potential bargaining chip: "We occupy ourselves a lot with theories and see ghosts everywhere" (ADAP B1/2, No. 88).[2] Briand said the whole question of monitoring, such as through the League of Nations after the removal of the Inter-Allied Military Commission of Control (IMCC), was "pure

---

1. See the mentions in ADAP B/1 Nos. 2, 11, 15, 16, 24, 33 110, 116, 225, 2270, 275, 276.
2. Briand told Stresemann about the thousands of files about German disarmament infractions that had been delivered to him by the War Ministry when he told the military of his intention to remove military control in Germany. Briand proceeded to throw them into the corner and asked to hear about on issues of genuine importance (ADAP B1/1, No. 94). He believed there were only a "few small questions" to resolve, after which he would have all military control lifted (ADAP B1/2, No. 94).

theory" and "academic." He reassured Stresemann that "No one is think-ing of investigation through the power of the League Council" because "no one would dream of an investigation in the case of a League Power." They would find a solution that corresponded to the needs of Germany, he promised (ADAP B1/2, No. 94; Stresemann, Vol. 3: 17–27).[3] As will be seen later, Briand thought of inspection as a simple face-saving device for public opinion, with little actual value. But he told Stresemann this as a sign of good-faith diplomacy. Finally, Briand did not propose breaking apart the evacuation of the Rhineland into a number of steps to maintain leverage, as he might have.

The two foreign ministers agreed that they would make a joint state-ment indicating that they had discussed a general settlement of out-standing issues and would recommend such a deal to their own cabinets. If they found support, the two countries would appoint expert commit-tees to deal with the technical details of a financial settlement and the evacuation (Kabinette Marx, Vol. 1, No. 83). The two statesmen were so pleased with their honest and open exchange and so optimistic about the prospects for peace that Briand said of the meeting, "Our souls were as white as the snow on Mt. Blanc" (Wright 2002: 377).

Stresemann returned home somewhat awestruck by the generosity of the French offer. The chancellor believed it was "almost too good to be true" (Kabinette Marx, Vol. 1, No. 83). But Stresemann had noted to Briand that "we both have to overcome glaciers." Whereas he had to get by President Hindenburg, Briand had to circumvent an even more dif-ficult obstacle—Poincaré, who had returned as French premier (Wright 2002: 377). The domestic political environment in France had shifted under Briand's feet. As long as the domestic political constellation in the three countries remained consistent, there were great gains to be made. French diplomacy under a conservative government would be very different.

THE FRENCH TURN: BRIAND AND THE
CONSERVATIVE UNION NATIONALE

The conservative Raymond Poincaré returned in July 1926, becoming both premier and finance minister, to stop the falling franc, along with a number of other rightist ministers such as André Tardieu and Louis Marin. Briand was again in the position of being the lone liberal in a

---

3. He maintained that it was necessary to have the League exercise a "certain control" but promised, "I agree in advance with what may be decided on the matter by the jurists, subject to your review"(Vermächtnis, Vol. 1: 17–27).

conservative coalition. Even though this meant the end of the Cartel des Gauches, Briand's Locarno policy was so domestically popular that he was essentially untouchable, and he stayed on in the Union Nationale government as foreign minister even though he ceded the premiership (Keeton 1987: 175). The German ambassador in Paris estimated that 75–80 percent of the French embraced Briand's appeasement policy (ADAP B1/2, No. 173). Briand recognized that in cabinet "he sits across from the intellectual elites of his political opponents" but believed that his high degree of support would nevertheless allow him to carry through his Thoiry scheme over Poincaré's objections (Kabinette Marx, Vol. 1, No. 82). Poincaré had never lived "among people," only "with files," and "pursues his ideas with tenacity," he told Stresemann. "But he does not know the feeling of the French people and he knows nothing of the spirit that is necessary for a new time" (ADAP B1/2, No. 94). The German foreign minister's only reservation about the deal at Thoiry was that stabilizing the franc would in turn strengthen Poincaré and allow him to stay on. Briand reassured Stresemann that Poincaré would soon fall. Only the foreign minister would be given credit for a diplomatic success of this type because "everyone knows that Poincaré does not like making concessions" (ADAP B1/2, No. 94; Kabinette Marx, Vol. 1, No. 83). Briand pledged to return home, touch base with his "party friends" and like-minded cabinet colleagues, and prepare the ground (Kabinette Marx, Vol. 1, No. 83; ADAP B1/2, No. 94). Stresemann doubted that Briand would succeed with this plan in a conservative cabinet but had little to lose by pursuing it (Kabinette Marx, Vol. 1, No. 75).

Briand vastly underestimated the conservative resistance. Poincaré was an economically orthodox finance minister and willing to let his foreign minister at least explore a deal that would make it easier to balance the budget and stabilize the franc. The German ambassador reported that the French financial situation was so deleterious that even the "wild right [news]papers" did not reject any potential deal with Germany outright (ADAP B1/2, No. 109). But when Briand returned from Thoiry, he was hammered in the cabinet for the extent of his proposed concessions. His colleagues lambasted his "personal" policy and reprimanded him for going beyond his guidelines (ADAP B1/2, No. 106). Marin, perhaps the most conservative member of the cabinet, organized a behind-the-scenes campaign of the right-wing press against Briand's ideas, saying that the plan would leave France defenseless in return for "financial trifles" (Keeton 1987: 173). The conservatives backed coercive diplomacy to secure more gains (ADAP B1/2, Nos. 119, 142, 156, 157, 173). The right wanted to drive a harder bargain for Rhineland evacuation, by insisting on German recognition of its eastern frontiers, a permanent system of inspection of disarmament, and a comprehensive reparations agreement

[168]

that would guarantee French receipts rather than the simple one-time payment foreseen by Briand (Keeton 1987: 220; ADAP B1/2, No. 109). The continued occupation of the Rhineland could be used as leverage to compel greater concessions. Briand, as Stresemann later noted, "had ventured too far" given the ideological character of his government (Stresemann, Vol. 3: 73–77). The conservatives had turned the tables on their cabinet colleague.

Briand was too domestically popular for the French government to simply reject the proposed deal. The cabinet, however, issued the most tepid of press statements. It simply acknowledged what was discussed at Thoiry, claimed that Briand did not "lay down even the barest outline of an agreement," and reiterated again that complete compliance on disarmament was necessary for early evacuation (Stresemann, Vol. 3: 27). In coercive bargaining style, the statement noted how difficult it would be for the deal to be arranged. The German ambassador called the communiqué a "product of embarrassment" (ADAP B1/2, No. 106; see also No. 173). The cabinet agreed to convene committees of experts but, as the Germans noted, stacked them with conservative opponents of Briand's liberal diplomacy (ADAP B1/2, No. 106). Briand put up a fight, speaking, in the words of one anonymous source, with "staggering conviction" (ADAP B1/2, No. 106). But he was forced to retreat. His own liberal style of diplomacy could not be maintained against conservative resistance.

Under Poincaré's strict financial stewardship, French finances improved quickly, more rapidly than anyone had anticipated. This suggests a simple structural account, that France had offered significant concessions only due to its bargaining weakness, concessions that it subsequently retracted when its economy recovered. Certainly the improving situation of France lessened conservative interest in a deal with Germany. But, major conservative opposition to Briand's liberal diplomacy had been evident before this rebound and Briand's proposals preceded the onset of the crisis. It seems almost certain that Poincaré's government would have rejected Briand's proposal regardless of France's financial circumstances. In private, Stresemann himself attributed the failure of the Thoiry plans largely to politics. The "idea that only the economic necessities of France could induce that nation to adopt such a policy is to take rather too exclusively material a view. I fancy that, having regard to the mentality not only of the French nation but also of other nations, if the old atmosphere of hatred still persists, it cannot be removed by any sort of financial services rendered by Germany" (Stresemann, Vol. 3: 41).[4]

---

4. The failure of the Thoiry proposal was overdetermined. The technical aspects of Briand's scheme, as Stresemann had prognosticated in his very first conversation with the foreign

Briand's position in the rightist Union Nationale government continued to deteriorate, leaving him ever more isolated. At a "Geneva tea party" on the sidelines of the December 1926 League Council meeting, Stresemann and Briand arranged for the final removal of the IMCC in exchange for the resolution of some contentious issues of disarmament (Jacobson 1972: 91–98). Withdrawing allied military inspection without some kind of replacement meant that the allies no longer had any on-site presence for detecting rearmament or a remilitarization of the Rhineland. France would only have the legal right to request the League Council for an ad hoc inspection in cases of suspected violation (Jacobson 1972: 91–98).

Conservatives in the cabinet, led by Tardieu, insisted that the cabinet telegram Briand in Geneva to warn him not to exceed his powers (Jacobson 1972: 102–3). Briand had to threaten to resign to overcome the cabinet opposition for the deal he had worked out with the Germans (Wright 2002: 382; Keeton 1987: 176). He complained to Stresemann that he "had gone home . . . with thorns" and Stresemann "with laurels" (Stresemann, Vol. 3: 119).

On his return, Briand fought back, defending his liberal diplomacy in testimony before the parliament (Keeton 1987: 225–26). Both sides had been trying to reach an agreement that benefitted each party through open and honest discussion. "It is true that on certain points there were differences of opinion between Stresemann and myself. A talk between two Ministers in the dining-room of an inn[5] cannot at one blow alter the position of France and Germany, and wipe out a blood-stained past. The essential point is that there shall be good-will on both sides; and that the nations shall be able to say—'At last they are getting together'"

---

minister, also helped sink the proposal (Kabinette Marx, Vol. 1, No. 89). The successful commercialization of the German railway bonds was predicated on adequate demand, which could be provided only by U.S. investors. Floating German bonds in the United States, however, required the authorization of the U.S. government, which was not interested in providing such permission unless the French first ratified a war-debt agreement that the two nations had recently negotiated (ADAP B1/2 No. 107, 119, Stresemann, Vol. 3: 41; Jacobson 1972: 87–90). Poincaré's rightist cabinet was hostile to the arrangement, which was concluded before it took up the reins of government, for emotional reasons. Conservatives, in particular, believed that France should not have to pay off loans to the United States considering the price paid in blood by its armed forces during the war on behalf of the Americans. Even if the U.S. government had been more forthcoming, however, there would have not been an agreement, due to Poincaré's coercive diplomacy. Stresemann later noted that the "alteration in the political situation *and* in the technical condition of the currency induced Herr Briand to ask me to abstain from positive proposals" (Stresemann, Vol. 3: 76, emphasis added).

5. In Thoiry, Stresemann and Briand had met at a small hotel.

(Stresemann, Vol. 3: 71–73). Nor was the occupation a bargaining chip that should be held to extract further concessions, as the French right felt it should be. "The occupation of the Rhineland is not a penalty. . . . The occupation can alter in character, and its duration can even be modified, if it has fulfilled its purpose," asserted Briand (Stresemann, Vol. 3: 72).[6]

By January 1927, however, Briand was forced in a statement that had been unanimously approved by the cabinet to publicly disavow any support for withdrawing French troops ahead of schedule (Jacobson 1972: 138). Briand promised to consult the cabinet in the future and even denied having ever supported early evacuation, claiming that the Thoiry plans had been suggested by Stresemann (Jacobson 1972: 103; Wright 2002: 404; Stresemann, Vol. 3: 57–59, 73–77). The foreign minister's wings had been clipped. The German ambassador wrote to Berlin, "Had he tried to go further with the Locarno policy, he would have suffered defeat" (in Jacobson 1972: 103). The Frenchman set his sights on the spring 1928 French elections, which he believed would oust the right from power and allow him to reinstate his liberal diplomacy (Jacobson 1972: 138, 146; Wright 2002: 390, 396; Stresemann, Vol. 3: 368). He asked the Germans for patience, stressing that he continued to be committed to the policy of understanding (ADAP B1/2, Nos. 156, 167, 173). Stresemann still trusted Briand, noting in a private memorandum that "however much a cynic he might seem to the outer world, [he] did in fact hold views that were based on an intention to bring about a Franco-German understanding" (Stresemann, Vol. 3: 41). He wrote, "I do not think there is much change in the man's own mind. But he knows that French public opinion would not tolerate his speaking in the sense of his former utterances" (Stresemann, Vol. 3: 41). The spirit of Locarno was put on ice due to conservative opposition.

THE GERMAN TURN: STRESEMANN AND THE FRENCH CONSERVATIVES

German diplomats in Paris stressed to their home office that Briand was isolated and that pushing the French too far would undermine their closest ally, someone genuinely driven by a belief in mutual gains (ADAP B1/2, Nos. 157, 167, 173). Only the Socialists in France firmly supported

---

6. The foreign minister even expressed admiration for Germany: "It has been accounted to me as an infamy that at Geneva I admitted a certain greatness and nobility in our former foe. If that is a blunder, then I regard myself as honoured by having committed it" (Stresemann, Vol. 3: 72).

the foreign minister (ADAP B1/2, No. 173). As the ambassador to France argued (and Stresemann accepted), the Germans could not get more from any other politician in France (Jacobson 1972: 116). Efforts should be made not to publicly embarrass him despite the short-term temptation because it would undermine long-term efforts (ADAP B1/2, Nos. 167, 173). This was classic realist diplomacy, pragmatic cooperation driven by instrumental self-interest.

Fear of undermining Briand at home and the shared hope that the French elections would work in his favor led Stresemann to refrain from publicly demanding at that time an immediate and unconditional evacuation of the Rhineland (Jacobson 1972: 138–39; Stresemann, Vol. 3: 180–82; Wright 2002: 382–82; Keeton 1987: 234). In an internal memorandum, Stresemann explained that he was handling the evacuation question publicly "only in the most general way, and always in a form that endeavoured to avoid creating any acute tension" so that "M. Briand should maintain the position of being able to do something soon, at least in the matter of the reduction of troops, without laying himself open to the reproach that he was giving way to Germany pressure" (Stresemann, Vol. 3: 149).

In public, Stresemann asked for a greater reduction of troops in the occupied zone but never a complete evacuation.[7] In speeches before the Reichstag in 1927, Stresemann defended Briand's sincerity and noted that novel ideas such as Briand's created conflicts between those "ahead of their time, and the rest, who are never more violent and ungrateful than towards those who utter a truth before the majority of the nation has given its *placet*" (Stresemann, Vol. 3: 63).[8] Stresemann directed his ill will toward the French premier rather than Briand. He asked, "What is the goal of Herr Poincaré, the Ruhr policy or the Locarno policy? One or the other is possible, but not one with the other" (VDR 326: 1101–9; see also Stresemann, Vol. 3: 179; Wright 2002: 406).

---

7. He used only moral pressure, in both private and public, arguing that the continuation of the occupation and the size of the contingents in the remaining zones were "not compatible with the spirit of Locarno" (Stresemann, Vol. 3: 116–19). It was an "anomaly" given the rapprochement transpiring between Germany and the western powers (Stresemann, Vol. 3: 143–44). "Either Locarno means peace on the western frontier or it does not have this meaning" (ADAP B1/2, No. 36). He told Briand privately, it "could not be understood why the peace between France and Germany needed to be backed by bayonets" (Stresemann, Vol. 3: 116–19).

8. In a speech, he proclaimed the significance of the fact "that the accredited representative of the French nation no longer regards the post-War policy hitherto pursued as compatible with the spirit of Europe today. This is the object for which Briand is resolved to work. He may meet with great difficulties in this struggle. But the mental wall is surmounted, and there has been much less opposition made than on many other occasions" (Stresemann, Vol. 3: 61–62).

Stresemann, however, was losing patience. The foreign minister cautioned privately in spring 1927, "Any further dilatoriness in these matters is impossible in the interest of both our foreign and internal policy. The centre-point of my foreign policy is the understanding with France, and this will be most seriously imperiled if something does not happen soon which can be taken as evidence that the French Government intends to continue it. . . . I cannot go on facing the Reichstag, when it again assembles, with vague promises that something will be done sometime" (Stresemann, Vol. 3: 149–50). He emphasized the "continuing regard which I have shown for Briand's situation" but that this "cannot go without reciprocation" (in Jacobson 1972: 116; see also Stresemann, Vol. 3: 143, 151).

The British were also growing tired of the coercive bargaining by France. Chamberlain sided with the Germans. In regards to troop reduction, he told Briand that the French had "behaved badly" and admitted that the allies were "guilty of a very ugly breach of faith" incompatible with the value creating that had prevailed (Jacobson 1972: 82). "I and all British opinion," he said to the French, believe that delaying troop reduction is "radically indefensible" (in Jacobson 1972: 82). He admitted to Stresemann that the British did not have "clean hands" (Jacobson 1972: 133) and had a "very bad conscience" (Stresemann, Vol. 3: 119–24). The German protests were "perfectly well-founded. The number of troops engaged was not justifiable" (Stresemann, Vol. 3: 119–24). At the June League Council meeting, in a "tea party" with Briand and Stresemann, he exploded, maintaining that Britain "could not acquiesce in this state of affairs. He wanted this question settled. . . . He could in no way counter the arguments put forward by the German Foreign Minister. . . . Herr Stresemann has the right to regard us in this matter as having given a common pledge to keep our express and solemn promises. It does not interest Herr Stresemann to know how many Belgian, English and French troops are still in the Rhineland; what interests him is the occupation as a whole. We must therefore meet and arrive at an agreed solution of this question" (Stresemann, Vol. 3: 168–69).

The British foreign secretary tried to broker a compromise without significant costs to either side. He urged the Germans to accept some sort of token inspection regime of the Rhineland to replace the IMCC as a face-saving device for the French that would facilitate an earlier evacuation (Jacobson 1972: 114). It would be a "very good bargain from the German point of view" if Germany permitted "a few gentlemen to kick up their heels in the Rhineland," he wrote to his colleagues (in Wright 2002: 383). Chamberlain, as a pragmatist, stressed that it would be more symbolic than substantive; this would be "nothing but a gesture" for Germany (Jacobson 1972: 133). He envisioned "giving the French the minimum that they need to satisfy their public opinion that evacuation is safe and asking nothing of the Germans either in form or substance which they could not accept with perfect equanimity and without any serious inconvenience" (Grayson 1997: 133).

But in January 1928 domestic circumstances in Germany compelled Stresemann to break the "gentlemen's agreement" to not raise the issue of the early and complete evacuation of the Rhineland until after the spring French elections (Jacobson 1972: 146). Axel von Freytagh-Loringhoven of the DNVP publicly attacked Stresemann in the Reichstag for his lack of diplomatic results, claiming it had led to a "cul-de-sac" (Wright 2002: 412; Jacobson 1972: 143). Although this opposition was hardly new, it had much more domestic political significance now because the DNVP had recently returned to the German cabinet as part of Chancellor Marx's second coalition. Stresemann had opposed the inclusion of the party, preferring some sort of arrangement with the Social Democrats who, even when in opposition, were always the most loyal supporters of his policy. As before, his calculations about party politics were based on considerations about what most favored the implementation of his realist diplomacy. But Stresemann was outvoted by others in the cabinet. Nevertheless, Stresemann was successful in his insistence that the DNVP explicitly pledge support for the Locarno treaty and his diplomatic efforts, as well as indicating their willingness to accept the concessions that might prove necessary to achieve early evacuation (Wright 2002: 395). The Marx government declaration on foreign policy described its "abandonment of the idea of revenge," replaced by a policy of "mutual understanding" (Strese-mann, Vol. 3: 114–15). Therefore, the speech by von Freytagh-Loringhoven, one of the most reactionary members of an already very conservative party, was a breach of the earlier commitment of his party.

In two public replies, Stresemann defended the gains of his policy so far and noted that the DNVP had not offered any realistic alternative. However, he also demanded for the first time publicly that the allies remove all their troops from the Rhineland. The occupation was an "anomaly"; the spirit of Locarno was not compatible with its "opposite." Alluding to Briand's famous speech at the September 1926 League Council meeting, he accused the French of exhibiting a "bit of hypocrisy." "Much has been said about discarding machine guns and cannons, but machine guns and cannons are still staring [Germany] in the face in the Rhineland," he observed. The maintenance of allied troops was a "psychological obstacle" to rapprochement. Stresemann expressed his willingness to discuss an exchange of premature withdrawal for some kind of advanced payment of reparations. But he explicitly stated that he would not agree to any "lasting measures that go beyond the Treaty of Versailles," by which he meant any French proposal of a permanent commission of inspection in the Rhineland beyond 1935, when all foreign troops were scheduled to be withdrawn. Stresemann had switched to distributive tactics, making extreme demands, drawing red lines, and using public pressure as bargaining leverage (VDR 371: 12490, 373: 12556–60; Jacobson 1972: 143–47; Wright 2002: 412; Stresemann, Vol. 3: 350). Coercive bargaining by France had induced similar tactics by Germany. Briand wrote Stresemann, "I was horrified at your speeches. . . . They stood my hair on end" (in Jacobsen 1972: 148).

In what became known as the "winter debate," the French foreign minister responded in kind with a speech before his own legislature, insisting that France needed guarantees of security and reparations before it could leave the Rhineland. Any assurance offered by Germany might not last past his government, and France needed something more permanent (Jacobson 1972: 150; Stresemann, Vol. 3: 352–54). Stresemann correctly attributed Briand's tone to his "disabilities in the Senate, and probably in the Chamber as well" (Stresemann, Vol. 3: 355). Of Briand's "personal goodwill I have no doubt," wrote the foreign minister (Stresemann, Vol. 3: 150); however, this was no longer enough to justify German moderation. The pattern continued.[9] A spirit of value claiming had replaced one of value creating.

Rather than weakening the conservatives, the spring elections in France consolidated the right. The French Socialists, the one party favoring immediate and unconditional evacuation of the Rhineland, lost seats, as did the Radical Socialists. In contrast, the rightist parties of Marin and André Maginot increased their number of seats and augmented their influence in the Union Nationale (Jacobson 1972: 226). The Radical Socialists acted as a moderating force in the cabinet but dropped out of the coalition later in the year (Jacobson 1972: 303–5). Briand stayed on as foreign minister. Knowing the domestic popularity of Briand's

9. At the League Council meeting in September 1928, the German Chancellor Hermann Müller, a Social Democrat, accused French policy of wearing a "double face": "In international negotiations the mutual confidence of States in each other is eloquently proclaimed, and mutual understanding between the nations is celebrated as an event; on the other side . . . in practice things remain as they were, and that not one of the barriers that have arisen as a result of the War has been wholly removed" (in Stresemann, Vol. 3: 395–96; see also Jacobson 1972: 195). Briand responded with what became known by the Germans as his "angry speech." Thinking that he personally had been called "two-faced," Briand launched a diatribe justifying French fears of a sudden German attack and their demand for security (Jacobson 1972: 197).

diplomatic efforts, Poincaré disingenuously endorsed his liberal diplomacy during the election campaign, going so far as to falsely claim paternity of the Thoiry scheme (Jacobson 1972: 162; Keeton 1987: 198, 232). Once the election was over, however, the declaration of government policy omitted what had become a standard reference to the spirit of Locarno and even expressed suspicions of German revisionism (Jacobson 1972: 171).

SECURITY DEPOSITS: COERCIVELY LINKING THE RHINELAND EVACUATION TO REPARATIONS

There was a simple package deal to be made between France and Germany. Germany's annual payments of reparations under the Dawes Plan, the provisional reparations deal reached in 1924, were scheduled to balloon shortly, potentially exceeding the capacity of Germany to pay. This was in the interests of neither France nor Germany, and the head of the international reparations authority, Parker Gilbert, recommended a new scheme that would permanently set the amount of reparations Germany would owe. In the meantime, France had begun the construction of the Maginot Line, the series of fortifications on its eastern border that conservatives genuinely (and incorrectly) believed would provide them a degree of permanent protection (Keeton 1987: 229, 306). The occupation of the Rhineland was therefore of decreasing value to them in terms of security, and there was an incentive to cash in on it while it still maintained value for Germany. The Rhineland was scheduled to be evacuated in 1935; every year that passed made an early evacuation less and less meaningful for Germany. France could trade premature withdrawal for a final settlement on reparations that would cover its war debts to the United States and Great Britain.

The type of diplomacy pursued by both France and Germany, however, inhibited such a solution, in stark contrast to the Locarno period. The Poincaré government employed a coercive bargaining approach. The premier proposed to use the continued occupation of the Rhineland as a bargaining chip to ensure reparations payments from Germany after the conclusion of any deal. He wrote Britain that "for the Allies, the Rhineland occupation remains the only effective insurance of reparations payments" (in Keeton 1987: 307).

Even as the occupation was declining in value due to its impending expiration and the perceived increase in French security, Poincaré, backed by his conservative colleagues in the cabinet, Tardieu and Marin, proposed that the evacuation of the Rhineland would begin only after Paris began to receive advance payments of reparations. The German debt would have to first be capitalized, commercialized, and gradually sold in the bond markets (Wright 2002: 413; Jacobson 1972: 157, 279, 301). A simple agreement on terms was not enough to begin the withdrawal; typical of a coercive bargainer, Poincaré insisted on, literally, seeing the money first. Even after the agreement went into effect, the evacuation would not proceed all at once. French troops would be gradually pulled out only if Germany continued to make its payments (ADAP B9, Nos. 139, 263; Stresemann, Vol. 3: 383–92; Jacobson 1972: 173–74, 193). By dividing up the withdrawal, France could extract more concessions from Germany.

Poincaré was transparent about his diplomatic style. He admitted to the German ambassador that security considerations no longer made a continued occupation necessary. But, under the terms of the Dawes agreement that had ended the Ruhr standoff, France no longer had the legal right to reoccupy German territory if Germany refused to pay. Therefore, France could abandon German territory only piecemeal if it were to maintain its leverage (ADAP B9, No. 139; Jacobson 1972: 173). As Stresemann described it, the occupation gave the French a "trump" that put France in a "power position." It was a valuable "deposit" (VDR 373: 12556–60). The German ambassador called it a "pawn" (Jacobson 1972: 171).

When the German ambassador asked for an evacuation of the second zone two years ahead of schedule as a demonstration of French intentions in the Locarno spirit, Poincaré refused. "The French would not understand if France, suddenly out of high heaven, made direct sacrifices to Germany," he said. "There must be an occasion." When the ambassador suggested that this might be a reward to the German people for their repudiation of the nationalists in the recent elections and the construction of a grand coalition with the SPD, the French premier replied that this "was scarcely such an occasion." "The French people demanded clearer reasons," he stated. They—meaning, of course, Poincaré—opposed "any acts of spontaneous accommodation" (ADAP B9, No. 139; Jacobson 1972: 173). Every concession has a price in coercive bargaining.

Stresemann, the realist, was disgusted with Poincaré's coercive diplomacy: "Not one of the responsible politicians in France has any real apprehension of Germany. The intention is to use the Rhineland as a bargaining point in order extract larger sums from Germany. Monsieur Poincaré, who decisively rejects the idea of Security, emphasizes the character of the Rhineland as a pledge for the fulfillment of a financial claim." It was a "very short-sighted pursuance of a hand-to-mouth policy, without any attempt to look further head" (Stresemann, Vol. 3: 42). The Germans cautioned Poincaré that he was overplaying his hand given that the evacuation was to end just a few years hence. Stresemann asserted genuinely that the incentive of Germany to maintain its financial creditworthiness would alone ensure that it paid its debts (Stresemann, Vol. 3: 383–92; ADAP B9, No. 263; Jacobson 1972: 193). But the French did not budge. In a coercive fashion, Poincaré even inflated his previous demands, asking for a permanent renunciation of any effort, even peaceful, by Germany to regain the territory of Alsace-Lorraine.

The French position was not a simple function of the structural bargaining position of France, however. French diplomacy was not endogenous to French power. This is evident in the fact that Briand had a different diplomatic style. Rather than proceeding by stages, as Poincaré envisioned, Briand advocated a total and comprehensive agreement (ADAP B9, No. 262; Stresemann, Vol. 3: 380–83; Wright 2002: 429). The French foreign minister attempted an integrative compromise. He suggested that the allies would evacuate troops from Coblenz as soon as a committee of financial experts was appointed to draw up a plan for a final financial settlement on German reparations, provided that Germany also consented to what he called a Commission of Verification and Conciliation. When experts arrived at a reparations settlement formally approved by the relevant countries, the third and final zone would be freed at once rather than over time (DBFP Series IA, Vol. 5, nos. 146, 152, 287; Jacobson 1972: 198, 233). The foreign minister disparaged his cabinet colleagues to his foreign counterparts. "The nationalists would always cry for the moon and it was better to ignore them and to search for some compromise," he said (DBFP IA, Vol. 5, No. 156). He confessed, however, that he was "compelled to take up a position in conformity with the mandate which he had from his Government." He promised that "so far as he was personally concerned, he would like to be able to meet the wishes of the German Government and he could assure the German Chancellor that he would approach the subject in the most liberal spirit" (DBFP IA, Vol. 5, No. 151).

This appears at first glance as a kind of coercive diplomatic exercise, adding an additional side payment from Germany. But the foreign minister did not believe that the commission had any real value for France, calling it a "ridiculous trifle" (Keeton 1987: 235) and a face-saving device for public opinion (Keeton 1987: 317) that would allow him to be more conciliatory on the other issues.[10] The Germans believed him (Jacobsen 1972: 299). Indeed, Poincaré placed little value on monitoring

10. Briand even said publicly, "You can never stop Germany from having a population of sixty million. And you can never stop such a country from being a great power. . . . You can try in vain anything you want" (in Keeton 1987: 225–26). This made inspection unrealistic. "A nation of sixty millions cannot be controlled permanently and with safety" (Stresemann, Vol. 3: 72).

and, therefore, did not want to expend any bargaining leverage to get it (Jacobson 1972: 156, 305). Briand went out of his way to make the body as inoffensive as possible to Germany. It was an "entirely new departure" (DBFP IA, Vol. 5, No. 287), different from previous "exaggerated" demands by the allies (ADAP B10, No. 208). The name was softened so that it did not mention *investigation*. It need not be resident in the Rhineland. Its representatives would be civilian in character and include a German delegate. It needed only to be permanent and to possess the power to conduct immediate inspections without German permission (DBFP IA, Vol. 5, Nos. 146, 156; ADAP B10, No. 199; Jacobson 1972: 295–97).

The British again sought to broker a pragmatic compromise by pressuring both sides. They continued to urge the Germans to accept a token verification commission (DBFP IA, Vol. 5, No. 158; ADAP B10, No. 208). Three to five representatives would suffice, they thought (ADAP B10, No. 188). Chamberlain suggested that the Germans should present the ideas as having been being suggested by Germany itself so as not to be regarded domestically as "an indignity put upon them by us" (DBFP IA, Vol. 5, No. 287). In bilateral meetings, however, the British simultaneously pushed the French to evacuate the second zone as a gesture, without any compensation from Germany (DBFP IA, Vol. 5, No. 158). Baron Cushendun, sitting in for an ailing Chamberlain, explained that "so far as the second zone was concerned the period was so nearly mature for its evacuation that it was really of very little bargaining value." Therefore, it was best used as an object of goodwill, conceded prior to formal negotiations so as to "create a better atmosphere" (DBFP IA, Vol. 5, No. 152). In British eyes, the French were attempting to squeeze too much out of Germany through their coercive diplomacy, making an agreement more difficult.

When Briand suggested his compromise, the Germans held firm as part of their shift to distributive tactics. Reestablishing territorial integrity had been the very point of Stresemann's diplomatic initiatives, and the pressure on the foreign minister had only increased. The leader of the Center Party, a reliable supporter of Stresemann's diplomacy in the past both in the Reichstag and in the cabinet, had publicly criticized the foreign minister's lack of results in the parliament, referring to the "undeniable failure of German foreign policy" (in Jacobson 1972: 229, see also 232; Wright 2002: 435; ADAP B10, Nos. 188, 199). This was the first defection of Stresemann's center and center-left support base. In his private correspondence, the foreign minister was very black. The occupation was "driving everybody back to the German Nationalists. The ground here is slipping away under my feet," he wrote. Locarno was a thing of the past, he lamented (in Jacobson 1972: 249–50).

Therefore, the foreign minister argued that it was inconsistent with the whole purpose of his policy of understanding, of no value to France, and impossible for the German government to accept a verification commission (ADAP B10, Nos. 188, 199). While in Geneva, Chancellor Hermann Müller officially inquired of his cabinet about the French proposal. The German ministers would consider a commission only under the conditions that it be terminated in 1935 (the year the occupation was set to end), restricted to the occupied zones (rather than the entire demilitarized zone), and exchanged for the complete removal of troops (Jacobson 1972: 197–98; DBFP IA, Vol. 5, No. 161). The Center Party threatened to leave the cabinet under any other terms (Jacobson 1972: 297).

In the face of French coercive bargaining, Stresemann instead backed the strategy laid out in a *Denkschrift* ("thought piece") by his state secretary, Carl von Schubert. The spirit of Locarno gave France a "covering cloak," allowing it to perpetuate the occupation without any public outcry by Germany, thereby removing from Germany the leverage it might gain by mobilizing sympathetic world opinion. Germany should demand a complete evacuation without any concessions in the area of reparations (Jacobson 1972: 164–68, 175–83; ADAP B10: 609–14; Wright 2002: 436). The government should also try to maintain an independence between the two questions because reparations were a much more complicated issue that involved other powers, most notably the United States, and would likely drag on, allowing the French to hold the Rhineland hostage indefinitely. In the face of these new circumstances brought about by a shift in French diplomatic style, Germany adjusted in a pragmatic fashion.

The German government recognized that France would never consent to this. The issues were de facto connected, but making such a positional commitment would put Germany in a stronger bargaining position when the two issues did become linked. Under no circumstances, however, would Germany commit to a final reparation settlement independent of a deal on the Rhineland (Jacobson 1972: 164–68, 175–83). The Germans also inflated their demands, insisting on a final settlement on the status of the Saar as part of any package (Stresemann, Vol. 3: 580; ADAP B12, No. 146; ADAP B10, Nos. 56, 208; Jacobson 1972: 171, 279, 292; DBFP IA, Vol. 5, No. 287). These were distributive tactics of a type that the German government had generally not engaged in under Stresemann because integrative negotiation was thought to be more fruitful. The Germans turned the tables on the French. The British noted the shift and complained that to separate reparations and evacuation was simply "not within the bounds of practical politics" (DBFP IA, Vol. 5, No. 151).

At meetings in Geneva in September 1928 and Lugano in December 1928, the British, French, and Germans discussed the issues of reparations and evacuation. Stresemann turned down a partial deal that would make an evacuation contingent on progress on reparations agreements, which could easily break down and leave the French with too much leverage (ADAP B10, No. 208). The Germans consistently opposed the linking of the two questions and denigrated the value of the occupation for France, never yielding (DBFP IA, Vol. 5, Nos. 149, 161). Just as insistently, the French emphasized "it would be useless to approach the problem from the point of view of demanding the immediate evacuation of the occupied territory without offering some substantial *quid pro quo*," as Briand explained it (DBFP IA, Vol. 5, No. 146). The most that the three powers could agree on in September 1928 was a set of technically separate and parallel negotiations on reparations, early evacuation, and a monitoring commission for the Rhineland. The first would be based on the report of a committee of experts (Jacobson 1972: 195–200; DBFP IA, Vol. 5, No. 161). This solution allowed the Germans to publicly claim that the issues were not linked and that evacuation could and should proceed without a prior agreement on reparations (Jacobson 1972: 201, 225). The French could simultaneously tell their home audience that there was a de facto link (Jacobson 1972: 202, 221, 227; Wright 2002: 433).

Briand did promise that the evacuation would begin immediately upon the convocation of the committee of experts (known as the Young Committee) and that negotiations on the final termination date of the occupation would continue even if financial discussions came to a standstill or failed (Jacobson 1972: 233). These commitments, however, were overturned by his more conservative colleagues, who favored coercive diplomacy. Even after the experts finished their deliberations, French troops stayed put. Holding the occupation issue hostage, Poincaré insisted that discussions on evacuation would begin only when the Young Plan was finalized, with withdrawal beginning after the German debt was successfully commercialized and sold in the private market (Jacobson 1972: 240). It was not until much later, in August 1929, that the powers convened in The Hague to negotiate a final liquidation of the war.

THE BRITISH TURN: LABOUR AND THE FRENCH CONSERVATIVES

In the interim, however, there was a major change in British domestic politics; another Labour government took power in May 1929. Although Labour still did not gain an absolute majority and governed again only as a minority with Liberal support, the election was the best result for the left ever and made Labour the largest party in Parliament for the first time in its history (Jacobson 1972: 280). It was a short-lived administration, governing for only twenty-seven months. But this gave it enough time to decisively influence Franco-German relations.

[181]

The Labour government was more ideologically committed to better treatment of Germany. Even before the end of the war, the party had condemned the harsh peace terms being contemplated and the exclusion of Germany from the League. It blamed the autocratic German leaders for the war rather than the German people and complained bitterly that the latter were paying too high a price for the sins of their officials. Labour objected to the eastern territorial settlement, which violated the German people's right to self-determination by placing German minorities in other countries, and the exploitative excision of valuable economic regions such as Silesia and the Saar (Labour Party 1919; also Winkler 1994: chap. 2). It was not that the party was "pro-German." Rather, it objected to the immorality of the peace settlement and its one-sided and, therefore, inegalitarian nature (Naylor 1969: 5). The Labour Party had a "tradition of sympathy for post-Versailles Germany, deriving from a characteristic concern for the underdog and from a rejection of the 'war guilt' thesis," writes David Carlton (1970: 34).

Before the election, Labour had castigated the Conservatives in the Commons for their European policy (Jacobson 1972: 209, 211, 214). In its manifesto, the party promised the "immediate and unconditional withdrawal of all foreign troops from the Rhineland, the continued occupation of which is indefensible in view of the fact that Germany has fulfilled her obligations under the Treaty of Versailles, that she is a member of the League of Nations, and that she is a signatory" of the Locarno and Kellogg-Briand treaties outlawing war (Labour Party 1928; also Jacobson 1972: 210, 242, 281–83). Germany had a "right" to the evacuation due to its good behavior (Jacobson 1972: 282). The French were not reciprocating German concessions.

The party had declared itself, even before the war ended, against the coercive use of the occupation, derisively calling it "the use of human beings as 'pawns'" (Labour Party 1919). France was, therefore, generally regarded by Labour Party members as perpetuating an unjust status quo. This led to a change in foreign policy goals. Arthur Henderson, now foreign secretary, told his permanent undersecretary that there could be "too much continuity in foreign policy" (Carlton 1970: 21). He had the party manifesto, *Labour and the Nation*, distributed to senior career bureaucrats, along with a note to make foreign policy consistent with it (Jacobson 1972: 282–83; Winkler 1994: 322).

The cabinet subsequently approved in July a decision that Britain would evacuate the Rhineland unilaterally, with a private deadline of Christmas that year. Henderson informed the French that "the examination of the problem of how to bring about the total evacuation of the Rhineland at the earliest possible date can no longer be delayed or made dependent on the settlement of contentious issues not immediately arising out of it" (DBFP IA, Vol. 5, No. 189; see also No. 300). The Germans were, of course, delighted with this prospect because it would increase pressure on the French to evacuate alongside their allies and reduce the French ability to use the occupation as leverage in financial negotiations (DBFP IA, Vol. 5, No. 300). The leftist British government also stated that the commission on verification "is in no way indispensable in view of the machinery already provided for by the League of Nations and by the Treaty of Locarno" and refused to support France if it insisted on any kind of inspection regime lasting past 1935 (DBFP IA, Vol. 5I, No. 189). The British had turned the tables on the French.

HOSTAGES IN THE HAGUE: NEGOTIATIONS ON REPARATIONS AND THE RHINELAND

At the Hague conference, faced with German intransigence and lacking British support, the French conceded on the commission issue, which, of course, Briand had never thought important. There would be no permanent inspection of the Rhineland. Instead, Briand proposed and the Germans accepted that the arbitration procedures set up in the Locarno treaty also be given the task of resolving disputes over any alleged infraction of German obligations on disarmament and demilitarization of the Rhineland (Jacobson 1972: 332; ADAP B12, Nos. 155, 178, 197; DBFP IA, Vol. 6, No. 326). But, although the British helped to put this issue to rest, their coercive bargaining on the issue of reparations threatened to wreck the conference. Chancellor of the Exchequer Philip Snowden revisited the numbers of the Young Plan, which were supposed to serve as the basis for the negotiation of the financial settlement. Snowden objected to the distribution of the total reparations receipts, particular the percentage of "unprotected" annuities that Britain would receive compared to France. These were the financial payments that the German government could not suspend even in the case of a crisis of the mark and capital flight out of Germany.

The British finance minister had received the endorsement of the cabinet prior to the conference to try to gain a larger share of the reparations pie. If he encountered resistance, however, he was obliged to report back to the cabinet. It would then advise him about the "degree of rigidity" to be taken, that is how much coercive bargaining to engage in. Snowden disobeyed these guidelines (Carlton 1970: 39). He was rebuked by James Ramsay MacDonald, the prime minister, in a telegram to the delegation: "I am relying . . . on you before break occurs to get into touch with me and perhaps we could arrange to meet before any action for adjournment is taken or if you prefer that one of you should meet me in London" (in

[183]

Carlton 1970: 44). But the message was mistakenly sent nonsecretly, and the entire conference learned of its content. This forced the prime minister to transmit a statement unequivocally backing the finance minister to restore his standing and credibility at the conference, making it subsequently impossible to rein him in (Carlton 1970: 45).

For his coercive bargaining, Snowden earned the acclaim of the permanent foreign office bureaucrats who accompanied him to The Hague. Maurice Hankey wrote, "The Chancellor the Exchequer is amazing. Never for one moment has he budged from his 100% demand, in public, in meetings with his colleagues, in private or (I ask myself) to himself! . . . One cannot but admire such fortitude, with all the great politicians in Europe. . . . If you were to ask me what the Chancellor would take, frankly I could not tell you—but I think it would be difficult to refuse 75% of our demand, if we ever got such an offer" (in Carlton 1970: 48). Not surprisingly, however, his Labour colleagues were upset at him for departing from their preferred style of reasoned dialogue. Lord Parmoor, now Lord President of the Council, threatened to resign. Beatrice Webb, a cabinet member, complained that the finance minister approached diplomacy like a conservative. Snowden was "playing up to the vulgar international individualism of Chamberlain, the Jingo Press—with the object of superseding J.R.M. [James Ramsay MacDonald]" (Carlton 1970: 45).

Henderson objected to coercive bargaining because it imperiled a value creating deal on the occupation and reparations. As Hugh Dalton, his aide, later explained, "a few millions are dust in the balance, compared with the gains of the early and complete evacuation which will also certainly follow swiftly on a general acceptance of the Young Plan" (Carlton 1970: 40, see also 48). Memoranda from the previous summer indicate that Henderson foresaw such a problem far in advance. He cautioned that if the Hague conference failed due to the British position on reparations, the British "would find themselves isolated and held up in the United States as the Powers who for petty and selfish financial motives had sacrificed the interests of Europe and kept alive the discredited system whereby Europe is still divided into the two camps of victors and vanquished" (DBFP IA, Vol. 6, No. 182). In other words, he thought Labour should pursue diplomacy consistent with its prosocial motivation, promoting joint gains through consideration of others' interests as well as those of Britain. The "financial reasons for such a rejection must be absolutely overwhelming to justify a course fraught with so many dangers to the future success of Great Britain's foreign policy of reconciliation and co-operation" (DBFP IA, Vol. 6, No. 182).

It is unclear why Snowden took such a line. Scholars have pointed to the difficult financial circumstances in Britain, in particular the unemployment level and the need for a minority government to attract the

[184]

votes of other parties. Reparations agreements also have distributive implications at home in a way that security arrangements do not. And, of course, Snowden's bureaucratic interest was in protecting the British budget, not British diplomatic standing. All these factors probably mattered. Nevertheless, it does appear that the chancellor was the exception to the rule. "No other incident of this sort marred the government's behavior," writes Michael Gordon (1969: 60). And it speaks for the psychological argument that the main supporters of the finance minister's negotiating style were outside the Labour government—the right-wing press and Conservatives (Carlton 1970: 51).

Snowden's coercive diplomatic style led to a prolonged deadlock with France. If Britain were to claw back a greater share of reparations receipts, the difference would have to mostly come out of the share of France. As a consequence, Briand stalled negotiations in the political committee dealing with the evacuation question. To apply leverage, the French foreign minister would not even begin discussions on the potential terms of a deal, such as a beginning date for the withdrawal of French forces (ADAP B12, Nos. 155, 161; Jacobson 1972: 316; DBFP IA, Vol. 6, No. 313). This stands in sharp contrast to the way that diplomacy at Locarno proceeded, in which issues were dealt with sequentially rather than being held in abeyance before agreements on others and positions were openly and honestly revealed. Had the spirit of Locarno prevailed, Briand would have explored the basis of one element of the package deal, even while maintaining that all was contingent on agreements on all the issues on the table. This contrast in diplomatic style reflects the different diplomatic style of the cabinets Briand represented at the two conferences. The foreign minister stressed that he was now in charge of the conservative coalition that Poincaré had recently left behind when he resigned for health reasons. Most of the ministers are "comparable to Graf Westarp," he said, in an allusion to the ultra-conservative German politician and supporter of coercive diplomacy (ADAP B12, No. 168).

Stresemann objected to the French line, reiterating at the conference the German view that the two issues were not, in fact, linked and that there was no reason why division over financial questions should impact progress on the political ones (ADAP B12, No. 158; DBFP IA, Vol. 6, No. 313). He declared this publicly to apply pressure (Stresemann, Vol. 3: 580–82). Stresemann threatened not to recommend any financial deal to his cabinet if the parties at the conference had not set a definitive end date for the occupation (ADAP B12, Nos. 155, 161, 168, 178; DBFP IA, Vol. 6, No. 316). With no reparation deal in place to induce the French to negotiate, however, the Germans had little leverage.

It was only that this point, in the face of the lack of cooperation by France, that Henderson dropped his bombshell. Representing Britain on the political committee dealing with the occupation question, he tried to coerce the French by announcing British plans to withdraw all their forces, regardless of the outcome of the reparation negotiations. The removal of troops would begin in mid-September, and all soldiers would be home before Christmas (ADAP B12, Nos. 157, 158; DBFP IA, Vol. 6, No. 316). Although military leaders had stressed to him that it would take months to even begin the evacuation, Henderson instructed them that the pull out was to commence in just a few weeks (ADAP B12, No. 167).

It is unclear whether this shift reflects a change in foreign policy substance or diplomatic style. As mentioned earlier, Labour did make better treatment of Germany a foreign policy goal. Despite this, the Labour government announced its policy at the conference only in response to French coercive bargaining, suggesting that the persistent French coercive bargaining had induced the same style on the part of the British, as expected by my theory. Reasoned dialogue is not based on unrequited concessions. Coercive bargaining induces coercive bargaining. In any case, given British leverage, the move helped unlink the two issues to some extent. The prospect of being left isolated in the Rhineland induced Briand to agree to begin the French withdrawal of the second zone alongside the British, irrespective of progress on reparations (Winkler 1994: 235).

The French still intended to save the final zone until after the ratification and implementation by all parties of a financial agreement, should it ever be concluded. And Briand still refused to name an end date for the occupation, leading Stresemann to suspect that the French would use the continued occupation as insurance against German nonpayment (ADAP B12, Nos. 157, 168, 178). Disingenuously, Briand stressed the logistical difficulties posed by moving troops in the winter (ADAP B12, Nos. 155, 196). More accurately, he noted that the French military wanted to buy time to finish the Maginot Line (ADAP B12, No. 161). The German foreign minister leaked the divisions between the allies to increase the public pressure on the French. This behavior stood in contrast to his previous preference for quiet and private diplomacy during the Locarno period (Jacobson 1972: 319).

France and Germany, now finally negotiating, were still engaged in value claiming. Two weeks into the conference, the French foreign minister finally proposed a date for the completion of the evacuation— October 1930. Stresemann deemed this unacceptable and countered with April 1, 1930 (ADAP B12, No. 188). Briand argued that he would be sacked if he accepted such an early date because it contradicted the statement he had made before parliament. He warned that he would be replaced by a thoroughly nationalistic and conservative government

[186]

(ADAP B12, No. 196; also Jacobson 1972: 327). Stresemann gave the same warning about what would happen in Germany if he conceded—the right would take over, undermining any efforts at Franco-German reconciliation (ADAP B12, No. 158). Rejecting the offer, he threatened to resign if Briand stayed firm (ADAP B12, No. 191). The use of threats and counterthreats was new for the two statesmen, who had never before engaged in such face-to-face value claiming. In a game of chicken, the two stubbornly held out for days before finally accepting June 30, 1930, as the termination date for the occupation, five years ahead of schedule.

The French and Germans had not reached a compromise through the open sharing of their positions and an exchange of benefits based on a desire for a mutually beneficial outcome. France and Germany found success at The Hague despite their negotiating styles, not because of them. At several points, it seemed that the entire set of negotiations would collapse. Unlike Locarno, The Hague was a combative conference. Had it not been for the Labour government's coercion of France, inducing it to move in the direction of Germany on the issue of the evacuation, the conference might very well have ended in failure. By shrinking the bargaining space of the French and creating at least the prospect of success, the British created the potential for a package deal. Indeed, without this diplomatic move, the two might otherwise have been so far apart that even a successful reparations deal would not have been enough incentive to settle the evacuation of the Rhineland.

Still the lowest-common-denominator bargaining between France and Germany meant that the final terms favored the more powerful French in a way that had not been true at Locarno. When value claiming negotiation prevails, deals tend to either fall through or reflect the distribution of power. Germany was forced to make some final financial concessions on reparations to bridge the gap between France and Britain. By reworking the timing of the payments, the Germans covered the difference between the final French and British positions (Carlton 1970: 50). The settlement on the occupation was accompanied by a final financial agreement in which the British clawed back 83 percent of the amount Snowden had demanded (Carlton 1970: 49), largely at the expense of Germany.

[8]

Additional Value

The Rise and Fall of the Israeli-Palestinian Peace Process

In this chapter, I extend the analysis by telling the story of two groups attempting to transcend what was largely perceived as an intractable conflict. The weaker group, having lost considerable territory through ill-advised military action and now occupied by the stronger group, made gestures toward peace, including the recognition of lost lands and a promise to end violent confrontation. Even though, in many ways, the weaker side had no other options due to its structural position, the moves toward conciliation were initiated by pragmatists in the group against the strident opposition of extremists who preferred coercive methods to force the stronger group out. A third group, with stakes in the peace and stability of the region and historical ties to the stronger group, attempted the role of honest broker, trying to lead the two sides toward compromise by institutionalizing a process of diplomatic exchange. Although helpful, the process yielded success only when a prosocially minded leftist government of the stronger group, instead of exploiting its leverage, engaged in a diplomatic process of openly and honestly exchanging information. A pragmatic-prosocial combination generated a value-creating spirit that yielded a win-win outcome for both sides in which the cessation of hostilities was exchanged for the promise of the gradual return of territorial sovereignty. The weaker side had parlayed a very weak hand into long-sought-after goals. A Nobel Prize was awarded.

Yet, even though all sides declared that a new spirit had emerged, the two groups found it difficult to consolidate their gains through future agreements when a rightist party returned to power in the stronger group. Even though its conception of the national interest was increasingly similar to that of the left, it used a different diplomatic style, coercive bargaining, that contributed to a value claiming dynamic between the two groups. Mutual recriminations and increasingly violent actions by both sides sidetracked the prospect of permanent peace for over a decade.

Readers might believe that they have already heard this story and in some ways they have. But it was largely repeated in a different part of the world decades later. There are remarkable parallels between the interwar relations of the European powers and the relations of the Israelis and Palestinians in recent decades that show the broader applicability of my theory. In this chapter, I apply the theory advanced in previous chapters to this more contemporary case, the rise and fall of the peace process. As was true in 1920s Europe, key events in Israeli-Palestinian relations cannot be understood solely in terms of the distribution of power and interests. In a different time and in a different part of the world, diplomacy was necessary to achieve the negotiation successes and, perhaps, even sufficient to bring about the failures.

In the late 1980s, the Palestinian Liberation Organization (PLO), the national movement for the Palestinian people that had engaged in terrorist and other military activities against the Israelis for decades, took tentative steps toward reaching a rapprochement with Israel. Pragmatists in the group succeeded in having it endorse a diplomatic settlement with Israel to form a Palestinian state located in territories taken by the Israelis in the 1967 war: the West Bank of the Jordan River, including East Jerusalem, and the Gaza Strip on the Mediterranean Sea bordering Egypt. Land would be traded for peace, as long called for by UN Resolution 242. The organization formally renounced the use of violence and gave up its claim to the rest of Mandatory Palestine, the territory carved out of the Ottoman Empire and administered by the British after World War I. This amounted to the acceptance of the existence of Israel on the land for which it fought a coalition of Arab states in 1948, a conflict that Israelis refer to as the War of Independence and Palestinians call Al-Nakbar ("the catastrophe"), which led to the exodus of hundreds of thousands of Palestinian refugees.

Like Stresemann, these pragmatists were willing to let go of their claims to former lands and renounce the use of aggression in the hopes that such moves would end the occupation. The PLO was bankrupt, militarily overmatched, and increasingly without international allies, yet only the pragmatists had the epistemic motivation that allowed the admission of these facts. Just as Germany, destitute and occupied after World War I, was nevertheless conflicted over the style of diplomacy to pursue after its military loss, so too were the Palestinians. Structure was not determinant.

Sensing an opportunity to create greater stability in the Middle East, an area of key strategic concern, the United States tried to bring the

Palestinians and Israelis together at the negotiating table. Just as the British had valued peace on the continent and had been willing to push their French allies to make concessions, so did the Americans approach the Middle East. Despite its greater strategic and affective ties with Israel, the George H. W. Bush administration (and later the Bill Clinton administration) took on the role of honest broker between both sides, urging both toward compromise. James Baker, the pragmatic secretary of state of the first Bush administration, wanted to institutionalize a process of diplomatic interaction between the two sides, just as Chamberlain had tried to do between France and Germany.

Yet, as was the case in 1920s France, real progress occurred only after the election in Israel of a leftist government, led by the Labor Party, which replaced the Yitzhak Shamir government, led by the rightist Likud Party, in 1992. A diplomatic back channel in Norway with PLO pragmatists led to the drafting of the Declaration of Principles, in which the two sides agreed to recognize one another, curb violence, and begin a gradual transfer of autonomy to the territories taken by Israel in 1967. Pragmatic statecraft was necessary on the Palestinian side. Instead of insisting, as they historically had, on a commitment to full Israeli evacuation all at once, they agreed as Stresemann had to accept a concession—the Israeli surrender of Gaza—as the first step in a long-term process toward returning the West Bank to Palestinian control. For their part, the prosocial Israelis, as the prosocial French had done for the pragmatic Germans, rewarded the Palestinians for their shift in diplomatic style. Rather than exploiting the greater leverage of Israel, the Labor government granted the Palestinians a foothold in the West Bank at the onset of the process and committed to a reasoned dialogue about a number of issues that Israel had previously refused to discuss, such as the right of return and the establishment of a Palestinian capital in East Jerusalem.

A Palestinian-Israeli agreement in the early 1990s was as unlikely as a Franco-German rapprochement in the 1920s. This was a hard case for diplomacy, one of the most intractable conflicts in recent history (Wanis-St. John 2011: 1–2). Even one of the greatest Israeli "doves," Shimon Peres, writes that at the time it "had become effectively impossible to conceive of borderlines that could be acceptable to a solid majority of Israeli opinion, let alone the Palestinians. That underlying confusion made the prospects of a negotiated settlement appear increasingly remote" (1995: 278). Ron Pundak, an academic who helped initiate the back channel in Oslo, later reminisced that the "baleful history between Israelis and Palestinians represents an almost insurmountable obstacle for conventional negotiations, taking as a point of departure the existing imbalance of power between the occupier and the occupied that impeded conventional negotiations" (2001: 32–33).

Despite these obstacles, a new "spirit of Oslo" facilitated over the next few years the establishment of a Palestinian Authority with autonomy over most of the major population centers in the West Bank, gains that persist today. The victory was particularly sweet for the PLO, which, like interwar Germany, redirected the political momentum and completely revived its sagging fortunes despite its lack of bargaining strength. The two sides worked toward these ends even in the face of suicide terrorism by Palestinian religious extremists against Israeli civilians and a brutal crackdown by Israeli security forces that negatively impacted the lives of ordinary Palestinians in a dramatic way.

Then, just as the return of Poincaré and the right to power in France interrupted the new negotiating dynamic that had emerged with Germany in 1926, the election of a Likud government in 1996 under Benjamin Netanyahu put the peace process on hold. Even though its conception of foreign policy goals demonstrated increasing convergence with those of the Israeli left, the Likud government used a diplomatic style of coercive bargaining. The prime minister insisted that the Palestinians take the first steps to push the peace process forward. Netanyahu sought to increase Israeli leverage over the territorial dimension of a final status agreement through the expansion of Israeli settlement activity in the West Bank, including in the very sensitive area of Jerusalem. Progress in the peace process was contingent on the spirit of negotiations that prevailed among the parties, not just on the foreign policy interests of the two sides. The peace process is a process, one that is contingent on the behavior of multiple parties, and style matters just as much as substance.

A last gasp at settling all the remaining issues on the table began under the leadership of Ehud Barak, who led a Labor government to Camp David in 2000 in the hopes of achieving a final status agreement with the Palestinians. Yet, as was the case at the Hague Conference of 1929, the Camp David Summit was marked by a spirit of value claiming, given the combination of coercive bargaining by the two sides. Barak's behavior appears to be something of an anomaly for the analysis presented in this book, yet his combination of coercive bargaining, on the one hand, and a greater willingness to compromise, on the other, makes sense given the political complexion of his government, which also included a number right-wing parties. In any case, the character of the interactions among the parties at the conference made it harder for the two sides to identify a zone of possible agreement between the two sides, and talks broke down.

The findings of this chapter must be regarded as more tentative than those of the previous chapters. Unlike for 1920s Europe, there is a dearth of primary documents available, leading me to rely more extensively on secondary sources and memoirs of the key participants. This makes it difficult to definitively establish the diplomatic styles used because the bottom lines of the various sides are sometimes very cloudy. For instance, it still cannot be determined whether there was a deal at Camp David that both sides preferred to the status quo.

This lack of documentation is particularly true of the Palestinian side, so my assessment of Israeli behavior stands on firmer evidentiary ground. Unlike Israel, the PLO and the Palestinian Authority are not transparent democracies. And for most of the period under study, both organizations were led by the enigmatic figure of Yasser Arafat, who maintained control by playing his high-ranking aides against each other. He empowered multiple negotiating teams, often with conflicting instructions, resulting in a Byzantine labyrinth that makes systematic analysis very difficult. Because the PLO and Palestinian Authority lacked a coherent ideological space and party structure akin to mature democracies, it is also impossible to identify those indirect manifestations of epistemic and social motivation among the Palestinian elites that would make us more confident in our measurement, separate from behavior.[1] For all these reasons, critics might rightly call this analysis Israeli-centric in its focus, if not its sympathies. Nevertheless, a strong case can be made that diplomatic styles are a necessary component of any explanation of the initiation, the successes and failures, and the collapse of the peace process.

PALESTINIAN PRAGMATISTS: ACCEPTING LAND FOR PEACE

Without a fundamental change in the goals of the PLO, there was no possibility of a diplomatic agreement, much less a lasting peace, with Israel. It was only in 1988, at the PLO leadership conference in Algiers, that the organization endorsed the principle of "land for peace" and a two-state solution to the conflict. The organization also condemned the use of terrorism in service of this goal; an agreement should be reached through diplomatic means (Meital 2006: 33; Rasler 2000; Segev 1998: 89). Prior to that point, the official position of the PLO was that its goal was the liberation of all of Mandatory Palestine. Because this territory included all existing Israeli territory, this goal amounted to a call for the elimination of a Jewish national home. Although the "land for peace"

---

1. There were also multiple external influences, such as the neighboring Arab countries of Egypt, Jordan, and Syria, whose diplomacy and foreign policies would be necessary for any complete account, but which I do not deal with here.

formula would require Israel to leave the West Bank and Gaza, the Palestinian acceptance of this principle as the basis for agreement amounted, in their eyes, to a significant concession—a state constituting only 22 percent of what they regarded as rightfully Palestinian territory. The new policy was tantamount to a recognition of the right of Israel to exist, a revision of the 1968 PLO Covenant (Meital 2006: 33; Segev 1998: 89). The move strongly parallels the initiative of the German realists in 1925 in which Stresemann offered France a nonaggression pact and simultaneously conceded that Germany had lost the territory of Alsace-Lorraine.

The new positions were pushed by PLO groups with all the characteristics of pragmatic realists, in particular a high level of epistemic motivation relative to their more rejectionist colleagues. In addition to purely egoistic considerations, they stressed the importance of prioritizing vital interests over peripheral considerations and the need to make painful trade-offs; self-consciously adopted an objective and unemotional appraisal of their environment, including the interests of other parties; and emphasized the necessity of thinking in terms of steps toward a long-term goal.

These pragmatists actively tried to understand the Israeli position and complained of the refusal of their peers to do so. In his memoirs, Mahmoud Abbas, the future successor to Arafat as Palestinian president and perhaps the most important Palestinian leader other than the chairman of the PLO during this period (also known by his *nom de guerre*, Abu Mazen), writes of his colleagues, "I discovered that none of them [members of Palestinian National Council, PNC] knew what they were talking about, that their knowledge of Israel was limited to the simple fact that it was the enemy against whom continuous war should be waged" (1995: 14). Ahmed Qurie (also known by his *nom de guerre*, Abu Ala), who later became prime minister of the Palestinian Authority, complained of Palestinians' cognitive closure "The majority of Palestinian leaders and opinion-makers adhered nevertheless to their old slogans, maintaining rigid positions which were based on confusion between politics and ideology" (2006: 35). He writes, "There was no intellectual dialogue and no attempt to understand" (Qurie 2006: 8). Abbas writes, "Our quarrel is with those who see the world from their own perspective and perceive history through their inherited dogmas" (1995: 39).

Abbas had some time before set out to better understand the Israeli position and to establish contact with more sympathetic Israelis, making him suspect in the eyes of many Palestinians (1995: 14).[2] By learning

---

2. "Foolishly, knowing nothing of the enemy was turned into a virtue, as if willful ignorance would somehow reduce his potency. Reading material about Israel was interpreted as evidence of Zionist tendencies," said Abbas (in Beilin 1999: 168).

about Israel, Qurie explains, the pragmatists "understood better than ever before Israel's hyper-sensitivity to the security issues which it held sacrosanct. We were ready to respond more positively to the internal fears with which Israel was obsessed" (2006: 75). This contrasted with the rejectionist view in which (in Abbas's words) "Israel was thought of as all-powerful, as the source of the disaster which had befallen the Palestinian people, as the Devil," (in Beilin 1999: 168).

Abbas was hardly sentimental or genuinely empathetic toward Israel. He and others had a proself motivation and based their position "on the basis of realities." The acceptance of "land for peace" "emanated basically from Arab impotence and the inability of Palestinians to liberate their homeland single-handedly," not a genuine sympathy or understanding of the Jewish position (Abbas 1995: 12). He did not complain that his compatriots did not commiserate with the Israeli plight, only that the "slogan, 'Know Thine Enemy' . . . was not acted upon" (Abbas 1995: 12). The empathy of the pragmatists was instrumental. Abbas writes of how he "let my views on how to deal with enemies infiltrate and to suggest ways of attaining our goal" (1995: 14). His position was realist, not liberal.

The Palestinian pragmatists also were not wide-eyed idealists. Although they were pessimistic about the chances for diplomacy to bear fruit, they did not let their beliefs prevent them from trying, the essence of epistemic motivation. "Pessimistically, we supposed that [deadlock] would be the most probable result," remembers Qurie (2006: 72). He notes that he "was gratified in theory that I might be able to initiate some kind of useful contact, but frankly I had no desire in practice to follow the idea through." He had actually never met an Israeli in person. Yet Qurie did not let this deter him: "I later learned the lesson that it was possible to reach peace and to cooperate, even with one's enemies" (2006: 41).

The pragmatist position was based on a careful cost-benefit calculation that the Palestinians would gain more through diplomacy than through force. Qurie writes, "We knew that many people in Israel had begun to feel, today perhaps more than ever before, that the cost of continuous confrontation with the Palestinians was too high. Palestinian public opinion had begun to show an inclination to accept a compromise based on the 4 June 1967 frontier lines, with a willingness to accept the coexistence of the two peoples. . . . An intensified and bloody confrontation would only inflict more pain on both sides" (2006: 73). This conclusion was not based on a principled opposition to violence, something made obvious by previous PLO actions. As a pragmatist, Abbas and others did not rely on only one method but adjusted to the circumstances. "I did not scorn the gun," he writes, but realized that there were other options (1995: 14). The means of coercive leverage, such as piggybacking on the spontaneous

1987 uprising in the territories, were declining in utility. The intifada (literally, the "shaking off") "had already outlived its purpose." Following reprisals by Israel, the "negative effects . . . began to outweigh the Intifada's benefits" (Abbas 1995: 35). There was simply not a military path to victory. "Experience has taught us that our continued refusal to recognize the existence of Israel will not bring us the freedom we seek," Qurie explained later (2006: 148).

As was the case with Stresemann's diplomacy, the new position of the PLO might be seen as an inevitable surrendering to realities, the recognition of the overwhelming disparity in power between the Palestinians and the Israelis and the impossibility of achieving the overly ambitious aims of the PLO. But, just as with interwar Germany, such a crude structural account misses the crucial point that only a certain moderate faction of the PLO was willing to admit such hard truths. Institutional changes within the PLO as well as the disastrous experience of the Lebanon War in 1982, in which the PLO was expelled by Israel, empowered this group within the leadership and allowed this change in the direction of the PLO (Rasler 2000; Qurie 2006: 75). Abbas writes that it "was . . . an honest and courageous view, which recognized the international climate, the limitations of the Arabs on the one hand and Israel's strength on the other" (1995: 12). Like the pragmatists discussed in previous chapters, these Palestinians saw the necessity of making painful concessions for long-term gains. There were plenty of members of the PLO, not to mention Islamicist groups, who vigorously opposed this path, often violently. Abbas confronted his colleagues who advocated the exclusive use of coercive means, daring a Palestinian compatriot, "Are you prepared to think with me without being restricted by 'red lines' and worrying about what we regard as forbidden?" (1995: 21).

The greater epistemic motivation of the pragmatists allowed them to more objectively realize their increasingly weaker position. Qurie claims that the Palestinians needed to "admit frankly to ourselves that our position was in reality infinitely worse than that of Israel" (2006: 74). His faction was "more flexible and receptive to the profound regional and international challenges which were under way, all of which had their effect on the situation of the Palestinians" (2006: 12, see also 35). The end of the Cold War deprived the PLO of its long-standing patron, the Soviet Union, precipitating a financial crisis. And the organization foolishly backed Saddam Hussein during the first Gulf War, putting it on the wrong side of an international coalition against Iraq that included most Arab nations. The Kuwaitis and Saudis expelled thousands of Palestinians in retaliation. During the Gulf War, the PLO budget declined 56 percent and the flow of funds to the territories declined from $120 million to $45 million (Rasler 2000; Behrendt 2007: 12, 21–22, 25;

Ross 2004: 48–49; Segev 1998: 89; Rabinovich 2011: 23; Barari 2004: 113; Qurie 2006: 35). For the pragmatists, this created the imperative to act quickly to reverse the decline in Palestinian fortunes. Echoing Streseman's thinking in early 1925, Qurie writes of using the "little leverage which remained to it to keep the Palestinian problem on the world agenda." He proposed to "reverse the isolation of the PLO, freeing it from the huge political financial burdens it bore as a result of the position adopted by the Palestinians in the Gulf War of 1990–91" (2006: 35).

The advocates of realistic, pragmatic statecraft understood themselves as such. Ahmed Qurie writes of an increasingly "mature national liberation movement, based on realism and moderation" (2006: 10). His faction aimed at being "flexible and pragmatic" (Qurie 2006: 75). Abbas writes of the "rational thinking behind the Palestinian peace initiative" (1995: 22); Qurie describes a "new Palestinian rationality" (2006: 12).

No Settling for Peace: The Coercive Bargaining of the Israeli Right

The Palestinians needed a partner, however, and Israeli domestic politics had been dominated in recent years by Likud, the main Israeli party of the right. Under the leadership of Prime Minister Yitzhak Shamir, Likud approached the conflict with the Palestinians with a zero-sum mind-set, the heuristic that characterizes coercive bargaining (Steinberg 1995). Shamir viewed a Palestinian state as "an option which we would fight with all our strength as bearing within it no less than the seeds of Israel's destruction" (1994: 200). Likud supporters were therefore deeply pessimistic about the possibility of a negotiated solution to the conflict (Rynhold and Waxman 2008: 22). Shamir demonstrated no empathy with the Palestinian cause. Dennis Ross, U.S. diplomat, perhaps the most important career bureaucratic player in the U.S. administration, writes, "[Shamir's] insensitivity to Palestinian needs and concerns mirrored Arafat's insensitivity and indifference to Israeli needs a decade earlier" (2004: 82).

Shamir rejected the basic trade-off of "land for peace" as requiring too great a sacrifice for Israel. He preferred "peace for peace."[3] To some

---

3. He complained that "not a year passed without some official proposal being made. . . . There were few if any new elements, just old proposals recycled, changed a bit, always centering on Israel's withdrawal from territory. . . . The Arab states and the PLO always insisting on what, however it was phrased, amounted to peace in exchange for territory; recognition in exchange for territory; never 'just' peace" (Shamir 1994: 175).

degree, this reflects Shamir's conception of Israeli national interests and his foreign policy goals. It indicates his satisfaction with the status quo and the low price he was willing to pay for peace. In addition, how Likud treated the territory issue also reflects its preferred diplomatic style. Shamir sought to increase Israeli leverage by rapidly expanding settlements in the territories, creating a fait accompli that would force the Palestinians to give up any hope for independence and compromise. He later admitted, "I would have carried on autonomy talks for ten years; meanwhile we would have reached half a million Jews in Judea and Samaria. Without this demographic revolution, there is no reason to hold autonomy talks" (in Rynhold and Waxman 2008; see also Rasler 2000: 713; Kurtzer et al. 2013: 28). The settler movement proceeded more rapidly under Shamir than any other previous Israeli government, with the prime minister setting a goal of 750,000 settlers, which would forestall the possibility of a viable Palestinian state (Segev 1998: 144). Likud was the party of the settlers but also the party that used the settlements as diplomatic leverage.

Shamir saw negotiations with the Palestinians as a game of chicken, as is typical of coercive bargainers. "The truth is that, in the final analysis, the search for peace has always been a matter of who would tire of the struggle first, and blink. Would it be the Arabs, finally accepting, as they had started to do, Israel's conditions for a genuine and lasting peace? Or one day, might an Israeli government . . . believing in the doctrine of 'land for peace,' giving way to impatience and political ambition, capitulate to Arab demands at the possible cost of Israel's future?" (Shamir 1994: 259). The prime minister took pride in his "reputation as a tough, committed negotiator" (Shamir 1994: 182). As a consequence, Shamir found it difficult to compromise even on the most minor of issues, much less make any major concessions that would be necessary for a long-term solution: "I regarded every loophole possibly left unblocked, every possibility of irrevocable damage being done to us, every yielding for the sake of being 'nice' or 'reasonable' that might constrict or distort Israel's stand as being of the utmost importance" (1994: 230).

Shamir demanded that the Palestinians prove their goodwill and intentions first by ending terror and the intifada (1994: 259). But, like Poincaré in 1920s France, he was unimpressed by his adversary's signals of reassurance, as we would expect given his low level of epistemic motivation. "I do not see, nor do I expect, any fundamental change," Shamir said. "They set up their organization to destroy Israel and when they conclude that this goal will not be achieved, they will disband" (in Abbas 1995: 28). The prime minister engaged in reactive devaluation, denigrating the significance of the steps taken by the PLO in Algiers.

The Likud commitment to coercive bargaining is perhaps most evident in its refusal to consider lifting the legal ban on meeting with any representatives of the PLO (Rabinovich 2011: 22; Sassley 2010; Shamir 1994: 200). Indeed, Shamir also refused to hold a dialogue with anyone deported from the West Bank or Gaza, any leader of the intifada, anyone who was not a permanent resident of the territories, or anyone from East Jerusalem because doing so would undermine the Israeli claim to the city. There were very few influential Palestinians who fit this bill (Segev 1998: 111). A refusal to talk is the antithesis of reasoned dialogue.

REPUBLICAN REALISM: U.S. PRAGMATIC STATECRAFT AND
VALUE CLAIMING OVER SETTLEMENTS

The beginning of what would become known as the "peace process" therefore had its origins in the United States. Following the triumphant U.S. victory over Iraq in the first Gulf War, the administration of George H. W. Bush tried to consolidate new-found stability in the Middle East by bringing Israel and its historical adversaries together for talks (Rabinovich 2011: 24). The Bush administration was dominated by Republican Party moderates naturally inclined toward pragmatic statecraft, best personified by Baker. Aaron David Miller (2008: 94), who participated directly as a high-ranking aide for the entire duration of the peace process, notes that a Nexus search of post-1989 news stories revealed 390 hits in which Baker's name appeared within thirty words of *pragmatic* or *pragmatism*. Baker himself wrote that "principles are fine, but if you're going to succeed in carrying them out, you need to be pragmatic" (in Miller 2008: 94).

Baker had all the characteristics of a realist diplomat. First, he had a proself social motivation. As Miller describes him, he was "not an empathetic guy. He didn't feel your pain. What he felt and intuited was your politics, your weaknesses and how to play them" (2008: 202). The Israelis agreed; "No sentiment there," an official said (in Miller 2008: 219). And Baker used an array of methods, adapting to the particular situation he faced. Miller calls this the "plain commonsense realization that American power and interests are multifaceted and complex and that the instruments needed to advance them require a careful, deliberate adjustment depending on circumstances" (2008: 194). Baker used diplomacy "to coerce, to reward, and to embarrass," a "combination of honey and vinegar" (Miller 2008: 218–19). Yet, as much as Baker adapted to constraints, he also believed in the ability of diplomacy to affect the outcome. Miller writes that Baker thought that "American efforts could actually make a difference and that he could make a deal" (2008:194). The secretary of state believed in diplomacy's value.

[198]

Baker used the same tactics as the center-right British government in the 1920s. Like Chamberlain, Baker thought of the U.S. role as one of an honest broker between the two sides, even if U.S. interests were much more closely aligned with Israel, just as British interests had been with France. He would criticize the Israelis in his meetings with Palestinians and do the opposite when he met Shamir (Miller 2008: 202). His "trash-talking to the Arabs about Israel helped build confidence in him," remembers Miller (2008: 221). Baker was also hard on both sides. He "used both incentives and disincentives to cajole and persuade both Arabs *and* Israelis" (Miller 2008: 202, emphasis added). Miller recounts one such instance: "Having blasted them the night before, he now gathered the Palestinians around him, much as a football coach would huddle with his players for a pregame pep talk. The yelling had stopped; the reassuring now began" (2008: 223).

Baker also urged moderation on both sides based on a realistic and objective appraisal of the situation. In a May 1989 speech before the *American Israel Public Affairs Committee* (AIPAC), a Jewish lobbying group, he called on both sides to make difficult admissions. To the Palestinians, he spoke of the "illusion of control over all of Palestine" (in Shamir 1994: 202). He advised them to recognize Israel and admit that violence will not work (Segev 1998: 109). He urged Israelis to accept the principle of "land for peace" and "to lay aside, once and for all, the unrealistic vision of a greater Israel" (in Miller 2008: 207; Kurtzer et al. 2013: 21; Shamir 1994: 202). He did the same privately. Regardless of any moral claims that the Palestinians might make, Baker told one of their delegations: "It's not a question of fairness or what is right. It's a question of reality" (in Kurtzer at al. 2013: 25). He told Shamir to avoid "digging one's heels in" (in Shamir 1994: 200).

The combination of the preference of the Israeli right for coercive bargaining and U.S. pragmatic statecraft resulted in value claiming negotiation. Just as the allies Britain and France had struggled to find agreement under a French conservative government, strong ties were not enough to bring the United States and Israel together over the Palestinian issue. The Israelis were prepared for such a confrontation. When meeting Baker for the first time, Shamir writes that he told Baker, "I thought he should know that he had been described to me as an 'ever-flexible pragmatist,' and I suspected that he had been told that I was an inflexible man of ideological principle" (1994: 200). Consistent with his coercive diplomatic style, Shamir did not back down despite his relative weakness. "If Mr. Baker thought for one moment that those Israelis who were determined not to trade their land for peace . . . would be influenced by his advice or agree that their vision was 'unrealistic,' he had badly misread them," remembers Shamir (1994: 203). Adapting, as pragmatists do, to

the diplomatic style of the other side, Baker responded with his own coercive tactics. Expressing indifference and aloofness, he publicly gave the
Israelis the number for the White House switchboard: "I can only say
'Take this number: 202-456-1414. When you're serious about peace, call
us" (in Shamir 1994: 203).[4]

The Americans particularly stressed the need to stop settlement activity as a necessary condition for any peace deal (Ross 2004: 82). Baker
said, "I don't think there is any greater obstacle to peace than settlement
activity" (in Kurtzer et al. 2013: 23). Bush called the issue "literally min-
iscule in importance compared to the objective of peace" (in Shamir 1994:
234). The question came to a head following the end of the Cold War.
Emigration to Israel from the former Soviet Union soared, increasing the
general population by 20 percent (Ross 2004: 82). The Israelis asked the
United States for $400 million in loan guarantees that would reduce bor-
rowing costs. Concerned that the Israelis would use the greater financial
flexibility to pursue settlement activity and encourage the new immigrants to establish homes in the territories, the Bush administration
asked for assurances that the Israeli government would disclose its ex-
penditures on settlements to make sure they did not increase.

The U.S. administration figured that, in their position of need, the Israelis would meet their commitments (Ross 2004: 83; Miller 2008: 224).
But, whereas a more pragmatic government might have done so, the
Likud government did not comply. The Israeli coercive bargaining induced value claiming negotiations between the two countries. Miller
writes, "let's not forget that Shamir was asking the United States for political backing without extending much reciprocity, particularly given
Israel's stonewalling on providing credible information on settlement
activity" (2008: 229). Bush became angry that the Israelis were allowing
Soviet immigrants to settle in the "occupied territory" of East Jerusalem,
a characterization that upset the Israelis (Segev 1998: 115). The pragmatic
Bush administration then adapted its tactics to Israeli actions. The president postponed the consideration of a subsequent request for $10 billion
in loan guarantees, demanding a freezing of settlements and the Israeli

---

4. Much as the British realists thought that French and German nationalists were undermining
their own national interests through their coercive bargaining, the realist-dominated
Republican administration thought that Shamir's diplomacy did not actually serve Israeli
ends. The Bush administration believed that, had Shamir granted tangible steps in the
direction of autonomy and stopped the most hated of Israeli practices, such as settlements and
checkpoints, the prime minister might have produced an indigenous Palestinian leadership
from the territories. This could have served as a viable alternative to the PLO, a long-standing
goal of Shamir (Kurtzer et al. 2013: 28).

endorsement of "land for peace" in exchange for their release. Shamir did not relent. He refused this effort at coercive linkage, calling it "blackmail" (Segev 1998: 131). The prime minister took a hard line, betting that he could use the leverage offered by the Jewish lobby in Congress against the Bush administration, leaving the Americans no choice but to compromise (Miller 2008: 225). But Bush did not back down either, complaining publicly about how a "thousand lobbyists on the Hill are working the other side of the question." "I don't care if I get only one vote," he proclaimed. "I believe the American people will be with me" (in Shamir 1994: 234). This cost the Bush administration significantly in terms of domestic politics because it provoked the U.S. Jewish community, but the Israelis lost the confrontation, as generally happens to the weaker side in value claiming negotiations (Segev 1998: 103).

LEARNING TO CRAWL: THE MADRID CONFERENCE

The Bush administration also had difficulties in securing its primary goal, bringing the two sides (as well as the historical Israeli antagonists Syria and Jordan) together for an international conference in Madrid sponsored by the United States and the Soviet Union in 1991. Shamir recalls, "There were bitter, prolonged disputes at almost every point about almost everything including what the gathering itself should be called" (1994: 239). Through extensive shuttle diplomacy, Baker eventually succeeded, but as Shlomo Ben-Ami, the Israeli foreign minister, recalls, "Shamir was practically dragged to Madrid by President Bush. The message was forcefully, by way of pressure and intimidation, brought home to him that he could have either America's friendship or the territories, not both" (in Kurtzer et al. 2013: 29). Shamir admits as much (1994: 228). There is unanimity among participants and secondary accounts that had it not been for U.S. pressure, Israel would never have consented to attending (Behrendt 2007: 16; Segev 1998: 147; Rasler 2000: 713; Peres 1995: 274; Qurie 2006: 36). Shamir worried that such an international gathering would put pressure on the Israelis to make concessions that would inevitably lead to the establishment of a Palestinian state. As a coercive bargainer, he wanted to avoid putting himself in a weaker position (Steinberg 1995: 176–80)

Despite U.S. pleas for the participants to engage in pragmatic diplomacy, however, the conference was marked by its spirit of value claiming (Ross 2004: 80).[5] Abbas writes, "Both sides had to resort to sending

5. In Spain, President Bush pleaded in his opening remarks for each side to practice pragmatic statecraft: "Peace will only come as a result of direct negotiations, compromises, give and

memoranda to each other expressing their respective viewpoints and demands" with little actual deliberation among the parties (1995: 89). Qurie complains that it amounted to a "dialogue of the deaf, grinding to a virtual halt amid a welter of mutual accusations" (2006: 36). There was no reasoned dialogue. Miller, who attended, writes, "Madrid came out of an environment in which the sides had no contact, no trust, no agreed-upon anything. In fact they were openly hostile and disdainful" (2008: 201). It "had as much warmth and good feeling as a shotgun wedding" (Miller 2008: 229). Given that the conference emerged from U.S. pressure rather than the combination of diplomatic styles conducive to value creating negotiation, this is not a surprise. Miller writes, "This time, Shamir, Assad and the PLO authorized a conference because they couldn't afford not to, and they weren't happy about it. Their concessions were made not to one another but to America and to Jim Baker" (2008: 203).

In the opening speeches, each side played to the cameras at home, repeating its grievances with no reference to or consideration of the legitimate needs of the other side. Shamir referred to the rightful claim of Israel to the "Land of Israel," meaning the West Bank. "We are the only people who have lived in the Land of Israel without interruption for nearly 4000 years. . . . We are the only people for whom Jerusalem has been a capital. We are the only people whose sacred places are only in the Land of Israel. . . . Only Eretz Israel, the Land of Israel, is our true homeland" (Shamir 1994: 238). The prime minister expressed no willingness to make concessions on territory or settlement activity: "It will be regrettable if the talks focus primarily and exclusively on territory. It will be the quickest way to an impasse" (Shamir 1994: 240). Instead of expressing consideration for the Palestinian and Arab positions, he accused them of pushing "Israel into a defenceless position and . . . to destruction. . . . The issue is not territory but our existence" (Shamir 1994: 240). He remembers, "I took my listeners . . . through the history of the Zionist claim to the Land of Israel . . . of the armed Arab rejection of it and deadly assaults upon the state that came into being and of Arab hostility to Israel'" (Shamir 1994: 239). The Palestinians, in turn, did no better. A PLO delegate declared, "We come to you from a tortured land and a proud, though captive people, having been asked to negotiate with our occupiers, but leaving behind the children of the intifada and a people under occupation and under curfew, who enjoined us not to surrender or forget"

---

take. . . . We come here to Madrid as realists. We don't expect peace to be negotiated in a day, or a week, or a month, or even a year. It will take time. Indeed it should take time." Consistent with the U.S. role as honest broker, he emphasized the legitimate concerns of both sides, the Israeli need for security and the Palestinian need for a territorial home (in Segev 1998: 97–98).

(in Segev 1998: 99). They made no promise to call off the intifada as a confidence-building measure.

Even though the Americans had forced Shamir to attend, they could not force him to negotiate. Ben-Ami explains that Shamir went to Madrid to "protect his possessions, not to negotiate them away" (in Miller 2008: 230). Shamir did not even understand the conference as a negotiation. He later referred to the "drama of this first historic *confrontation* between Israel and its neighbors which offered an unparalleled background for the retelling of our story to a worldwide audience" (Shamir 1994: 236, emphasis added). As the Palestinians saw it, Madrid was "little more than a platform for the intransigence of the right-wing Likud government" (Qurie 2006: 36).

In the substantive bilateral negotiations that followed in Washington between the Israelis and Palestinians, the pattern continued. Each side made maximalist and inflated demands. The Palestinians wanted all the land that Israel had seized in 1967, the end to settlements, the right of return for all Palestinian refugees, and a capital in East Jerusalem. Israel rejected all these demands, even at one point denying the existence of the Palestinians as a separate Arab people (Segev 1998: 133).

Nevertheless, the Madrid conference was significant and perhaps a necessary condition for the diplomatic successes that followed. It was the first time that Arabs had sat across from Israelis since the Camp David Accords were reached in 1978 (Segev 1998: 101) and the first time ever that Israelis, Syrians, Jordanians, and Palestinians had come together at the same table (Miller 2008: 195). For his part, Baker never had any illusions that Madrid would lead to any dramatic deals in the short term. The secretary of state saw this "as a way to break taboos and create an investment trap that would keep Arabs and Israelis at the table for a long time" (Miller 2008: 217). He later said its "real significance was that it happened at all. It was not a substantive breakthrough, but it was a procedural one" (in Kurtzer et al. 2013: 30).

Baker was trying to lay the institutional foundation for future value creating negotiation, much like pragmatic foreign secretary Austen Chamberlain's vision of using the League of Nations as a regular meeting place for the French and Germans. This reflected the long-term perspective of the Bush administration, characteristic of pragmatic diplomacy. "It wasn't about reaching agreements or wrestling with the tough issues," writes Miller. "In fact, Baker tried to finesse or kick down the road every contentious issue that might constitute what he called a deal-breaker." He told his team, "'Boys, you need to crawl before you walk and walk before you run'. . . . For Baker, the goal on this hunt was to get them to the table" (Miller 2008: 21). Baker had a "negotiator's mindset, a tendency to see the world of power and politics in terms of problems to be solved, managed or deferred" (Miller 2008: 193).

[203]

A PARTNER FOR THE PALESTINIANS:
THE DIPLOMATIC STYLE OF LABOR

U.S. statecraft was responsible for institutionalizing a process that allowed cover, time, and space for diplomacy to continue until domestic political conditions in Israel shifted to make the possibility of value-creating negotiation more likely (Miller 2008: 233). The Americans were waiting for a new Israeli government with a new diplomatic style (Rabinovich 2011: 26). In 1992, the left-wing Labor Party came to power. Miller writes that the fact that Baker paid little attention to the post-Madrid negotiations until Yitzhak Rabin, the Labor candidate, defeated Shamir in June 1992 "was all you needed to know. At best, Madrid was intended as a stage-setter" (2008: 195). When Labor replaced Likud, according to Dennis Ross, the U.S. envoy to the peace process, "it was if a great weight had been lifted off the body politic. Hope was alive again. Expectations soared about peace being possible" (Ross 2004: 84).

The Palestinian pragmatists were also buoyed (Abbas 1995: 53). "We knew that Likud would not take one single step towards a settlement, and so we became doubly interested in the preparations for the elections that were announced in June 1992," Abbas recalls (1995: 90). Leading Palestinians had gone so far as to quietly coordinate their activities to benefit Labor in the election (Segev 1998:135). For instance, Abbas instructed Palestinians to avoid raising the issue of Jerusalem because this would "do Likud a great service because it can then claim that there is no common ground for negotiation" (1995: 60–61). He did not anticipate major substantial changes to Israeli positions but, rather, a different diplomatic approach. "We expected that the victory of Labor and its allies would bring in a new style of negotiating and novel ideas to it," explains Abbas (1995: 92).

There is universal agreement in the literature on Israeli-Palestinian relations that the election of Labor was a necessary condition for progress in peace talks in the early 1990s. Nevertheless, most accounts stress the different foreign policy preferences of the parties involved (Rasler 2000; Sassley 2010; Abbas 1995: 53; Behrendt 2007: 65; Kydd and Walter 2002; Hermann and Yuchtman-Yaar 2002; Rabinovich 2011: 28; Segev 1998: 152; Barari 2004: 104–5; Telhami 1996; Steinberg 1995). Likud, according to this argument, was less willing to cede territory in exchange for peace because it valued peace less and territory more than Labor did. The former was more attached to the notion of *Eretz Israel* ("Land of Israel"). For Likud, Judea and Samaria (which the rest of the world calls the West Bank) rightfully belongs to the Jews by divine mandate. This was the site of the biblical Jewish kingdom and the cradle of early Jewish civilization. Although Likud leaders frequently argued that ceding any of the West Bank would endanger Israeli security by creating a base for terrorists and making it easier for a joint Arab attack, the real objection of the party to any territorial concessions was the "profound emotional and symbolic value" of the area, which made it more difficult to let it go. As such, Likud valued the status quo more highly (Miller 2008: 209).

For Labor, the Land of Israel was, according to Sassley's (2010), "expendable," tradable for other more high-ranking priorities. Yossi Beilin, a key Labor figure who features centrally in the narrative that follows, writes of his early political awakening, "I saw how unimportant the occupied territories were to us, and how to a great extent we had become the prisoners of our own conquests. . . . I decided to work inside the Labor Party towards strengthening the peace camp within it" (1999: 11). In this view, withdrawing from the territories was a prerequisite for maintaining Israel as a liberal democratic state. Maintaining control over the Palestinians morally corrupts the Jews, threatening the Israeli commitment to human rights and engendering the hatred of its Arab neighbors (Sassley 2010; Waxman 2008). This was particularly true given the demographic changes occurring in the region; that is, the Arab birthrate has been much higher than the Jewish birthrate. Evacuating the West Bank and Gaza would help bring about peace.

If the political parties approached the negotiations differently because they had different evaluations of the value of different assets, then this is a foreign policy rather than a diplomatic account. There is little doubt that there were differences in the Labor and Likud conceptions of Israeli foreign policy interests; nevertheless, such differences can also be overstated. There has been an increasing consensus between the two parties, Labor and Likud, that demographic considerations make a permanent annexation of the West Bank impossible (Rynhold and Waxman 2008). Certainly Likud liked to claim in the early 1990s that Labor would quickly trade away the West Bank for an illusory peace (Shamir 1994), but even at that time, the plans offered by the two parties for dealing with the issue were remarkably similar. Both endorsed some sort of Palestinian autonomy. Likud leaders said as early as 1986 that "it is our aspiration that [the Palestinians] will be able to run their affairs by themselves" (Shamir 1994: 167). Shamir's national unity government proposed elections in the occupied territories to provide representatives with whom the Israelis could negotiate the creation of a self-governing administration (Shamir 1994: 195; Segev 1998: 108).

Also, the two major Labor figures at the time, Yitzhak Rabin and the more dovish Shimon Peres, opposed the creation of a sovereign Palestinian state as being too dangerous for Israeli security. This was part of the official 1992 party platform (Steinberg 1998: 223). Their positions on the return to the 1967 borders, the disposition of the settlements in any permanent agreement, and the indivisibility of Jerusalem were also identical to those of Likud (Peres 1995: 262–64; Segev 1998: 152; Barari 2004: 83; Behrendt 2007: 64, 72; Ben-Yehuda 1997: 205). Following his election, Rabin pledged publicly that he would attempt to conclude an autonomy agreement with the Palestinians that would grant the Palestinians local authority over internal matters. Elections would be held, as in the earlier plans endorsed by Likud and that offered by Shamir's apparent heir, Benjamin Netanyahu (1993: 351–53). Beilin describes the Palestinian position of establishing a state with Jerusalem as its capital, the return of the Palestinian refugees, and dismantling the Jewish settlements as "a prospect which the Labor Party obviously could not countenance" (1999: 21). As Wanis-St. John concludes, the Rabin government "held fast to the key assumption of the previous Likud government: that Palestinian self-government could only have functional attributes and no territorial sovereignty" (2011: 107).

Labor differed substantially, however, in terms of its diplomatic style, which was liberal rather than coercive. Rather than feigning indifference to draw out negotiations and extort greater concessions, Rabin promised the interim agreement within six to nine months. He believed an agreement on elections could be concluded by December 1992 and one on the extent of the jurisdiction of the new entity by February 1993, with elections to be held in May 1993 (Segev 1998: 158). He also gave the Palestinians a firm time line for the conclusion of a final status accord. There would be a five-year transition period, with final status talks beginning three years into the process on the basis of the principle of "land for peace" (Abbas 1995: 57; Behrendt 2007: 68, 84; Segev 1998: 149; Rabinovich 2011: 29). Shamir had simply proposed to hold elections and talk after, holding future concessions as bargaining chips to secure a better deal (Ross 2004: 56). Labor also expressed a greater willingness to talk directly to the PLO. In January 1993, the government repealed the law making it illegal for Israelis to meet with PLO officials (Meital 2006: 32; Wanis St-John 2011: 90; Behrendt 2007: 66). This contrasted sharply with Shamir's efforts to forestall reasoned dialogue with most of the main political players in Palestinian politics.

Finally, Labor was willing to make preliminary concessions on the settlement issue that reduced its bargaining leverage. The Rabin government largely froze building upon taking office, cancelling 6,500 new housing units that had been approved by Shamir, although it did vow to complete the 10,000 units that had already begun and allowed building without public financing (Segev 1998: 149, 152; Behrendt 2007: 35, 64, 68). Although this was not a blanket ban, the Bush administration subsequently allowed the $10 billion in loan guarantees to Israel because of the new diplomatic style of Labor. A senior Bush adviser later stated that "the difference in this case was the difference between Shamir and Rabin; Rabin demonstrated to us that he was determined to reach a settlement; that's why we were prepared to look the other way"(in Kurtzer et al. 2013: 34).[6] The pragmatic Americans were reciprocating the prosocial Israeli gesture in a value creating spirit.

These behaviors emerged naturally from the prosocial motivation of the Labor party and are those we would expect from a leftist political party. Foreign Minister Shimon Peres outlines his conception of negotiations as positive rather than zero-sum in character. He remembers, "I felt that the peace process until now had been based on a misconception: instead of negotiating over the substance of peace and the benefits that would accrue from it—for all the parties—we had been dealing solely with the price to be paid for peace with the decades-old causes of the conflict. I thought that unless our people were given a new sense of the situation, it would be hard for them and, therefore, for their leaders to shake loose from the rigid thinking that was still the residue of the old world" (Peres 1995: 275). Peres described the essence of liberal diplomacy at the time, "Negotiations are an exchange of gestures instead of an exchange of blows. . . . Instead of coming with outstretched swords and a mouth full of abuses, you come to negotiations with goodwill. We will, of course, be making gestures, and I expect the Palestinians will also do so" (in Behrendt 2007: 76). The foreign minister expressed an interest in a deal in which both sides benefited: "We definitely want to persuade our neighbors that we are serious about the need to attain an arrangement and to make a decision in the course of 1993 so as to shorten the suffering of all sides: ours and theirs" (in Behrendt 2007: 77).

Yossi Beilin, who became Peres's deputy foreign minister, also approached the issue with the mind-set that an agreement that satisfied both sides was possible but would require active engagement and discussion with the Palestinians. "My working hypothesis was that the dispute *could* be solved, there *was* somebody to talk to, namely the PLO, and there *was* something to discuss if both sides were prepared to be creative," he recounts (Beilin 1999: 46). The Israelis needed to remain open to the possibility lest cognitive closure blind them to opportunities for peace. Beilin writes, "I understood that the concept 'Nobody to

6. President Bush announced, "I am delighted that we have agreed on an approach that would assist these new Israelis, without frustrating the search for peace. . . . The prime minister has persuaded me that Israel is sincere about peacemaking. . . . We see a very different approach to settlements. We salute the prime minister for his courage. I know it wasn't easy" (in Segev 1998: 156).

Chapter 8

talk to, nothing to discuss' developed after the Khartoum conference[7] as a new Israeli consensus was correct only in part, and when there *had* been someone to talk to and something to discuss, we had still been trapped in a different mind-set" (1999: 11). Beilin expressed his prosocial motivation directly. He has liberal moral foundations: "I always believed that all human beings were created of the same matter and that my rights were in no way superior to those of the boy offering to black my army boots in exchange for a few coppers on my way through Gaza." This, however, was not simple capitulation to Palestinian demands. Beilin adds, "Nor was I numbered among those who were so impetuously calling for unilateral withdrawal in the immediate post-war period" (1999: 10).

Prime Minister Rabin expressed these prosocial sentiments publicly in a statement before the Israeli Knesset in July 1992 after taking power. He addressed the Palestinians directly: "To you, the Palestinians in the territories, our foes today and our partners to a peaceful coexistence tomorrow, I wish to say: We have been fated to live together on the same patch of land. . . . We lead our lives with you, beside you, and against you. . . . We offer you the fairest and most viable proposal . . . an autonomy, with all its advantages and limitations. You will not get everything you want. Neither will we. . . . Don't lose this opportunity that may never return. Take our proposal seriously—to avoid further suffering, humiliation and grief" (in Segev 1998: 147).

Rabin was himself more of a pragmatist than were other key leaders in the Labor Party, consistent with his position on the right of his party (Makovsky 1996: 87; Steinberg 1995: 187). Rabin and Peres had long been the poles of the centrist and more left-leaning parts of the party. Therefore, it not surprising that, whereas Peres was the "dreamer and visionary," Rabin was the "pragmatist" and "political realist," writes Segev (1998: 163; see also Ben-Yehuda 1997: 203). No other than Henry Kissinger noted how Rabin was "relentless in separating the chaff from what is essential" (Segev 1998: 147). Ross also noted his pragmatism (2004: 92). Indeed it was Rabin's centrism that was responsible for his victory over Peres for leadership of the Labor Party before the 1992 elections. Party members thought he would better attract moderate voters due to his historically harder line on conflicts with Arab neighbors (Rabinovich 2011: 29; Segev 1998: 143–44; Makovsky 1996: 83; Steinberg 1995: 187). In addition, Rabin had been the head of the armed forces in the great 1967 Israeli military victory.

---

7. In this 1967 conference, the Arab countries rejected negotiations with, recognition of, and peace with Israel, even after their crushing military defeat.

[208]

Rabin seems to have come to the conclusion that peace talks were necessary due to practical necessity—out of realism rather than an a principled commitment to reasoned dialogue. Although as defense minister under the national unity government headed by Shamir he had ruthlessly repressed the intifada, the experience also seems to have convinced him that the status quo was too costly for both sides (Rabinovich 2011: 31; Rasler 2000; Miller 2008: 259; Makovsky 1996: 84–85, 95). The costs of continued confrontation outweighed the potential but uncertain benefits of peace. While Shamir understood the uprising as indicating again the existential threat to Israel, thereby assimilating the events so they were consistent with his overall heuristics (Shamir 1994: 182), the more epistemically motivated pragmatist Rabin changed his position as a consequence of the experience. He came to understand the intifada as the expression of national aspirations that could not be contained forever (Sassley 2010). Rabin said that Palestinians "who carry on their shoulders the burden of the intifada deserve our attention. They are our interlocutors" (Segev 1998: 147; see also Ben-Yehuda 1997: 210).

THE DECLARATION OF PRINCIPLES: CREATING VALUE IN OSLO

Pragmatists in the Palestinian camp were more open to these signals sent by the Israeli government, which we would expect given their higher level of epistemic motivation. Qurie told his leadership, "Coming, as they do, after a long history of enmity, conflict and mistrust, these remarks carry a significance that merits your deep and serious consideration, especially after the long period of duplicity on the part of successive Likud governments" (2006: 45). He judged that a "new level of political maturity" had emerged in Israel, "or at least in the Labor Party," and that the opportunity for a deal "might easily be lost if it were not grasped at the right time" (Qurie 2007: 73). Abbas agreed that this "chance will never be repeated to implement self-rule" (1995: 62).

Abbas reached out to Rabin following the election. He wrote the new prime minister that the Palestinians "are in complete agreement with you about the need for urgent and intensive action in the coming negotiations." He drew a distinction between Rabin and the previous government, having been "disturbed by the announcement of [Foreign Minister Moshe] Arens and Shamir that they intend to negotiate for ten years without achieving a result" (Abbas 1995: 64). Rather than denigrating the significance of his statements, Abbas paid tribute to Rabin's "courage in presenting some positive ideas to achieve a solution during an election campaign, which was characterized by demagogy, bigotry and obstinacy" (1995: 63). He informed Rabin that the PLO had "advocated self-restraint on the eve of the elections so that Shamir could not arm himself against you" (Abbas 1995: 65).

The combination of pragmatic statecraft among key Palestinian leaders and prosocially motivated Israelis with their realistic prime minister created the conditions for value creating negotiation in 1993. What became known as the Oslo process was initiated by Yossi Beilin, the deputy foreign minister, who without the knowledge of his superiors authorized unofficial contacts between two Israeli academics and PLO officials to explore ideas about the general outlines of an agreement. Beilin was the founder of the Mashov Caucus of Labor, a progressive faction that sought to move the party to the left on domestic and social issues. For years, he had sought out contacts with Palestinians to better understand their positions and identify possible bases for compromise between the two sides (Wanis-St. John 2011: 83; Makosvky 1999: 97–100). He recalls, "My objective at this stage was to increase as far as possible the number of 'kosher' interlocutors, to identify possible common denominators and arrive at informal accords with the Palestinian leadership, thus proving to Peres, Rabin and the institutions of the Labor Party that agreement really was attainable" (Beilin 1999: 21). Beilin was optimistic: "The investment in talks with the Palestinian leadership in the territories and in Jerusalem had paid dividends in enabling me to gain a better understanding of the problems, the emotions, the 'other man's mind'" (1999: 46). Abbas coordinated the Palestinian team from Tunis. Qurie served as the chief Palestinian negotiator in Norway.

Both sides approached these secret discussions, made possible through the generosity of the Norwegian government, with the mind-set conducive to value creating. Beilin writes, "Our guiding principle throughout the talks was to try to avoid conventional negotiating tactics, where the parties begin with speeches intended to mark out the distance between them and then move towards compromise. We tried to locate the limits beyond which the other side could not go, to understand what our own limits were, and to strive towards the construction of broader options in which both sides would have room to manoeuvre" (1999: 68). Ron Pundak, one of the Israeli academics who began the talks, writes that the "goal was to work towards a conceptual chance which would lead to a dialogue based, as much as possible, on fairness, equality and common objectives. . . . For many years, the two peoples had been locked in a zero-sum relationship, in which every victory by one side was considered a defeat for the other. 'Oslo', by contrast, was guided from the start by efforts to create as many win-win situations as possible, notwithstanding a balance of power that was tipped heavily in Israel's favor" (2001: 32–33). Qurie writes of the need to "break away from the circle of mutual suspicion which had historically been dominant in the position of both sides"

(2006: 80). Abbas, who monitored the process from Tunis and who would eventually participate directly, compared these discussions to the official and more public negotiations ongoing in Washington that had been fruitless up to that point: "We therefore had to devise another style for the Oslo channel" (1995: 115).[8]

The Israelis did not withhold their bottom line in an effort to extract a better deal. Pundak described how the Israelis constructed their first proposal: "So we did not draft an Israeli position, we drafted . . . something which we believed could be already a first construction for a bridging draft and then it became, after amendments . . . the first joint draft declaration of principles" (in Behrendt 2007: 51). Yair Hirschfeld, his colleague, noted that they "always strove to emphatically take into account the Palestinian position" (in Behrendt 2007: 51).

Based on early successes, Beilin informed his boss, Peres, about the existence of the talks. Soon after, Peres informed Rabin, who allowed the talks to continue. Two Israeli officials were brought in, Joel Singer and Uri Savir, making the channel official. It was the first time that the Israeli government had ever formally negotiated with the PLO. Rabin directed his negotiating team not to engage in the stalling that is part of coercive bargaining: "I want you to keep the ball rolling all the time. . . . Don't act in a manner that would halt the negotiations. You have to be extremely patient. Try to avoid bogging down on principle issues. On the contrary, try to seek formulae that would be fair to both sides. Just keep up the momentum" (in Segev 1998: 168). Peres told them similarly to "wrap it up fast. . . . Don't let the Oslo track become like chewing gum" (1995: 295).

The Palestinians were willing for the first time to separate the peace process into a number of stages, negotiating an interim settlement and postponing a final deal for a period of time. The earlier insistence on knowing the entire contours of a final deal was part of a coercive bargaining strategy. The Palestinians wanted to secure maximum Israeli concessions on all the important issues—final borders, a Palestinian

8. Maher el-Kurd, one of the participants, recounts that the Palestinians came to the conference with a pragmatic style, focused on tangible issues on which there was actually a chance for agreement: "We realized if we want to talk about 1948, about historical rights, 1967, refugees, displaced, water rights, then of course we would not get anywhere. In our consideration there was a historical brief moment that needed to be utilized. . . . When we had the first meeting with Hirschfeld and Pundak we told them: let's not talk about the past, let's not talk about who occupied the land and who made the aggression. . . . Let's talk about what we can achieve if we can achieve it in the coming five years and create a momentum and an interest on both sides in making peace based on the two state solution" (in Behrendt 2007: 50). The Israelis stated the same position (Segev 1998: 195).

capital in East Jerusalem, the right of Palestinians to return—all up front, getting the most from the limited bargaining leverage they had. Otherwise, they risked the interim settlement turning into a final one (Peres 1995: 67; Beilin 1999: 67, 132). This time, however, they accepted that these contentious issues would be postponed for the final status talks, with agreement on the easiest issues first (Qurie 2006: 79). This was indicative of pragmatic statecraft. "We would seize what advantage we could in the near future, while never losing sight of our long-term goals," Qurie recounts (2006: 76).

The embrace of pragmatic statecraft also enabled the Palestinians to accept the principle of "Gaza first." Instead of the Israelis granting autonomy to the West Bank and Gaza all at once, they would relinquish Gaza as a good-faith gesture. The Palestinians had previously denigrated such a concession as worthless, a way for the Israelis to appear forthcoming while shedding what was actually a burden (Qurie 2006: 81). The Gaza Strip was unimportant for Israeli security, had no historical or symbolic significance for the Jewish people, and had few settlements to dismantle. Qurie explains the worry that "withdrawal from Gaza might turn out to be not only the first but also the last step in Israel's withdrawal. . . . We were concerned that Israel's colonial mentality, expansionist policies and devious negotiating strategies might incline it to embroil us deeply in the Gaza issue while at the same time strengthening its hold on the West Bank and Jerusalem" (2006: 81).

However, in the Oslo track, the Palestinian pragmatists decided to look at the Gaza issue differently: "We made the effort to set aside our suspicion that Israel wanted to hold on to territory at all costs, and to believe that Israel's desire to withdraw from Gaza was real," writes Qurie (2006: 81). It was regarded as a preliminary demonstration of Israeli intentions that would create a precedent that applied to other lands. Qurie highlighted the gains rather than the potential perils, such as the psychological boost it would provide for the Palestinians. "Our strategy was to present withdrawal from Gaza as a move which would have benefits both for ourselves and for the Israelis. Thus, we ended the situation in which negotiation was seen as a zero-sum game" (Qurie 2006: 82).

The Oslo negotiations were marked by the reciprocity so important for value creating. Although the Palestinians consented to defer several key issues to the final status talks, the Israelis made the concession of discussing them at all. Even as they stressed, for instance, that Jerusalem would remain undivided, the Israelis agreed that the final status of the city would be the subject of negotiations. Had they been engaged in coercive bargaining, they would have demanded that Palestinians give up any claim to East Jerusalem as a precondition for negotiating (Behrendt 2007: 54; Peres 1995: 287). Beilin writes, "Naturally, we did not guarantee our willingness to compromise on these issues, any more than on those of frontiers and Jewish settlements and other questions, but the very fact that these issues were now on the agenda was enough to solve a series of problems which had prevented agreement on autonomy since discussions on the subject had begun following the 1979 peace treaty with Egypt" (1999: 69).

To ease Palestinian concerns that "Gaza first" would become "Gaza last," Peres offered a bigger downpayment (Beilin 1999: 65; Makovsky 1996: 35). As Peres admits in his memoirs, Palestinian suspicions about the eagerness of Israel to shed itself of Gaza were not unfounded. The region suffered from tremendous overcrowding and poverty and tied up large numbers of Israeli troops without increasing Israeli security. "In all honesty, nobody wanted Gaza," he writes (Peres 1995: 278–79). Nevertheless, the Israelis might have held on to Gaza as a bargaining chip had they been practicing coercive bargaining. Not only did the Israelis relinquish the strip of territory, they suggested that Gaza autonomy be accompanied simultaneously by a Palestinian foothold in the West Bank. Peres offered Jericho "as a sign of our intent to continue negotiations" (in Makovsky 1996: 35; see also Peres 1995: 136; Behrendt 2007: 92; Beilin 1999: 69; Segev 1998: 180). The area contained a large Palestinian refugee population and no Israeli settlements; however, holding the city did serve an important security purpose for Israel because it lay on the border with Jordan. It also had religious significance for Israelis, making the offer much more than an empty gesture (Behrendt 2007: 88–92; Segev 1998: 197, 202).

The Israelis also offered an accelerated timetable for granting autonomy to Gaza and Jericho, to begin within three months of the signing of a declaration of principles, and a fixed date for the beginning of final status talks. The Israelis refrained from using a coercive linkage strategy. Beilin wanted to ensure that the transfer of autonomy was *not* made contingent on agreement over the framework for the elections to a new Palestinian council that would govern the areas, which would probably prove difficult to conclude. He also preferred to have a five-year period for the conclusion of all outstanding issues written into the interim agreement "so that the [Menachem] Begin ploy, of postponing the permanent settlement indefinitely, would not be repeated" (Beilin 1999: 69). Beilin came up with the idea of a "ticking clock"—early withdrawal from Gaza and Jericho and the beginning of final status talk after two years, with a permanent settlement to be concluded within three years (Beilin 1999: 77; Peres 1995: 286).

For their part, the Palestinians offered to be flexible on Israeli security (Segev 1998: 198). Although the Israeli Defense Forces (IDF) would be withdrawn from the major cities as autonomy was granted, they would be allowed to protect the settlers and Israeli citizens, meaning that they could reenter evacuated territory without having to secure Palestinian consent if this proved necessary to fight terrorism (Makovsky 1996: 67). "My instructions are that in matters of security I am to be open to your suggestions. . . . But please . . . don't declare the entire West Bank a security area," Qurie told Peres (in Peres 1995: 289; see also Segev 1998: 206).[9] Their willingness to make these concessions was a key factor convincing Rabin of the possibility of an agreement, which was a necessary condition for keeping the track alive. He said, "On four or five major issues, they agreed to [things] I had doubted they would agree to. . . . First, Jerusalem under Israeli control and outside the jurisdiction of the Palestinians for the entire interim period. Second, [retaining all Israeli] settlements. Third overall Israeli responsibility for the security of Israelis" (in Makovsky 1996: 66).

The negotiations were not free from coercive bargaining. Consistent with my analysis, however, coercive bargaining begat coercive bargaining. After officials from the Israeli government took over from the academics, they objected to some of the provisions in the earlier drafts, the most important being the creation of an international trusteeship to govern Gaza. For the Israelis, this was tantamount to an endorsement of a future Palestinian state, which genuinely went past their red lines. The Palestinians rescinded some of their concessions, such as giving up the ability of East Jerusalem residents to run for positions on the Palestinian Council, something the Israelis also could not have accepted regardless of diplomatic style (Makovsky 1996: 71). And they demanded control of the bridge from Jericho into Jordan and an extraterritorial road between Gaza and the West Bank (Qurie 2006: chaps. 10–14; Behrendt 2007: 84–92; Beilin 1999: 104–5; Abbas 1995: 166–69; Makovsky 1996: 59–64). In a new draft, Qurie introduced twenty-five amendments to the official Israeli proposal, claiming that he had the same right to backtrack as the Israelis (Qurie 2006: 196). Qurie remembers the "bitter satisfaction": "Now, I thought, they are drinking from the same cup they gave us to drink from in past rounds" (2006: 197). The other Israeli delegate, Joel Singer, later complained that "instead of moving toward you, like in any other negotiation, they move *beyond* their opening position, so that you are almost at their opening positions as negotiations move on" (in Makovsky 1996: 60). Qurie denigrated the significance of the Israeli offer as "occupation in a different form and using different methods" and

---

9. The bottom line for Israel on this issue is another indication that the distinction that has been made between Labor and Likud on foreign policy goals—with Likud allowing only "functional" autonomy and Labor willing to grant "territorial" autonomy—has been overstated (Makovsky 1999: 122–23).

threatened to "wait ten more years to obtain a reasonable agreement acceptable to us" (2006: 213).

Consistent with my analysis, the value claiming dynamic that emerged precipitated crises that almost undermined the negotiations (Beilin 1999: 105; Makovsky 1996: 61). The Israeli representative, Uri Savir, accused the Palestinians of deliberatively crossing Israeli red lines and demanded they withdraw the draft. Otherwise, the Israelis would shut down the back channel. "We will not accept this method of negotiation," he said (in Qurie 2006: 203). Movement toward an agreement reemerged only when the Palestinians stepped back from the brink and returned to value creating.

The final product of the Oslo negotiations, a Declaration of Principles on an Interim Self-Government Arrangement, indicated the intent of the PLO and the Israeli government to negotiate an interim framework granting autonomy to the West Bank and Gaza via a gradual process beginning with the handover of Gaza and Jericho. The first withdrawal of the IDF would occur in just three months. Negotiations over subsequent withdrawals from the major Palestinian urban centers would begin immediately. Israelis promised three "further redeployments," withdrawals from the West Bank, but of unspecified size and timing. In "early empowerment," the new Palestinian government would control the six functions of education, health, social affairs, taxation, tourism, and internal security, even before elections to the Palestinian Council, a legislative body. Once the council was constituted, military government by Israel would be dissolved. A mechanism was to be worked out later allowing for the participation of East Jerusalem residents in elections, a major concession by the Israelis. Final status negotiations on security, borders, refugees, and the status of Jerusalem would begin no later than the third year of the interim period, to be concluded no later than five years after the first withdrawal. During this period, the Israelis would also refrain from expanding the settlements but would not remove any during the interim period (Segev 1998: 213, 349; Behrendt 2007: 2–3, 85; Peres 1995: 293; Wanis-St. John 2011: 110). The announcement of the Declaration of Principles was accompanied by a letter from Arafat to Rabin indicating the acceptance by the PLO of the right of Israel to exist, a letter from Arafat to the Norwegians calling on the Palestinians to end the violence, and a letter from Rabin to Arafat recognizing the PLO as the legitimate representative of the Palestinian people.

Qurie, the Palestinian negotiator who was present from start to finish in Norway, writes that Oslo was a "great international event, world-changing in a way true only of such major events as the fall of the Berlin Wall in 1990" (2008: 13). Just as the French and Germans had made reference to the new type of negotiating that had emerged between the two

[215]

sides in a neutral location, the spirit of Locarno, so too did the Israelis and Palestinians (Pundak 2001: 32). This new "spirit of Oslo" was a remarkable outcome, particularly for the PLO, whose bargaining leverage had been extremely limited. Much as Stresemann had done for Germany in the 1920s, the diplomatic style of pragmatic statecraft had brought the PLO back from the brink of extinction despite its limited power. There was elation on the Palestinian side when agreement was reached: "we could hear them cheering and weeping, and we knew that they were hugging one another," reports Peres (1995: 299). Qurie wept at the signing ceremony in Washington. It was only because of the pragmatists that the Palestinians did not succumb to their usual behavior, "to never miss an opportunity to miss an opportunity," as the popular saying went. Abbas defended the achievements of his team against opponents with a rhetorical question befitting a realist: "Could you have gotten more?" (in Makovsky 1996: 77).

Moreover, just as Franco-German cooperation in the 1920s had depended on the liberal diplomacy of France, the Oslo agreement required a prosocial partner in Israel. Much as Stresemann had sought out Briand at the Locarno Treaty–signing ceremony, Qurie sought out Peres to thank him effusively for his efforts. And like Briand, Peres responded to Qurie "sincerely [that] we had no wish to rule over the Palestinian people" (Peres 1995: 302). Arafat paid tribute to Peres as well. He was "capable of saying things and doing things on behalf of the Palestinians that many Arab states would neither say nor do" (Peres 1995: 302). The Israelis had not coerced the Palestinians when they were at their weakest (Segev 1998: 215). Shamir, the former Likud prime minister, complained about this very aspect of the Labor diplomatic style.[10] An agreement such as the Oslo Accords, for better or for worse, probably would not have been possible with an Israeli government that preferred coercive diplomacy. The agreement passed by a single vote in the Israeli Knesset in September 1993 following a unanimous decision by the cabinet to approve the declaration (Meital 2006: 36).

The achievements in Oslo are all the more striking in light of the situation on the ground in the territories during the talks. The fall of 1992,

---

10. "Bankrupt, increasingly discredited in the Arab world—his intifada, though hard for Israel to bear, solved nothing and was harder yet for the Palestinians, with no prospect of success on any front and not even the USSR to help him—Arafat was literally saved by Rabin and Peres. I am sure that he knows as well as I do that if Israel had only been a little more patient, as I had urged for so long, the PLO would have very soon collapsed in any case—and, a bitter foe gone, we would have moved on, along a safer, infinitely better road to new relationships in the Arab world" (Shamir 1994: 260).

directly prior to the discussions in Norway, was marked by violence in the territories. Rabin, who also served as defense minister, closed off the West Bank, preventing 120,000 Palestinians from going to work in Israel, and reinforced the IDF presence in the territories (Makovsky 1996: 89–90). He also cracked down on Hamas and Islamic Jihad militants, deporting four hundred into Lebanon. And when Lebanon refused to receive them, leaving them to starve and freeze in the winter cold, Israel suffered a monumental public relations crisis (Behrendt 2007: 71; Segev 1998: 132, 181, 191; Rabinovich 2011: 35). This was not a most promising case for diplomatic success.

Rabin's behavior was due to his pragmatic approach, most his high level of epistemic motivation, something stressed in every account of his decision-making style. Although he was, like Shamir, a long-standing opponent of direct dialogue with the PLO, the prime minister had concluded that, realistically, only the PLO had the power to conclude a binding agreement with the Israelis (Barari 2004: 82, 95; Rasler 2000: 714; Segev 1998: 192). This was a painful admission. "This may not be pleasant," he said, "but it is a fact" (in Ben-Yehuda 1997: 208). Rabin also distrusted Arafat. In 1974, he had even given orders to have him killed. But he did not let this impede him from exploring the possibility of value creating negotiation between the sides (Segev 1998: 158, 193). Rabin asked rhetorically, "What can we do? Peace you don't make with friends, but with very unsympathetic enemies. I won't try to make the PLO look good. It was an enemy, it remains an enemy, but negotiations must be with enemies" (in Ross 2004: 92).[11] Rabin was pessimistic, yet in keeping with the high level of epistemic motivation that is part of pragmatic statecraft, he did not allow this skepticism to create closed-mindedness (Makovsky 1996: 119). He "doubted anything would come of Oslo," writes Peres. "Nonetheless, he gave me, and the talks, a chance" (Peres 1995: 285; see also Beilin 1999: 136–37). The prime minister's stewardship might have been a necessary condition for the Israeli government to approve the agreement. Whereas Peres had the vision, only Rabin had the credibility at home on security because of his military pedigree (Barari 2004: 93; Makovsky 1996: 87).[12]

---

11. The prime minister later described the difficulty of shaking Arafat's hand at the signing ceremony in Washington: "I knew that the hand outstretched to me . . . was the same hand that held the knife, that held the gun, the hand that gave the order to shoot, to kill. Of all the hands in the world, it was not the hand that I wanted or dreamed of touching" (in Sassley 2010: 710). Yet he did exactly that.

12. It was undoubtedly helpful, perhaps necessary, that the Oslo talks were secret because this eliminated the public pressure on the participants that probably would have forced them to break off discussions in light of this escalation of violence on the ground (Wanis-St. John

Chapter 8

THE SPIRIT OF OSLO: NEGOTIATING THE INTERIM AGREEMENT

Value creating negotiation persisted after the signing of the Declaration of Principles. The Cairo Agreement of May 1994 identified the terms of the transfer of Gaza and Jericho to the Palestinians. On July 1, 1994, Arafat crossed into the Gaza Strip from the Sinai Peninsula and took charge of the Palestinian Authority, marking the first time in Middle Eastern history that Palestinians governed Palestinians. The twenty-four-member Palestinian Authority assumed thirty-one executive and legislative functions, including the ability to issue passports and create its own police force. It could even have "routine dealings" with foreign states and international organizations, although it could have no embassies or consulates abroad (Segev 1998: 359). These had not been easy negotiations, with strong disagreements, particularly over the extent of territory granted in Jericho and concerning control over crossings from the border city into Jordan (Segev 1998: 352).

In September 1995, the two sides reached agreement on what became known as Oslo II. The Interim Agreement on the West Bank and Gaza Strip elaborated the expansion of self-government and established the Palestinian Council (Meital 2006: 43). It divided the West Bank into three zones with various degrees of Palestinian sovereignty. In Zone A, which comprised the major cities of the West Bank, the Palestinians would exert full control. In Zone B, 450 small towns and villages where 65 percent of the Palestinians resided, the authority would govern but security would be jointly administered with the Israeli army. Zone C was to remain under Israeli control, the final disposition to be settled during final status negotiations with a series of periodic military redeployments during the interim phase (Segev 1998: 376; Rabinovich 2011: 45). Zone C included Israeli military installations and settlements that comprised 70 percent of the land but contained only 50,000 Palestinian residents. This was a value creating solution because the land most vital for Israeli security contained the fewest Palestinians. Although the peace process is often regarded as a failure, there were, as Miller notes, "real gains made on the ground, particularly Israeli withdrawal from six West Bank cities and towns by the end of 1995" (2008: 261). These gains persist today (Meital 2006: 40).

2011). Nevertheless, it would be wrong to attribute the success purely to the quality of the negotiations rather than the nature of the participants. This would miss the fact that the back channel owed its existence to the diplomatic styles of the two sides. The talks were initiated by Beilin, who was committed to a liberal dialogue. The opportunity was seized by Palestinian pragmatists. The originally informal and always highly secretive nature of negotiations was endogenous to individual-level psychological attributes of the Palestinians and Israelis.

The achievements are all the more remarkable in light of the backdrop of negotiations—a massive escalation of violence. Hamas and Islamic Jihad rejected the basic compromise of "land for peace" inherent in the Oslo process and sought instead the creation of a Palestinian state consisting of all of Mandatory Palestine. The groups attempted to derail the peace process through suicide bombings and other attacks on the Israeli military and ordinary civilians. Hamas launched its first series of attacks just three weeks after the signing of Oslo I and its second series following the signing of the Cairo Agreement (Kydd and Walter 2002). This was a level of violence greater than in the days of the first intifada. During those six years, 172 Israelis had been killed; during the early days of Oslo from 1993 to 1996, more than 300 Israelis died (Rabinovich 2011: 48).

In response, the Israelis closed Gaza off from Israel to provide greater security, leaving thousands unable to travel to work in Israel, and delayed the release of prisoners (Segev 1998: 363). Right-wing Israelis also conducted terrorist attacks, most notably the massacre by a former Israeli captain of twenty-nine Palestinian worshippers at the Tomb of the Patriarchs in Hebron in February 1994, which precipitated an international crisis and the temporary stationing of an international observer force (Meital 2006: 39; Rabinovich 2011: 27; Segev 1998: 355). Retaliation by IDF made it extremely difficult politically for Arafat to secure the two-thirds support necessary for the revision of the PLO Charter, promised as a condition of Oslo I and then Oslo II (Segev 1998: 361).

It is difficult to judge the Palestinians' thinking during this period because the available sources are insufficient. It is clear, however, that the peace process would have stalled were it not for the diplomatic style of the Labor government. The terrorist activities did not lead the Israeli government to reverse course because Arafat was not seen as directly responsible for the violence (Kydd and Walter 2002). Rather than using a crackdown on terror as a precondition for extracting greater concessions from the Palestinians, key Israeli officials expressed understanding for Arafat's plight, deserved or not. Peres stated that "although Israel does not expect the [PLO] to produce 100 percent success, it would like to see 100 percent effort" (in Kydd and Walter 2002: 282). Rather than linking the two issues, Rabin and Peres promised to "fight terrorism as though there is no peace process" and "continue the peace process as though there is no terrorism" (Segev 1998: 380). As Miller remembers, after Oslo, "For the next two years their negotiators solved problems. They lived, laughed, yelled, and cried together against the backdrop of missed deadlines, terror, violence and continuing mutual suspicion. They became friends . . . [and] pushed the Oslo process uphill against the laws of political gravity" (2008: 260).

Rabin also faced heavy domestic opposition. Likud took a strong stand against the peace process (Rabinovich 2011: 60; Inbar 1998: 39). Benjamin

Netanyahu, the Likud leader, claimed it laid the foundation for a Palestinian state that would threaten the existence of Israel. "Arafat will devour Jordan and assimilate its army. . . . You are strengthening our enemies and weakening us," he claimed (in Qurie 2008: 19). Oslo II barely passed in the Knesset, and right-wing opponents began major demonstrations across Israel. Rabin paid for his fortitude with his life; he was assassinated by another Israeli, a radical opponent of the peace process, on November 4, 1995.

A wave of terrorist attacks in February and March 1996, the most significant since the Cairo Agreement, killed 102 and wounded over 80 Israelis (Kydd and Walter 2002). In less than three weeks, Peres's lead of 20 points over Netanyahu, the Likud candidate, in the upcoming prime ministerial election evaporated. Promising "peace with security," the Likud leader emerged victorious over Rabin's heir in the 1996 election, largely as a result of the actions of Palestinian spoilers (Rabinovich 2011: 53; Barari 2004: 59; Steinberg 1998: 210–11).

FROM SHALOM TO SHLEP: THE NETANYAHU GOVERNMENT, THE AMERICANS, AND THE PALESTINIANS

The new Israeli government was composed of a coalition whose common denominator was opposition to the peace process as it currently stood. Netanyahu embraced the same zero-sum framing of the situation that guided Shamir. The Palestinian issue was a question of the very survival of Israel: "It will not do to obscure the primacy of this existential opposition to Israel as the driving force of the Arab-Israeli conflict," he wrote (Netanyahu 1993: 331). The Arabs would simply use peace as a bargaining asset of value to trade for something else in a coercive bargaining style. "Many Arab leaders who profess a desire for 'peace' think of it as a *means* to an end, such as regaining lost territory or securing military supplies from the West. . . . For much of the Arab world, peace is a coin with which one pays in order to get something else" (Netanyahu 1993: 337). Rather than explore the possibility of a mutually beneficial agreement, Netanyahu presumed that the terms that would provide Israeli security would not be acceptable to the Palestinians (Netanyahu 1993: 284).[13]

13. He claimed that if Israeli needs for hot pursuit, control of the Jordan Valley, and early warning stations were met, there would be nothing left for the Palestinians. "Israeli's retention of these boundaries is of course incompatible with the incessant calls for a Palestinian state on the West Bank," he wrote (Netanyahu 1993: 343). The Palestinians would insist on the right to protect their own borders with their own army and not allow a foreign military presence (2).

Like Shamir, Netanyahu had no sympathy for the Palestinian position. He rejected the "neat symmetry imposed on their respective needs and desires. These commentaries hold that Israel's demand for Arab recognition of its right to exist should be met in exchange for various Arab demands, especially for land. Yet to treat these demands as symmetrical, as the two sides of an equation, is to ignore both history and causality" (Netanyahu 1993: 331). Netanyahu claimed the very notion of "land for peace" was unfairly imbalanced, favoring the Palestinians: "What kind of a 'compromise' is it for one side to renounce one hundred percent of its claims and the other side to renounce zero percent?" And his framing of the situation was decidedly unpragmatic, stressing the moral superiority of the Israeli position: "What kind of a moral position is it to say that the failed aggressor should be given back all the territory from which he launched his attack?" (Netanyahu 1993: 292).

Again, we might conclude that Netanyahu simply had different preferences based on different foreign policy goals. He was the son of a prominent revisionist Israeli scholar who put forward claims to the entire West Bank as rightfully belonging to Israel. Yet, although Netanyahu complained about the peace process, before it even had begun he had sketched a solution that differed little from what ultimately emerged from the Oslo track. In his 1993 book, he endorsed the "fullest possible autonomy" for Gaza and self-government in the urban areas where most Palestinians lived, with jurisdiction over commerce, education, religion, health, and social welfare. He had proposed that sparsely populated territory remain under Israeli military control and that the army have access to the West Bank to crack down on terrorism (Netanyahu 1993: 350–53). Two years before Oslo II, Netanyahu had sketched out the same agreement.

Therefore, to the extent that Netanyahu's bottom line, and that of Likud, differs from that of Labor, the differences between the two sides are generally overstated. There is a strong case to be made that a major, perhaps the most important, division between Labor and Likud is in diplomatic style. When he became prime minister, Netanyahu did not seek to dismantle the core elements of the Oslo agreements that had already been implemented. He recognized "established facts on the ground. I am forced to accept them as starting points" (in Rabinovich 2011: 61; see also Inbar 1998: 38). Miller, the U.S. diplomat, focuses on Netanyahu's style rather than his substance in distinguishing his government from Labor: "I'll be more grudging and it will take longer, but I'll hold my base because they'll see how hard I can resist" (2008: 271). Ross says the same: "[Netanyahu] hoped he could move very slowly and through attrition give up less than the Labor Party—demonstrating that he was superior to others because in the end he could manage peace but at a lower price" (2004: 493).

[221]

Whereas Labor significantly curtailed settlement activity to send a signal of cooperative intentions, the Likud government accelerated building to create facts on the ground that strengthened the Israeli bargaining position. On taking office, Netanyahu removed the freeze on new activity, announcing the building of 1,500 new units in the West Bank with the goal of increasing Israeli numbers in the territories by 10 percent (Ross 2004: 263; Qurie 2008: 20, 52). Qurie complained that "Israel's underlying motive seemed to be . . . continuing to undermine the notion of a truly viable independent Palestinian state by covering the Palestinian territories with more and more Israeli settlements" (2008: 34).

In addition, Netanyahu put a break on the peace process. He pledged to continue negotiating but refused to begin final status talks as previously agreed in light of Palestinian violations of their commitments. The prime minister insisted on "reciprocity" (Rabinovich 2011: 61; Barari 2004: 124; Inbar 1998: 40–41; Steinberg 1998). Although at first glance this might seem to indicate a prosocial commitment to value creating in which both sides would benefit, Netanyahu used Palestinian noncompliance as a reason to stall the process of negotiations and extract more concessions from the Palestinians. Pundak, who had participated in the early Oslo talks, writes, "The main weapon in his campaign against the Palestinians was the mantra that the Palestinian side was not fulfilling its part of the agreements; and therefore Israel would not implement its part" (2001: 33). Qurie, who negotiated directly with Netanyahu, complains, "When we met, Netanyahu had frequently raised the notion of reciprocity, claiming it was the Palestinians who never implemented their commitments. . . . Whatever he was offered, he would ask for more, or suddenly discover he had wanted something else all along, in order to avoid having to agree with us on any issue" (2008: 52). He summarizes, "All in all, Netanyahu's three years in office were a wretched time for the peace process. It was a nightmare not only for the Palestinians but also for many level-headed Israelis" (2008: 19).

Beilin criticizes Netanyahu, comparing the Labor conception of reciprocity with that of Likud. "In any agreement, reciprocity is taken for granted; no party wants to fulfill its side of a contract without the compliance of the other side. However, in a political agreement, you are both a party to the agreement and its judge. It is necessary to sometimes turn a blind eye to a minor breach in order to sustain the agreement itself." This distinguished Netanyahu's coercive bargaining from a style of pragmatic statecraft: "It might be acceptable, in private life, to insist on complete reciprocity in every interaction. But the truth is that nobody will appreciate this, and you will be seen as an unrealistic person. . . . If you allow the other side to breach an agreement in a way that goes against your national interest, then you are not a responsible leader. But if you turn a blind eye to something which is marginal because you know that down the road there are more important things, then you are a realistic leader" (Beilin 2004: 57).[14]

Just as the shift from a liberal to a coercive bargaining style in France following the triumph of Locarno induced a change in the spirit of negotiating that prevailed with Germany, value claiming emerged between the Israelis and Palestinians. Although some blame surely also lies with Arafat, who never demonstrated the commitment to fighting terrorism that might have convinced others of his sincere intentions, the diplomatic style adopted by Israel is also certainly a necessary component for explaining the stall in the peace process that occurred so quickly following the ascent of Likud into office.[15]

Even though the structural circumstances had not changed, the shift from value creating to value claiming negotiations undermined the peace process. Qurie writes that "we had the depressing sensation that our relations with Israel were regressing to the point from which we had set out, years before. The relationship between Israel and the Palestinians declined from the modest level of understanding and partial reconciliation that had been achieved into an escalating and debilitating

---

14. The Americans were not pleased either. Ross describes the period, in which the "shared assumptions that had guided U.S. and Israeli policy would no longer exist—Martin [Indyk, ambassador to Israel] on a daily basis would now be dealing with people who did not see the Palestinians as partners" (2004: 258). The Americans adjusted their expectations. "We understood that not much more than interim issues could be worked through with Netanyahu and Arafat," writes Miller (2008: 270). "All of us saw Bibi [Netanyahu] as a kind of speed bump that would have to be negotiated along the way until a new Israeli prime minister came along who was more serious about peace" (Miller 2008: 274).

15. Statements made by Qurie in his meeting with Ariel Sharon, the Israeli foreign minister, echoed those made by Stresemann to the French following Poincaré's return. Qurie stressed that Palestinian diplomacy was premised on receiving tangible benefits and that the Israeli failure to seriously negotiate would force the Palestinians to reconsider their approach. "The progress of the Palestinian Authority is predicated on the end of occupation and cooperation over security. The advent of the present Israeli government has placed this project in doubt and has held up the developments that were scheduled" (Qurie 2008: 39). When Sharon placed blame on the Palestinians, referring to Arab actions even as far back as the 1930s, Qurie tried to reorient him toward present concerns: "Last time, we lost. This time, we shall both lose. We do not want to argue about who won and who lost" (40). In the face of coercive bargaining by the Israelis, the Palestinians also dug their heels in, despite the greater power of Israel. "You hold all the cards and have the power on the ground. If you want security, I can offer you the arrangements and measures that will guarantee you that. But, I am not prepared to cede more land to you, as this is all I have left" asserted Qurie (43). As Sharon detailed the list of Palestinian failures, Qurie responded with his own list (Qurie 2008: 57).

confrontation with the Netanyahu government over the building of new settlements and other issues" (2008: 21). U.S. Secretary of State Madeleine Albright referred to a "crisis of confidence between the two sides" that "was turning a situation in which each problem seemed solvable into one where there was endless dispute over every small detail" (in Beilin 2004: 70). Thomas Pickering, U.S. undersecretary of state for political affairs, put it more colloquially, "We have gone from Shalom to Shlep" (in Beilin 2004: 73). Itamar Rabinovich refers to the shift in the spirit of negotiations to explain the deterioration: "At the core of the original Oslo process had been the idea that time was needed to make a transition from conflict and hostility to a settlement predicated on compromise and partnership." After Netanyahu's ascent to power, "Any concessions made and cooperation secured were offered grudgingly. Both parties presumed they were locked in conflict, and each acted to maximize its position in the West Bank and in East Jerusalem" (Rabinovich 2011: 76).

When the two sides were able to reach agreements, such as the protocol of 1997 to implement the long-delayed withdrawal of Israeli forces from Hebron while still guaranteeing the security of the small Israeli settlement there, Netanyahu quickly offset these concessions by taking unilateral steps that would please his right-wing base (Miller 2008: 263, 271; Ross 2004: 281). To secure the support of his cabinet for this first withdrawal from West Bank territory by a Likud leader, the prime minister agreed to the construction of 6,500 housing units for 30,000 Israelis in Har Homa near East Jerusalem, a highly inflammatory move given Palestinian aspirations for a capital there (Barari 2004: 123; Beilin 2004: 63–65; Rabinovich 2011: 66).

The other major agreement between the two sides was forced on the Israelis by the Americans. The coercive bargaining style of Likud created the need for U.S. brokering. "After three years of watching a functioning process from the sidelines, we were playing the mediator's role now," writes Miller (2008: 269; see also Qurie 2008: 70; Ross 2008: 267).[16] Like Shamir, Netanyahu did not adjust to structural circumstances, pursuing coercive diplomacy even vis-à-vis the powerful Americans. President Clinton complained, "He thinks he is the superpower and we are here to do

16. The diplomatic style of the Labor government had made U.S. involvement somewhat superfluous. Miller writes that "instead of having to push futilely on a door that the first Yitzhak (Shamir) slammed shut, Clinton's team had merely to knock on a door that the second Yitzhak (Rabin) had already opened (2008: 247). The Americans were aware of but not involved with the Oslo track. Although they hosted the signing ceremony for the Declaration of Principles at which Arafat and Rabin famously shook hands in the White House Rose Garden, this was the extent of their involvement at the time.

whatever he requires" (in Ross 2004: 261). Just as the left-wing Labour government in Britain, despite its preference for liberal diplomacy, assimilated in behavior to the coercive bargaining style of France, its close ally, in the late 1920s, so did the Democratic Clinton administration start to change its diplomatic style. Coercive bargaining induced coercive bargaining. The Americans began to blame the Israelis for the lack of progress in the peace process. They complained about Israeli stubbornness on the tiniest of concessions and threatened to end their involvement (Beilin 2004: 75, 89).

The United States sought to accelerate the three further Israeli military withdrawals that had earlier been promised to the Palestinians before the completion of the interim agreement. The president pushed a transfer of 13 percent of West Bank land on the Israelis (Beilin 2004: 75; Rabinovich 2011: 78–79; Qurie 2008: 65); the Israelis countered, in coercive diplomatic fashion, with 9 percent (Rabinovich 2011: 80). At the Wye River Summit, hosted by the Americans in 1998, the Israelis agreed to two more redeployments, provided that the Palestinians took further steps toward curbing terrorism (Beilin 2004: 76; Qurie 2008: 63). The negotiations were marked by value claiming between the United States and Israel. Beilin describes the scene as "raised voices, crises" with "the Israelis packing their bags to return home, only to unpack and remain" (2004: 77). The United States called the prime minister's bluff, making travel arrangements for his departure (Qurie 2008: 72). Netanyahu "flooded the negotiations with unrealistic demands," even of the Americans, such as the release of an American caught spying for Israel (Qurie 2008: 67). In the end, the United States prevailed, with Israel accepting an agreement almost identical to that which the Americans had proposed. Value claiming favors the more powerful side.

Nevertheless, although the Americans could lead the Israeli horse to water, they could not make it drink. Netanyahu's cabinet assented to the Wye memorandum only after insisting that it approve each redeployment sequentially, giving the Israelis greater ability to leverage the process for more Palestinian concessions. The prime minister still needed Labor votes to approve the agreement in the Knesset. Afterward, Netanyahu found it impossible to implement the agreement due to pressure from his party and from other right-wing coalition partners in the cabinet. When he ordered the first redeployment, the coalition collapsed (Miller 2008: 275–76; Barari 2004: 121–26; Beilin 2004: 80–81). Miller writes, "It may well be that Wye's greatest consequence was to bring about, quite unintentionally, the demise of Netanyahu's government, which broke apart over the agreement he signed" (2008: 276). This happened despite the fact that 80 percent of the Israeli public supported it (Ross 2004: 461–62). Whereas the Rabin government had been brought down by Palestinian terrorists, the Netanyahu government succumbed to internal right-wing opposition. Indeed, Hamas and Islamic Jihad had been very quiet for most of the Likud term in office, leading some to argue that Netanyahu's positions slowed the peace process enough so that it was unnecessary for the Palestinian extremists to play a spoiler role (Rabinovich 2011: 77; Kydd and Walter 2002).

BARGAINING BY BARAK: QUASI-COERCIVE DIPLOMACY BY LABOR

Elections returned Labor to power in Israel, generating very high expectations for the new prime minister, Ehud Barak. The former head of the Israeli armed forces was considered an heir to Rabin, a military man committed to peace while still keeping Israel safe. Abbas said, "We can now make peace. These are our natural partners" (in Ross 2004: 492). The Americans were optimistic as well. "At the time . . . administration officials believed there was a historic opportunity for an agreement. "Bibi [Netanyahu] was out, Barak was in, and overnight expectations in Israel, among the Palestinians, and within our administration were sky-high about the prospects for peace. We were back in business," writes Ross (2004: 494). Yet Barak's diplomatic style was deeply conflicted. On the one hand, he was similar to his Labor predecessors in his commitment to finding a mutually beneficial agreement; on the other, he was unsure of the Palestinian commitment to a final peace deal.

Barak promised to "leave no stone unturned and to open all avenues" (Meital 2006: 56) and prepared the Israelis for the "painful concessions" that would be necessary (Meital 2006: 53). Rather than feigning pessimism, he declared, "I am always optimistic. . . . I do not know of another way to deal with life in our region" (in Sher 2006: 5). He was, in Pundak's estimation, "rationally left-wing" with empathy for the Palestinian desire for a state, going as far as to admit that he would have been a freedom fighter had he been a Palestinian (2001: 37). Behind the scenes he told his team, "We are on the brink of some of the most difficult decisions of this decade, if not of the history of this country. We do not really know how far we can go in terms of reaching a reasonable balance between the needs of one side and the needs of the other. It is important to be aware of the need to change our own perceptions" (in Sher 2006: 25). Like Rabin before him, Barak set an ambitious timetable for the conclusion of the final status talks long delayed by Netanyahu, hoping for a deal within twelve to fifteen months (Meital 2006: 55; Malley and Agha 2001). At Sharm el-Sheikh in September 1999, he secured grudging Palestinian acceptance to conclude an agreement within a year (Meital 2006: 58; Rabinovich 2011: 102).

Barak's key advisors and negotiators were some of the most committed doves in Israel, and they approached the negotiations with a liberal diplomatic style of reasoned dialogue. Gilead Sher writes,

> I used to first listen attentively in order to be able to analyze the positions of the other side, its interests and intentions. The ability to connect with the people sitting across from me did not dilute my mission, which was to achieve the best possible results as defined in the strategic objectives of the leadership. I found out that empathy for the arguments of my interlocutors often helped overcome real and imaginary obstacles. Shlomo Ben-Ami and I made an effort to be fair and accurate in presenting the positions of the other side, as we understood them. By so doing, we attempted to increase the chances that they would trust the veracity of the positions we presented. (2006: 19–20)

The team was prepared for a value creating solution satisfactory for both sides. "It was clear that the negotiations should be based on a 'give and take' on the core issues," writes Sher. "This should be done without compromising the vital interests of Israel while looking for the widest possible common denominator between the members of the Palestinian leadership" (2006: 61).

Yet Barak was not sure that the Palestinians were willing to make reciprocal concessions and did not want to reveal the Israeli bottom lines unless he was sure that a deal was at hand (Malley and Agha 2001: 69). He explained later, "Essentially, I insisted that despite our desire to try every chance for an agreement, and perhaps because of it, if we reached the last leg of an agreement, it was vital that we know if we had a partner before we continued to hand over assets" (Barak 2003: 86–87). Barak saw the final status talks as a "window of opportunity" at the close of which "we will know where we stand" (in Meital 2006: 55). The Israeli prime minister was willing to make tough choices if Arafat was, but he was not sure that Arafat would be. Barak had the idea of "unmasking" Arafat (Meital 2006: 72) to see if he was indeed a "Palestinian [Anwar] Sadat" who could end the conflict (Pressman 2003: 11; see also Rabinovich 2011: 88).

This uncertainty about Palestinian intentions induced the use of coercive bargaining tactics. Publicly Barak issued his "five Nos," positional commitments on the major issues in the final status talks (Malley and Agha 2001: 69; Meital 2006: 57; Sher 2006: 58). There would be no return to the 1967 borders, no division of Jerusalem, no systematic dismantling of settlements, no foreign army west of the Jordan River, and no right of return for Palestinian refugees (Pressman 2003). These positions were close to actual Israeli bottom lines rather than a gross inflation of Israeli demands. Nevertheless, simply making such claims seems to have been an effort to drive a hard bargain.

In keeping with this strategy, Barak did not initially complete the third redeployment promised in the Wye agreement, opting to withhold the territory for bargaining leverage in the final status agreements (Meital 2006: 55; Malley and Agha 2001: 65; Pundak 2001: 31–32). Sher explains, "Barak was convinced that Israel's final withdrawal from the Occupied Territories should be tied to far-reaching agreements on the core issues of the conflict, namely territorial boundaries, refugees, Jerusalem, water rights and security arrangements. But the magnitude of the gaps between Israeli and Palestinian positions on these issues led Barak to believe that it was wrong to move forward with implementing the Israeli further redeployment before the disputed issues were further explored and the gaps between the polarized positions narrowed" (2006: 2).

Yet Barak, unlike Netanyahu and Shamir, was holding back on Israeli positions so that he could ultimately make great compromises. "Precisely because he was willing to move a great distance in a final agreement (on territory or on Jerusalem, for example), he was unwilling to move an inch in the preamble (prisoners, settlements, troop redeployment, Jerusalem villages)," write Malley and Agha (2001: 63). Sher explains, "Conceding additional territories without reaching an agreement on these core issues would leave Israel without any assets to negotiate. The only incentive for the Palestinians to relinquish their claim for the Right of Return of Palestinian refugees to Israel, would involve transferring a substantial amount of territory as part of a comprehensive peace agreement. Barak assessed that discussing the Right of Return when most of the territory had already been transferred to the Palestinians would leave us empty-handed in the negotiation process" (2006: 2).

The natural corollary of Barak's goal of negotiating a permanent settlement that would finally uncover Arafat's true face was to push for a high-level summit (Malley and Agha 2001: 67). Sher writes, "It was only at this point, [Barak] believed, that Arafat would reveal his true intentions" (2006: 2). Barak instructed his advisors to "tell the Palestinians discreetly that we Israelis are built for a settlement 'in one fell swoop.' All the issues, all the subjects, all the pain . . . we are not built for agreements in stages, in which we will have to make continual political down payments" (in Freilich 2012: 154). This was a "boom-or-bust" approach (Miller 2008: 280; see also Rabinovich 2011: 87). The Americans originally resisted, feeling that the proper preparation had not been done, but ultimately consented. "We went to Camp David on his word," remembers Secretary of State Albright (in Miller 2008: 280).

Barak's diplomatic style seems to have reflected both individual characteristics and domestic political pressures. When the prime minister had been in Rabin's cabinet as the head of the IDF, he had been genuinely skeptical of the Oslo process, even abstaining from the interim agreement that ceded territory in exchange only for Palestinian promises to curtail terrorism (Freilich 2012: 173; Malley and Agha 2001; Pundak 2001: 36; Rabinovich 2011: 101; Meital 2006: 53). Barak later wrote of his period as military chief, "I stopped a one-sided process that had developed since the Oslo accords were signed, a process in which Israel gave up tangible assets in exchange for vague promises about the nature of relations in the future. When I was still a new minister in the Rabin government, I campaigned in government votes against that pattern of behavior. The Netanyahu government, with Sharon as foreign minister, continued to sign agreements that transferred assets for promises (Hebron and the Wye River agreement) and even handed over assets (Hebron)" (Barak 2003: 86).

The Labor Party was also much weaker in the Barak government than previously under Rabin and Peres. Labor won only 26 seats in the parliament of 120. Barak's coalition included a much stronger presence of right-wing parties that seems to have significantly affected the diplomatic style of his government (Pundak 2001: 36–37; Sher 2006: 43, 48; Stinnett 2007). The other left-wing parties did not provide an absolute majority in the Knesset, and the prime minister had built a coalition that excluded Likud but incorporated a number of religious and right-wing parties, such as Shas, the National Religious Party (NRP), and Yisrael Ba'aliya, that preferred coercive bargaining (Rabinovich 2011: 88; Barari 2004: 127). This was also part of a political calculation. "Prime Minister Yitzhak Rabin had paid a tremendous political (and physical) price by alienating the Israeli right wing and failing to bring its members along during the Oslo process. Barak was determined not to repeat that mistake," write Malley and Agha (2001: 63). Barak stressed that "he could not allow himself at this stage to sidestep his party colleagues from the left" (Sher 2006: 25). In many ways, Barak's diplomatic style was the perfect blend of the tendencies of the parties in his coalition.

This partly explains why Barak delayed the third redeployment. "He did not want to estrange the Right prematurely or be (or appear to be) a 'sucker' by handing over assets, only to be rebuffed on the permanent status deal. . . . If Israelis and Palestinians reached a final agreement, all these minor steps (and then some) would be taken; on the other hand, if the parties failed to reach a final agreement, those steps would have been wasted and would cost precious political capital" (Malley and Agha 2001: 63). Pressure from the United States led Barak to ultimately concede to a third redeployment in exchange for a Palestinian agreement to quickly begin the final status talks (Malley and Agha 2001: 67; Freilich 2012: 164). Shas abstained from approving this agreement, however, and the NRP voted against it (Meital 2006: 59). Although the redeployment was approved by the Knesset, the prime minister delayed the withdrawal by two months (Freilich 2012: 164). David Levy, the minister of foreign affairs and a former member of Likud who had broken away from his party, pleaded with Barak not to rush to a summit: "We still have nothing and we are tearing the coalition apart" (in Sher 2006: 32). Along with Nathan Sharansky, the leader of the NRP and minister of the interior, Levy called for red lines at the summit. Sharansky threatened to resign if a conference were held (Freilich 2012: 165–69), and Levy pledged not to attend (Sher 2006: 56). Sharansky also was responsible for Barak's decision to shut down a back channel negotiation with the Palestinians, which had been exploring a final status framework on the basis of the terms set out in Stockholm in 1995. The NRP leader publicized its content and claimed Israel had conceded too much (Rabinovich 2011: 102; Meital 2006: 65).[17]

Ultimately, however, Barak was still unsuccessful in holding the right in his coalition, which broke apart before the Camp David Summit even began due to differences over the peace process (Rabinovich 2011: 104). Shas, the NRP, and Yisrael Ba'aliya all voted to bring down the government (Sher 2006: 42). Because the prime minister was directly elected, he was not compelled to put together another coalition but was forced to call for elections to be held in December 2000. He imagined fighting the election on the basis of the deal he brought back home from Camp David. If Barak won the election, he would put the issue to a public referendum (Sher 2006: 48–49; Freilich 2012: 165–67). The need to bring home a deal that would win over moderate voters in such a campaign probably also affected his diplomatic style, moving it toward coercive bargaining.

MASKS IN MARYLAND: VALUE CLAIMING AT CAMP DAVID

It was in the very nature of the final status talks that they would be difficult. They dealt with the most sensitive issues, those that the Israelis and Palestinians had postponed because they could not yet figure out a

---

17. Pressure from the right in the coalition was also responsible for Barak's decision to delay the agreed transfer of three East Jerusalem villages, including Abu Dis, to Palestinian control as a confidence-building exercise favored by the Americans before the summit (Freilich 2012: 166; Sher 2006: 31; Miller 2008: 294). Clinton was furious at the Israeli actions (Malley and Agha 2001: 67). Although Barak blamed the outbreak of violence that had accompanied Al-Nakba festivities, domestic politics were to blame (Meital 2006: 63–64). The prime minister told Sher, "If it will pacify the NRP and Israel B'Aliya, I will not transfer Abu Dis at this stage" (in Sher 2006: 48).

solution. As a consequence, negotiations were bound to be more distributive and zero-sum in nature, encouraging value claiming by both sides. It is unclear whether there even is a zone of possible agreement between the Israelis and Palestinians, a deal that both would prefer to the status quo. In any case, the character of negotiations that prevailed at Camp David in 2000 did not facilitate its discovery. Diplomatic styles helped to undercut the chance for peace.

A number of analysts maintain that Barak's coercive bargaining before and at Camp David undermined the Palestinians' belief that he was willing to make the compromises necessary for peace, encouraging them to use a similar diplomatic style. Pundak claims Barak "did not understand that while trying to 'remove Arafat's mask in order to see if Arafat could make tough decisions,' he actually unveiled an ugly Israeli face which had not been conditioned to pay the necessary price for peace" (2001: 39). His style "was completely wrong. . . . Barak should have presented the principles underlying what eventually became his proposed solutions . . . in the early stages of negotiations. . . . Instead, Barak dragged his feet and treated the talks like a Persian market . . . fearing he would 'expose' his positions too early in the game" (Pundak 2001: 39). Arafat was suspicious of Barak's strategy, believing that he was trying to create an atmosphere of pressure and impose an unfair settlement (Malley and Agha 2001: 64). Should talks break down, Arafat would be blamed (Meital 2006: 66). Malley and Agha write, "Designed to preserve his assets for the 'moment of truth,' Barak's tactics helped to ensure that the parties never got there. His decision to view everything through the prism of an all-or-nothing negotiation over a comprehensive deal led him to see every step as a test of wills, any confidence-building measure as a weakness-displaying one. Obsessed with Barak's tactics, Arafat spent far less time worrying about the substance of a deal than he did fretting about a possible ploy. Fixated on potential traps, he could not see potential opportunities" (2001: 74).

Even Sher partly blames the prime minister: "This pattern of brash behavior by Barak would repeat itself numerous times in the upcoming months, severely hampering efforts to restore the trust between the two sides" (2006: 4). In particular, Barak's failure to comply with interim agreements raised doubts about his willingness to deliver during the final status talks. Barak's policies confused the Palestinians. He appeared serious and determined to reach an agreement but also spoke in "right-wing code" (Pundak 2001: 36). Although Barak's style is certainly not the only factor responsible, it can be safely said that, when the two sides arrived at Camp David, a value creating mind-set was not present.

At Camp David, Barak could only hold back the Israeli bottom lines while simultaneously presenting Arafat with an attractive ultimatum that would reveal his intentions if Israeli positions were put forward by the Americans as U.S. ideas (Meital 2006: 76). Clinton administration officials therefore shuttled between the cabins of the two sides brokering the talks. Arafat and Barak met only once at Camp David during the several weeks of negotiations (Rabinovich 2011: 82). The Israelis deemed any commitments they made as hypothetical and revocable in the absence of a reciprocal concession (Rabinovich 2011: 107; Malley and Agha 2001: 67). Barak's team negotiated on the basis that "nothing is agreed until everything is agreed" (Sher 2006: 2; Pressman 2003: 7). The Israelis were obsessed even before Camp David with leaks that could reveal the compromises that they were willing to make, undermining public support for peace. Consequently, they wrote very little down (Sher 2006: 42; Freilich 2012: 171; Meital 2006: 83). For all these reasons, as Malley and Agha write, the Palestinians saw Barak's generous proposals as "neither generous, nor Israeli, nor, indeed, as an offer" (2001: 62).

Although accounts differ, the Israelis offered the Palestinians (indirectly through the Americans) all of the West Bank save an annexation of somewhere between 9 and 10 percent of territory so that 80 percent of the Israeli settlers could be incorporated into Israel. The Israelis did not offer a one-to-one exchange of land, although they were ready to cede 1 percent of current Israeli territory as compensation. This was a better deal than had been discussed in Stockholm, where the Israelis proposed a 12 percent annexation with no territorial swaps (Rabinovich 2011: 106; Freilich 2012: 163). The Israelis wanted a temporary military presence in the Jordan Valley, including early warning stations but reduced their demand that the Israeli military presence last for twenty years. Palestine would be demilitarized. The Israeli position on refugees, however, had not changed. Committed to the preservation of the Jewish character of Israel, representatives refused to recognize a right of return but were willing to concede to a family reunification program that would allow a small number of Palestinians to return to their ancestral homes. Other refugees would be free to settle in the new Palestinian entity and other Arab countries (Pundak 2001: 40; Freilich 2012: 159–62; Pressman 2003; Malley and Agha 2001: 69; Rabinovich 2011: 107; Meital 2006: 78).

Barak's most striking concession, however, was on Jerusalem. Previously committed, like all Israeli leaders before him, to the indivisibility of the city, Barak was willing to give the Palestinians a capital in East Jerusalem with sovereignty over the Christian and Muslim quarters of the old city and "permanent custodianship" of (although not sovereignty over) the Temple Mount, known to Muslims as Haram al-Sharif, the

[232]

third holiest site in Islam (Pundak 2001: 40; Freilich 2012: 159–62; Pressman 2003; Malley and Agha 2001: 69; Rabinovich 2011: 107; Meital 2006: 78).

For their part, the Palestinian delegation wanted a return to 1967 borders with the possibility of territorial swaps on an equal, one-to-one basis. East Jerusalem would be the Palestinian capital, and Palestinians would exert sovereignty over the Temple Mount, although they were willing to concede ownership of the Western Wall and the Jewish Quarter of the Old City to the Israelis. Although the Palestinians wanted an Israeli recognition, in principle, of the right of return, they were willing to limit it in practice out of respect for the demographic and security interests of Israel (Pundak 2001: 40; Freilich 2012: 159–62; Pressman 2003; Malley and Agha 2001: 69; Rabinovich 2011: 107; Meital 2006: 78).

The Palestinians never responded definitively to the "U.S." proposals. The Palestinians expressed no appreciation for Barak's concessions on Jerusalem, seeming to pocket the concession with reciprocation. Accounts seem to indicate that personal rivalries among the negotiating team, a lack of preparation, and Arafat's indecision contributed to their passiveness (Dajani 2005). In any case, whether this was the intent or not, the Israelis and Americans understood Palestinian behavior as coercive bargaining. Barak complained, "[Arafat] did not negotiate in good faith; indeed, he did not negotiate at all. He just kept saying 'no' to every offer, never making any counterproposals of his own" (Pressman 2003). Shlomo Ben-Ami, an Israeli negotiator recalls, "The whole time [at Camp David] we waited to see them make some sort of movement in the face of our far-reaching movement. But they didn't" (in Pressman 2003: 12). Even Pundak, whose account is generally more sympathetic to the Palestinians, accuses the Palestinians of "foot-dragging, passivity and contradictory positions" (2001: 41). "Throughout the negotiations, the Palestinian team conveyed a feeling that there was no end to Palestinians demands and that this pressure would continue to increase as an agreement came closer," a tactic "designed to extract every possible concession prior to signing" (Pundak 2001: 43). The Americans also faulted Arafat. Ross remembers, "Throughout the course of the Oslo process, Chairman Arafat was extremely passive. His style was to respond, not initiate ideas. That is a good tactic, especially for a weaker party that feels it has little to give. If it was only a tactic, it should have stopped when serious ideas or package proposals were put on the table" (Ross 2001). Arafat expressed indifference to reaching a deal. When Albright stressed that Arafat was losing the opportunity to create his own state, he responded, "I already have state. . . . If Barak does not want to recognize this now, I do not care if it is recognized even in twenty years. Our situation is like the one in South Africa, the whole world supports me" (Sher 2006: 67). Palestinians even expressed doubts about the holiness of the Temple Mount for Jews, going as far as to claim that there was never a Jewish temple on the site (Pundak 2001: 43; Haberman 2001).[18]

The combination of coercive bargaining by both sides produced value claiming negotiations in which both refused to reveal information and dug their heels in (Miller 2008: 202). "Bottom lines and false bottoms: the tension, and the ambiguity, were always there," write Malley and Agha (2001: 69). "Barak feared that everything he would say would be committing himself, and Arafat would say nothing at all," Ross summarizes (in Haberman 2001). Malley and Agha write, "Barak's strategy was predicated on the idea that his firmness would lead to some Palestinian flexibility, which in turn would justify Israel's making further concessions. Instead, Barak's piecemeal negotiation style, combined with Arafat's unwillingness to budge, produced a paradoxical result" (2001: 72). Value claiming led to a game of chicken in which each side was waiting for the other side to make the first move. Barak said at the summit, "If we put our final positions on the table, there will be no way back. But if they would move toward us, we would move forward" (in Sher 2006: 70). Arafat felt the same. "The mutual and by then deeply entrenched suspicion meant that Barak would conceal his final proposals, the 'endgame,' until Arafat had moved, and that Arafat would not move until he could see the endgame" (Malley and Agha 2001: 72). The deadlock could not be broken.

Following the breakdown of negotiations at Camp David, the Clinton administration launched a last-minute effort to secure a deal before the president left office. In the end, however, time ran out. The second intifada began in October 2000. Street action was accompanied by devastating suicide bombings starting in December 2000 (Pressman 2006; Kydd and Walter 2002). The Barak government continued to negotiate with the Palestinians in the early days of the uprising, but the prime minister suffered a crushing election loss to Ariel Sharon in February 2001. As was

---

18. Although President Clinton, personally mediating between the two sides, expressed frustration with the Israelis, he was more upset with the Palestinians for their diplomatic style. Clinton said to Ahmed Qurie, "Don't simply say to the Israelis that their map is no good. Give me something better! . . . This is a fraud. It is not a summit. I won't have the United States covering for negotiations in bad faith. Let's quit! . . . If the Israelis can make compromises and you can't, I should go home. You have been here fourteen days and said no to everything. These things have consequences" (in Malley and Agha 2001: 71). At another point, when Qurie repeated the well-rehearsed Palestinian case for rightful return of all land held in 1967, Clinton exploded, "You are not acting with integrity . . . and you are breaking my agreement with Arafat and Barak. You are not acting in good faith. This is no way to manage negotiations!" (in Sher 2006: 68).

the case with Netanyahu, Sharon's victory had been thought unlikely before the increase in violence (Barari 2004: 132). But given the bloodshed, combined with the Israeli public's strong reaction to Arafat's perceived lack of good faith at Camp David, Sharon won by almost a two-to-one margin. The Israeli public was almost unanimous in its belief that the Palestinians had initiated the violence to extract additional concessions, exploiting Barak's willingness to make historic concessions (Bar-Tal and Sharvit 2007). By the end of 2000, 70 percent believed that the Palestinians did not accept the very existence of Israel (Hermann and Yuchtman-Yaar 2002; see also Waxman 2008).

The violence of the second intifada was less spontaneous and proceeded with more active leadership from Arafat's political party, Fatah, than the first had. The actual role of key Palestinian leaders in planning the uprising is the subject of dispute, but it is clear that Arafat did exploit it and made no effort to suppress it (Rabinovich 2011: 109). The Al-Aqsa brigades, declaring themselves the military wing of Fatah, fought alongside Hamas and the Islamic Jihad. This explains why, although support for the peace process declined across the political spectrum, polls show that the fall was particularly precipitous for the left. This is another example of the behavioral assimilation in diplomatic style that occurs when the other side is regarded as not reciprocating. Barak believed that Arafat walked away from a deal very close to Palestinian demands and deliberately turned to terrorism (Pressman 2003: 10). He later echoed the importance of reciprocity in value creating negotiation: "We don't have a partner. Frustrating or not, that's a fact. Peace and agreements are like a tango. They take two. In war, all it takes is the will of one side" (Miller 2008: 329). Shlomo Ben-Ami, the foreign minister under Barak, later wrote, "We . . . did not expect to meet the Palestinians halfway, not even two-thirds of the way, but we expected to meet them somewhere" (in Rabinovich 2011: 115). Following the failure at Camp David, Barak became the first Israeli leader to publicly propose the construction of a security barrier between the Israeli and Palestinian populations (Waxman 2008).

Ariel Sharon ruthlessly repressed the intifada, using targeted assassinations of Hamas officials, regular military incursions into autonomous Palestinian territory, checkpoints and curfews, home demolitions, and mass arrests. After a bombing of a Passover seder dinner in March 2002, the IDF retook areas that had been given full sovereignty under the Oslo II agreements and surrounded Arafat's headquarters in Ramallah. The second intifada was far more deadly than the first, with 3,189 Palestinians and 92 Israelis losing their lives. In addition, the Palestinian economy was destroyed (Pressman 2006). Sharon also began the construction of the security barrier separating Palestinians from Israelis. The peace process was dead.

[235]

[9]

Searching for Stresemann

THE LESSONS OF THE 1920s FOR DIPLOMACY AND
THE MIDDLE EAST PEACE PROCESS

There is a reason why scholars of international relations have not devoted significant attention to the 1920s. The maelstrom of the 1930s sucks up all the intellectual oxygen. It is somewhat natural that some, if not the most, cataclysmic events in world history—the Great Depression, the eliminationist Nazi regime, and World War II—attract more interest. Yet there is a lot to learn from the 1920s as well, both about what could have been in Europe and what could still be in the Middle East.

It is by no means certain that had Germany, France, and Britain continued down the diplomatic path forged by Stresemann, Briand, and Chamberlain, that Europe and the world at large would have avoided the rise of fascism in Germany. Their actions surely could not have averted the Great Depression and perhaps not even rise of nationalism that followed in its wake. And it seems that there was no deal that would have left Adolf Hitler satisfied, short of war. The Führer was sui generis. The world had never seen such a destructive force before and will, it is hoped, never see anything like it again. The problems of Europe in the late 1930s, after Hitler's rise, did not have diplomatic solutions.

Nevertheless, I contend that, if there had been an alternative historical path that preserved the peace, it would have followed the lines drawn by those three statesmen, supported at home by those who embraced their diplomatic styles. Germany was particularly important. The greatest chance for peace was the preservation of that domestic coalition in Germany that had supported Stresemann's rapprochement with Western Europe, a Baptist-bootlegger alliance of the left and the center-right. It was across this domestic tightrope that Stresemann is seen guiding Germany on the cover, trying to bring Germany safely across the abyss toward peace. If there is to be a lasting peace between Israel and the Palestinians, recent history shows that a similar partnership in Israel will be a necessary (although not a sufficient) condition.

As detailed in chapter 4, Stresemann did his best to attract the support of the nationalist right, which preferred a coercive diplomatic style to reach the same goals—an alteration of the eastern borders of Germany, new colonies, and the end of occupation by France. He was unable to do so. Instead he had to rely on the center-left, in particular the Social Democrats. Stresemann's center-right did not have the numbers he needed in the parliament without the German left. And in such a polarized political climate, both internationally and domestically, the Social Democrats alone could not pull it off. It required the cover provided by Stresemann, who could credibly claim to speak for those Germans who were not "internationalists" in any ideological sense. He and his DVP could not be accused of being traitors to Germany (although the nationalists tried). This is the great virtue of a diplomatic coalition that crosses the political spectrum.

That Stresemann was able to attract the support of the SPD indicates the distinction made between liberals and realists in international relations theory is overdrawn. Historically in international relations theory, realism is contrasted to liberalism. The two form the bookends of courses on international relations. Michael Williams calls it "one of the oldest and most pervasive contrasts" (2005: 129). Classic realists in the field—Edward Carr (1964), Hans Morgenthau (1948), and Robert Osgood (1953)—situate their arguments against liberal utopianism. Despite this, liberal reason and pragmatic rationality are similar in that they both involve careful deliberation to see things as they really are, as opposed to unthinking, noncalculating, emotional, subjective, and passionate decision making (Berki 1981). The two diplomatic styles differ in that the former involves a genuine consideration of, although not a capitulation to, the interests of others in a genuine effort to reach a mutually beneficial outcome (Zacher and Matthew 1995). Nevertheless, where state interests align, realists would offer identical advice about the merits of diplomacy. Realism is ultimately more pessimistic than liberalism about the ability to transcend the nature of power politics (Zacher and Matthew 1995; Rathbun 2010); however, this does not foreclose the possibility of, many times, there being significant mutual interests among states other than alliances against a common foe. All realists should agree that conflict can be needlessly expensive and distract from the core vital interests of a country. A. J. H. Murray writes of realism, "the national interest is defined so as to incorporate an obligation to self-limitation and tolerance. The statesman is obliged to define interests in terms compatible with those of other states" (1996: 104). Realists are, in terms used by Ken Booth and Nicolas Wheeler, not "transcenders" of state conflict, nor are they "fatalists." Rather, they are "mitigators" of state conflict (Booth and Wheeler 2008: 11).

[237]

Although in theory realism and liberalism might be very different, in practice they are often on the same side. The true opponents of a liberal diplomacy (and foreign policy) are the nationalist advocates of coercive bargaining. Center-right realists, although sharing the egoistic orientation of the far right, often have more in common with the left in terms of their policy agendas. In practice, we should not think of realists in crude terms as militaristic saber-rattlers, as we often mistakenly do but, instead, as the shrewd pragmatists they are. They are often the best friends to liberals who need to shore up their domestic political base.

Neglecting the qualitative difference in diplomatic style between pragmatic realists and coercive bargainers leads to faulty empirical conclusions. In the case of 1920s Germany, both constructivists and structural realists have argued that Stresemann was ultimately no different from other nationalist politicians of his era and would have backed Hitler's rise to power, as other prominent conservatives did. Stresemann was "fairly typical," according to Jeffrey Legro (2005: 96). "It is not difficult to imagine the pragmatic Stresemann, had he lived and remained in power, traveling the same path to Hitler that the Heinrich Brüning, Franz von Papen, and Kurt von Schleicher governments followed" (Legro 2005: 96). If this assessment is true, Stresemann and the DVP were not practitioners of pragmatic statecraft, and Briand and the Cartel des Gauches had no real epistemic motivation but, rather, were idealistic dupes tricked by the cagey foreign minister into believing what they wanted to believe.

Both Legro (2005) and Dale Copeland (2000) argue that the 1920s demonstrate a seamless continuity with prewar nationalist and militaristic policies of Germany (and those of Hitler afterward). Legro attributes this to cultural factors; Copeland attributes it to structural pressures derived from geography and the balance of power. From this, Legro concludes that, even under Stresemann, the return of Germany to great power status "would ultimately rest on the renewal and use of military power in the service of territorial expansion" (2005: 94). Copeland states that "it is hard not to conclude that this 'man of peace', had he commanded the military power of Germany in 1939, would have reignited the heroic *Drang nach Osten*" (2000: 124).

Both are wrong. Legro and Copeland reach their empirically indefensible conclusions because they lack the proper conceptual tools. They are unable to distinguish realism from nationalism and pragmatic statecraft from coercive bargaining. As a consequence, international relations scholars are still searching to establish an accurate picture of Stresemann.

Stresemann was not a genuine advocate of European integration. The hagiographies of the early 1930s after his untimely death were indeed off the mark. The foreign minister was pursuing only national goals, not European ones. But this does not make him a likely ally of fascism. That is a false dichotomy. As Jonathan Wright explains, "Stresemann did not believe that the League had transformed the nature of international relations. . . . He distinguished his policy from the illusions of those on the left as well as the right" (1995: 127). Stresemann did want major changes in the postwar system; however, that is something different entirely from arguing that the foreign minister was a wolf in sheep's clothing.

Legro makes reference to Stresemann's acknowledgment that Germany had no choice but to pursue a peaceful policy of revision given the heavily skewed distribution of power; however, this is hardly equivalent to Stresemann's advocating another war had Germany been stronger. In fact, there is almost no evidence that the foreign minister had such a strategy in mind and much evidence that he did not. Stresemann was contemplating peaceful solutions when he spoke of the "free hand" (Stresemann, Vol. 2: 88–95) he would have in the east after any rapprochement with the west (Wright 2002: 313; Cohrs 2006: 228). France and Britain would provide the diplomatic backing to negotiate border changes; "I am not thinking of war in relation to the eastern question," he stated (in Wright 2002: 345). Wright argues, "He never tried to predict that future in detail, though there are [no indications] that he thought of a new German military empire in Europe" (2002: 378–79).

In fact, Stresemann thought more could be accomplished through diplomacy than through force. He said privately to his DVP allies, "The only policy which can succeed is that which aims to become a worthwhile ally for other nations, so as at the moment of becoming a useful ally to receive from the other side *what you never get* with old, buried guns" (in Wright 2002: 285, emphasis added). Stresemann opposed the use of force not out of principled reasons, of course, but from pragmatic and utilitarian ones consistent with his realism. That does not make him a Hitler or even a garden-variety German nationalist of the type that populated the DNVP. He wrote, "One could imagine a German foreign policy which is based on forgetting nothing and having only one goal: to recover Germany's old position. Even if Germany were a military power, one would have to be clear in conducting such a policy that one would thereby bring back to life an alliance of the whole world against Germany" (Stresemann, Vol. 2: 157–59; Wright 2002: 325). Those few allusions by Stresemann to the use of force as the ultimate arbiter were always made in the same context, in efforts to gain adherents on the nationalist right to his style of diplomacy, as in conversations with military leaders such as General Hans von Seeckt (Wright 1995: 121–29). In his infamous letter to the crown prince, he identified a number of long-term objectives for Germany, including unification with Austria (Stresemann, Vol. 2: 159, 503–6). This should not be surprising. After all, as a rightist politician, he had a proself motivation in diplomacy. Nevertheless,

Stresemann never made any commitment to a forceful change. Even before nationalist crowds, he spoke of a "carefully considered policy to find a way, working with other nations, to re-establish the right of self-determination where it is violated" (in Wright 2002: 378; ADAP, B1/2: 665–69). As a consequence, von Seeckt and those like him disliked and distrusted Stresemann immensely and frequently spoke of removing him from power (Gatzke 1954: 13, 37–38).

It is true that "by design" (Copeland 2000: 123) the Locarno treaty did not lock in the eastern borders of Germany. But Stresemann was always upfront with his interlocutors about wanting those lines redrawn. He just did not imagine that force was necessary to do so. The very fact that Stresemann negotiated such a treaty indicates that he did not view it as merely a scrap of paper. If the foreign minister truly had had such designs, why did he not simply negotiate a treaty guaranteeing the status quo in the east, thus lowering the guard of the allies, and strike when Germany was ready?

Stresemann did, indeed, know about the limited covert rearmament programs of the Reichswehr, but he put little stock in it. "I consider all the elaborate games to recover power secretly as total nonsense. You cannot produce heavy artillery or build a thousand planes secretly, that damages our foreign policy without bringing us anything," he said at the time (in Wright 2002: 285). Stresemann tolerated the covert programs so as not to provoke a powerful domestic adversary. For the foreign minister, the merits of limited rearmament lay in repressing a potential internal socialist revolution, not in overturning the geographical status quo (Gatzke 1954: 25).

The foreign minister's biographer, Jonathan Wright, concludes, "It is unthinkable that he would have embarked on the same policy, which was a denial of everything he stood for." Stresemann said of Hitler in 1923 that the future Führer was "only able to destroy" (in Wright 1995: 131). Legro and Copeland are confused by what Wright calls his "consummate blend of statesmanlike argument and nationalist rhetoric" and distracted by the latter (2002: 346).

Israel is still searching for its Stresemann, or more broadly, for a strong party backing pragmatic statecraft on the center-right. The search for Stresemann's true nature as historical figure is ultimately an academic debate, but finding his equivalent in Israeli politics could go a long way toward ending the protracted conflict with the Palestinians. With the Labor Party decimated in parliamentary strength, some pragmatic statecraft is the best hope on the Israeli side for a final status agreement with the Palestinians.

In the early years of the new millennium, it appeared that Israel might indeed have found such a political figure and force in the form of Ariel

Sharon. Even as he ruthlessly repressed the intifada, the new prime minister plotted a political exit strategy. While the peace process was frozen, Prime Minister Sharon announced in December 2003 a significant unilateral move—a total withdrawal of the IDF from the Gaza strip and the dismantling of all settlements there as well as four settlements in the northern West Bank. This disengagement would require relocating thousands of settlers (Rynhold and Waxman 2008: 35). This was a significant departure from the coercive diplomatic style of previous Likud administrations in that it released a bargaining chip without a concession from the Palestinians (Freilich 2012: 177; Rynhold and Waxman 2008: 33; Bar-Siman-Tov and Michael 2007: 275). Sher Arian and Michael Shamir write, "The call for unilateral actions negated decades of Zionist demands for recognition and negotiation as conditions for concessions" (2008: 700).

Sharon's actions were indicative of a commitment to pragmatic statecraft, a different diplomatic style (Waxman 2008; Rabinovich 2011: 129; Arian and Shamir 2008: 700). The prime minister had come to the conclusion that demographic realities made it impossible for Israel to continue to hold the territories while still retaining the Jewish identity of Israel (Freilich 2012: 180; Bar-Siman-Tov and Michael 2007: 264–65). "Disengagement recognizes the demographic reality on the ground specifically, bravely and honestly," said Sharon (in Rynhold and Waxman 2008: 25). Ehud Olmert, his ally and the mayor of Jerusalem, said of his plan, "Above all hovers the cloud of demographics" (in Rynhold and Waxman 2008: 23). The prime minister had also determined, in light of the second intifada, that the Palestinians could not be suppressed forever (Freilich 2012: 180; Bar-Siman-Tov and Michael 2007: 264–65). Palestinians and Israelis were in a deadlock detrimental to both sides. Sharon famously declared, "I think the idea that it is possible to continue keeping 3.5 million Palestinians under occupation . . . is bad for Israel. . . . Controlling 3.5 million Palestinians cannot go on forever" (in Waxman 2008).

Sharon was carefully ranking priorities. He distinguished between "goals worth fighting for, because they are truly vital, like Jerusalem, the big settlement blocs, the security areas and preservation of Israel's character as a Jewish state, as opposed to objectives which we all clearly know will not be achieved and which most of the public is justifiably unwilling to sacrifice a great deal for" (Freilich 2012: 179). Disengagement from these areas would allow Israel to focus its interests on "trying to save as much as possible of Judea and Samaria" (Freilich 2012: 179). The prime minister was pragmatically cutting Israeli losses.

The prime minister's decision was particularly surprising given Sharon's history as a patron of the settler movement and a hard-liner when it came to dealing with the Palestinians and other Arab adversaries (Rabinovich 2011: 129). When he was foreign minister, he had urged the

[241]

settlers to "run and grab the hills" after the Wye agreement (Rynhold and Waxman 2008: 26). In this way, he was very similar to Stresemann, who during World War I had been a virulent German nationalist.

There had been signs of Sharon's pragmatism in his earlier stint as foreign minister under Netanyahu. In discussions with Qurie, he said, "I am inclining towards a restricted but definite objective that would be achievable. This will not be peace, but a stage below it, a kind of truce. We need an entity made up of geographically linked territories under the Palestinian Authority" (Qurie 2008: 45). Sharon was settling for coexistence not peace, conflict management not conflict resolution (Rynhold and Waxman 2008: 26). Israelis would take the bird in the hand.

Sharon's plan created a huge division in the Likud Party between party moderates and the right wing, suggesting the familiar divide based on epistemic motivation observed in previous chapters. The center-right embraced Sharon's pragmatic statecraft, whereas the far right did not (Rabinovich 2011: 130; Miller 2008: 322; Kurtzer et al. 2013: 159). The prime minister submitted his plan to the Likud Party for a referendum, which it rejected in May 2004. Netanyahu and four other cabinet ministers had issued a joint statement opposing disengagement. An amended plan, in which the cabinet would decide whether and which settlements to dismantle in four consecutive steps, was passed (Freilich 2012: 184–88; Bar-Siman-Tov and Michael 2007: 267–72). This was the same staged solution, preserving bargaining leverage, that had emerged from the Likud cabinet deliberations after the Wye River summit. Even so, the Knesset held two votes of no confidence in which fifteen of forty Likud members defected, voting against Sharon. In the fall, Netanyahu resigned from the cabinet and contested the Likud leadership on a program of opposition to disengagement. The rebel ranks included half of the Likud parliamentarians.

Sharon's diplomatic style of pragmatic statecraft therefore required left-wing support. Sharon brought Labor into a national unity coalition in December 2004 when the right-wing NRP resigned (Freilich 2012: 188–89). As was the case in Germany in the 1920s, the Israeli left and center-right formed a Baptist-bootlegger coalition against the right based on differences in diplomatic style. Labor had fought the 2003 elections on a program of disengagement in light of its belief that it no longer had a Palestinian partner (Arian and Shamir 2008; Rynhold and Waxman 2008; Freilich 2012: 178). Dov Waxman writes that the alignment "took the policy of territorial withdrawal from the Left, and the Right's skepticism about the possibility of achieving Israel-Palestinian peace and pessimism about the ability of Israelis and Palestinians to live together" (2008: 89). By September 2005, 8,000 settlers had been removed from twenty-one settlements in Gaza and four in the West Bank, some through force.

The divisions in Likud were so profound that in November 2005 the prime minister announced his departure from Likud and the creation of an alternative party, called Kadima. Public opinion polls showed that voters who defected from Likud to Kadima had a different diplomatic style than those who stayed with the traditional Israeli party of the right. Kadima supporters were only slightly less pessimistic about the likelihood of reaching an agreement with the Palestinians than were Likud loyalists but were much more skeptical than Labor voters. Yet, like Labor voters, they largely endorsed Sharon's disengagement plan, whereas Likud voters did not. Kadima voters were a "specific combination of the Left and the Right: a growing willingness for compromise from the Left together with deep mistrust of the Palestinians . . . from the Right." It was a "pragmatic middle ground" (Shamir et al. 2008).

Sharon's gamble paid off, but he was not able to enjoy the victory. Before the 2006 Knesset elections that yielded a plurality for his party and ultimately a governing coalition with Labor and Shas, he suffered a debilitating stroke. In yet another parallel between the two periods, the poor health of this unlikely leader of the pragmatic center-right deprived him of his chance to make history (Stresemann died in 1929 at the relatively young age of fifty-one). In Israel, Ehud Olmert took up the position of prime minister and head of the new party. The former mayor of Jerusalem, along with Tzipi Livni, his new foreign minister, and others, had shifted his diplomatic thinking based on pragmatism—what he perceived as irreversible demographic trends and the lack of a viable military solution to the conflict (Freilich 2012: 180). "Above all hovers the cloud of demographics," he said before becoming prime minister (in Miller 2008: 23; Rynhold and Waxman 2008: 23). Aaron Miller describes him as "smart, centrist, and pragmatic" (2008: 356).

Under Kadima leadership, the Israelis announced a "convergence plan," withdrawing from the outer settlements in the West Bank and consolidating an Israeli state with the large settlement blocs closer to Israel proper (Rabinovich 2011: 163–64; Kurtzer et al. 2013: 214). Ideally this was to be negotiated with the Palestinians; however, Olmert would go forward unilaterally as well. In November 2007, the Israelis came to the table with the Palestinians in Annapolis, Maryland, under the tepid and inattentive brokering of the George W. Bush administration (Kurtzer et al. 2013: 226). Subsequent talks nevertheless demonstrated flexibility on both sides. Olmert was willing to consider accepting up to 15,000 Palestinian refugees in exchange for a Palestinian pledge to end the conflict as well as to place the Holy Basin (the Old City of Jerusalem and the adjacent area) under the control of a trusteeship of Saudi Arabia, Jordan, the United States, Israel, and Palestine. The differences between the two sides on territory narrowed considerably, with Israel indicating a much greater willingness to swap land in exchange for annexing major settle-ment blocs (Rabinovich 2011: 176–80; Kurtzer et al. 2013: 228–31).

Abbas, now the president of the Palestinian Authority, never formally responded to the Israeli proposals, and before the peace process could gain momentum, Olmert was forced to resign due to corruption charges. With Livni unable to form a coalition, new elections were held in Febru-ary 2009 that, although yielding another plurality for Kadima, saw Ben-jamin Netanyahu return as prime minister.

Early in his new tenure, Netanyahu for the first time endorsed a two-state solution to the conflict with the Palestinians. Were diplomacy only about foreign policy goals and not at all about style, this might have led naturally to negotiations and a final peace settlement. As I have argued, however, diplomatic style is also crucial, and Netanyahu embraced the coercive bargaining approach that was evident in his first term as prime minister. The first few years of his second stint were marked by very public disagreements with U.S. President Barack Obama about ending Israeli settlement activity as a precondition for starting peace talks that bring to mind the disputes between Shamir and President George H. W. Bush in the early 1990s. If Netanyahu is to bring peace, he will have to disassociate himself from the political right he has always called home and stake out a new political base allowing for pragmatic diplomacy.

Of course, this is not the only major problem to be solved before there can be a final peace agreement. The control of Hamas over Gaza looms large over any negotiations. And any progress is likely to precipitate a new wave of violent spoiler behavior from Palestinian extremists, which will tempt the Israelis to respond forcefully.

Observers generally believe that any final agreement between the two sides will approach that put together by President Clinton in his last days of office. Clinton proposed a Palestinian state consisting of 94–96 percent of the territory of the current West Bank with a compensation of 1–3 percent of Israeli territory so that the major Israeli settlements could be incorporated into Israel. Jerusalem would be divided, with the Pales-tinians controlling the Arab and Christian parts of the city and the Israe-lis the Jewish parts. The Temple Mount, however, would be under Palestinian sovereignty, with the Israelis holding the Western Wall. Is-rael would recognize the suffering of the refugees but would not be obliged to see to their return (Rabinovich 2011: 111–16; Meital 2006: 83–88; Malley and Agha 2001: 74; Pressman 2003). Indeed, that bridging proposal bears a striking resemblance to the Abbas-Beilin framework that arose in 1995 (Beilin 1999: 155; Rabinovich 2011: 51). Beilin writes of those talks, "The best solution for either side is one that the other cannot accept. So, in the end, a solution has to be found whereby each side con-cedes part of its dream. Not all of it. . . . In the Stockholm track we tried to square this circle. Our aim was to grant to each side what it considered most important, so long as this did not damage the interests of the other" (1999: 187). The talks were value creating in nature, demonstrating "remarkable creativity while protecting the core interests of each nation" (Beilin 1999: 155).

This should make us cautiously optimistic. Differences in interests are sometimes impossible to bridge, thereby imposing a structural impediment to peace that no agency can alter, at least not in the short to medium term. In contrast, diplomacy is something over which decision makers exert agency. Diplomacy can add value, if leaders let it.

References

Primary Sources

ADAP   Akten zur deutschen auswärtigen Politik, 1918–1945.
——. 1994. Serie A, Band XII (1. Januar bis 25. April 1925). Göttingen: Archiv des Auswärtigen Amtes (cited as ADAP A12).
——. 1995. Serie A, Band XIII (27. April bis. 13. August 1925). Göttingen: Archiv des Auswärtigen Amtes (cited as ADAP A13).
——. 1995. Serie A, Band XIV (14. August bis 30. November 1924). Göttingen: Archiv des Auswärtigen Amtes (cited as ADAP A14).
——. 1966. Serie B, Band I,1 (Dezember 1925 bis July 1926). Göttingen: Archiv des Auswärtigen Amtes (cited as ADAP B1/1).
——. 1968. Serie B, Band I,2 (August bis Dezember 1926). Göttingen: Archiv des Auswärtigen Amtes (cited as ADAP B1/2).
——. 1976. Serie B, Band IX (1. Mai bis 30. August 1928). Göttingen: Archiv des Auswärtigen Amtes (cited as ADAP B9).
——. 1977. Serie B, Band X (1. September bis 31. Dezember 1928). Göttingen: Archiv des Auswärtigen Amtes (cited as ADAP B10).
——. 1978. Serie B, Band XII (1. Jun ibis 2. September 1929). Göttingen: Archiv des Auswärtigen Amtes (cited as ADAP B12).
BDFA   British Documents on Foreign Affairs. 1993. Part 2: *From the First to the Second World War*, Series F, Vol. 17: *Europe*. Bethesda, MD: University Publications of America.
CC   Conclusions of the British cabinet, sometimes providing a summary of discussions. Minutes are numbered sequentially throughout the year, with the last two digits of the year in parentheses.
Cmd. 2169 Parliamentary Command Paper 2169, *Papers Respecting Negotiations for an Anglo French Pact*. 1924. London: His Majesty's Stationery Office.
CP   Cabinet Papers circulated to ministers. Papers are numbered sequentially throughout the year, with the last two digits of the year in parentheses.
DBFP   Documents on British Foreign Policy, 1919–1939.
——. 1966. Series Ia, Vol. 1: *The Aftermath of Locarno, 1925–1926*. London: Her Majesty's Stationery Office (cited as DBFP IA, Vol. 1).
——. 1973. Series Ia, Vol. 5: *European and Security Questions, 1928*. London: Her Majesty's Stationery Office (cited as DBFP IA, Vol. 5).

——. 1975. Series Ia, Vol. 6: *The Young Report and the Hague Conference: Security Questions, 1928–1929*. London: Her Majesty's Stationery Office (cited as DBFP IA, Vol. 6).

——. 1985. First Series, Vol. 26: *Central Europe and the Balkans 1924; German Affairs 1924*. London: Her Majesty's Stationery Office (cited as DBFP I, Vol. 26).

——. 1986. First Series, Vol. 27: *Central Europe, the Balkans and Germany, January– October, 1925; The Conference of Locarno, October 1925*. London: Her Majesty's Stationery Office (cited as DBFP I, Vol. 27).

DD   Documents diplomatiques: Documents relatifs aux négociations concernant les garanties de sécurité contreune aggression de l'Allemagne (10 janvier 1919–7 decembre 1923). 1962. Paris: Ministère des Affaires Étrangère.

FO 371   Political files of the British Foreign Office. "W" refers to Western Europe.

Hansard. London: Her Majesty's Stationery Office (British parliamentary record).

Henderson, Arthur. 1925. *Labour and the Geneva Protocol* (pamphlet).

Kabinette Luther   *Akten der Reichskanzlei Weimarer Republik: Die Kabinette Luther I and II*, Vols. 1–2. 1977. Edited by Karl-Heinz Minuth. Boppard am Rhein: Harald Boldt Verlag.

Kabinette Marx   *Akten der Reichskanzlei Weimarer Republik: Die Kabinette Marx III und IV*, Vol. 1. 1996. Edited by Günther Abramowski. Boppard am Rhein: Harald Boldt Verlag.

Labour Party. 1919. *Labour and the Peace Treaty* (pamphlet).

——. 1928. *Labour and the Nation* (election manifesto).

Locarno-Konferenz   *Locarno-Konferenz 1925: Eine Dokumentensammlung*. 1962. Berlin: Ministerium für Auswärtige Angelegenheitender Deutschen Demokratischen Republik.

PRO 30/69.   James Ramsay MacDonald and predecessors and successors: Papers. 1793–1937. London: The National Archives.

Stresemann   *Stresemann, Gustav: His Diaries, Letters and Papers*, 3 vols., 1935–40. Edited by Eric Sutton. New York: Macmillan.

VDR   *Verhandlungen des Deutschen Reichstags*. Berlin: Norddeutscher Buchdruckerei (German parliamentary record).

Vermächtnis   *Vermächtnis, der Nachlaß in drei Bänden*. 1932. Vol. 2: *Locarno und Genf*. Edited by Henry Bernard, Wolfgang Goetz, and Paul Wiegler (German version of Stresemann's diaries and papers).

SECONDARY SOURCES

Abbas, Mahmoud. 1995. *Through Secret Channels*. Reading, UK: Garnet Publishing.

Adler-Nissen, Rebecca. Forthcoming. "EU's New Diplomats: Symbolic Power, the Diplomatic Field, and the EU's External Service." *Review of International Studies*.

Altemeyer, Robert. A. 1998. "The Other 'Authoritarian Personality.'" *Advances in Experimental Social Psychology* 30: 47–91.

Arian, Sher, and Michal Shamir. 2008. "A Decade Later, the World Had Changed, the Cleavage Structure Remained: Israel 1996–2006. *Party Politics* 14(6): 684–705.

Axelrod, Robert, and Robert O. Keohane. 1985. "Achieving Cooperation under Anarchy: Strategies and Institutions." *World Politics* 38(1): 226–54.

Baker, Kenneth. 1993. *The Faber Book of Conservatism*. London: Faber and Faber.

References

Barak, Ehud. 2003. "I Did Not Give Away a Thing." *Journal of Palestine Studies* 33(1): 84–87.

Barari, Hassan A. 2004. *Israeli Politics and the Middle East Peace Process, 1988–2002*. London: Routledge Curzon.

Barnes, John. 1994. "Ideology and Factions." In *Conservative Century: The Conservative Party since 1900*, edited by Anthony Sheldon and Stuart Ball, 315–46. Oxford: Oxford University Press.

Baron, Jonathan. 1994. *Thinking and Deciding*. Cambridge, UK: Cambridge University Press.

Bar-Siman-Tov, Yaacov, and Kobi Michael. 2007. "The Israeli Disengagement Plan as a Conflict Management Strategy." In *The Israeli-Palestinian Conflict: From Conflict Resolution to Conflict Management*, edited by Yaacov Bar-Siman-Tov, 261–82. New York: Palgrave Macmillan.

Bar-Tal, Daniel, and Keren Sharvit. 2007. "A Psychological Earthquake in the Israeli-Jewish Society: Changing Opinions Following the Camp David Summit and the Al-Aqsa Intifada." In *The Israeli-Palestinian Conflict: From Conflict Resolution to Conflict Management*, edited by Yaacov Bar-Siman-Tov, 169–202. New York: Palgrave Macmillan.

Barnea, Marina F., and Shalom H. Schwartz. 1998. "Values and Voting." *Political Psychology* 19(1): 17–40.

Beersma, Bianca, and Carsten K. W. De Dreu. 1999. "Negotiation Processes and Outcomes in Prosocially and Egoistically Motivated Groups." *International Journal of Conflict Management* 10(4): 385–402.

Behrendt, Sven. 2007. *The Secret Israeli-Palestinian Negotiations in Oslo: Their Success and Why the Process Ultimately Failed*. London: Routledge.

Beilin, Yossi. 1999. *Touching Peace: From the Oslo Accord to a Final Agreement*. London: Weidenfeld & Nicolson.

——. 2004. *The Path to Geneva: The Quest for a Permanent Agreement, 1996–2004*. New York: RDV Books.

Ben-Yehuda, Hemda. 1997. "Attitude Change and Policy Transformation: Yitzhak Rabin and the Palestinian Question, 1967–95. In *From Rabin to Netanyahu: Israel's Troubled Agenda*, edited by Efraim Karsh, 201–24. London: Frank Cass.

Berger, Stefan. 1994. *The British Labour Party and the German Social Democrats, 1900–1931*. Oxford: Clarendon Press.

Berki, Robert N. 1981. *On Political Realism*. London: Dent.

Berman, Sheri. 2006. *The Primacy of Politics: Social Democracy and the Making of Europe's Twentieth Century*. Cambridge, UK: Cambridge University Press.

Berridge, Geoffrey R. 2001. "Machiavelli: Human Nature, Good Faith, and Diplomacy." *Review of International Studies* 27(4): 539–56.

Booth, Ken, and Nicolas J. Wheeler. 2008. *The Security Dilemma: Fear, Cooperation and Trust in World Politics*. New York: Palgrave Macmillan.

Bull, Hedley. 1977. *The Anarchical Society: A Study of Order in World Politics*. New York: Columbia University Press.

Carlton, David. 1970. *MacDonald versus Henderson: The Foreign Policy of the Second Labour Government*. New York: Humanities Press.

Carnevale, Peter J., and Edward J. Lawler. 1986. "Time Pressure and the Development of Integrative Agreements in Bilateral Negotiations." *Journal of Conflict Resolution* 30(4): 636–59.

Carnevale, Peter J., and Dean G. Pruitt. 1992. "Negotiation and Mediation." *Annual Review of Psychology* 43: 531–82.

Caprara, Gian Vittorio, Shalom Schwartz, Christina Capanna, Michele Vecchione, and Claudio Barbaranelli. 2006. "Personality and Politics: Values, Traits, and Political Choice." *Political Psychology* 27(1): 1–28.

Carr, Edward H. 1964. *The Twenty Years' Crisis, 1919–1939*. New York: Harper and Row.

Clingan, C. Edmund. 2010. *The Lives of Hans Luther, 1879–1962: German Chancellor, Reichsbank President, and Hitler's President*. Lantham, MD: Lexington Books.

Cohrs, J. Christopher, Barbara Moschner, Jurgen Maes, and Sven Kielmann. 2005. "The Motivational Bases of Right-Wing Authoritarianism and Social Dominance Orientation: Relations to Values and Attitudes in the Aftermath of September 11, 2001." *Personality and Social Psychology Bulletin* 31(10): 1425–34.

Cohrs, Patrick O. 2004. "The Quest for a New Concert of Europe: British Pursuits of German Rehabilitation and European Stability in the 1920s." In *Locarno Revisited: European Diplomacy, 1920–1929*, edited by Gaynor Johnson, 33–58. London: Routledge.

——. 2006. *The Unfinished Peace after World War I: America, Britain and the Stabilisation of Europe, 1919–1932*. Cambridge, UK: Cambridge University Press.

Copeland, Dale. 2000. *The Origins of Major War*. Ithaca: Cornell University Press.

Craig, Gordon A. 1978. *Germany, 1866–1945*. New York: Oxford University Press.

Craig, Gordon A., and Alexander L. George. 1983. *Force and Statecraft: Diplomatic Problems of Our Time*. New York: Oxford University Press.

Cross, Mai'a K. Davis. 2007. *The European Diplomatic Corps: Diplomats and International Cooperation from Westphalia to Maastricht*. New York: Palgrave Macmillian.

Dajani, Omar M. 2005. "Surviving Opportunities: Palestinian Negotiating Patterns in Peace Talks with Israel." In *How Israelis and Palestinians Negotiate: A Cross-Cultural Analysis of the Oslo Peace Process*, edited by Tamara Cofman Wittes, 39–80. Washington, DC: United States Institute of Peace Press.

Davis, Christina L. 2004. "International Institutions and Issue Linkage: Building Support for Agricultural Trade Liberalization." *American Political Science Review* 98(1): 153–69.

de Callières, François. 2000. *On the Manner of Negotiating with Princes*. Boston: Houghton Mifflin.

De Cremer, David, and Paul Van Lange. 2001. "Why Prosocials Exhibit Greater Cooperation than Proselfs: The Roles of Social Responsibility and Reciprocity." *European Journal of Personality* 15: 5–18.

De Dreu, Carsten K. W., Bianca Beersma, Katherine Stroebe, and Martin C. Euwema. 2006. "Motivated Information Processing, Strategic Choice, and the Quality of Negotiated Agreement." *Journal of Personality and Social Psychology* 90(6): 927–43.

De Dreu, Carsten K. W., and Terry L. Boles. 1998. "Share and Share Alike or Winner Take All?: The Influence of Social Value Orientation upon Choice and Recall of Negotiation Heuristics." *Organizational Behavior and Human Decision Processes* 76(3): 253–76.

De Dreu, Carsten K. W., and Peter J. Carnevale. 2003. "Motivational Bases of Information Processing and Strategy in Conflict and Negotiation." *Advances in Experimental Social Psychology* 35: 235–90.

De Dreu, Carsten K. W., Ellen Giebels, and Evert Van de Vliert. 2000. "Social Motives and Trust in Integrative Negotiation: The Disruptive Effects of Punitive Capability." *Journal of Applied Psychology* 83(3): 408–22.

De Dreu, Carsten K. W., Sander L. Koole, and Frans L. Oldersma. 1999. "On the Seizing and Freezing of Negotiator Inferences: Need for Cognitive Closure

Moderates the Use of Heuristics in Negotiation." *Personality and Social Psychology Bulletin* 25(3): 348–62.

De Dreu, Carsten K. W., Sander L. Koole, and Wolfgang Steinel. 2000. "Unfixing the Fixed Pie: A Motivated Information-Processing Approach to Integrative Negotiation." *Journal of Personality and Social Psychology* 79(6): 975–87.

De Dreu, Carsten K. W., Bernard N. Nijstad, and Daan van Knippenberg. 2008. "Motivated Information Processing in Group Judgment and Decision Making." *Personality and Social Psychology Review* 12(1): 22–49.

De Dreu, Carsten K. W., and Gerben A. Van Kleef. 2004. "The Influence of Power on the Information Search, Impression Formation, and Demands in Negotiation." *Journal of Experimental Social Psychology* 40(3): 303–19.

De Dreu, Carsten K. W., and Paul A. M. Van Lange. 1995. "The Impact of Social Value Orientations on Negotiator Cognition and Behavior." *Personality and Social Psychology Bulletin* 21(11): 1178–88.

De Dreu, Carsten K. W., Laurie R. Weingart, and Seungwoo Kwon. 2000. "Influence of Social Motives on Integrative Negotiation: A Meta-Analytic Review and Test of Two Theories." *Journal of Personality and Social Psychology* 78(5): 889–905.

Der Derian, James. 1987. "Mediating Estrangement: A Theory for Diplomacy." *Review of International Studies* 13(2): 91–110.

Deutsch, Morton. 1960. "The Effect of Motivation Orientation upon Threat and Suspicion." *Human Relations* 13: 123–39.

Dietelhoff, Nicole, and Harald Müller. 2005. "Theoretical Paradise: Empirically Lost? Arguing with Habermas." *Review of International Studies* 31(1): 167–79.

Downs, Anthony. 1957. *An Economic Theory of Democracy.* New York: HarperCollins.

Doyle, Michael. 1997. *Ways of War and Peace: Realism, Liberalism and Socialism.* New York: Norton.

Duckitt, John. 2001. "A Dual-Process Cognitive-Motivational Theory of Ideology and Prejudice." *Advances in Experimental Social Psychology* 33: 41–113.

———. 2006. "Differential Effects of Right Wing Authoritarianism and Social Dominance Orientation on Outgroup Attitudes and Their Mediation by Threat from and Competitiveness to Outgroups." *Personality and Social Psychology Bulletin* 32(5): 684–96.

Duckitt, John, and Kirstin Fisher. 2003. "The Impact of Social Threat on Worldview and Ideological Attitudes." *Political Psychology* 24(1): 199–222.

Duriez, Bart, and Alain Van Hiel. 2002. "The March of Modern Fascism: A Comparison of Social Dominance Orientation and Authoritarianism." *Personality and Individual Differences* 32: 1199–213.

Dworkin, Ronald M. 1977. *Taking Rights Seriously.* Cambridge, MA: Harvard University Press.

———. 1985. *A Matter of Principle.* Cambridge, MA.: Harvard University Press.

Eley, Goeff. 2002. *Forging Democracy: The History of the Left in Europe, 1850–2000.* Oxford: Oxford University Press.

Etzioni, Amitai. 1962. *The Hard Way to Peace: A New Strategy.* New York: Crowell-Collier Press.

Fearon, James D. 1994. "Domestic Political Audiences and the Escalation of International Disputes." *American Political Science Review* 88(3): 577–92.

———. 1995. "Rationalist Explanations for War." *International Organization* 49(3): 379–414.

———. 1998. "Bargaining, Enforcement, and International Cooperation." *International Organization* 52(2): 269–305.

Feldman, Stanley. 2003. "Enforcing Social Conformity: A Theory of Authoritarianism." *Political Psychology* 24(1): 41–74.

Feldman, Stanley, and Karen Stenner. 1997. "Perceived Threat and Authoritarianism." *Political Psychology* 18(4): 741–70.

Fordham, Benjamin O. 1998a. *Building the Cold War Consensus: The Political Economy of U.S. National Security Policy 1949–51.* Ann Arbor: University of Michigan Press.

——. 1998b. "Economic Interests, Party, and Ideology in Early Cold War Era U.S. Foreign Policy." *International Organization* 52(2): 359–96.

Freilich, Charles D. 2012. *Zion's Dilemmas: How Israel Makes National Security Policy.* Ithaca: Cornell University Press.

Fry, William R. 1985. "The Effect of Dyad Machiavellianism and Visual Access on Integrative Bargaining Outcomes." *Personality and Social Psychology Bulletin* 11(1): 51–62.

Gartzke, Erik. 1999. "War Is in the Error Term." *International Organization* 53(3): 567–87.

Gatzke, Hans Wilhelm. 1954. *Stresemann and the Rearmament of Germany.* Baltimore: Johns Hopkins Press.

Gaubatz, Kurt Taylor. 1991. "Election Cycles and War." *Journal of Conflict Resolution* 35(2): 212–44.

Gerring, John. 1998. *Party Ideologies in America 1828–1996.* New York: Cambridge University Press.

Gewirth, Alan. 1983. "The Rationality of Reasonableness." *Synthese* 57(2): 225–47.

Glaser, Charles L. 1994. "Realists as Optimists: Cooperation as Self-Help." *International Security* 19(3): 50–90.

——. 2010. *Rational Theory of International Politics: The Logic of Competition and Cooperation.* Princeton: Princeton University Press.

Golec, Agnieszka, and Christopher M. Federico. 2004. "Understanding Responses to Political Conflict: Interactive Effects of the Need for Closure and Salient Conflict Schemas." *Journal of Personality and Social Psychology* 87(6): 750–62.

Gordon, Michael R. 1969. *Conflict and Consensus in Labour's Foreign Policy, 1914–1965.* Stanford: Stanford University Press.

Graham, Jesse, Jonathan Haidt, and Brian A. Nosek. 2009. "Liberals and Conservatives Rely on Different Sets of Moral Foundations." *Journal of Personality and Social Psychology* 96(5): 1029–46.

Graham, Jesse, Brian A. Nosek, Jonathan Haidt, Ravi Iyer, Spassena Koleva, and Peter H. Ditto. 2011. "Mapping the Moral Domain." *Journal of Personality and Social Psychology* 101(2): 366–85.

Grathwol, Robert P. 1980. *Stresemann and the DNVP: Reconciliation or Revenge in German Foreign Policy, 1924–1928.* Lawrence: Regents Press of Kansas.

Grayson, Richard S. 1997. *Austen Chamberlain and the Commitment to Europe: British Foreign Policy, 1924–29.* London: Frank Cass.

Haberman, Clyde. "Dennis Ross's Exit Interview." *New York Times*, March 25, 2001.

Haidt, Jonathan, Jesse Graham, and Craig Joseph. 2009. "Above and Below Left-Right: Ideological Narratives and Moral Foundations." *Psychological Inquiry* 20(2): 110–19.

Haidt, Jonathan, and Craig Joseph. 2004. "Intuitive Ethics: How Innately Prepared Intuitions Generate Culturally Variable Virtues." *Daedalus* 133(4): 55–66.

Hall, Hines. 1978. "Lloyd George, Briand and the Failure of the Anglo-French Entente." *Journal of Modern History* 50(2): 1121–38.

References

Hearnshaw, Fossey J. C. 1967. *Conservatism in England: An Analytical, Historical and Political Survey*. New York: Howard Fertig.

Hermann, Tamar, and Ephraim Yuchtman-Yaar. 2002. "Divided Yet United: Israeli-Jewish Attitudes toward the Oslo Process." *Journal of Peace Research* 39(5): 597–613.

Hiden, John. 1996. *The Weimar Republic*. New York: Addison Wesley Longman.

Howard, Rhoda E., and Jack Donnelly. 1986. "Human Dignity, Human Rights and Political Regimes." *American Political Science Review* 80(3): 801–17.

Iedema, Jurjen, and Matthijs Poppe. 1994. "Effects of Social Value Orientation on Expecting and Learning Others' Orientations." *European Journal of Social Psychology* 24(5): 565–79.

Inbar, Efraim. 1998. "Netanyahu Takes Over." In *Israel at the Polls, 1996*, edited by Daniel Judah Elazar and Shmuel Sandler, 33–53. London: Frank Cass.

Inglehart, Ronald. 1977. *The Silent Revolution: Changing Values and Political Styles among Western Publics*. Princeton: Princeton University Press.

Inglehart, Ronald, and Scott Flanagan. 1987. "Value Change in Industrial Societies." *American Political Science Review* 81(4): 1289–319.

Jacobson, Jon. 1972. *Locarno Diplomacy: Germany and the West, 1925–1929*. Princeton: Princeton University Press.

——. 2004. "Locarno, Britain, and the Security of Europe." In *Locarno Revisited: European Diplomacy, 1920–1929*, edited by Gaynor Johnson, 11–32. London: Routledge.

Janoff-Bulman, Ronnie. 2009a. "Political Attitudes and Complexity: Responses from a Motivational Perspective." *Psychological Inquiry* 20: 177–82.

——. 2009b. "To Provide or Protect: Motivational Bases of Political Liberalism and Conservatism." *Psychological Inquiry* 20(2–3): 120–28.

Janoff-Bulman, Ronnie, Sana Sheikh, and Kate G. Baldacci. 2007. "Mapping Moral Motives: Approach, Avoidance and Political Orientation." *Journal of Experimental Social Psychology* 44: 1091–99.

Jervis, Robert. 1970. *The Logic of Images in International Relations*. Princeton: Princeton University Press.

——. 1976. *Perception and Misperception in International Politics*. Princeton: Princeton University Press.

——. 1989. "Rational Deterrence: Theory and Evidence." *World Politics* 41(2): 183–207.

Jönnson, Christer, and Martin Hall. 2005. *Essence of Diplomacy*. New York: Palgrave Macmillan.

Jost, John T., Jack Glaser, Arie W. Kruglanski, and Frank J. Sulloway. 2003. "Political Conservatism as Motivated Social Cognition." *Psychological Bulletin* 129(3): 339–75.

Jugert, Philipp, and John Duckitt. 2009. "A Motivational Model of Authoritarianism: Integrating Personal and Situational Determinants." *Political Psychology* 30(5): 693–719.

Kahneman, Daniel. 2003. "Maps of Bounded Rationality: Psychology for Behavioral Economics." *American Economic Review* 93(5): 1449–75.

Kanagaretnam, Kiridaran, Stuart Mestelman, Khalid Nainar, and Mohamed Shehata. 2009. "The Impact of Social Value Orientation and Risk Attitudes on Trust and Reciprocity." *Journal of Economic Psychology* 30(3): 368–80.

Kayser, Jacques. 1960. "The Radical Socialist Party as a Party of Government in the Third French Republic." *Parliamentary Affairs* (13): 318–28.

Keeton, Edward D. 1987. *Briand's Locarno Policy: French Economics, Politics and Diplomacy, 1925–1929*. New York: Garland.

Keiger, John. 1997. *Raymond Poincaré*. Cambridge, UK: Cambridge University Press.

——. 2004. "Poincaré, Briand and Locarno: Continuity in French Diplomacy in the 1920s." In *Locarno Revisited: European Diplomacy, 1920–1929*, edited by Gaynor Johnson, 95–107. London: Routledge.

Kelley, Harold H., and Anthony J. Stahelski. 1970. "Social Interaction Basis of Cooperators' and Competitors' Beliefs about Others." *Journal of Personality and Social Psychology* 16(1): 66–91.

Kemp, Katherine E., and William P. Smith. 1994. "Information Exchange, Toughness and Integrative Bargaining: The Roles of Explicit Cues and Perspective Taking." *International Journal of Conflict Management* 5(1): 5–21.

Keohane, Robert O. 1984. *After Hegemony: Cooperation and Discord in the World Political Economy*. Princeton: Princeton University Press.

——. 1989. "Neoliberal Institutionalism: A Perspective on World Politics," in *International Institutions and State Power: Essays in International Relations*, edited by Robert O. Keohane, 1–20. Boulder: Westview Press.

Kimmel, Melvin J., Dean G. Pruitt, John M. Magenau, Ellen Konar-Goldband, and Peter J. D. Carnevale. 1980. "Effects of Trust, Aspiration, and Gender on Negotiation Tactics." *Journal of Personality and Social Psychology* 38(1): 9–22.

Kitschelt, Herbert. 1988a. "Left-Libertarian Parties: Explaining Innovation in Competitive Party Systems." *World Politics* 40(2): 194–234.

——. 1988b. "Organization and Strategy of Belgian and West German Ecology Parties: A New Dynamic of Party Politics in Western Europe?" *Comparative Politics* 20(2): 127–54.

——. 1994. *The Transformation of European Social Democracy*. New York: Cambridge University Press.

Kitschelt, Herbert, and Staf Hellemans. 1989. "The Left-Right Semantics and the New Politics Cleavage." *Comparative Political Studies* 23: 210–38.

Kitschelt, Herbert, and Anthony McGann. 1995. *The Radical Right in Western Europe: A Comparative Analysis*. Ann Arbor: University of Michigan Press.

Kramer, Roderick M., Marilynn B. Brewer, and Benjamin A. Hanna. 2004. "Collective Trust and Collective Action: The Decision to Trust as a Social Decision." In *Trust and Distrust in Organizations: Dilemmas and Approaches*, edited by Roderick M. Kramer and Karen. S. Cook, 357–89. New York: Russell Sage Foundation.

Kramer, Roderick M., Pamela Pommerenke, and Elizabeth Newton. 1993. "The Social Context of Negotiation." *Journal of Conflict Resolution* 37(4): 633–54.

Krasner, Stephen D. 1991. "Global Communication and National Power: Life on the Pareto Frontier." *World Politics* 43(3): 336–66.

Kreuzer, Marcus. 2001. *Institutions and Innovation: Voters, Parties, and Interest Groups in the Consolidation of Democracy—France and Germany, 1870–1939*. Ann Arbor: University of Michigan Press.

Kruglanski, Arie. W., and Donna M. Webster. 1996. "Motivated Closing of the Mind: 'Seizing and 'Freezing.'" *Psychological Review* 103: 263–83.

Kuhlman, D. Michael, and Alfred F. Marshello. 1975. "Individual Differences in Game Motivation as Moderators of Preprogrammed Strategy Effects in Prisoner's Dilemma." *Journal of Personality and Social Psychology* 32(5): 922–31.

Kuhlman, D. Michael, and David L. Wimberley. 1976. "Expectations of Choice Behavior Held by Cooperators, Competitors, and Individualists across Four

Classes of Experimental Games." *Journal of Personality and Social Psychology* 34(1): 69–81.

Kupchan, Charles. 2010. *How Enemies Become Friends: The Sources of Stable Peace.* Princeton: Princeton University Press.

Kurtzer, Daniel, Scott B. Lassensky, William B. Quandt, Steven L. Spiegel, and Shibley Z. Telhami. 2013. *The Peace Puzzle: America's Quest for Arab-Israeli Peace, 1989–2011.* Ithaca: Cornell University Press.

Kydd, Andrew H. 2005. *Trust and Mistrust in International Relations.* Princeton: Princeton University Press.

Kydd, Andrew H., and Barbara Walter. 2002. "Sabotaging the Peace: The Politics of Extremist Violence." *International Organization* 56(2): 263–96.

Larson, Deborah Welch. 1997. *Anatomy of Mistrust: U.S.-Soviet Relations during the Cold War.* Ithaca: Cornell University Press.

Legro, Jeffrey. 2005. *Rethinking the World: Great Power Strategies and International Order.* Ithaca: Cornell University Press.

Liebrand, Wim, Ronald Jansen, Victom Rijken, and Cor Suhre. 1986. "Might over Morality: Social Values and the Perception of Other Players in Experimental Games." *Journal of Experimental Psychology* 22(3): 203–15.

Lindsay, Thomas F., and Michael Harrington. 1974. *The Conservative Party, 1918–1970.* New York: St. Martin's Press.

Lipset, Seymour M., Paul F. Lazarsfeld, Allen H. Barton, and Juan Linz. 1954. "The Psychology of Voting: An Analysis of Political Behavior," in *Handbook of Social Psychology,* edited by Daniel Gilbert, Susan Fiske, and Gardner Lindzey, 1124–175. New York: McGraw Hill.

Lohmann, Susanne. 1997. "Linkage Politics." *Journal of Conflict Resolution* 41(1): 38–67.

Lynch, Marc. 2002. "Why Engage? China and the Logic of Communicative Engagement." *European Journal of International Relations* 8(2): 187–230.

Makovsky, David. 1996. *Making Peace with the PLO: The Rabin Government's Road to the Oslo Accord.* Boulder: Westview Press.

Malley, Robert, and Hussein Agha. 2001. "Camp David: Tragedy of Errors." *Journal of Palestine Studies* 31(10): 62–75.

Marks, Sally. 1982. "Ménage à Trois: The Negotiations for an Anglo-French-Belgian Alliance in 1922." *International History Review* 4(4): 524–52.

Marquand, David. 1977. *Ramsay MacDonald.* London: Jonathan Cape.

Martin, Lisa L. 1992. *Coercive Cooperation: Explaining Multilateral Economic Sanctions.* Princeton: Princeton University Press.

——. 1994. "Heterogeneity, Linkage, and Commons Problems." *Journal of Theoretical Politics* 6(4): 473–93.

McClintock, Charles G. 1972. "Social Motivation: A Set of Hypotheses." *Behavioral Science* 17(5): 438–54.

McClintock, Charles G., and Wim B. Liebrand. 1988. "Role of Interdependence Structure, Individual Value Orientation, and Another's Strategy in Social Decision Making: A Transformational Analysis." *Journal of Personality and Social Psychology* 55(3): 396–409.

McClosky, Herbert, and Dennis Chong. 1985. "Similarities and Differences between Left-Wing and Right-Wing Radicals." *British Journal of Political Science* 15(3): 329–63.

McCrillis, Neal R. 1998. *The British Conservative Party in the Age of Universal Suffrage: Popular Conservatism, 1918–1929.* Columbus: Ohio State University Press.

McGinnis, Michael D. 1986. "Issue Linkage and the Evolution of International Cooperation." *Journal of Conflict Resolution* 30(1): 141–70.

McKibben, Heather. Forthcoming. *Play by the Rules or Change Them? The Dynamics of State Bargaining Strategies*. New York: Cambridge University Press.

Meital, Yoram. 2006. *Peace in Tatters: Israel, Palestine and the Middle East*. Boulder: Lynne Rienner.

Mercer, Jon. 1996. *Reputation and International Politics*. Ithaca: Cornell University Press.

Messick, David M., Suzanne Blom, Janet P. Boldizar, and Charles D. Samuelson. 1985. "Why We Are Fairer than Others." *Journal of Experimental Social Psychology* 21(5): 480–500.

Messick, David M., and Charles G. McClintock. 1968. "Motivational Bases of Choice in Experimental Games." *Journal of Experimental Social Psychology* 4(1): 1–25.

Miller, Aaron David. 2008. *The Much Too Promised Land: America's Elusive Search for Arab-Israeli Peace*. New York: Bantam Books.

Miller, Suzanne. 1976. "Grundwerte in der Geschichte der deutschen Sozial-demokratie." *Aus Politik und Zeitgeschichte* 11: 16–31.

Mitzen, Jennifer. 2005. "Reading Habermas in Anarchy: Multilateral Diplomacy and Global Public Spheres." *American Political Science Review* 99(3): 401–17.

Mitzen, Jennifer, and Randall Schweller. 2011. "Knowing the Unknown Unknowns: Misplaced Certainty and the Onset of War." *Security Studies* 20(1): 2–35.

Mommsen, Hans. 1989. *The Rise and Fall of Weimar Germany*. Chapel Hill: University of North Carolina Press.

Moravcsik, Andrew. 1998. *The Choice for Europe: Social Purpose and State Power from Messina to Maastricht*. Ithaca: Cornell University Press.

Morgan, T. Clifton. 1990. "Issue Linkages in International Crisis Bargaining." *American Journal of Political Science* 34(2): 311–33.

Morgenthau, Hans. 1948. *The Politics among Nations: The Struggle for Power and Peace*. New York: A. A. Knopf.

Morrow, James D. 1999. "The Strategic Setting of Choices: Signaling, Commitment and Negotiation in International Politics." In *Strategic Choice and International Relations*, edited by David Lake and Robert Powell 77–114. Princeton: Princeton University Press.

Müller, Harald. 2004. "Arguing, Bargaining and All That: Communicative Action, Rationalist Theory and the Logic of Appropriateness in International Relations." *European Journal of International Relations* 10(3): 395–435.

Murray, A. J. H. 1996. "The Moral Politics of Hans Morgenthau." *Review of Politics* 58(1): 81–107.

Murray, Shoon K. 1996. *Anchors against Change: American Opinion Leaders' Beliefs after the Cold War*. Ann Arbor: University of Michigan Press.

Muthoo, Abhinay. 1999. *Bargaining Theory with Applications*. New York: Cambridge University Press.

Narizny, Kevin. 2007. *The Political Economy of Grand Strategy*. Ithaca: Cornell University Press.

Nash, John F. 1953. "Two-Person Cooperative Games." *Econometrica* 21(1): 128–40.

Naylor, John F. 1969. *Labour's International Policy*. London: Weidenfeld and Nicolson.

Neale, Margaret A., and Alison R. Fragale. 2006. "Social Cognition, Attribution, and Perception in Negotiation: The Role of Uncertainty in Shaping Negotiation

Processes and Outcomes." In *Frontiers in Social Psychology: Conflict and Negotiation*, edited by Leigh Thompson, 27–54. New York: Psychology Press.

Netanyahu, Benjamin. 1993. *A Place among the Nations: Israel and the World*. New York: Bantam Books.

Neumann, Iver B. 2003. "The English School on Diplomacy: Scholarly Promise Unfulfilled." *International Relations* 17(3): 341–69.

——. 2012. *At Home with the Diplomats: Inside a European Foreign Ministry*. Ithaca: Cornell University Press.

Nicolson, Harold. 1937. *Curzon: The Last Phase, 1919–1925: A Study in Post-War Diplomacy*. London: Constable and Company.

——. 1980. *Diplomacy*. Oxford: Oxford University Press.

Nincic, Miroslav. 2011. *The Logic of Positive Engagement*. Ithaca: Cornell University Press.

O'Connor, Kathleen M., and Peter J. D. Carnevale. 1997. "A Nasty but Effective Negotiation Strategy: Misrepresentation of a Common-Value Issue." *Personality and Social Psychology Bulletin* 23(5): 504–15.

Odell, John S. 2000. *Negotiating the World Economy*. Ithaca: Cornell University Press.

Olekalns, Mara, and Philip L. Smith. 2009. "Mutually Dependent: Power, Trust, Affect and the Use of Deception in Negotiation." *Journal of Business Ethics* 85(3): 347–65.

Olekalns, Mara, Philip L. Smith, and Rachael Kibby. 1996. "Social Value Orientations and Negotiator Outcomes." *European Journal of Social Psychology* 26(2): 299–313.

Osgood, Charles. 1962. *An Alternative to War or Surrender*. Urbana: University of Illinois Press.

Osgood, Robert. 1953. *Ideals and Self-Interest in America's Foreign Relations: The Great Transformation of the Twentieth Century*. Chicago: University of Chicago Press.

Oudin, Bernard. 2004. *Aristide Briand*. Paris: Perrin.

Owen, John M. 1997. *Liberal Peace, Liberal War: American Politics and International Security*. Ithaca: Cornell University Press.

Paese, Paul W., and Robert D. Yonker. 2001. "Toward a Better Understanding of Egocentric Fairness Judgments in Negotiation." *International Journal of Conflict Management* 12: 97–186.

Peres, Shimon. 1995. *Battling for Peace: A Memoir*. New York: Random House.

Piurko, Yuval, Shalom H. Schwartz, and Eldal Davidov. 2011. "Basic Personal Values and the Meaning of Left-Right Political Orientations in 20 Countries." *Political Psychology* 32(4): 537–61.

Pouliot, Vincent. 2008. "The Logic of Practicality: A Theory of Practice of Security Communities." *International Organization* 62(2): 257–88.

——. 2010. *International Security in Practice: The Politics of NATO-Russia Diplomacy*. New York: Cambridge University Press.

Pressman, Jeremy. 2003. "Visions in Collision: What Happened at Camp David and Taba?" *International Security* 28(2): 5–43.

Pruitt, Dean G., and Steven A. Lewis. 1975. "Development of Integrative Solutions in Bilateral Negotiation." *Journal of Personality and Social Psychology* 31(4): 621–33.

Pundak, Ron. 2001. "From Oslo to Taba: What Went Wrong?" *Survival* 43(3): 31–45.

Putnam, Robert D. 1973. *The Beliefs of Politicians: Ideology, Conflict and Democracy in Britain and Italy*. New Haven: Yale University Press.

——. 1988. "Diplomacy and Domestic Politics: The Logic of Two-Level Games." *International Organization* 42(30): 427–60.

Qurie, Ahmed. 2006. *From Oslo to Jerusalem: The Palestinian Story of the Secret Negotiations.* New York: I. B. Tauris.

——. 2008. *Beyond Oslo, the Struggle for Palestine: Inside the Middle East Peace Process from Rabin's Death to Camp David.* New York: I. B. Tauris.

Rabin, Matthew. 2002. "A Perspective on Psychology and Economics." *European Economic Review* 46: 657–85.

Rabinovich, Itamar. 2011. *The Lingering Conflict: Israel, the Arabs and the Middle East, 1948–2011.* Washington, DC: Brookings Institution Press.

——. 2011. "'Cheap Talk' Diplomacy, Voluntary Negotiations, and Variable Bargaining Power." *International Studies Quarterly* 55(4): 1003–23.

Rapport, Aaron. 2012. "The Long and Short of It: Cognitive Constraints on Leaders' Assessments of 'Postwar' Iraq." *International Security* 37(3): 133–71.

Rasler, Karen. 2000. "Shocks, Expectancy Revision and the De-Escalation of Protracted Conflicts: The Israeli-Palestinian Case." *Journal of Peace Research* 37(6): 699–720.

Rathbun, Brian C. 2004. *Partisan Interventions: European Party Politics and Peace Enforcement in the Balkans.* Ithaca: Cornell University Press.

——. 2007. "Hierarchy and Community at Home and Abroad: Evidence of a Common Structure of Domestic and Foreign Policy Beliefs in American Elites." *Journal of Conflict Resolution* 51(3): 379–407.

——. 2010. "Is Anybody Not an (International Relations) Liberal?" *Security Studies* 19(2): 2–25.

——. 2012. *Trust in International Cooperation: International Security Institutions, Domestic Politics and American Multilateralism.* Cambridge, UK: Cambridge University Press.

Reus-Smit, Christian. 1999. *The Moral Purpose of the State: Culture, Social Identity, and Institutional Rationality in International Relations.* Princeton: Princeton University Press.

Risse, Thomas. 2000. "'Let's Argue!': Communicative Action in World Politics." *International Organization* 54(1): 1–39.

Ross, Dennis. 2004. *The Missing Peace: The Inside Story of the Fight for Middle East Peace.* New York: Farrar, Straus and Giroux.

Rothbart, Myron, and William Hallmark. 1988. "In-Group and Out-Group Differences in the Perceived Efficacy of Coercion and Conciliation in Resolving Social Conflict." *Journal of Personality and Social Psychology* 55(2): 248–57.

Rotter, Julian B. 1980. "Interpersonal Trust, Trustworthiness and Gullibility." *American Psychologist* 35(1): 1–7.

Rynhold, Jonathan, and Dov Waxman. 2008. "Ideological Change and Israel's Disengagement from Gaza." *Political Science Quarterly* 123(1): 11–37.

Sartori, Anne E. 2005. *Deterrence by Diplomacy.* Princeton: Princeton University Press.

Sassley, Brent E. 2010. "Affective Attachments and Foreign Policy: Israel and the 1993 Oslo Accords." *European Journal of International Relations* 16(4): 687–709.

Schei, Vidar, and Jorn K. Rognes. 2003. "Knowing Me, Knowing You: Own Orientation and Information about the Opponent's Orientation in Negotiation." *International Journal of Conflict Management* 14(1): 43–59.

Schelling, Thomas C. 1966. *Arms and Influence.* New Haven: Yale University Press.

Schultz, Justin W., and Dean G. Pruitt. 1978. "Effects of Mutual Concern on Joint Welfare." *Journal of Experimental Social Psychology* 15(5): 480–92.

Schultz, Kenneth A. 2001. *Democracy and Coercive Diplomacy.* New York: Cambridge University Press.

References

———. 2005. "The Politics of Risking Peace. Do Hawks or Doves Deliver the Olive Branch?" *International Organization* 59(1): 1–38.

Schwartz, Shalom H. 1992. "Universals in the Content and Structure of Values: Theoretical Advances and Empirical Tests in 20 Countries." *Advances in Experimental Social Psychology* 25: 1–63.

———. 2007. Universalism Values and the Inclusiveness of Our Moral Universe." *Journal of Cross-Cultural Psychology* 38: 711–28.

Schwartz, Shalom H., Gian Vittorio Caprara, and Michele Vecchione. 2010. "Basic Personal Values, Core Political Values, and Voting: A Longitudinal Analysis." *Political Psychology* 31(3): 421–52.

Schweder, Richard A., Nancy C. Much, Manamohan Mahapatra, and Lawrence Park 1997. "The 'Big Three' of Morality (Autonomy, Community, and Divinity), and the 'Big Three' Explanations of Suffering." In *Morality and Health*, edited by Allan M. Bandt and Paul. Rozin, 119–69. New York: Routledge.

Sebenius, James K. 1983. "Negotiation Arithmetic: Adding and Subtracting Issues and Parties." *International Organization* 37(2): 281–316.

Segev, Samuel. 1998. *Crossing the Jordan: Israel's Hard Road to Peace*. New York: St. Martin's Press.

Sending, Ole Jacob. 2011. "United by Difference: Diplomacy as a Thin Culture." *International Journal* 66(3): 643–59.

Shamir, Michal, Raphael Ventura, Asher Arian, and Orit Kedar. 2008. "Kadima—Forward in a Dealigned Party System." In *The Elections in Israel*, edited by Alan Arian, 15–43. New Brunswick, NJ: Transaction Publishers.

Shamir, Yitzhak. 1994. *Summing Up: An Autobiography*. Boston: Little, Brown and Company.

Sharp, Paul. 2009. *Diplomatic Theory of International Relations*. Cambridge, UK: Cambridge University Press.

Sher, Gilead. 2006. *The Israeli-Palestinian Peace Negotiations, 1999–2001: Within Reach*. London: Routledge.

Smith, Jeremy. 1997. *The Taming of Democracy: The Conservative Party, 1880–1924*. Cardiff: University of Wales Press.

Sorenson, Ritch L., Eric A. Morse, and Grant T. Savage. 1999. "A Test of the Motivations Underlying Choice of Conflict Strategies in the Dual-Concern Model." *International Journal of Conflict Management* 10(1): 25–44.

Stambrook, Fred G. 1968. "'Das Kind': Lord D'Abernon and the Origins of the Locarno Pact." *Central European History* 1(3): 233–63.

Stanovich, Keith E., and Richard F. West. 1998. "Individual Differences in Rational Thought." *Journal of Experimental Psychology* 127(2): 161–88.

———. 2000. "Individual Differences in Reasoning: Implications for the Rationality Debate."*Behavioral and Brain Sciences* 23 : 645–726.

Steinberg, Gerald. 1995. "A Nation That Dwells Alone?: Foreign Policy in the 1992 Elections." In *Israel at the Polls, 1992*, edited by Daniel Judah Elazar, 175–200. Lanham, MD: Rowman and Littlefield.

———. 1998. "Peace, Security and Terror in the 1996 Elections." In *Israel at the Polls, 1996*, edited by Daniel Judah Elazar and Shmuel Sandler, 209–34. London: Frank Cass.

Steinel, Wolfgang, and Carsten K. W. De Dreu. 2004. "Social Motives and Strategic Misrepresentation in Social Decision Making." *Journal of Personality and Social Psychology* 86(3): 419–34.

Steiner, Barry H. 2004. "Diplomacy and International Theory." *Review of International Studies* 30(4): 493–509.

[259]

Stenner, Karen. 2009. "Three Kinds of 'Conservatism.'" *Psychological Inquiry* 20(2–3): 142–59.

Stinnett, Douglas. 2007. "International Uncertainty, Foreign Policy Flexibility, and Surplus Majority Coalitions in Israel. *Journal of Conflict Resolution* 51(30): 470–95.

Stouten, Jeroen, David De Cremer, and Eric van Dijk. 2006. "Violating Equality in Social Dilemmas: Emotional and Retributive Reactions as a Function of Trust, Attribution and Honesty." *Personality and Social Psychology Bulletin* 32(7): 894–906.

Telhami, Shibley. 1996. "Israeli Foreign Policy: A Realist Idealist-Type or a Breed of Its Own?" In *Israel in Comparative Perspective*, edited by Michal Barnett, 29–49. Albany: SUNY Press.

Tetlock, Philip E. 1983a. "Cognitive Style and Political Ideology." *Journal of Personality and Social Psychology* 45(1): 118–26.

———. 1983b. "Policy-Makers' Images of International Conflict." *Journal of Social Issues* 39(1): 67–86.

———. 1984. "Cognitive Style and Political Belief Systems in the British House of Commons." *Journal of Personality and Social Psychology* 46(2): 365–75.

———. 1988. "Monitoring the Integrative Complexity of American and Soviet Policy Rhetoric: What Can Be Learned?" *Journal of Social Issues* 44(2): 101–31.

———. 1998. "Social Psychology and World Politics," in *Handbook of Social Psychology*, edited by Daniel Gilbert, Susan Fiske, and Gardner Lindzey, 870–89. New York: McGraw Hill.

———. 2005. *Expert Political Judgment*. Princeton: Princeton University Press.

Tetlock, Philip E., and Anthony Tyler. 1996. "Churchill's Cognitive and Rhetorical Style: The Debates over Nazi Intentions and Self-Government of India." *Political Psychology* 17(1): 149–70.

Thompson, Leigh, and George Loewenstein. 1992. "Egocentric Interpretations of Fairness in Interpersonal Conflict." *Organizational Behavior and Human Decision Processes* 51(2): 176–97.

Tollison, Robert D., and Thomas D. Willett. 1979. "An Economic Theory of Mutually Advantageous Issue Linkages in International Negotiations." *International Organization* 33(4): 425–49.

Tomlinson, Edward C., Brian R. Dineen, and Roy J. Lewick. 2009. "Trust Congruence among Integrative Negotiators as a Predictor of Joint-Behavioral Outcomes." *International Journal of Conflict Management* 20(2): 173–87.

Trager, Robert F. 2010. "Diplomatic Calculus in Anarchy: How Communications Matters." *American Political Science Review* 104(2): 347–68.

Turiel, Elliot. 1983. *The Development of Social Knowledge: Morality and Convention*. Cambridge, UK: Cambridge University Press.

Unger, Gérard. 2005. *Aristide Briand*. Paris: Fayard.

Van Hiel, Alain, and Ivan Mervielde. 2003. "The Measurement of Cognitive Complexity and Its Relationship with Political Extremism." *Political Psychology* 24(4): 781–801.

Van Lange, Paul A. M. 1999. "The Pursuit of Joint Outcomes and Equality in Outcomes: An Integrative Model of Social Value Orientation." *Journal of Personality and Social Psychology* 77(2): 337–49.

Van Lange, Paul A. M., and D. Michael Kuhlman. 1994. "Social Value Orientations and Impressions of Partner's Honesty and Intelligence: A Test of the Might versus Morality Effect." *Journal of Personality and Social Psychology* 67(1): 126–41.

References

Van Leeuwen, Florian, and Justin H. Park. 2009. "Perceptions of Social Dangers, Moral Foundations, and Political Orientation." *Personality and Individual Differences* 47(3): 169–73.

Voeten, Erik. 2001. "Outside Options and the Logic of Security Council Action." *American Political Science Review* 95(4): 845–58.

Walters, Francis P. 1952. *History of the League of Nations*. Vol. 1. London: Oxford University Press.

Wanis-St. John, Anthony. 2011. *Back Channel Negotiation: Secrecy in the Middle East Peace Process*. Syracuse: Syracuse University Press.

Waxman, Dov. 2008. "From Controversy to Consensus: Cultural Conflict and the Israeli Debate over Territorial Withdrawal." *Israel Studies* 13(2): 73–96.

Watson, Adam. 1981. *Diplomacy: The Dialogue between States*. New York: Routledge.

Webster, Donna M., and Arie W. Kruglanski. 1994. "Individual Differences in Need for Cognitive Closure." *Journal of Personality and Social Psychology* 62: 1049–62.

Weingart, Laurie R., Jeanne M. Brett, Mara Olekalns, and Philip L. Smith. 2007. "Conflicting Social Motives in Negotiating Groups." *Journal of Personality and Social Psychology* 93(6): 994–1010.

Wheeler, Nicholas J. 2013. "Investigating Diplomatic Transformations." *International Affairs* 89(2): 477–96.

Williams, Michael C. 2005. *The Realist Tradition and the Limits of International Relations*. Cambridge, UK: Cambridge University Press.

Wilson, Glenn D. 1973. "A Dynamic Theory of Conservatism." In *The Psychology of Conservatism*, edited by Glenn D. Wilson, 257–65. London: Academic Press.

Winkler, Henry R. 1994. *Paths Not Taken: British Labour and International Policy in the 1920s*. Chapel Hill: University of North Carolina Press.

Wolfers, Arnold. 1940. *Britain and France between Two Wars: Conflicting Strategies of Peace since Versailles*. New York: Harcourt Brace.

Wright, Jonathan. 1995. "Stresemann and Locarno." *Contemporary European History* 4(2): 109–31.

——. 2002. *Gustav Stresemann: Weimar's Greatest Statesman*. Oxford: Oxford University Press.

Yarhi-Milo, Keren. 2014. *Knowing Thy Adversary: Leaders, Intelligence Organizations, and Assessments of Intentions in International Relations*. Princeton: Princeton University Press.

Zacher, Mark, and Richard Matthew. 1995. "Liberal International Relations Theory: Common Threads, Divergent Strands." In *Controversies in International Relations Theory*, edited by Charles Kegley, 107–50. New York: St. Martin's Press.

Index

Abbas, Mahmoud, 201, 204, 209, 226, 244; epistemic motivation of, 193; proself motivation of, 194; pragmatic statecraft of, 194–196, 209–211, 216

Arafat, Yasser, 192–193, 215–220, 223–224, 227–228, 231–235

Baker, James, 202, 204; pragmatic statecraft of, 190, 198–200, 203; proself motivation of, 198; switch to coercive tactics, 200

Barak, Ehud, 226–235; coercive bargaining by, 226–228, 231–234; pressure from right, 229–230; reasoned dialogue of, 226–227

Beilin, Yossi, 205, 207–208, 210–213, 218, 222–223, 244; reasoned dialogue of, 207

Belgium, 63, 68–69, 104, 109, 119, 137, 139, 164

Ben-Ami, Shlomo, 201, 203, 227, 233–235

Bismarck, Otto von, 74, 91, 98–99, 155

Bloc National, 56, 62, 72, 75, 111, 114, 122; proself motivation of, 56, 60. *See also* Poincaré, Raymond

Briand, Aristide, 61–63; pressure from right, 65, 168–171, 178, 185; reasoned dialogue of, 112, 122, 135–136, 145–147, 149–151, 165–167, 170–171, 178–179; prosocial motivation of, 112, 145

Britain: honest broker role, 118, 131–135, 141, 165, 173–174, 179; inter-party disagreements, 72–73; position on occupation, 164, 173, 179, 182, 185–186. *See also* Conservative Party; Labour Party

Bush, George H. W., 10, 190, 198–201, 203, 206–207, 244

Camp David summit, 230–235

Cannes conference, 61–66, 69, 72, 75–76

Cartel des Gauches, 168, 238; placating right, 114–117, 119, 121; reasoned dialogue of, 76–83, 90, 118–122; shared interests with right, 74–75, 90, 110

Center Party of Germany, 101, 128, 155, 179

Chamberlain, Austen: as honest broker, 118, 131–135, 141, 165, 173–174, 179; plan for Concert of Europe, 89, 104–105, 122; pragmatic statecraft of, 89, 101–106, 131–135, 141, 151–152; proself motivation of, 102–103

Clinton, Bill, 190, 224–225, 230, 232, 234, 244

Churchill, Winston, 107–108

coercive bargaining, 4, 14–16, 25, 34–36; by British left, 185–186; by British right, 60, 62–65, 68–69; by French right, 60–62, 65–68, 113, 163, 167–169, 176–177, 181, 185; by Germany, 127–128, 155–157, 163, 174–175,